MACKENZIE KING

IN THE AGE OF THE DICTATORS

Roy MacLaren

MACKENZIE KING

IN THE AGE OF THE DICTATORS

Canada's Imperial and Foreign Policies

McGill-Queen's University Press

Montreal & Kingston | London | Chicago

© McGill-Queen's University Press 2019

ISBN 978-0-7735-5714-7 (cloth)
ISBN 978-0-7735-5811-3 (ePDF)
ISBN 978-0-7735-5812-0 (ePUB)

Legal deposit second quarter 2019
Bibliothèque nationale du Québec

Printed in Canada on acid-free paper that is 100% ancient forest free (100% post-consumer recycled), processed chlorine free

We acknowledge the support of the Canada Council for the Arts, which last year invested $153 million to bring the arts to Canadians throughout the country.

Nous remercions le Conseil des arts du Canada de son soutien. L'an dernier, le Conseil a investi 153 millions de dollars pour mettre de l'art dans la vie des Canadiennes et des Canadiens de tout le pays.

Library and Archives Canada Cataloguing in Publication

Title: Mackenzie King in the age of the dictators : Canada's imperial and foreign policies / Roy MacLaren.
Names: MacLaren, Roy, author.
Description: Includes bibliographical references and index.
Identifiers: Canadiana (print) 2019004800X | Canadiana (ebook) 20190048158 | ISBN 9780773557147 (hardcover) | ISBN 9780773558113 (ePDF) | ISBN 9780773558120 (ePUB)
Subjects: LCSH: King, William Lyon Mackenzie, 1874-1950. | LCSH: Dictators—History—20th century. | LCSH: Canada—Foreign relations—1914-1945.
Classification: LCC FC580 .M33 2019 | DDC 971.063/2—dc23

In memory of my father, Wilbur Glen MacLaren, an eighteen-year-old gunner in a Prince Edward Island battery, who survived severe wounds at Passchendaele in October 1917, thanks in large part to the care of German prisoners of war who had been pressed into service as Canadian stretcher-bearers.

Contents

Acknowledgments ix

Chronology xi

Illustrations follow page 84

1 The Beginnings of the Affair 3

2 Asian Apprenticeship 12

3 Leadership Manoeuvres 31

4 Chanak and All That 41

5 Canada at the League of Nations 56

6 The Advent of the Dictators: Mussolini 62

7 The Advent of the Dictators: Hitler 68

8 King and Abyssinia: The Muddle 82

9 King and Abyssinia: The Domestic Scene 102

10 King and Abyssinia: The End 123

11 Appeasement 153

12 A Berliner in Berlin 171

13 Appalling Mischief 186

14 The End of the Affair 231

15 A Good Bit of Wool 252

Notes 263

Bibliography 289

Index 307

Acknowledgments

I thank first Henry Newton Rowell Jackman for his intellectual and practical support for this book. The idea arose in part from our frequent conversations about Canadian public policy during the interwar years. Hal Jackman, liberal in his many benefactions, is untiring in his commitment to helping others realize their full potential. A great Canadian, as was his grandfather before him.

Elizabeth Riddell-Dixon, granddaughter of Walter Riddell, was helpful in discussing her grandfather's role in recognizing the imperative need, before and after the Second World War, to construct and realize the potential of collective security.

Ellice Evans of Mount Allison University showed exemplary dexterity as well as both patience and comprehension in readying the manuscript for review and publication.

Amanda Wagner, of the splendid Robarts Library in the University of Toronto, demonstrated an inventive flexibility in applying the sometimes elusive disciplines of technology to the disciplines of writing history – and did it with unfailing humour and wit.

Courtney Lundigran of Trinity College Library in the University of Toronto displayed a rare understanding of how to identify sources electronically, a skill that has somehow eluded me.

Neville Thompson of the University of Western Ontario, an expert in the history of public policy in the British Commonwealth in the interwar years, was always constructive and stimulating in his suggestions and analyses.

No author could want a better editor than Mark Abley of McGill-Queen's University Press. Remarkably well informed and imaginative at the same time, he, a notable author himself, was wonderfully supportive.

My wife, Susan Eleanor MacLaren, was unfailingly constructive in her many contributions to the final draft of this manuscript.

To them all I am most grateful.

Chronology

Dec. 1874	birth of William Lyon Mackenzie King
1900	King appointed deputy minister in the Department of Labour
Sept. 1907	anti-immigration riot in Vancouver
1908	King meets with President Theodore Roosevelt in Washington three times in discussion among Great Britain, the United States, and Canada on the exclusion of Japanese immigrants
1908	King elected to parliament in a by-election
1909	King appointed deputy minister of labour
1911	Liberals defeated in general election
1914	King hired as head of industrial research at the Rockefeller Foundation
1914	Mussolini forms Fasci Rivoluzionari d'Azione Internazionalista
1917	general election held on conscription issue, King defeated in York North
1918	King publishes *Industry and Humanity*
Aug. 1919	King elected leader of the Liberal Party
Jan. 1920	League of Nations founded
1921	Liberals win general election and King becomes prime minister
Sept. 1922	Chanak incident
Oct. 1922	Mussolini's March on Rome King Victor Emmanuel III asks Mussolini to form the new government
1925	Italy becomes a one-party state

1925	Liberals hold on to power in general election with the support of Progressives
1926	parliamentary elections abolished in Italy
1926	Liberals win plurality of seats in a general election
1926	Balfour Declaration recognizes independence of dominions within the British Empire
Feb. 1929	Lateran Treaty between Vatican and Italian government
July 1930	R.B. Bennett becomes prime minister as Conservatives win general election
	King now leader of the opposition
1931	Statue of Westminster codifies independence of dominions
Jan. 1933	Hitler becomes chancellor of Germany
Oct. 1933	Germany withdraws from League of Nations
Nov.–Dec. 1934	Italian-Abyssinia border incident at Welwel
Oct. 1935	Liberals win a majority in general election
Oct. 1935	Italy invades Abyssinia
Dec. 1935	Hoare-Laval Pact
Mar. 1936	Germany reoccupies demilitarized Rhineland
May 1936	Italy captures Addis Ababa and proclaims Italian Empire
1936–39	Spanish Civil War
Oct. 1936	Rome-Berlin Axis
June 1937	King visits Hitler
Mar. 1938	*Anschluss*, unification of Austria with Germany
Sept. 1938	Czech crisis, Munich Agreement to hand over Sudetenland to Germany
Mar. 1939	German occupation of Czechoslovakia
Apr. 1939	Italian invasion of Albania
May 1939	Pact of Steel between Italy and Germany
Aug. 1939	Molotov-Ribbentrop non-aggression pact between USSR and Germany
Sept. 1939	Germany invades Poland
Sept. 1939	Britain and France declare war against Germany
Dec. 1939	British Commonwealth Air Training Plan agreement signed
June 1940	Italy declares war against Britain and France

MACKENZIE KING

IN THE AGE OF THE DICTATORS

1

The Beginnings of the Affair

This book is about the policy or the policies of the prime minister of Canada, William Lyon Mackenzie King, toward the European dictators Benito Mussolini of Italy and Adolf Hitler of Germany, during the 1920s and 1930s, and the domestic ramifications thereof. But it also reaches back to 1900, when King arrived in Ottawa, and ends with the declaration of the Second World War. As reflected in his voluminous diary, however, in no affirmative sense did he offer his fellow Canadians an active, positive, creative foreign policy before the Second World War – and little enough during and after it. One Canadian historian, writing at the end of the war, neatly described King as being convinced that "the supreme task of statesmanship was to avoid enunciating a foreign policy."[1] Another observed that he, "having secured with disconcerting ease recognition of Canada's right to an independent role in the world, was left with undeveloped convictions about what to do next."[2] To many subsequent observers and readers of his diaries, King appeared to pursue two foreign policies during the interwar years, one for French Canada and another for English Canada.

Whatever foreign policy or policies Canada did have during those two decades were of King's near-exclusive formulation. From the institution of his first government during the last days of December 1921, King retained for himself the external affairs portfolio (as did Sir Wilfrid Laurier, Sir Robert Borden, Arthur Meighen, and R.B. Bennett). He seldom if ever looked to his cabinet colleagues – other than to Ernest Lapointe, his long-serving minister of justice and indispensable Quebec lieutenant – for comment or advice. And he most decidedly discouraged parliamentary or other debate of foreign affairs. Any such discussions, he told his diary and even some members of parliament, would only create mischief, confusion, and division between English and French Canada. That parliament must decide on

Canada's external affairs became King's public mantra, but at the same time he worked to ensure that there would be no parliamentary debate if it could possibly be avoided. He consistently denied parliament the information on which it could base informed discussion of foreign affairs, and even the occasions to do so. In any case, a Liberal-dominated parliament could be counted on to support whatever King himself decided.

When King became prime minister at the end of December 1921, he brought with him three foreign policy preoccupations: (1) Canada's place in an evolving British Commonwealth of Nations; (2) its membership in the recently established League of Nations; and (3) its relations with the United States.

Happily, the third preoccupation, that of sharing a continent with the United States, could be reduced to proclaiming that "We are for friendly relations with the United States."[3] In fact, King remained throughout his life wary of Washington, convinced that "it was the secret aim of every American leader, including Franklin Roosevelt, to dominate Canada and ultimately to possess the country."[4] His wariness was shared to a degree in Quebec where French-speaking Canadians valued a province capable of protecting and perpetuating their distinct traditions and culture. Their transformation and integration into a homogeneous English-speaking society, as Franklin Roosevelt later urged on King, had been rejected in Confederation.

The approach of the Liberal Party toward the other two foreign policy priorities, the British Commonwealth and the League of Nations, was determined to a degree by the rejection, especially in an isolationist Quebec, of any Canadian involvement in what were seen as either Britain's imperial wars or collective security obligations of the League of Nations. Beyond Quebec, there was also widespread revulsion among ten million war-weary Canadians at the idea of more bloody conflict and more spending on military forces. During King's 1919 quest for the leadership of the Liberal Party upon the death of Sir Wilfrid Laurier – whose policy successor he regarded himself – he declared his commitment to the British Empire, although "in imperial relations we are opposed to centralization. We are advocates of British unity based upon human relations, rather than upon governmental machinery, unity based upon self-government and the quality of the British community of nations." About the newly born League of Nations, he was cautiously vague, contenting himself with "We are in sympathy with the movement to substitute friendly co-operation for conflict and jealousy in international relations with all countries."[5]

As for the rest of the world, King had no policy toward Latin America, thereby avoiding having to choose between the United States and Latin American republics in their perennial disputes. Publicly he offered the excuse that membership in the Pan American Union was open only to republics. His view of Asia was shaped by the controversies over the immigration to Canada of "cheap peoples," with attendant difficulties in relations with both Britain and the United States, that had marked his term as, first, deputy minister (1900–08), and subsequently (1909–11) minister of labour (his only ministerial appointment). Africa, in his thinking, simply did not exist – aside from the Union of South Africa, a fellow if distant and recent dominion of the British Commonwealth. Africa was an obscure plaything of imperial powers and, as in the case of the British in Egypt and India, should be left to them.

Four ancillary points should also be made about King's dual foreign policy and his lack of any real and consistent leadership during his many years as secretary of state for external affairs and as prime minister.

First, King's lack of a single, dynamic foreign policy was not the result of staying at home, as was the case with many postwar isolationists both in Canada and especially in the United States. In fact, among prime ministers before the advent of transoceanic airlines, he was remarkably well travelled. As early as 1899–1900, he had visited Britain, France, Germany, and Italy and had lived in the United States. In 1906 and 1908 he was again in Europe and in 1908–09 he was in India, Japan, and China. During the interwar years he was frequently in Geneva, Paris, Brussels, Rome, and Berlin, as well as London and Washington. But no understanding of isolationism or collective security that he may have acquired during his constant travels outweighed his commitment to retaining for the Liberal Party the electoral support which he saw as essential for the unity of Canada and its place in the British Empire.

Second, Canada had no foreign ministry to speak of before the Second World War. King failed to build a foreign service capable of providing the policy analyses, reasoned counsel, or even accurate relaying of messages that are the minimal desiderata of any foreign service. Even if he, wearing his hat as secretary of state for external affairs, had wanted to put forward a single, active, and constructive foreign policy, he did not equip himself with the apparatus to do so. During the interwar years, there was only a corporal's guard of neophyte career diplomats to staff the handful of missions abroad and the minute headquarters of External Affairs in Ottawa. To make matters worse, as the British high commissioner in Ottawa rightly observed, the undersecretary of state for external affairs, O.D. Skelton, "is not a good administrator and his office is badly organized."[6] What passed as the department was trammelled by the undersecretary's administrative failures, as well as his mounting opposition to his own minister's policies and his untiring efforts to frustrate them. One senior diplomat, Hume Wrong, decried "the woeful state of the Department" while from Canada House in London, Lester Pearson lamented that the undersecretary had no interest in "personnel and organisation problems" nor would he "fight for his men" (no woman until the latter half of the twentieth century), both serious failings in a deputy minister who was expected to lead in building a foreign service to support a clear foreign policy.[7] By 1939, on the eve of war, Pearson concluded that under Skelton the Department of External Affairs was simply "in one crude phrase in a mess – worse than I had expected."[8]

Third, given such an inadequate foreign service, King might have availed himself of information available in London at the regular briefings of high commissioners by the Dominions Office and in the proffered "prints" of selected dispatches from British missions abroad. However informative and perceptive the Foreign Office briefings and dispatches were, they were suspect in the jaundiced eyes of King and especially of Skelton. Foreign Office "prints" might mislead – or even worse be intended to mislead – Canadians. At Canada House in London in the late 1930s, Pearson recorded how both King and Skelton feared that "my independent sturdy Canadian attitude could be weakened ... and I might be lured into the Whitehall net" by reading such material and attending Foreign Office briefings.[9] The result was that, with so few posts abroad on the one hand and eschewing information from London on the other, King through the 1920s and into the 1930s relied in large part on newspapers, Canadian Press wire reports (which were frequently digests of the American Associated Press), and Canadian Broadcasting Corporation (CBC) news bulletins.

The fourth, and most striking, element in King's erratic approach to foreign affairs in the interwar years, including his blind support for Anglo-

French attempts at appeasement of the dictators, is the almost total absence in his voluminous diaries of recognition of the awfulness of war. His dual foreign policy, if it can be called that, reflected a deep desire to avoid war, but he leaves the impression that his commitment was not centred on the need to save women, men, and children from death or other attendant horrors of the killing fields, but rather on the desirability of avoiding constitutional difficulties within Canada. One searches in vain in King's diary for any passage similar to British prime minister Neville Chamberlain's profound hatred of war as the ultimate evil. The following passage serves as an example of Chamberlain's "never again" convictions: "When I think … of the seven million of young men who were cut off in their prime, the thirteen million who were maimed and mutilated, the misery and sufferings of the mothers or the fathers … in war there are no winners, but all are losers."[10] The sole book that Chamberlain wrote was about his infantry subaltern cousin, Norman, machine-gunned to death on the Western Front.

To say that King was himself unsoldier-like – to the point of all but avoiding Canadian battlefields and memorials during his many visits to France and Belgium – is no explanation. Even if his enthusiastic support in the late 1930s for appeasement of the dictators is deemed defensible, it should be recognized that he supported appeasement for the wrong reason. And if that were not enough, King prided himself on never having said anything derogatory about Hitler or Mussolini until war itself came. For example, he convinced himself that what he saw as the obstinacy and inflexibility of the Czechoslovaks made them and not Hitler responsible for the Sudetenland crisis of 1938. As for the League of Nations, he portrayed it as having caused the Second World War, not the dictators. To say anything else, King feared, might alienate Quebec and isolationist voters elsewhere in Canada, threatening the Liberal majority in the House of Commons. Better to say nothing.

This book is not a biography of Mackenzie King. It is an account of how he handled his favourite subject, foreign affairs, over four decades, and more particularly how he regarded Mussolini and Hitler during much of that time. But at least something needs to be said here about those aspects of his complex private life, as recorded in his diaries, that influenced his thinking as Canada's foreign minister. One aspect is his adoration of his mother. That she had a massive influence on her elder son, the second of her children, will be obvious to any reader of his extensive diary or of several biographies.

Pre-eminently, Charlotte Gray, in her *Mrs. King*, offers a convincing analysis of their convoluted, exaggerated, and fundamentally bizarre relationship, a relationship that had a life-long impact on King (he regarded his father as amiably ineffectual).

Isabel Mackenzie King died in December 1917, age seventy-four (King had celebrated her birthday by almost smothering her with seventy-four kisses[11]). It has been estimated that, in her son's 50,000-page diary,* begun in 1893, there are more than one thousand reverential passages about her and many about conversations with her from the Great Beyond (she was by far his most frequent and reassuring extraterrestrial interlocutor). Yet the myriad diary references do not tell us much about what she said; much more is about King's life-long adoration of her. At age twenty-five he recorded in his diary, "I do love her so much. She is so bright, cheerful, good, happy and lovely. She has so much grit and courage in her. I have met no woman so true and lovely in every way as my mother."[12] She was simply "the purest and sweetest soul that God ever made."[13]

King strove to live up to his mother's high expectations of him. It was to her as early as 1901 that he had "whispered … 'I might become the Premier of this country.'"[14] For her son to become prime minister would be the ultimate vindication of her father, William Lyon Mackenzie (1795–1861). Isabel was fiercely loyal to his memory and proud of his leadership in the failed rebellion of 1837 against the reactionary Tory Family Compact in Upper Canada. Her father's inconsistent leadership in his reform commitments did not lessen her pride. As the thirteenth of his thirteen children, she had shared his near poverty while in exile in the United States (where he became a citizen). An amnesty allowed him to return to Toronto in 1851 when he again became a member of the provincial legislature. William Lyon Mackenzie, the "Firebrand," died thirteen years before his grandson's birth. One recent biographer has defined his long and controversial political career as marked by an "overwhelming urge to reform everything, his suspicion of all in power and his fierce pride in his own independence [which] suggests that Mackenzie's only decided policy was *je suis contra*."[15]

---

*The original diaries, a mixture of longhand and typewritten, of 50,000 pages, are in Library and Archives Canada (LAC) in Ottawa, along with a later typewritten version of approximately 30,000 pages. George Henderson, in his admirable *W.L. Mackenzie King: A Bibliography and Research Guide*, places the total at 60,000 pages.

King would tell himself or anyone who might listen sympathetically that his grandfather's rebellion was not, repeat not, against the British Empire as such. King had a life-long admiration for the Empire, but was against the narrowly based oligarchy of local landowners and officials in Upper Canada who had served themselves rather than others. In that way, he saw a model for himself in his maternal grandfather, whom he regarded as in the great British tradition of defining the democratic rights of the people. Mackenzie had contributed to the development of responsible government in Upper Canada, embodied in the elected assembly rather than in the governor-in-council. For King, the liberal tradition of "parliament will decide" had been enhanced, not denied, by his maternal grandfather's reform career. But at the same time, King saw a parallel if less evident model for himself in his paternal grandfather who came to Canada in the British army and served against Mackenzie and other rebels. "He was a soldier of the Queen, and the grandson of the rebel never forgot the other family tradition of loyalty to the Crown ... The reconciliation of the opposing backgrounds of his parents was fundamental to Mackenzie King's Liberalism. And the reconciliation often concealed a mass of contradictory attitudes."[16]

Mackenzie King was born in Berlin, Ontario, in 1874. Popularly regarded as "the German capital of Canada," about two-thirds of its inhabitants – and King's classmates – were estimated to be of German descent, but nothing of their rich heritage in the arts or sciences appears to have rubbed off on him. He records little about and certainly no intimacy with his German-speaking classmates in his later journal. Living in his close-knit, devout Presbyterian family, dominated by his ambitious mother (who concentrated her endless ambitions for her children primarily on him), he does not seem to have sought any friendships among his largely Lutheran contemporaries. His mother remained his sole lodestar.

At the universities of Toronto, Chicago, and eventually Harvard, King fulfilled his parents' academic expectations. All that, however, must only be preliminary to a long and distinguished career in government, worthy of the grandson of William Lyon Mackenzie. But King did not enter the public service in that guise. Entrance was still heavily influenced by whom one knew, and it was not his mother but his father who opened the way.

King had first crossed to Europe in 1899 on a Harvard University travel grant. After a winter spent partly in London and Berlin, he was in Rome in June 1900 when a telegram arrived from William Mulock offering him the appointment of editor of the projected *Labour Gazette* (to be modelled on the British periodical of the same title). King, with some uncertainty, accepted, having decided to decline a likely appointment at Harvard. Mulock, then a Liberal member of parliament as well as chancellor of the University of Toronto, was shortly to become postmaster general and soon thereafter concurrently the first minister of labour. More to the point, he was a long-time friend of King's lawyer father, John. Two years before, he had commissioned Mackenzie King to prepare reports on labour conditions, especially abuses, in several industries.

From Rome, King telegraphed his acceptance of the editorial appointment, assuring himself that it was but the first step – as in fact it was – on his way to a ministerial appointment and ultimately to his remarkably long premiership. Within two months of his arrival in Ottawa, he was appointed deputy minister of labour at the young age of twenty-six. For the following eight years, as a senior public servant, he learned intimately the ways of the dominion government and the devices and desires of the Liberal Party, becoming an advocate of constructive labour-management conciliation and innovative legislation in the settlement of industrial disputes. In 1906 he went again to London, this time to discuss with the colonial secretary, Lord Elgin, and the undersecretary for the colonies, Winston Churchill (whom he had first met in Ottawa in 1900), fraud and other malpractices among Canadian immigration agents in Europe. On his return from London, King wrote to a coming Conservative candidate in Britain, Leopold Amery, "The Empire must grow, not be manufactured." (King had first met Amery in Ottawa before Amery's marriage in 1910 to a Canadian. She was the sister of Hamar Greenwood, King's 1895 classmate at the University of Toronto.) Presumably King had in mind Joseph Chamberlain's proposed manufacturing of an imperial customs union. For a liberal imperialist like himself, "It is how best to further that growth which is the problem."[17]

For King the eleven years between his appointment in 1900 by Laurier as the first deputy minister of labour until his defeat as minister of labour in the election of September 1911 was a highly instructive time. He learned at first hand how the British Empire functioned and how within it the status of Canada as a self-governing colony had developed since Confederation in 1867, forty years before. The early-twentieth-century world of gradual evolution was to be changed profoundly by the disaster of the First World War, but King's unexpected apprenticeship in foreign affairs took place in the prewar years amid empires, precarious balances of power, entangling alliances, and, in the unparalleled British Empire, the elaboration of dominion status. King's prewar decade as deputy minister, and especially his direct excursion into foreign affairs in 1908, confirmed him as an exponent of a liberal British Empire, an attitude that he retained throughout his long political career. He anticipated with satisfaction that Canada itself would soon succeed the United Kingdom as the lead nation of the Commonwealth.

When King's debut in international affairs was suddenly and unexpectedly launched in 1908, Canada had no foreign ministry. Within the Empire it had complete autonomy for, *inter alia*, fiscal and immigration policies and trade promotion, including from 1894 a trade commissioner service abroad, but only in 1909 did it create its own miniscule Department of External Affairs. At first it largely occupied itself – always in accord with the Foreign Office – with extra-imperial consular matters, the issuance of passports (all signed personally by the governor general), and protocol questions. Exchanges with London on matters imperial were reserved for the governor general, the prime minister, and the periodic imperial conferences. Laurier set a precedent by choosing to double as his own secretary of state for external affairs, a decision that opened the way for Mackenzie King to regard foreign affairs as his personal fiefdom.

2

Asian Apprenticeship

In 1907, the year before King resigned as deputy minister of labour to stand for parliament, he became involved in the challenge posed by mounting opposition in British Columbia to immigration from Asia, a problem with imperial implications that was becoming acute, especially with a national election pending. In the absence of a diplomatic service, King, as deputy minister and after June 1909 as minister of labour, played an unexpected and heady role in trilateral discussions at the most senior levels among the United States, Canada, and the United Kingdom over the increasingly vexed question of migrants from Japan and China and, in Canada's case, from India as well.

Avner Offer, in his incongruously titled *The First World War: An Agrarian Interpretation*, gives a detailed analysis of King's involvement in the prewar Asian immigration controversies. He rightly places King's sudden and unexpected introduction to the world of diplomacy in the context of the evolving imperial transformation of the United States, the United Kingdom, and Japan and, more specifically, the growing opposition on the west coast of North America to Asian migration. "By the turn of the century the demand for exclusion was about five decades old and the principle well and truly established that Asians were not acceptable. Canada, the United States, New Zealand and Australia had all enacted legislation to restrict or prevent the entry of non-whites and all of them discriminated against Asiatic residents already in place by denying them some rights, subjecting them to special taxes, denying them some forms of legal protection and preventing male residents from acquiring wives from overseas."[1]

King's diplomatic apprenticeship took place against this background as well as that of accelerating economic growth and imperial thinking in all three countries. The United States had expanded territorially after the

Mexican-American War of 1846–48, which resulted in American sovereignty over Texas. Following the Spanish-American War of 1898, it had become an even greater imperial power with the acquisition of the Philippines, Puerto Rico, and several Caribbean and Pacific islands including Hawaii, as well as suzerainty over Cuba. Japan emerged as a major regional if not yet a world power, the first Asian country to be so recognized. The United Kingdom was attempting to respond to emerging nationalist movements in India that challenged the over-stretched Raj. India also expressed discontent over the exclusion in one part of the British Empire of people from another part, a violation of the principle of equality under the crown. With Australasia even less welcoming to Asian migrants than Canada, it was an additional problem that the Raj did not need.

London had for more than a decade valued its 1894 Treaty of Commerce and Navigation and its more recent and comprehensive alliance of 1902 with the rising maritime power of Japan. Japan had defeated the armed might of Russia in 1905, for racists an astonishing victory of yellow people over white.

> Ever since the Anglo-Japanese alliance of 1902, and more so since the Russian naval defeat at Tsushima, Japan had been a cornerstone of British strategy. Japan's presence in the Far East held in check the other European powers in the region, especially Russia and Germany. It made it possible for Britain to withdraw its naval forces to face the German threat. Britain's big trade with China, the security of Hong Kong, India, Ceylon, Malaya and Australia, all came to rest on the understanding with Japan. And while the alliance neutralized the Russian threat to India, the Japanese example stimulated the yearning for independence there. It placed the United States and Britain at odds in the Far East, and gave rise to tensions in India, in Russia, in China and in Australia.

> King was so innocent of strategy that, on arrival in Britain in March 1908, he was astonished to discover that there was an Anglo-German naval rivalry.[2]

In Canada, King came to recognize that the increasing demand in British Columbia for the exclusion of Asian immigrants was not simply a worrisome local or partisan problem. It had broad imperial dimensions, as well as implications for Canada-United States relations. From 1854 the United Province of Canada, eager to attract settlers, especially qualified farmers, had sent immigration agents to Europe, but certainly not to Asia. "Coolies" from China had played an indispensable if ill-rewarded role in the hazardous construction of the Canadian Pacific Railway through the Rockies, but were neither invited to bring their families nor to stay. From India came mainly Sikhs, among them Indian army veterans of the Soudan campaigns, in search of a better life in another part of the British Empire; they were subjects of the Queen as much as Canadians were. But it was Japanese immigrants (some making their way indirectly to the United States via Hawaii and Canada) who gave the greatest concern on both sides of the border. Along the Pacific coast they were seen as working hard for little money and living frugally, leaving white workers convinced that their own standard of living and that of their families would be undermined by the arrival of yet more "cheap peoples." No one in Canada attempted to answer the question put by a Canadian observer of the exclusion of Asian immigrants. "It cannot be his colour, for we admit the Negro; it cannot be his religion, for we admit the Doukhobour and the Mormon; it cannot be his morals, for we have no standard gauge for morality; it cannot be his untruthfulness; it cannot be his disregard for law and order. If, then, he is sober, industrious, law-abiding, thrifty, what more would we have?"[3]

That was not the way that Robert Macpherson, the Liberal member of parliament for Vancouver City, saw the question. In August he wrote to Laurier, "I would like very much to keep this country White and I would also like to keep it Liberal, but it is impossible to keep either one of the two unless the Japs are peremptorily told that they must carry out their understanding with your government."[4] Laurier replied, "The Japanese has adopted European civilisation, has shown that he can whip European soldiers, has a navy equal man-for-man to the best afloat [i.e., the Royal Navy] and will not submit to being kicked and treated with contempt as his brother from China still meekly submits to."[5] Hamar Greenwood, King's classmate at the University of Toronto, now at Westminster as an MP and parliamentary private secretary to Winston Churchill, then undersecretary for the colonies, cautioned in a widely reported speech to the Empire Club in Toronto that "It is impossible to treat the subjects of the Mikado ... in any way that will humiliate them ... We have to change our whole idea of inferior races ... You can deal as you like with the Chinaman for he is a patient fellow. He has no great government behind him ... I believe in a white Canada ... in strengthening the white portions of the Empire. But … you must not forget that you have an imperial responsibility."[6]

For Canada, the imperial dimensions of which Greenwood spoke complicated unrest over Asian immigration on the west coast. The Anglo-Japanese Treaty of Commerce and Navigation of 1894 had included a reciprocal provision for the movement and residence of nationals between the two countries, emigration from Japan to the United Kingdom not being seen as a real or potential problem. Dominions were free to subscribe or not to the treaty. Certainly Australia and New Zealand did not do so, but Laurier, in search of trans-Pacific markets for western grain, did, with the added provision that Canada was free to restrict Japanese immigration to Canada along the lines of a restrictive provision in a contemporary United States-Japan trade agreement. That Laurier and others in central and eastern Canada saw trade advantages arising from the treaty did nothing to lessen the fear of the "Yellow Peril" on the Pacific coast where it had become the paramount political issue. British Columbia premier Sir Richard McBride called for "Mongolian exclusion." Robert Borden, the leader of the opposition in Ottawa, declared that "the Conservative Party stands for a white Canada," a sentiment shared by another future Conservative prime minister, the Calgary MP R.B. Bennett: "We must not allow our shores to be overrun by Asiatics and become dominated by an alien race."[7] Even the more measured Laurier, with his eye on the pending election, was reluctant to surrender whatever standing the Liberal Party still had in BC. "I have very little hope of any good coming to this country from Asiatic immigration of any kind." Mackenzie King, MP, shared his leader's misgivings about Liberal fortunes on the west coast, readily agreeing that Canada should remain a white man's country.

In the western United States there was yet stronger opposition to immigration from Japan. King's unexpected foray into foreign affairs began with a visit to Ottawa in January 1907 by Elihu Root, the secretary of state and former secretary of war in President Theodore Roosevelt's administration. Given each dominion's responsibility for its own immigration policies and procedures, Root went to Ottawa rather than to London to explore how Canada and the United States might best collaborate to reduce or eliminate local political and racial agitation against Japanese immigration. He recognized that there was no practicable way for the United States to close to Asian immigrants the decidedly porous US frontier with Canada, so he called on its good neighbour to join in denying entry to North America of all Asian immigrants. That heavy-handed proposal left Laurier in the invidious position of trying to deal concurrently with political tensions in British Columbia, London's imperial priorities with Japan and India, and Root's loaded questions.

While the prime minister reflected on the approaching election, violence in British Columbia became increasingly likely, prompted in part by the Asiatic Exclusion League of California, which had become active in the province. On 7 September, before Laurier had decided what to do, the anti-immigration agitation in Vancouver culminated in a rowdy demonstration that became a riot. Both Ottawa and London viewed this violence with consternation. The prime minister's immediate public response was to portray it as essentially a labour and not a racial problem (it did, in fact, begin as a labour march that got out of control).

Hamar Greenwood, who fortuitously had been in Vancouver directly before the riot, promptly set out the parallel concerns of the foreign and colonial offices in his Empire Club speech in Toronto on 13 September. There was no mistaking his message: the immigration problem on the west coast was not only a Canadian problem; it was an imperial problem. "Owing to the overwhelming defeat of Russia by an Oriental power, the sudden rise of Japan and, following that, the Oriental immigration question on the Pacific Coast, the Dominion suddenly came within the arena of foreign politics, and to-day you have the danger zone of the world, insofar as our own Empire is concerned, shifted from the Northwest Frontier of India … to the Pacific Coast of this Dominion." Senator Robert Jaffray, the owner of the *Globe*, followed Greenwood: "As Britishers … the people on the Pacific Coast must do what they could to make Canada a white man's country, but it was not by riot or lawlessness that they would succeed in doing so."[8]

Six weeks after the riot, King, as deputy minister of labour, was sent by Laurier to Vancouver as a one-man royal commission to recommend compensation for Japanese victims of the violence and vandalism (larger Chinese claims were dealt with later) and, less formally, to gain with a Japanese consul a first-hand impression of the post-riot situation.* The British ambassador in Washington and the governor general sent their own reports

---

*As deputy minister of labour, King arranged for the publication of his twenty-two page report on the damages to Japanese property and his eighteen-page report on damages to Chinese property by the King's Printer in 1908 (Henderson, *W.L. Mackenzie King*, 78).

to London and the mob violence received coverage in the newspapers of Britain, Japan, and the United States. For King the riot and his successful commission in Vancouver were to mark the beginning of a three-year involvement in Asian emigration to North America (not merely to Canada) and, more broadly, the place of Canada in an evolving British Empire.*

Following King's return to Ottawa from Vancouver, Laurier's next step was to send Rodolphe Lemieux, Mulock's successor as postmaster general and minister of labour (and hence King's minister), to Tokyo in mid-October to seek a commitment from Japan that it would restrict the flow of its immigrants to Canada, a practice that would be compatible with the priorities of both Canada and the British Empire. As the order-in-council of 12 October 1907 appointing Lemieux stated, he was "to discuss the situation with His Majesty's Ambassador at Tokyo and Japanese authorities, with the object, by friendly means, of preventing recurrence of such causes as might disturb happy relations which have … existed between the subjects of the King in Canada and elsewhere, and the subjects of the Emperor of Japan."[9] Lemieux succeeded in concluding such a gentlemen's agreement on 23 December 1907. Benefiting from the indispensable counsel, comprehension, and contacts of the experienced British ambassador, Lemieux was assured in writing, before his return to Ottawa in mid-January 1908, that the number of Japanese immigrants to Canada would not exceed four hundred annually. The Japanese government undertook to enforce the limit itself rather than suffer the humiliation of seeing Japanese applicants excluded by white countries.

At the same time, President Theodore Roosevelt, the belligerent "Rough Rider" of the Spanish-American War in Cuba and a pronounced admirer of Japanese prowess – describing Japan in a message to Congress "as one of the greatest of civilized nations" – canvassed behind the scenes the prospects for a trilateral approach to the vexed question of Asian migration that would somehow defuse the situation in the Pacific coast states and at the same time reduce the possibility of a bilateral clash with Japan. In California, anti-immigration agitation and legislation, fuelled in large part by labour unions, included controversial school segregation of students of Japanese background. Roosevelt dispatched his secretary of labor to the west coast. He recommended

---

*King's seventy-nine-page Harvard doctoral thesis of 1909 was entitled "Oriental Immigration to Canada."

that Japan curtail its emigration in return for California restoring unrestricted school admission.

At this point Roosevelt came up with the surprising idea that Britain could solve the Japanese immigration problem for him. He had a curiously ambivalent attitude toward Britain. In 1898, at the time of the Spanish-American War, he had declared that "I hope to see the Spanish flag and the English flag gone from the map of North America [including Canada?]." Ten years later, although fully conscious that Britain and Japan had become allies (reaffirmed by the Anglo-Japanese Alliance of 1902), Roosevelt was reputed to be too proud to be seen seeking British support in what he regarded as a difficulty that United States power alone should be able to resolve, while at the same time convinced that Britain might more readily settle the immigration problem by virtue of being Japan's ally.

William Howard Taft, the secretary of war and later successor to Roosevelt as president, was on his second Pacific tour when Lemieux was disembarking in Tokyo. Taft reported to Roosevelt that the Japanese minister of war had described to him how, on a visit to Vancouver ten years, before he had foreseen labour tensions. The Canadian foreign minister had told him "how the very serious situation in Vancouver, BC, made it necessary for them to take further steps to prevent additional immigration into that country." Assuming erroneously that Britain was responsible for Canadian immigration practices, Taft advised Roosevelt to leave the problem to Britain, Japan's ally, to resolve. Roosevelt had the United States ambassador to Japan contact Lemieux in Tokyo to propose that Britain, Canada, and the United States join in a "common cause," a proposal that Lemieux courteously suggested should be discussed not with him but with London as well as Ottawa.

Lemieux having in effect declined Roosevelt's idea of Canada initiating a trilateral approach to Japan, the president, aware of the riot in Vancouver some months before, pondered how he might employ a Canadian as interlocutor with both Japan and Britain for his own ends, despite the fact that the United States and Britain had earlier encountered difficulties over settling the Venezuelan/British Guiana border and the creation of the Republic of Panama to permit the US construction of a canal (completed in 1914). A Harvard friend suggested to Roosevelt that he invite King to call when he would be in Washington in January 1908. Against the background of war talk in Washington and his decision to transfer the navy's battle fleet from its home waters in the Atlantic to the Pacific, the president came to see King as a possible *interlocuteur valable* with the British government.

Laurier and King were not wholly surprised at Roosevelt's unlikely approach. Lemieux had alerted them by telegram from Tokyo of the US ambassador's query. King, although a public servant and not a responsible minister as Lemieux was, was well informed of the details of his minister's visit to Japan. Despite his lingering dissatisfaction with the flaccid performance of Britain in the Alaska boundary settlement of 1903 and his understandable suspicions of American intentions, Laurier agreed to King's acceptance of the invitation from the president. Perhaps Laurier had in mind the desirability of appearing cooperative when he was himself pondering the negotiation of a reciprocal trade agreement with the United States, but MacGregor Dawson, in his biography of King, later regarded his selection with some skepticism. "Even the most charitable could never have described King as an expert. The truth was that the [embryonic] Canadian [foreign] service did not contain anyone to challenge King's knowledge, such as it was … although doubtless there were a number of immigration officials who had some familiarity with Far Eastern relations. In the country of the blind, the one-eyed man was king" (pun perhaps intended).[10]

Elihu Root, the US secretary of state who had raised the immigration exclusion question in Ottawa one year before, suggested that zones be created for Asian immigrants in various parts of the world with suitable climates, but King could not ignore the ethical aspect. "Of course there was to be considered the doctrine of our common humanity … but … we might well say that the peace of the family was sometimes best kept … by brothers and their families not sharing the one household. Mr Root said: 'In regard to brotherhood, because I recognize my neighbour as a brother, I am not thereby obliged to allow him to come into my yard and do what he wishes with my property, to plant his seeds in my garden and take what he can out of my soil.'"[11]

For the next three months, King, with Laurier's reluctant accord, was placed in contact with the highest levels of government in both London and Washington. According to King's detailed diary entries, Roosevelt clearly stated his goals during three visits to Washington. Not too subtly, he had said at their first meeting that if by chance "you were going to England I would give you some strong messages to take to Sir Edward Grey [the foreign secretary]. I would have you tell him that ... he could do much for the cause of peace, not that we want to ask the help of the British, but the Japanese must learn that they will have to keep their people in their own country. Britain is her ally, a word ... might go far ... I decided to send the fleet into the Pacific [for the first time]; it may help them [the Japanese] to understand that we want a definite arrangement."[12]

Convinced that Japan was not observing its earlier "gentlemen's agreement" with the United States to limit emigration, Roosevelt had decided to dispatch the "Great White Fleet" of sixteen battlewagons around the world – from the Atlantic into the Pacific via Cape Horn – as one part of his determined effort to stop Asian immigration once and for all. He also speculated for King that if Britain did not act with the United States in promoting a settlement, he anticipated a threat to the unity of Canada in that the states west of the Rockies might join with British Columbia to form an independent republic of the Pacific (that Roosevelt would, apparently with a straight face, advance the idea that the three Pacific states might successfully secede from the Union only forty years after one of the bloodiest civil wars in history was remarkably imaginative). With Japan, Roosevelt declared that he would "deal politely, be conciliatory, but carry a big stick." The Great White Fleet, despite British reservations, was later received enthusiastically in an Australia chronically uneasy over its isolation and courteously in a Japan secure in the conviction that impossibly long lines of communication would render a conflict with the United States unlikely.*

The mood in Washington, King reported to the governor general and to Laurier on his return to Ottawa, was that a US war with Japan had suddenly become possible. "The whole tone of the President's talk ... was that we must have absolutely what we are demanding or war ... be prepared for war and be ready for it on a moment's notice ... [Root] fears the possibility of war in the immediate future. There will be war for sure if the Japanese do not see what this country wishes done and do it quickly."[13] Although he did not say so explicitly, was Roosevelt threatening war with a British ally and hence, if it came to war, expecting Britain to stand clear?

---

*In one of their conversations, Roosevelt asked King, "If the population of the country [Australia] is not increasing ... how can it defend itself against the blackbird and the yellow skin?" His solution? If "she cannot get the peoples of the northern part of Europe, [she should] take Italians or ... bring in Portuguese, but bring in white races and people the land with them" (King diary, 31 January 1908. See also Heere, "Japan and the British World 1904–14.").

King recorded Roosevelt as saying, "You should impress upon the British that there is a common interest in this matter. If the Japanese recognize that there is a common interest, there will be peace."[14] Or was Roosevelt saying that if the British government failed to press its ally Japan to stop immigration to North America, he for his part would do nothing to hinder the separation of British Columbia from the Canadian confederation and with the support of the three Pacific coast states see it become a new state of the Union?

In January 1902 when Britain and Japan had negotiated a military alliance to supplement their commercial treaty of 1894, Britain had proposed a provision that if either signatory was attacked by one other country [e.g., the United States] the other signatory would maintain a benevolent neutrality, but if attacked by two, the other signatory would declare war in support of its ally. In the wake of the 1905 Russo-Japanese treaty of Portsmouth, New Hampshire (presided over by Roosevelt), Britain and Japan amended their alliance to specify that either would come to the other's assistance if attacked by one other nation. Far-fetched though it now seems, Roosevelt may have worried that this revision could conceivably require Britain to line up with its valued Japanese ally against an unprovoked attack by the United States. He told King that "it was hard to say what purpose may not be in the brain of those little yellow men. [That Japan] is heading for war appears to be certain."[15] The security of British assets in the Asia-Pacific region, he implied, had come to rest upon good relations among Japan, Britain, and the United States, who could soon be at odds.

Laurier was unimpressed with what he dismissed as Roosevelt's "flam" (as in flimflam), but he recognized that it was in Canada's own interests to send King back to Washington to explore further the president's far-fetched idea of having a Canadian civil servant act for the United States at ministerial-level discussions with Britain amid the threatening unrest on the Pacific coast of North America. More incredibly, King, on his second visit to Washington, realized that Roosevelt would not hesitate to distort the truth to make it appear that it was Canada and not the United States that was seeking the involvement of London to resolve a US problem with Japan. And that incredible invention is what in fact Roosevelt attempted to pursue. The sardonic comment of Lord Grey, the governor general, in keeping London informed, was apposite: "up comes [to Ottawa] a letter in which the President tells Sir Wilfrid Laurier that he will be glad to come to the assistance of

Canada! The whole story would be laughable if it were not an interesting illustration of American methods."[16] The other Grey – Sir Edward, the foreign secretary – also dismissed any idea of a Japanese threat. "He pointed out that a war between Japan and the United States was logistically almost impossible and that North America was well beyond the military reach of Japan. Japan had no designs on North America. More positively, the [Anglo-Japanese] alliance was based on the tacit British understanding that Japan would have a free hand … in Korea and Manchuria."[17]

Nevertheless, King warned Lord Grey and Laurier that "if war broke out between the United States and Japan, the residents of Vancouver … would turn to the United States for protection." Indeed, King suspected that "one of Roosevelt's designs in fanning up the tension with Japan was to detach British Columbia and bring it over into the United States."[18] He told John Morley, the secretary of state for India, that "Nothing would suit the purposes of the Americans better … than some trouble should break out in Vancouver [over Japanese immigration] at the time the American fleet reached San Francisco … it would demonstrate that the whole problem of Oriental immigration was one in which the interests of the two countries [were] the same." He also described how "There were people in British Columbia only too interested in creating the impression that because of the distance … Ottawa did not appreciate the situation on the Pacific coast and were indifferent to it." Further, "there were other persons who were [convinced] that there was no use of the people of British Columbia looking to Ottawa for help, that the Anglo-Japanese alliance made it impossible for them [the British] to take any action."[19]

In later years King remained convinced that all US presidents sought to possess Canada. Theodore Roosevelt had said that he wanted to banish "the English flag" from North America. In his mind, could Japanese intransigence, matched by the arrival of the US battle fleet in the Pacific, be a sufficient platform for anti-immigration advocates on both sides of the border to seek a permanent solution through the US acquisition of the immigration staging post of British Columbia?

After King had made a third and final visit to the belligerent Roosevelt, Laurier agreed, again without enthusiasm, that, as the president had requested, he would make King available to go to London in early March 1908 to discuss various matters, including implicitly the approaches to Canada that the United States had made in both Tokyo and Washington to involve Britain in the problem of restricting Japanese immigration to North America. In addition, Laurier took the occasion to instruct him to tell the British government that the immigration of Indians to Canada "must be stopped. If Britain did not arrange to keep the Indians out of Canada, Canada would be forced to do it herself."[20] In his own musings about the exclusion of Asian immigrants, King asked himself, "as one who believed in Christian teachings, whether a nation which called itself Christian could take a stand on [i.e., support] a question of restriction." That fundamental question King evaded by rationalizing support for exclusion on economic grounds. "So far as the labouring classes were concerned the question was an economic question and not a race question ... the standard of living of our people would be seriously menaced by the competition of persons of a lower standard."[21]

Such thinking prompted King to speculate on Canada's need for a navy to protect its shores from, *inter alia*, unwanted immigrants and to demonstrate thereby to the United States that it was capable of controlling its own borders. Foreshadowing the difficult naval debates that were to become acrimonious over the next five years, King concluded, "We might as well face this situation squarely ... by [either] contributions to the British Government or by the beginning of a navy of our own ... [but] I do not mean that we would act in any way independently of the British."[22]

From the middle of March 1908, King spent a month in London seeing Balfour, Grey, Elgin, Churchill, and a host of other MPs, including Amery and Greenwood, and less enthusiastically the octogenarian high commissioner, Lord Strathcona.* Offstage King was especially pleased to see again Violet Markham, the affluent Liberal social reformer whom he had met three years before during her visit to Governor General Lord Grey (who was something of a mentor for King). Thereafter she frequently gave him advice and money, although on this occasion she deplored the Anglo-Japanese alliance and "Japan ever having defeated Russia, that it was the defeat of a white people by a yellow."[23]

The British government responded surprisingly readily to King's request for restrictions on Indian migration to Canada, although it did so with a certain unease arising from the fact that the would-be migrants would see

---

*King had become wary of what he saw as Churchill's self-centred nature: "It is Churchill rather than the movement with which he is identified that is the mainspring of his conduct" (Dawson, *William Lyon Mackenzie King*, 162).

themselves as British subjects seeking to join other British subjects overseas. Drawing on his own convictions, King added more optimistically that "Laurier recognized the obligations and responsibilities of Empire, as well as its advantages ... all being of one household, we should endeavour to quietly settle our differences among ourselves ... the outsider [the United States] need not have anything whatever to do with it."[24] Later King went further: "I am beginning to see the essential need of Canada shaping her policy from a national view-point ... Let her remain part of the Empire ... [but] let her become a nation or other nations [i.e., the United States] will rob her of this right."[25] He remained deeply suspicious of Roosevelt's real purpose in exaggerating Japan's intentions: he wanted "to detach British Columbia and to bring it over into the United States." He told Laurier that a war between Japan and the United States "would be the beginning of the disruption of the Canadian Dominion."[26]

King speculated for his various British interlocutors on just how far Roosevelt would use the war scare to curtail immigration from Japan. Lord Bryce, the wise and patient British ambassador, soon reported that the Japanese were already moving to defuse the situation. In the case of Canada, they were continuing their undertaking to Lemieux. In the case of the United States, they were now fully implementing their existing "gentlemen's agreement," leading to a sharp decline in arrivals by the end of 1908. At that point, the problem of Japanese immigrants having been, at least for the time being, resolved, Roosevelt promptly lost interest in Laurier, King, and Canada. King returned from London pleased with himself, but he also recorded his admiration for the British ministers and officials who had received him so sympathetically and so candidly, as they themselves anticipated the renewal in 1911 of their 1894 Treaty of Navigation and Commerce with Japan.[27]

Racial opposition to Asian immigration, however, lingered on the west coast of Canada. As late as 1914, Prime Minister Robert Borden saw continuing partisan profit in declaring his dissatisfaction with what he termed the limited measures taken by the Laurier government to exclude Asian immigrants. The Conservative member for Vancouver City, H.H. Stevens, who had won the seat from the Liberals, stated, "We cannot allow indiscriminate immigration from the Orient and hope to build up a nation ... on the foundations upon which we have commenced our national life."[28] Borden instructed the acting high commissioner in London (Strathcona having recently died in office) to inform both the colonial and foreign secretaries "that public opinion in this country will not tolerate immigration from Asiatic countries and that even more drastic measures and regulations will if necessary be provided in order to prevent an influx."[29] Within a few months, the First World War, in which Japan became a valued ally of the United Kingdom, ended Borden's threat of drastic measures.

What is one to make of all the racial agitation that formed the extraordinary advent of King's long and cherished involvement in foreign affairs? Certainly it is odd that he never appears to have referred to it and specifically to Theodore Roosevelt in later life – but then again there was always much that was odd about King. The present author makes no claim to have read the forty thousand or more pages of his diary that follow his encounters with Theodore Roosevelt, but a canter through them leaves the impression that even during the extended periods that he spent in the United States between 1911 and 1919, King made no journal comments about him. Why? Perhaps he reflected that in the aftermath of Liberal defeat in the September 1911 "reciprocity election," it would be the better part of wisdom not to dwell on the fact that Roosevelt had lied to Laurier and to the British, as well as to himself. But given the remarkable and heterogeneous revelations that King habitually included elsewhere in his diary, both about himself and others, diplomatic reticence is hardly a convincing explanation. King was always eager to consort with the high and mighty in the United States as well as in Britain and was later notably diffident to Theodore Roosevelt's cousin, Franklin. Perhaps he simply concluded that to be candid about the Rough Rider even in the privacy of his diary might be impolitic, although he remained remarkably candid about others.

If King's prewar devotion to the British Empire needed any reinforcing – which it did not – the extraordinary experience with Theodore Roosevelt would have stimulated it. Asian immigration being of little or no interest to French Canada, King did not need on this occasion to look over his shoulder at Quebec, as Borden would later put it. Throughout, he praised the governor general and British ministers and officials and he happily recorded in his diary their praise for him and his satisfaction at his debut in international affairs. Certainly against the pre-First World War emergence of the United State as an imperial power and the postwar confusions of the Paris Peace Conference, the episode remains, as it were, a bubble in time. It is an odd episode left dangling in the prewar relations of the three countries.

King's diary for the decade between his election to parliament in 1908 and the end of the First World War in 1918 has a more impersonal, a more arm's length air about it than it has for the more prolific and emotional later years. More specifically, his detailed diary of his unlikely visits to Roosevelt and his related trips to Britain read like paraphrases of official reports, a civil servant's record for later reference. Much of the spontaneity, candour, and personal revelations that mark his postwar diary are not yet present. There are even fewer adoring references to his mother and messages from the Great Beyond, intensified only in later years.

Long before 1918, however, King repeatedly recognized that he had been ordained by God to be prime minister of Canada with a direct and significant role in solving the world's many problems. Amid such imaginings – which only grew in time – King has been seen by some apologists as being influenced by the heyday of occultism, which emerged in the late nineteenth century, culminating in the grief of families everywhere during and after the First World War.

In any event, why King displayed unwonted reticence in his diary about Theodore Roosevelt and his machinations may be left to the reader's speculation, but two transcendent elements in his prewar, anglophile thinking are central to any understanding of his later international excursions. The first is that he was a confirmed, life-long liberal imperialist. Certainly not a tory imperialist, but a liberal imperialist who believed that a British Empire was a good thing. It was where Canada belonged, although largely in response to Quebec he would occasionally add that imperial centralists, more numerous in his imaginings than in reality, had to be watched. For all his twists and turnings, he ended his life as he had begun it, an ardent, if politically prudent, monarchist and imperial advocate.

The second abiding element in King's pre-First World War thinking was his lifelong skepticism – to put it at a minimum – about the intentions of the United States toward Canada. When in late 1935 he hurried to complete Bennett's negotiation of a trade agreement with the United States, he assured his American interlocutors that if he had to choose between a British path and an American in international relations, he would choose the American, a claim which was all nonsense. Forty years after Theodore Roosevelt had lied in portraying Canada rather than the United States as seeking the assistance of Britain in resolving Asian immigration problems, King retained a fundamental conviction that the United States wanted to take over Canada. How much better it was to be a dominion in the British Empire!

In his immigration debut, King had won the support of the governor general and of many Liberals, pre-eminently Laurier himself. On his return from London in April 1908 he secured, with "the Unseen Hand of God as his guide," the Liberal nomination in Waterloo North (which included his birthplace, Berlin). Five months later, on 21 September 1908, he resigned as deputy minister of labour and in the election of 26 October 1908 became the Liberal member for his home constituency. His mother, employing rather unusual syntax, shared her delight with him: "you are going on with a work that your grandfather strove hard to throw the best part of his life into, and now you will have the advantage of a more enlightened people to deal with … 'My political career' has a ring about it that rouses all my nature and [I] … trust I may be spared to see [you] gain the love of your followers, and in fact to see you as a regular Gladstone."[30]

Upon his election in Waterloo North, King hastened to ask Laurier to make him minister of labour with his own separate department, but Laurier wisely afforded him time to prove himself in the peculiar environment of the House of Commons. Much of the seven months from King's election to his appointment as minister of labour on 2 June 1909, was, however, spent outside Canada. According to the British embassy in Washington, the United States was not yet done with King. Curiously, Washington, not London, had before the Canadian election sought his appointment as a British Empire delegate to a conference in Shanghai of the International Opium Commission. King had seen something of the opium trade at the time of the riot in Vancouver two years before, but that fleeting encounter was hardly enough to explain Washington's request for his participation in the Shanghai conference. In any event, Laurier again concurred.

Only six weeks after being elected a member of parliament, King was away from the House of Commons from early December 1908 to May 1909. During those five months, he again saw in London many senior parliamentarians and officials, including the foreign secretary, Sir Edward Grey, whom he had called on in March as well as in 1906. As was the case later in Calcutta (Delhi did not become the capital of India until 1912), King's visit to London could be seen as a "goodwill mission" in recognition that the various interests of the United States, Canada, and Britain had been successfully resolved by the restrictive actions of the governments of Japan and India in stopping immigration to North America (as for China, in 1903 Canada had imposed an impossibly high head tax on would-be immigrants). In Japan after the Shanghai opium conference, King reviewed the all but total emigration restrictions with the Canadian trade commissioner in Yokohama, W.T.R. Preston (who had been chief immigration agent in London), although he had earlier advocated to his minister, Lemieux, the continuation of a "modest" degree of Japanese immigration to Canada. He also carefully recorded his gratitude, as Lemieux had already done, for the unfailing assistance of the British ambassador with whom he shared his conviction that the root cause of the anti-Asian immigration sentiment in British Columbia was not racist but economic or even climatic. "So far as the labouring classes were concerned, the question was an economic question and not a race question ... The economic conditions of which it was the outcome were the standard of living of our people which would be seriously menaced by the competition of people of a lower standard."[31] To a senior member of the Chinese government, he explained in a wonderfully self-serving manner that the exclusion of the Chinese would really help to make China "the greater industrial power of the future."[32]

The Shanghai conference of the International Opium Commission achieved little during its three-week duration, but King came away from it with two general conclusions: first, that he had a useful – perhaps even unique – role to play as interlocutor between Britain and the United States and, second, that conference diplomacy was not at all to his liking. Better to have "a policy of each nation negotiating its own settlements ... with countries concerned,"[33] an attitude that he was to pursue in his "good will" visits to Peking and Tokyo in April, and to replicate at the League of Nations twenty-five years later.

With the suspension of his involvement in international affairs in 1909 and his defeat in the election of 1911, King's focus for the next decade was on North America. Strangely, as noted above, he does not appear to have referred subsequently in his journal to his unique encounters with Theodore Roosevelt, notable though his comings and goings to Washington and London were. Possibly in time he concluded, rightly, that those events clearly belonged to another era, distinct from the very different postwar world in which he would make his way toward the prime ministership.*

---

*King recalled in October 1935 for the newly arrived Japanese minister to Canada some of the officials he had met during his visit to Tokyo in 1909, but he made no reference to Theodore

Following his travels in Asia, King was made a Commander of the Order of St Michael and St George upon the recommendation of Lord Grey – to his own gratification and to the envy of older and longer serving senior public servants. He had made a name for himself in Ottawa and even in London during his eight years as deputy minister of labour. In his two years as minister of labour between his return from Asia and his defeat in the election of 1911, King advisedly concentrated on domestic matters, including legislation intended to ameliorate working conditions by, for example, limiting the workday to eight hours. Other measures included improved technical education and methods of settling labour disputes through conciliatory conversations. Against that background, he told his diary at the time, "God has a great work for me in this Dominion, maybe at some time to be its Prime Minister."[34] Accordingly he stayed away from two major issues in parliament that did have international implications but were unpopular in his constituency of Waterloo North. Laurier's initiative, foreshadowed as early as the 1902 imperial conference, to create a Canadian navy (rather than make a direct financial contribution to the overstretched Royal Navy as Australia and New Zealand had done) was seen by many voters in Quebec – and Waterloo North – as carrying with it the potential to embroil Canada in overseas conflicts. Two years before, King had recognized the need for naval protection of Canada's long shoreline, but for domestic reasons he prudently kept out of the 1910 naval controversy, speaking about the Liberal approach only in 1913.

The second major issue leading up to the 1911 election was a proposed reciprocity trade agreement with the United States, seen as having the potential to lead to free trade benefiting Canadian farmers but not vulnerable manufacturers. Laurier's bilateral trade initiative would define the election

---

Roosevelt (King diary, 24 October 1935). He did, however, record that on returning to office in 1935, he had inherited "a serious tariff conflict" with Japan, which prompted him to describe Canada's relations with Japan as being "commercial in character but ... at one time of sufficient acuteness to take on political implications" (21 May 1937, *DCER*, 6: 154). It is also possible that in proposing himself to the governor general in 1938 as the leader of a British Empire peace mission to Japan, he envisaged contacting officials whom he had met thirty years before. Finally, King may have had in mind his 1909 visit to Japan when, in reviewing in 1945 the terrifying potency of the atomic bombs dropped by the United States on Hiroshima and Nagasaki, he took some consolation in observing to his diary that "it is fortunate that the use of the bomb should have been upon the Japanese rather than upon the white men of Europe" (King diary, 9 August 1945).

of 1911, but King took little part in the increasingly heated debates during which, in much of English Canada, Laurier was accused of abandoning the motherland for the scarlet woman to the south. Since Waterloo North was home to a number of small manufacturers, King adopted, when forced to it, a position that was convoluted and vaguely protectionist – and ambiguous and occasionally contradictory, as would frequently be the case in the future.

3

Leadership Manoeuvres

Countering any prolonged period of unemployment and after careful soundings, King accepted an invitation from the Rockefeller Foundation in New York to serve as a well-paid consultant on labour and, more broadly, public relations, which were not strong points in the managerial repertoire of John D. Rockefeller, Jr. King passed much of the next eight years in the United States, although he retained his personal residence in Canada and his Liberal nomination in York North (Ontario) because God, he was certain, had singled him out as a future prime minister. He was thus remote physically and mentally from the turmoil and carnage of the First World War, which had spread across Europe, and from the suffering and despair that was the price of Canada's all-out war effort. In the United States (which did not enter the war for almost three years) he did not see, day after day, the toll in Canadian dead and wounded reported in Canadian newspapers. He was never in uniform and he had no friends in uniform who did not return (but then he had no intimate friends beyond the deceased Bert Harper, a university friend and Ottawa colleague, and later Joan Patteson, the wife of an Ottawa banker). Nor was his family involved in the war: his brother Max, a physician, was an invalid in Arizona. In short, King knew nothing at first hand of the loss and agony that the war meant to most Canadians.

King's diary recounts little of how he understood the First World War and no perception of the dire challenges that faced Prime Minister Borden during the years of seemingly endless slaughter and the subsequent confusions, contradictions, and contrivances of the Paris Peace Conference, where the various aims of the victors were never reconciled. In struggling with questions of what place Canada should fill in the world, including in a rapidly evolving and overstretched British Commonwealth, Borden successfully sought membership for Canada in both the International Labour Organization

(ILO) and the League of Nations, which were intended to ensure that there would never again be a similar holocaust. At the wartime imperial conferences and at the Paris Peace Conference he thought in depth – at least to the extent that his failing health permitted – about the confused and virtually insoluble problems left by the war and the potential of the proposed League of Nations to address them. His leadership during the war and above all during the compulsory military service crisis of 1917 won for Canada a significant place in international affairs which Canada might have retained if King, following Borden and his successor Arthur Meighen, had felt able to pursue such a role. But King did not do so. He constantly looked over his shoulder at Quebec rather than offering all Canadians leadership in recognizing the role that their country could play in the new world of collective security. Instead he spent much of his eight years out of office in the United States, thinking about labour relations instead of international relations, both wartime and postwar, which in time would mean that he would abandon the League of Nations and back into the Second World War for the wrong reasons.

When Borden's union government was re-elected in the "khaki" election of 17 December 1917, King, now in York North, was among the many defeated Liberal candidates. With Laurier's subsequent resignation and the leadership convention of the Liberal Party – its first – in August 1919, King, convinced that he would succeed Laurier, adopted a remarkably leisurely approach, visiting his York North constituency only twice that year and spending four months in Britain as well as more time in New York. It is a comment on the inadequacies of the other three candidates that at the convention a man could be elected leader who had passed a substantial part of the past eight years in another country – and had no war record to recommend him to English Canada. Among his preparations for the October 1919 election, King sought a journalist to compose laudatory articles or even a biography, in large part to refute criticisms that he had been an eminent "slacker" during the war who had not done his duty to Canada. He wrote to John Lewis of the *Toronto Daily Star*, "there would be everything to gain, and nothing to lose, were you to make something … of the constructive service which I rendered industry on this continent and through industry, the fighting armies at the front … Instead of feeling the least apologetic as to the part I played … in the way of improved relations between Capital and Labour … there were fewer men on the continent who rendered a larger service."[1]

Not forty years old when the war began in August 1914, King could have volunteered for a civilian or military staff or other non-combatant job, but he never showed any inclination to do so. As the nominated Liberal candidate in North York, King had not, however, avoided entirely the most searing of wartime political controversies: the conscription crisis of 1917. Although apparently agreeing in principle with Borden that conscription was the fairest way to end the manpower crisis and, according to some observers, even offering in vain his services to Borden and his Union Government, he eventually followed Laurier in opposing the Military Service Act as a threat to national unity, a factor that he decided must take precedence over all else, including the pressing need for reinforcements for units at the front.* In the fraught election of December 1917, which reflected the deep division between English and French Canada over conscription, King was defeated in his York North constituency (the day before his mother died) where he had campaigned briefly and circumspectly. The defeat of the Liberals was not, however, the end of King's political ambitions. His work in the United States not only rendered him affluent, especially when coupled with funds from his friends Violet Markham and Peter Larkin, but also resulted in his heavy (in all senses of the word) tome on labour relations, *Industry and Humanity*, published in November 1918, the last month of the war, a book he so admired that he hoped it would qualify him to be a member of parliament in the United Kingdom rather than in Canada. (His University of Toronto classmate, Hamar Greenwood, had achieved this status a decade before.)

King's dual approach to Canada's place in an evolving British Empire was crucial to his success in winning the Liberal leadership in 1919. Without most of Quebec's sixty-five seats in the House of Commons, he could not have hoped to win the leadership and form a stable government. He never forgot Laurier's pledge to the people of Quebec, and indeed to all Canadians, limiting imperial military cooperation, but it seems he had no recollection of the 1907 statement of Frederick Borden, Liberal minister of militia, that

---

*The Ottawa journalist Grattan O'Leary, in his *Recollections of People, Press and Politics*, was convinced that King "offered himself for Sir Robert Borden's Union Government in 1917 and was turned down. The story infuriated King all through his political life and he went to great lengths to lay it by the heels, probably on account of its absolute truth. I had the story from Meighen himself and there is no doubt whatever that King offered his services to Borden in 1917" (88). See also MacFarlane, *Ernest Lapointe*, 22.

in any imperial conflict Canada was "not bound to take part if we do not wish to do so."[2] In his self-imposed struggle against real or imagined imperial centralists during the two interwar decades, King was, for his own partisan purposes, in pursuit of a will-o'-the-wisp. There were, in fact, few imperial centralists in London holding any major office: the former dynamic colonial secretary Joseph Chamberlain was permanently incapacitated by illness in 1906, and the influence of his disciple Alfred Milner was limited by his posting as high commissionership in distant South Africa. Fewer still were those who believed that Britain could dictate to the dominions. There were, of course, many British who, in acclaiming the substantial contribution of the dominions to Allied victory in the First World War, hoped that in any future major conflict they would again be alongside Britain. Yet King, to the gratification of Liberals in Quebec, spent inordinate amounts of time knocking down imperial centralist straw men. Robert Borden accurately summed up King's performance at the imperial conference of 1923: "Mr King was continually looking over his shoulder at Quebec and sought evasion of responsibility in a futile and nebulous verbosity."[3] Borden's successor, Arthur Meighen, was even more succinct about King's approach to the imperial relationship: "he was forever bursting heroically through open doors."[4]

In fact, the United Kingdom had long made it clear that there were few in Whitehall or Westminster who harboured any imperial centralist ambitions. Lord Carnarvon, the colonial secretary, said as early as 1870 that "Our relations to Canada have been and are political rather than colonial."[5] The long-serving Liberal prime minister, William Gladstone, whom King's mother had so much admired, had not wanted colonies at all. They were a financial drain and a foreign policy liability. Arthur Balfour, the Conservative prime minister in 1904, proclaimed that over the "self-governing colonies of the Empire ... no office in this country has any control at all."[6] Seven years later, he was even more emphatic: "The most serious thing that could happen for the integrity of the British Empire is to interfere ... with the absolute self-governing integrity of the colonies over the seas."[7] And if that was not clear enough, Balfour offered the analysis that the legislatures of the dominions "are independent Parliaments, absolutely independent, and it is our business to recognize that, and to frame the Empire upon the co-operation of absolutely independent parliaments."[8] The Liberal prime minister H.H. Asquith focused on foreign affairs in rejecting in 1911 an enthusiastic proposal from New Zealand, presented at the 1911 imperial conference, for an imperial council of state (the imperial centralists, such as they still were, being mainly in the dominions rather than in Whitehall or Westminster): "It would impair if not altogether destroy the authority of the Government of the United Kingdom in such matters as the conduct of foreign policy … That authority cannot be shared." To that conference he explained, "We each of us are, and we each of us intend to remain, master of our own household."[9]

The idea of a common imperial foreign policy – at least in broad terms – had resurfaced during the First World War, chiefly among the dominions themselves. For Borden, the Imperial War Cabinet provided a model for imperial consultation during the postwar years. "Ministers from six nations [of the Empire are] … responsible to their respective parliaments … Each nation has its voice upon questions of common concern, each pursues unimpaired its perfect autonomy." With dominion and British troops serving side by side, the Canadian government stated toward the end of the war, "Our people are proud to be doing their share, but it is evident that … we should at the same time have a voice in all decisions regarding matters of common concern," a stance that in time led to dominion participation at both the Paris Peace Conference and the League of Nations.[10] In short, Canada would participate in the British Commonwealth, as envisaged in Resolution IX of the Imperial War Conference of Dominions and India, with an adequate voice in foreign policy and in foreign relations. What was intended in detail by this unanimous wartime resolution (e.g., what was meant by "adequate") was left for a postwar special constitutional conference that never took place, given the demands, distortions, and difficulties of the complex Paris peace negotiations; painful economic adjustment; and a feeling that it was perhaps futile to attempt to formulate quasi-legal definitions of who in the flexible Empire was responsible for what. To be sure, when Borden, with serious if unspoken reservations, brought to the House of Commons on 2 September 1919 the Treaty of Versailles, it was the Liberal House leader who declared, "We are not a nation in the true sense of the term. We are part of a great Empire of which we are proud, and we are nothing else." W.S. Fielding, who had been Laurier's minister of finance, was even more outspoken in his attack on the Conservative prime minister: Conservatives, not Liberals, were attempting "to break up the British Empire."[11]

It was the British Foreign Office, and not the dominions, that primarily set its face against any postwar attempts to arrive at a common imperial foreign policy. A memorandum to the Liberal prime minister Lloyd George in 1920 echoed Asquith's thoughts of 1911: "Directly the Dominions begin to have strong feelings about general foreign policy, we are up against a fundamental issue, because no [British] Government, which is responsible for foreign affairs, can possibly undertake to subordinate its views to those of other people unless they are willing to share the responsibility for, and the consequences of, policy."[12] Similarly, Lord Curzon, the Conservative foreign secretary from 1922 to 1924, who along with the Liberal Winston Churchill was seen for a time by an apparently intimidated and insecure Mackenzie King as an imperial centralist par excellence, echoed the Liberal Asquith in stating that there could be no limitations placed by the dominions on the freedom of the United Kingdom to pursue whatever foreign policy appeared to be in its own interests. If a dominion wished to join in any specific British foreign policy initiative, it was welcome to do so, but if not, it was of course free to go its own way, as Britain itself was. The idea of a common imperial foreign policy, if it ever had much substance, certainly did not reside in the Foreign Office.

Successive prime ministers and foreign secretaries made it clear that the United Kingdom could not let its foreign policy be decided by others, including the dominions. Consultation would be welcome in a cooperative empire, but at the end of the day, London alone would decide for the United Kingdom its foreign policy, as Ottawa was free to do for Canada, Canberra for Australia, etc. In the 1920s, however, King, for partisan purposes, occasionally depicted to his cabinet (but seldom to parliament) and to Quebec (but seldom to English-speaking Canada) a perfidious Albion intent upon foisting a common foreign policy on the hapless dominions. Later, as noted below, he even forbade the high commissioner in London to attend briefings at the Foreign Office: such activities might be seen in Quebec as Canada participating in an embryonic imperial council, confirming imperial centralist control.

King carefully avoided any public acknowledgment of the fact that no foreign secretary attempted to impose a common foreign policy on the dominions. Doing so would have deprived him of his self-portrayal, chiefly for the benefit of Quebec, as the Bunyan-like figure of Mr Standfast vanquishing imperial centralists in whom no virtue resided. That bizarre self-portrait made such good politics for the Liberals in Quebec that King, prompted by Lapointe, never wholly gave it up, although in the late 1930s he increasingly looked over his other shoulder at English Canada, playing down any lingering suspicions about imperial centralists as war approached (he was, however, still imaginatively detecting imperial centralists in a war-exhausted Britain until his death in 1950).

With the counsel of Ernest Lapointe, King's early posturing and platitudes about imperial centralists paid off handsomely in Quebec. A member of parliament since 1904, Lapointe's standing in Quebec had greatly increased as a result of his opposition to Borden's controversial naval bill of 1911 and his even more controversial Military Service Act of 1917. By the Liberal leadership convention in August 1919, he had become something of a king maker (pun intended). He in effect delivered the Quebec vote to King in the leadership convention and again in the election of late 1921. Ever thereafter he controlled the Quebec caucus to the degree that King would write after his death in late 1941 that "but for him, I would never have been Prime Minister, nor would I have been able to hold office as I had held it through the years."[13]

With its votes, Quebec clearly expressed its views on Canada's involvement in foreign wars or imperial naval needs or, above all, the hated enactment of conscription by Conservatives slavishly committed to the British Empire. In the December 1921 election, two years after King had become leader, the Liberals took all sixty-five seats in Quebec; in 1925 they took sixty; in 1926 again sixty. In what they saw as an aberration in their defeat in the election of 1930, the Liberals still took a majority, forty of Quebec's sixty-five seats. In the 1935 election they regained sixty of the sixty-five.

Throughout the 1920s and into the mid-1930s, King was also influenced by O.D. Skelton, a professor of political science at Queen's University and a pronounced isolationist who saw his coveted role as undersecretary of state for external affairs as including "stiffening" his insecure minister in his real or assumed suspicions of imperial centralists, although why King appeared insecure after his elevated excursions in prewar Washington and London is unclear. King did, however, tell his diary of his great satisfaction at having become an "internationalist [with] ... a wider outlook than some of my fellow-countrymen have enjoyed," in part the result of "my post-graduate training at Chicago, Harvard and abroad, and my many visits to England, my trip to the Orient."[14]

By contrast, isolationist policies and even neutrality seemed to Skelton the only route for a postwar Canada to follow. He attempted to exploit such sentiments in Quebec, varying in origin although they were, for his own ends. King, however, differed fundamentally from Skelton in never losing sight of the allegiance to the British Commonwealth that was widespread in the eight other provinces and which he himself shared. Unlike his deputy minister, King always eschewed the word "independence." With his eye on English Canada, he habitually spoke instead of "autonomy" within the British Commonwealth of Nations. But that did not satisfy some of his critics in English Canada, who saw "autonomy without a clear statement of national foreign policy... [as] little better than a policy of drift, of indecision or isolation."[15]

Skelton had convinced himself that behind every interwar British initiative – constitutional, economic, or military – lay a dark intent to introduce a consolidation of the Empire. "There can be little doubt that Skelton was almost pathological of English Tory imperialism in a manner that smacks of the rejected and irrational."[16] Vincent Massey, the Canadian high commissioner in London from 1935 to 1946, was convinced that Skelton "had a strong and lasting suspicion of British policy and an unchanging coldness towards Great Britain ... he was anti-British."[17] Professor George Glazebrook of the University of Toronto was not impressed with his fellow academic: "a narrow-minded, extreme autonomist ... who is nervously jealous of what he suspects as English 'superiority.'"[18] Skelton's eventual successor as undersecretary of state for external affairs, Norman Robertson, bound for Oxford University in 1923, met King and Skelton on their way to the imperial conference of that year. He was equally unimpressed. He wrote to his parents in Vancouver that Skelton was "extremely dull and if he isn't saturated clean through with dullness then he was also rather discourteous." As for King, he was simply "hopelessly undistinguished."[19]

King remained sensitive to political moods across the country, while Skelton concentrated on attempting to loosen those few formal ties that Canada still had with Britain and the Commonwealth, an irrational goal that some have speculated may have arisen in part from his Irish background. To gather as many votes as possible in Quebec, King in his early years as prime minister went along with a certain amount of Skelton-like rhetoric, but he was equally aware that many Canadians of British descent – he was, of course, one himself – still had strong cultural and sentimental, if not direct family ties with the United Kingdom. And English-speaking Canadians had many more votes in total than French-speaking Canadians. Accordingly, as the low, dishonest decade of the 1930s wore on, King increasingly rejected Skelton's more extreme isolationism and even neutrality, instead offering ad nauseam his favourite paradox that loosening the ties of the dominions to Britain in fact enhanced their allegiance to a commonwealth of equals.

Of one thing King was certain: the extraordinary parliamentary influence of Quebec in the aftermath of the First World War. In the early 1920s, he had convinced himself that "Quebec dominates the House of Commons." However, his efforts to please or at least placate Quebec opinion did not reflect either a genuine regard for French-speaking Canadians or any particular confidence in them. Like Skelton, he made no attempt to understand or discuss their motives, sentiments, and ambitions, relegating to Lapointe all things Québécois. On arrival in Ottawa in 1900 as a public servant, King had lamented that it was "a great shame that so much French should be perpetuated around here."[20] Jack Pickersgill, one of his able secretaries on loan from External Affairs in the late 1930s and later himself a Liberal cabinet minister, is only one of many who affirmed that King knew little about French Canada. "Certainly he had no affinity with French culture, a sketchy and superficial knowledge of the language, and all the Protestant intolerance of Catholicism."[21] On this at least Skelton and King were at one. King agreed with Skelton that "the widest possible knowledge of English" was essential for a "common Canadian consciousness [since] this is and will be overwhelmingly an English-speaking country." No bilingualism or biculturalism for Skelton, who sought to use "good old Ernest" Lapointe not for Quebec's but for his own isolationist ends.

King was content to leave politics in Quebec to Quebecers – and to his Quebec viceroy – but he never lost sight of the province's all-important sixty-plus seats. His primary goal was to retain the support of Quebec by presenting himself there as something of an isolationist and to paint the Tories as unrepentant imperialists who, during the latter part of the war, had imposed compulsory military service. Or to put it another way, the difficulties in formulating a coherent foreign policy between English and French Canada were so great that it was better to have two vaguely enunciated foreign policies, one for Quebec and one for English Canada – or on occasion no foreign policy at all.

But conciliating Quebec was not King's only electoral challenge. To complicate matters, the election of 1921 resulted in a Liberal minority government due to the unexpected success of a newly constituted agrarian party, the National Progressive Party. It drew on the recent successes of the provincial United Farmers Party in forming the governments in Ontario,

Manitoba, and Alberta. King sought a merger with the Progressives, but not a coalition, which he abhorred. But here, as in Quebec, foreign affairs intruded upon domestic affairs. Wary of European entanglements and committed to tariff-free trade with the United States, many of the autonomist-minded supporters of the Progressives had also been opposed to compulsory military service, which among other things they had seen as removing essential labour from their farms.

The Progressive leader, T.C. Crerar, a former conscriptionist Liberal and minister in Borden's union government, had worked with his wartime Liberal colleague from Toronto, Newton Rowell, in attempting to chart a course that would bring the Liberals and the Progressives together, but the Progressives stood in the 1921 election as a separate party, winning sixty-four of the 245 seats in the House of Commons, as many seats – all but one – as Quebec had. With their sixty-four seats, the loosely organized National Progressive Party became the second largest party in parliament. Accordingly, they were for the moment hardly less important to King than the sixty-five seats in Quebec.

At the same time, King balanced his preoccupation with Liberal electoral fortunes in Quebec with his support for the efforts of Rodolphe Lemieux, the speaker of the House of Commons (and the negotiator of the prewar emigration agreement with Japan) to conclude an accord with France for the assignment in perpetuity of 250 acres at Vimy Ridge as the site of the principal Canadian war memorial and one of the greatest monuments of the First World War. It was politically advantageous to have a French Canadian speaker in the lead (an early manifestation of King's mantra "Parliament will decide"), but he confided to his diary that despite continuing criticism of his lack of wartime service and his uneasy relations with veterans' organizations, the land "would have never been acquired by Canada but for my efforts."[22]

4

Chanak and All That

Eight months after King formed his first government at the end of 1921, a contrived incident (not a real crisis) in Turkey came to him as an opportunity to show himself to Quebec and the Progressives as always dependable against machinations of imperial centralists, while at the same time demonstrating to English Canada his basic commitment to the Empire.

By the autumn of 1922, the wartime coalition government in London was in a vulnerable state. Lloyd George, a Liberal, still presided over it, but a majority of its members were Conservative. Although their leader, Austen Chamberlain, the president of the council, remained loyal to the Liberal prime minister, an increasing number of Conservative members, especially the younger undersecretaries, were becoming restless, believing that it was time to withdraw from the ambiguous coalition of wartime imperatives and reassert their separate party identity and integrity. Lloyd George himself was still widely acclaimed as "the man who won the war," but by late 1922, in the view of many Conservative MPs, the electoral negatives of continuing the wartime coalition outweighed the historical positives.

The British economy, severely disrupted and depleted by world war, was maimed by economic depression, including severe unemployment. Victory had brought few rewards, but had fostered substantial unease. The Treaty of Versailles was already seen by some – Maynard Keynes and even Lloyd George himself pre-eminent among them – as carrying within it the seeds of future strife. The treaty was only one manifestation of the increasingly differing views and mutual suspicions that soured the postwar relations of the erstwhile allies, Britain and France, over a range of issues. Concurrently, Lloyd George's supposed settlement of the "troubles" in Ireland had pleased few, Liberals believing that he had delayed far too long in offering Ireland Dominion Home Rule and diehard Conservatives believing that he had surrendered Ireland to the gunmen. Closer to home there were allegations that the prime minster had been engaged in the scandalous wholesale of honours for both party and personal gain, leading intimates to say that they "had never seen him so much worried about anything."[1] And overarching all else was the disconcerting postwar growth in electoral support for the Labour Party at the expense of the Liberal.

In these highly unpromising circumstances, a worried Lloyd George became even more preoccupied with how to keep his coalition government afloat. Expansion of social programmes was not an option for the hard-pressed Treasury in pre-Keynesian days. Lloyd George was, however, well aware of the time-honoured political ploy that foreign ventures could, if cleverly manipulated, distract the attention of voters from their domestic discontents. Accordingly, he promoted international conferences in Cannes and Genoa, ostensibly to resolve the already contentious problems of war reparations, the place of the new Soviet Union in the comity of nations, and the fragile European economic recovery. But his excursions into multilateral diplomacy were not satisfactory. Neither conference was a success in itself – or proved to be the desired distraction. As Lord Curzon's biographer colourfully put it, "Mr Lloyd George returned from Genoa not more, but less secure than he had been when he started. At any moment a match might be laid to a powder train which would blow up his Government, and by the irony of fate it was Mr Lloyd George himself who in the end struck and applied the match."[2]

The immediate powder train was a concoction of the Liberal Winston Churchill, the secretary of state for the colonies, and his louche Conservative friend, Lord Birkenhead, the lord chancellor. Desperate to keep the coalition government afloat when they had nowhere else to go, they regarded a confrontation with an aggressive Turkey, intent on annulling by force the Treaty of Sèvres, as a promising way of distracting the attention of disgruntled voters from domestic issues and doing down restless Conservative backbenchers. Not for the first time, military glory abroad was seen as uniquely able to lessen disharmony at home. Middlemas and Barnes have written, "In the overheated imagination of the triumvirate, the challenge [to Turkey] ... might be the very occasion that could bring together the British electorate in supporting the coalition government. It was itself a highly speculative initiative, especially when British forces were so over-stretched across the Empire."[3]

By mid-1922, the aborted peace treaty of Sèvres, a signal failure of Lloyd George's Middle East and pro-Greek policies, had provoked a resurgence of Turkish nationalism, led by Mustafa Kemal, the hero of Gallipoli. Allied "spheres of influence" in Turkey had been recklessly allocated at Versailles to France and Italy, but the French and Italian governments, with a war-weary population and postwar economic uncertainties, had understandably effectively abandoned their spheres in the face of resurgent Turkish nationalism. Greece also had an assigned – and unrealistic – sphere. It attempted to retain its influence in the expectation that Lloyd George would yet again blindly support it against Turkey, which he hated, as he had done before the First World War. But the Turks easily drove the Greeks out of Smyrna and proceeded toward the neutral zone of the Dardanelle Straits, which had been declared open to all shipping. Standing in their way at the town of Chanak, near the strait's neutral zone, was a small British garrison (the even smaller French and Italian garrisons having hurriedly departed).

On 15 September 1922, the British cabinet, at the urging of the scheming triumvirate of Lloyd George, Churchill, and Birkenhead, decided to confront Mustafa Kemal by reinforcing the garrison at Chanak with, it was hoped, the renewed assistance of France and Italy and possibly even of Australia and New Zealand, the Anzacs of Gallipoli fame who were as always concerned to see the imperial sea route through the Mediterranean to Suez and to the East remain secure. But somehow Lloyd George's cypher telegram seeking support against the Turks was instead sent to *all* the dominions. Its relevant passage was, "I should be glad to know whether Dominion Government wish to associate themselves with the action we are taking and whether they would desire to be represented by a contingent … we cannot forget that Gallipoli Peninsula contains over twenty thousand British and Anzac graves … The announcement that all or any of the Dominions were prepared to send contingents … would undoubtedly in itself exercise a most favourable influence on situation."[4] Lloyd George's private secretary and long-serving mistress, Frances Stevenson, thought otherwise. "L.G. … asked me to take down from Churchill the text of what I realised was to be a telegram asking for the [Dominion] Governments support in the event of a war with Turkey. I was horrified at the unwisdom of the message, conveying as it did the prospect of renewed warfare on a grand scale."[5] Her immediate reaction was entirely justified by events. "The cabinet's brinkmanship … aroused a storm of protest. The reckless triumvirate …

was widely accused of warmongering to distract public attention from problems at home."[6]

Lloyd George's telegram to the dominions was confidential, but the following day, 16 September, Churchill prepared a press release. It was cleared only with Lloyd George and not the cabinet. Curzon later confirmed to Mackenzie King that such a "manifesto ... was not a normal occurrence and that it was issued without the knowledge or approval of the Cabinet."[7] And to the Conservative Bonar Law, the chancellor of the exchequer, it was clear in any case that Britain could not police the world alone.

Churchill's *en clair* press release overtook the slow-moving cypher telegram of the prime minister to all the dominions. As King at great length subsequently told the 1923 imperial conference, he had first learned of the British cabinet's decision of 15 September (it was, after all, a late summer weekend in Ottawa, not a good time for the manual decyphering of telegrams) from a *Toronto Star* reporter's account of Churchill's press release and not from Lloyd George's telegram. On the basis of Churchill's press statement, King could at once go public. He could refer to Chanak openly, exploiting it publicly in displaying his anti-centralist stance to the Progressives and Quebec, something that he would have been unable to do if he had received only Lloyd George's confidential message.

Within forty-eight hours of receiving both the press release and the confidential message, King and his cabinet realized that "the decision to fight the Turks" was not a grand foreign policy initiative at all, but a ludicrously parochial ploy in the highly uncertain British domestic political scene. On 17 September King recorded that "the whole business is mostly a Lloyd George election manoeuvre." The following day, after a full cabinet meeting (only Lapointe was absent, at the League of Nations Assembly in Geneva), he added that "all [the cabinet ministers] were inclined to feel whole business an 'election scheme' of Lloyd George and Co."[8] Accordingly, that evening King told both the press and the British government that he was requesting background papers and, of course, parliament would decide. Only New Zealand and Newfoundland had indicated that they would be prepared to send contingents. The British reply to King's telegram reflected that Canada was not in fact a target for assistance. The Canadian press baron Lord Beaverbrook noted that "Churchill cabled that there would be no war. Contingents would not be required." (Beaverbrook's reference is to a telegram of 18 September from Churchill to King in which he said that "There is no probability of a serious war ... It seems most improbable that actual need for despatching contingent will arise.")[9] That reply, joined with the fact that the cabinet recognized that the whole business was an election scheme, effectively negated any consideration of Canadian involvement. According to the *Toronto Globe* of 18 September, "the feeling of the Government ... is that the situation in the Near East does not now and is not likely to call for any military participation by Canada."[10]

In London, Beaverbrook fully recognized that Lloyd George, prompted by his two cohorts in recalling how Britain had rallied behind him during the First World War, "foolishly believed that a state of war against Turkey would unite Conservatives and Coalition Liberals, silence the two opposition Parties, and justify an appeal to the electors with a whopping majority for his leadership."[11] Stanley Baldwin, the president of the Board of Trade, agreed. He recalled for King at the 1923 imperial conference that

> England and the Empire were in the hands of three dangerous men, all intoxicated with their own cleverness and love of power, and prepared to sacrifice everything to it; foolish and blind even to the point of believing that they could win an election by bringing on another war. They were determined to have war with Turkey and were doing everything in their power to bring it about; they felt that if they could once launch war they could then appeal to the people and come back as a government triumvirate ... The message that was sent to the Dominions had never been shown to the Cabinet. Lloyd George pretended that he had not seen it, but there was no doubt that he had. Churchill had drafted it, but Birkenhead and Lloyd George were equally responsible for it; it was part of the campaign of war and the election manoeuvre which they had planned.[12]

Sir Horace Rumbold, the British high commissioner in Constantinople, was in no doubt who was behind the fuss. He wrote to a friend in London, "We realized of course that there was a war party in the cabinet headed by Lloyd George, with the support of Winston Churchill and Birkenhead."[13]

John Campbell, the biographer of Birkenhead, aptly encapsulated the public reaction in Britain: "the Cabinet's brinkmanship – highlighted by Churchill calling publicly for Dominion support – ... aroused a storm of protest ... The reckless triumvirate ... was widely accused of warmongering to distract public attention from problems at home ... The evidence amounts to a serious charge that the leading personalities of the Coalition really did want to involve Britain in renewed war with Turkey ... The best explanation is that they were seized collectively by that summer madness which so often affects tired administrations as their term expires."[14] And Hamar Greenwood, the Ontario-born Liberal minister in Lloyd George's government, later told King that "Churchill, Lord Birkenhead, and Lloyd George had all been out dining pretty well that evening [14 September] and the decision to fight the Turks and to send out the appeal to the Dominions to aid in preventing the advance of the Turks was made under those conditions" (in cabinet a skeptical Greenwood had urged that an "appeal to the Dominions" should be sent – if at all – only to Australia and New Zealand).[15] Four months after the event and well before the 1923 imperial conference, King summed up to his diary the whole sorry business: "The more one goes into the matter, the clearer it becomes that Lloyd George, Churchill and others were out to try an Imperialist game to help the Coalition politically ... there seems good reason to believe that our action prevented actual war ... To have had the privilege of sharing in such a work is worth all that one suffers in political life."[16]

The absurdity of attempting to put such a bellicose venture before profoundly war-weary people was soon reflected in a wholly negative reaction in Britain itself. Any idea of renewing war with Turkey was decisively ended three weeks later by a sensible agreement of 11 October 1922 between Kemal and General Sir Charles Harington, the British commander on the ground, an agreement endorsed by Rumbold, the high commissioner in Constantinople and a future able ambassador in Berlin, assisted by Nevile Henderson, another future ambassador in Berlin, but not so able. In another week Lloyd George and his ramshackle coalition were in turn rejected by a "revolt of the [Conservative] Under Secretaries." Instead of strengthening the coalition government, the election scheme had become the final nail in its coffin. Curzon's biographer described what happened. "In the minds of the public ... the Government, or some members of the Government at any rate, were leading them to the brink of war and to the simultaneous determination that in no circumstances would they follow them there."[17] Curzon recorded in his diary that while Lloyd George, Churchill, and Birkenhead excelled themselves in jingo extravagance, four other Conservative ministers concerted with Baldwin and himself "until we either defeated the plot or resigned in common [and brought down the government]. On the morrow came the news that [Rumbold and] Harington had … saved the situation"[18] by their refusal to deliver the triumvirate's ultimatum to Turkey, for which they were duly thanked by Law's incoming government. In short, Curzon regarded the "plot" as "a gross and ridiculous exaggeration."[19]

At any point, King, if he had wished, could have returned a prompt and flat "no" to this ridiculous appeal. There were certainly precedents for him to do so. Allied intervention in the Russian Civil War at the end of the world war, long and strenuously pursued by Churchill despite the Tsarist regime being rightly seen as despotic and corrupt, had been terminated thanks in part to Borden's clear "no" to Churchill's request for the continued participation of Canadian units in the Allied intervention force. Borden, like Sir John A. MacDonald at the time of the Soudan debacle of 1885, had no trouble in saying "no," a response to British wars formulated by a Liberal militia minister in 1907 as "we were not bound to take part if we do not wish to do so."[20] Further, the recognition by King and his cabinet from the first days of the incident that Chanak was merely an "election scheme of Lloyd George and Co.," opposed by many of his own cabinet, would alone have justified a prompt Canadian "no." Lapointe had reported from the League in Geneva, "Appeal to Dominions deemed not judicious everywhere. Press strongly hostile to war. Seems untrue that France and Italy have agreed. British Government likely changing its attitude."[21]

But King knew a domestic political opportunity when he saw it. Here, not five years after the searing conscription crisis of 1917, was a rare occasion to demonstrate to Quebec and to the Progressives alike that the Liberal Party could be relied on never to be a toady of imperial centralists. King did his best to depict the Conservative leader, Arthur Meighen, as engaging in "jingo Tory militarism." Unlike King and his cabinet, Meighen had not learned that Chanak was merely an "election scheme," but even he proclaimed in a speech in Toronto, "There is no suggestion at all that we should send armed forces across the sea. Britain merely sought a declaration of solidarity on the part of the Dominions."[22] At the same time, King was careful to keep his political balance between English and French Canada. For Quebec he presented himself as opposed to imperial centralists. For Ontario and the Maritime provinces in particular he pledged that, there being no prior commitments made by his government, parliament would decide – which was to say that if Britain was itself threatened, parliament would decide to go to its aid. Knowing that Chanak was no such threat, King made much of the dominion's autonomy – he always avoided the word independence – within the Empire. That should more or less satisfy most Canadians, who could read into his equivocal and obscure formulae what they would. Long after Chanak, he continued to make the most of his response that parliament must decide, later listing it as a "lasting service [to the Empire] by [my] stand on the Near East question" and still talking about it during the 1939 negotiations of the British Commonwealth Air Training Plan and again in 1948 when he rejected Canadian participation in the Berlin airlift.

The public disclosure of the Chanak political scheme offered King an early opportunity to demonstrate to Quebec and to Progressives that his government would concentrate on domestic issues and keep the country out of foreign wars – as long as they were no threat to Britain itself. And he made certain that Lapointe was always well primed to report back to Quebec on his leader's anti-imperial-centralist stance. King took the occasion of his embarkation in Quebec City for the 1923 imperial conference to make a speech – in English – lauding Laurier's understanding of the "secret" of Canadian unity: a balanced equilibrium of something for English Canada and something for French Canada. Chanak also led King to conclude privately to his diary that "it would be a good thing for England if she could get rid of Lloyd George, Churchill, Birkenhead … I would not be surprised if Churchill were on a spree. He has overshot the mark. Lloyd George will diminish in stature from now on. He was never a truly great man. He was a betrayer of men and principles."[23] And King had not regarded Lloyd George as a true Liberal since the day he had chosen to head a coalition government dependent on Conservatives to remain in office.

King and his cabinet recognized that the Chanak nonsense had been from the beginning a devious scheme to win the British election set for 15 November. In fact, the electorate ejected the unholy triumvirate of Lloyd George, Birkenhead, and Churchill from office and brought in the new all-Conservative and anti-Chanak government of the more clear-headed Bonar Law. That did not deflect King from making a show of his disgruntlement when lecturing the imperial conference of 1923. Of course in the presence of Lapointe, he stressed the need for "great care … in respect to issuing any statements from the British Government … to the peoples of the Dominions over the heads … of the Governments concerned."[24] Also at that conference, Skelton described to J.W. Dafoe of the *Manitoba Free Press* that Baldwin had informed King that "last year [Lloyd] George, Churchill and

Birkenhead were determined to have a war with Turkey for electioneering purposes and that it was Canada's refusal to play up to the lead that spoiled their plans."[25] Skelton had it right about the triumvirate using a threat of war for electioneering purposes, but it was not Canada's response that had spoiled their plans.* It was the opposition of the British people themselves and many in the British government and, above all, the good sense of the British high commissioner in Istanbul and the general commanding the garrison at Chanak that had quelled the farce.

Chanak revealed inadequacies in imperial communications, but the fault was not all on the British side; King, as secretary of state for external affairs, had avoided facilitating exchanges with London of information or opinion on foreign affairs, which in his view should be limited to direct prime minister-to-prime minister communication. If King had wanted more details about what was actually going on beyond what was available in newspapers, the Foreign Office could have provided them. Moreover, in 1922 he could have sent as high commissioner in London a more perceptive political interlocutor than his personal financial benefactor Peter Larkin, an affluent retired tea magnate who had also privately supplied funds to Laurier and Lapointe. In contrast, Australia sent to London a former prime minister who initiated a dependable communications link with both the Cabinet and Foreign Office, but to King, anything of that sort smelled of the imperial centralism so abhorred, Lapointe assured him, by Quebec.

Internationally, the opera buffa of Chanak was finally settled by a second and more durable peace treaty with Turkey (replacing the abortive Treaty of Sèvres), renegotiated by Curzon at Lausanne between November 1922 and July 1923. Three months later, at the 1923 imperial conference in London, presided over by Stanley Baldwin, who had become prime minister upon the fatal illness of Bonar Law, King told Curzon and his fellow premiers of his gratification that Canada had not been invited to participate in the Lausanne negotiations. "We took and we take no exception to not being invited ... we have no exception to take to the course that was adopted."[26] With an eye on both western Canada and Quebec, King explained his stance

---

*Nevertheless, as late as 1928 Mackenzie King was still repeating to the House of Commons that at the 1923 imperial conference "we were told that but for the action of Canada ... a second great European conflict might have taken place" (Canada, Parliament, House of Commons Debates, 26 March 1928, 1715).

with one of his notable dualisms: "Our attitude is not one of unconditional isolation, nor is it one of unconditional intervention."[27]

King's lament about Chanak was a small part of his long and arid statement of 8 October to the 1923 imperial conference.* Only a small fraction was about foreign affairs. Instead, he spoke at great length about essentially domestic matters, including water levels in the Great Lakes, fisheries, liquor traffic questions with the United States, and Asian immigration, although he did include a passage about "Relations of Various Parts of the Empire in Foreign Policy." Most of this verbose passage had been prepared by Skelton, eagerly trailing his coattails at the conference for a senior appointment in Ottawa. In his statement King was taking "steps to dissociate his government from collective imperial responsibilities, and began also to make a critical distinction between imperial diplomacy as a whole and Canada's own particular external affairs, for which alone the Dominion would be accountable."[28] The essence of King's foreign affairs statement was that while "it is possible to consult on matters of overwhelming and enduring common interest; it is not possible to consult on the great range of matters of individual and shifting concern." He elaborated, primarily for the ears of Ontario and the maritime provinces, that "there are some matters which more immediately affect us than do other parts of the Empire and over which we desire an immediate and direct control, nevertheless, we are equally appreciative of the fact that there are great common interests in which all of us have an equal concern and are equally ready to share."[29] He concluded with a statement, both brief and convoluted, that was to form the leitmotif found in most of his later major musings about Canada's place in the British Empire. Although exceedingly circumspect about saying it, he pledged without elaboration that Canada would come to Britain's aid in the case of "a clear and present danger."

That was King's final word on international affairs in the formal sessions of the 1923 conference, but Chanak did come up informally when he lunched with Winston and Clementine Churchill and Admiral Sir Roger and Lady Keyes on 23 October. In King's presence, Clementine Churchill expressed surprise – disingenuously or otherwise – that her husband's statement about Chanak had been released to the press before the dominions had had time

---

*An edited version takes a total of twenty-three pages in volume three of *Documents on Canadian External Relations*.

to decypher Lloyd George's earlier confidential telegram. Her husband, disconcerted or otherwise, explained briefly that he had acted as he did because he expected fighting to begin immediately. Not having much else to say in the wake of the well-deserved failure of the triumvirate's crass political stratagem, that was that. With the success of the common sense diplomacy of Rumbold and Harington and with the election only three weeks off (in which Churchill would be defeated), there was clearly nothing to be gained by continuing to discuss Chanak.

Leopold Amery, first lord of the admiralty, who was married to a Canadian, was not impressed by King's performance at the 1923 imperial conference: "King's chief aim was to avoid committing himself to anything."[30] An Australian official at the conference was even more condign: "Surely no man can claim credit for having done so much as Mackenzie King to damage what remains … of the fabric of the British Empire. His efforts to make capital out of his domestic nationalism are analogous to a vandal who pulls down a castle in order to build a cottage."[31] The consultant Skelton, on the other hand, was quick with congratulations to the uneasy King since he himself had written the statement, but it later earned memorable derision from the Canadian historian C.P. Stacey. "Its most curious feature is the fact that it represents the plan for a unified foreign policy as an entirely British scheme … and says no word of the Canadian share in it. There is absolutely no reference to Sir Robert Borden's long campaign for a 'voice' for Canada in the formation of Imperial policy … A whole decade of determined Canadian effort in the field of external policy [by Borden and Meighen] is wiped from the record … Skelton's paper may have been good politics, but it was very bad history. In effect, if not in intent, it was mendacious."[32]

As the conference wore on, King flattered himself by thinking that "I am helping to make History in the lines along which I am defining relations between different parts of the Empire." In fact he was, as was often the case, bursting through an open door.[33] From 1923 he continued to pursue publicly in Quebec a policy that smelled of isolationism, but in Ontario and elsewhere in English-speaking Canada he clove, when pushed to it, to the Empire: Canada would come to Britain's aid if it were seriously threatened. He made no real effort to square his differing statements to Quebec and Ontario: in the end, although it was not always evident, he came down on the side of the Empire, while dexterously reassuring Quebec that he was making no commitments, a technique that Meighen for one never mastered.

Before leaving London to return to Ottawa, King had become uneasy at appearing to Ontario voters as too pro-Quebec and too negative to the British. He had approached the conference "filled with terror,"[34] despite having worked confidently with several leading British ministers fifteen years before over Asian migration. At the conclusion of the conference, he endeavoured to repair any bridges in need of repair by apologizing to the foreign secretary for his behaviour. He described to his diary how he had said to Curzon – who had made him "shudder" – "possibly I had been too persistent in pushing forward my point of view. To this Curzon said I was overcritical of myself; that I had displayed great candour and great courtesy and was most helpful."[35] To his wife, Curzon's account of their conversation was quite different (which is not surprising since Curzon had already shared with her his impression of King as "obstinate, tiresome and stupid").[36] King, he told her, "said that he had come to the conference with a violent prejudice against me … [but] he had been profoundly impressed by my courtesy and affability, knowledge of the subject and eloquence … in future he would follow everything that I said and did with intense interest and regard. I nearly sank into the ground with surprise."[37]

Three years later, shortly before the October 1926 imperial conference, Skelton, now undersecretary of state for external affairs, recorded privately his impression that King was still insecure and irresolute. During the very different prewar years Laurier had carried the ultimate responsibility for imperial relations, not King. Now King did. Presumably that was one reason why in Skelton's private opinion he was again "very nervous and lacking in self-confidence." All that King had learned in his prewar diplomatic apprenticeship, and his familiarity with British ministers, had apparently faded in the face of assuming ultimate policy responsibility in markedly different imperial circumstances. More fundamentally, his persistent unease in imperial discussions arose from his concern that it might become evident that he was saying one thing in Ontario and something else in Quebec. Before embarking for Southampton, however, he blandly sought (again in English) to reassure a Quebec City audience – and perhaps himself – that Lapointe and he "were going to the conference in a spirit of goodwill towards Great Britain and towards all the Dominions … we had not a single grievance … no particular demands to put forward."[38]

At the 1926 imperial conference, again of course in the presence of Lapointe and this time also of the prominent and affluent anglophile Ontario Liberal,

Vincent Massey, shortly to be minister in Washington, King decided that he had gone far enough in concentrating on Quebec's policy preoccupations (by then the Progressive Party had gratifyingly all but disappeared, largely into the Liberal fold). He became a little more public in his support of the British Commonwealth. In so speaking to the conference, he tacked toward the majority view among English-speaking voters in Canada. Echoing his statement of three years before about Canada's positive response to any "great and clear call to duty," King repeated, carefully and again without fanfare, his pledge that "if the situation arose Canada would do her part."[39] He sought to reassure the conference – and English Canada beyond – that the Liberal government, while supporting "autonomy" for Canada within the Empire (as the Conservative Borden had done before him) rejected an "independent" status for the dominions as vaguely advocated by South Africa and the Irish Free State (but strongly opposed by Australia and New Zealand).

As tangible evidence of his support for improved imperial communications, he pledged Canada's financial and other support for a network of airships to improve imperial communications: "we have … been thrilled … It is difficult to find words wherewith adequately to describe it [the proposal]; it was fascinating, one would be inclined to use the word 'romantic'… it is prophetic."[40] Otherwise, King intentionally used up much of his time in 1926 as he had in 1923 by talking to his homologues about things domestic rather than imperial or international. Instead of responding to the repeated efforts of Leopold Amery (then first lord of the admiralty) to focus on a greater sense of cohesion among dominions, he concentrated on water levels at Lake of the Woods, regulation of broadcasting, and prevention of smuggling. Australia was better pleased with King's statement about additional limitations on Chinese and Japanese immigration. Almost two decades after his first involvement with that issue, King was well aware that the Conservative opposition in Ottawa, eager to gain support in British Columbia, was advocating complete exclusion of Japanese immigrants, as had been done in the United States two years before. His government's response was more liberal; it had reduced the total number from 400 annually to 150.

At the conclusion of the 1926 conference, King welcomed a notably flexible statement by Arthur Balfour, the former prime minister and now lord president of the council. His declaration, which led directly to the Statute of Westminster of 1931, drew on his prewar recognition of the equality of all self-governing members of the British Empire. Its members "are autonomous communities within the British Empire, equal in status, in no way subordinate one to another in any aspect of their domestic or external affairs, though united by a common allegiance to the Crown, and freely associated as members of the British Commonwealth of Nations."[41] The final formulation of autonomy in the 1931 statute was made only after the Conservative R.B. Bennett had become prime minister, but King remained convinced that his own performance at both the 1923 and 1926 imperial conferences had been instrumental in Balfour's formulation, concluding again that "God's help was present. He carried me through,"[42] with the gratifying result that the "The Imperial Conference has helped to give me a place in History."[43] Many Toronto Liberals and the Toronto press did not, however, share King's self-satisfaction, censuring him for going too far in his autonomy stance. King countered with a dinner for 500 at the King Edward Hotel at which the cabinet, Lapointe included, attended to hear him deny for two-and-a-half hours that he had said or done anything to lessen the unity of the Empire.[44] The imperial conference had in fact "revealed foundations of national autonomy and imperial unity deeper, broader, and more enduring than many had dreamed." He did not speak that way in Quebec.

At the same time that King was beginning to have some doubts about his deputy minister's apparent isolationism, Skelton was finding the prime minister something of a disappointment in imperial relations. At the 1923 imperial conference King had not always followed his advice and had needed "stiffening" in his ambiguous public attitude toward Britain. By 1926, according to a *Manitoba Free Press* correspondent, King "has spent most of the time eating with duchesses" – a not uncommon practice among prime ministers, later pursued pre-eminently by the Scottish crofter Ramsay Macdonald when prime minister (King had first met him in 1899 in both Chicago and Toronto). And frequently he had "Luncheon with a duke ... dinner ... with some Lord, perhaps a dance at night and weekends in the country."[45] King was running true to form. A royalist to the core, he was throughout his years as prime minister rapturous about the romance of the monarchy and all the spectacular pageantry and history that went with it.

Neither King nor Skelton understood Quebec nor could they conceivably fashion an appeal to it to recognize the benefits of collective security under the League of Nations or of imperial defence collaboration. For Skelton, an isolationist and even a neutralist, "The Irish and Mr Lapointe" and not his own minister, "are our only sure-fire reliables."[46] In another three years King recognized that "Skelton is at heart against the British Empire, which I am not. I believe in the larger whole, with complete independence of the parts united by cooperation in all common ends."[47] In so saying, King was voicing one part of his balancing act between the differing interests and convictions of English and French Canada – at least as he understood them. Given his ignorance of the language, culture, and priorities of Quebec, he necessarily relied heavily on Lapointe for guidance through the unfamiliar and, to him, arcane byways of French Canada. Fortunately for King, there was no television (or other electronic gadgets) to confront. He held very few press conferences and the few that he did convene were carefully controlled. He avoided discussions of foreign relations in parliament, almost until the eve of the Second World War, rightly secure in his conviction that parliament would in the end do what he told it to do. From those basic positions King never moved.

5

Canada at the League of Nations

The League of Nations was founded on 10 January 1920. Mackenzie King and Ernest Lapointe, like Sir Robert Borden and many other Canadians, had initially viewed membership in the League as a vehicle to display to the world Canada's postwar autonomy within the British Commonwealth of Nations. The significant contributions of the dominions and India in the First World War had opened the way to their postwar membership in the League and the International Labour Organization, membership which had been hailed by nationalists as, among other things, an assertion of sovereignty. Britain would no longer represent the dominions in international organizations, which would presumably in turn foster in Canadians a new and closer interest in international affairs.

Borden, who had clarified Canada's evolving postwar international status by taking Canada into the League, remained for the rest of his life its advocate, eventually becoming in retirement the president of League of Nations Society in Canada, but he too had always kept Quebec in mind, with its deeply held misgivings about possible implications of collective security under the League. Both Borden and King were wary of becoming involved through League membership in European conflicts, distinct in their minds from shared imperial interests. The rub was that the League's Covenant contained commitments no more welcome to isolationists than were the real or supposed imperial commitments of the past. Borden, Meighen, and King agreed broadly in their distrust of those clauses in the League's Covenant that, in certain defined circumstances, would pledge member states to consider participating in collective sanctions, initially economic and ultimately military, against a deemed aggressor.

In the language of multilateral diplomacy, Article X of the League Covenant pledged member states to "preserve as against external aggression the territorial integrity and … independence of all Members." Article XVI went on to say what should be done by the League in the way of sanctions against a recognized aggressor, forward commitments that had been too much for isolationists in the postwar United States. Partly for that reason, in March 1920, a final resolution seen as opening the way to United States membership in the League failed to receive the necessary two-thirds support in the Senate. The League had thereby been dealt a near-mortal blow at its inception, rendering it in time in the eyes of King and other skeptics a largely European and hence fundamentally limited organization. Yet a fellow Liberal, Newton Rowell, who had served as a minister in Borden's wartime union government, saw European politics as the very reason why the League had to be supported. He told the first assembly of the League in 1920, "it was European policy, European statesmanship, European ambition, that drenched this world with blood."[1] The League of Nations was, in short, the only alternative to a second world war.

The absence of the United States also raised questions dating back to its architects' original concept of economic and military sanctions. President Woodrow Wilson had been a principal author of Article X, believing it to be crucial to the League's role as international peacekeeper, but Borden had from the beginning recognized the opposition in Canada. He understood well that most if not all of Quebec's sixty-five seats in the postwar House of Commons would continue to elude the Conservative Party for a long time to come. To begin to counter Quebec's deep suspicions of his party, Borden attempted to take a major role in the 1919 negotiations that finally led to a formal Canadian resolution – which failed by the single vote of Persia – that would have reformulated League sanctions and hence collective security.

For his part, Mackenzie King, having striven to convince Quebec that membership in the British Commonwealth of Nations carried no obligations to engage in imperial military excursions, eventually became equally vocal in his opposition to any such apparent obligations in membership in the League of Nations. In London in 1923, in line with his 1918 book *Industry and Humanity*, he described to Lord Robert Cecil, a major architect of the League, how much he valued it as a place to talk. "The great thing about the League of Nations [is that] it is teaching all countries a common language – using language in a broad sense, of like concepts and ideas."[2] Accordingly, he put through the House of Commons on 21 June 1926 a special resolution stating that "before His Majesty's Canadian Ministers … signify acceptance of any ... agreement involving military or economic sanctions [by the League], the approval of the Parliament of Canada should be secured."[3] Throughout the next decade, he remained determined to demonstrate to Quebec in particular that he had recognized on behalf of Canada no collective security obligations, however some might interpret the League Covenant. It would always be for parliament to decide. For King, with his eye on Quebec, membership in the League was not to be a case of out of the imperial frying pan into the League fire.

Given the failure of Borden and others to revise formally the League's Covenant, King responded to isolationists in Quebec and elsewhere by rejecting any interpretation of the Covenant that committed member states to military sanctions against a deemed aggressor. His solution was not to pursue any further attempts to rescind the doctrine of collective security, but rather to regard the League as a forum for talk, for conciliation and negotiation, and not for coercion, just as he had long been convinced that industrial peace would emerge from conversations between employers and employees. In this light he wrote to a friend in the United States, "I am heart and soul for a League of Nations, imperfect as the beginnings of its organization must necessarily be."[4]

At the same time, two of the more prominent supporters of the League in public life were Quebec Liberals: Ernest Lapointe, minister of justice, and Raoul Dandurand, government leader in the Senate. Both were convinced that while membership in the League affirmed for all to see Canada's autonomy in the British Commonwealth, a close watch had to be kept on any ambitions of other League members to move from talk to action, to back collective security decisions with economic and even military sanctions. Lapointe, as a later president of the League of Nations Society in Canada (succeeding Borden and Sir George Foster), was tireless in presenting to Quebec Canada's membership as underlining its freedom from anachronistic imperial centralist constraints. King, however, was in time to worry that Lapointe might project in Geneva an exaggerated interpretation of Canada's independent place in the collaborative British Commonwealth, a stance that would be unwelcome in English Canada – and to King himself. In 1927, fearing that a French Canadian might go too far in proclaiming reservations about the League's powers, King conceded reluctantly to Lapointe's demand that Senator Dandurand be a candidate for a three-year term on a non-permanent seat on the League Council. Lapointe, who had himself been a delegate to the

League Assembly in 1922 and 1923, went to the point of threatening King with resignation if he did not support the election of Dandurand, who would keep his eye on the League.

For Ontario, the ever-cautious King, wanting to keep his own eye on Dandurand and on the League itself, and after a visit to Ottawa by British prime minister Stanley Baldwin, stood for election in 1928 to one of the honorific six vice presidencies of the League Assembly. To the House of Commons in February 1929, he set forth for the benefit of English Canada his government's attitude toward the League. "Canada perhaps as much as any country in the world is united in its efforts to further the work of the League of Nations … We, who are supporting so splendidly the work of the League in all its activities, will wish to see that work strengthened and furthered."[5] In the election of July 1930, the Conservatives defeated King's Liberals, so it was for the new prime minister, R.B Bennett, to show how splendidly or otherwise Canada was supporting the League. Although Bennett himself was later determined to display support for the League, despite contrary advice from isolationists and Skelton in particular, his government got off to an uncertain start in its League policy.

On the other side of the globe, the military dictatorship in Japan, intent on garnering essential raw materials wherever and however it could in what it presented as a "Greater East Asia Co-Prosperity Sphere," staged the Mukden incident in September 1931, following conflict between Russian and Chinese forces in Manchuria. After seizing the city, Japanese units spread out across the ill-governed Chinese territory of Manchuria and also later clashed with Chinese forces in Shanghai, aggression that was in time to lead to a full Sino-Japanese war. In September 1932 the Chinese government brought Japan's seizure of Manchuria before a special assembly of the League of Nations, but amid the distractions of the economic depression, little consensus or even interest emerged in Geneva concerning what, if anything, should be done. The United States, long committed to China, at least via its missionaries and entrepreneurs, and not a member of the League, attempted to cooperate with it, but the League's major members displayed little enthusiasm for engaging in an unedifying dispute in a remote corner on the other side of the world from Geneva.

Canada was soon seen as pro-Japanese. Its delegate to the special assembly was Charles Cahan, Bennett's secretary of state (not to be confused with secretary of state for external affairs, a cabinet post which the new prime minister, like his predecessor, had retained for himself). Walter Riddell, who from 1925 had served as Canada's advisory officer at both the International Labour Organization and at the League of Nations, later recalled, "Many years previously he [Cahan] had represented Canadian financial interests in certain hydro-electric developments in Mexico and had very decided views regarding countries with weak or unstable Governments. He shared the common view that China was one of these countries and therefore he had a great deal of personal sympathy with Japan." Riddell, disconcerted by Cahan's independent stance, informed Ottawa that upon the minister's arrival in Geneva,

> I gave him a copy of our instructions ... and said that they seemed to cover the ground very well as I felt the chief task of the Assembly was to try to uphold the new system of peaceful settlement of international disputes ... I also told him that the Government desired to be kept continuously informed of the progress of the negotiations ... From the standpoint of collective security the result [of the Assembly's deliberations] was bad. It had given comfort to an aggressor who had taken the law of nations into its own hands ... This is the very opposite of what our instructions had been intended to do. I therefore took the first opportunity to urge upon the Canadian Government that they should correct the misleading impression regarding their attitude.[6]

Bennett accepted the advice of Riddell and that of the acting undersecretary for external affairs, Norman Robertson (Skelton being absent in London), to correct the misleading impression left by Cahan's speech. In a statement to the League Assembly, Riddell voiced Canada's support for an ad hoc commission (the Lytton commission) that eventually condemned the Japanese aggression, but did little else. Japan created the puppet state of Manchuko and withdrew from the League.

In a brief debate in the House of Commons, both King, now leader of the opposition, and J.S. Woodsworth of the Cooperative Commonwealth Federation (CCF) endorsed Riddell's statement in Geneva, in some part as a means of embarrassing the new Conservative government. King did not draw on his prewar understandings of Japan and China or his acceptance of the traditional conviction in London that the friendship of the industrial and militaristic Japan was key to the maintenance of the British Empire across Asia, particularly through lightening the load on the Royal Navy. Short of publicly disavowing one of his senior ministers, Bennett was left with no option but to explain that "he did not think it would be wise ... that we should endeavour, with the slight knowledge that we possess, either to blame or praise this country or the other in matters so serious as those involved in the differences between Japan and China."[7] The failure of the League membership to support a decisive collective security response to Japan's aggression was not lost on Mussolini and the leader of the ambitious Nazi party in Germany, Adolf Hitler.

6

The Advent of the Dictators: Mussolini

Mackenzie King's first personal encounter with a dictator was in 1928 on his third visit to Italy. With the House of Commons not sitting in the late summer of 1928, he embarked for a Europe now generally enjoying at least modest postwar economic recovery, Germany being the major and worrisome exception. As prime minister, he went to Europe partly to head Canada's small delegation to the League of Nations and to sign the United States-inspired Kellogg-Briand peace pact, which the Japanese in Manchuria would soon ignore. Fortuitously, the pact asked nothing of Canada. After his customary visits to London and Paris and his brief sojourn in Geneva, King went on a private visit to Rome where, twenty-eight years before, Mulock had telegraphed him his offer of the editorship of the *Canada Labour Gazette*.

Like many of his contemporaries, King marvelled at the economic progress made by Italy under the dictator Benito Mussolini. Near chaos had ruled in the immediate postwar years (to the point that a highly disgruntled Italy had withdrawn from the Paris Peace Conference) until Mussolini's Blackshirts had staged their dramatic march on Rome in October 1922 and set Italy on its road to becoming a great, or at least a greater, power. The year 1929 – the year following King's visit – marked the apogee of Mussolini's long career as a dictator. He had vanquished the communists and displaced ineffective democrats.

Italy's relations with nearly all the nations of Europe were in a state of happy tranquility. The British were demonstrating their customary reserved friendliness, the French were giving few signs of alarm, and the Austrians were settling into a relationship of amity with their protector south of the Alps … Even the Yugoslavs were enjoying a sense of precarious *détente* … in February 1929, Mussolini scored the most substantial success of his whole career – the signature of the accords with the Vatican. This amicable settlement … had enormous repercussions throughout Europe and the Catholic world: the thesis that Mussolini was essentially a moderate and constructive statesman now seemed to have found irrefutable confirmation.[1]

Yet no one, including the garrulous and vainglorious dictator himself, had any clear idea of what fascism was. Richard Evans, the historian of the Nazi regime in Germany, has written that "Italian Fascism was violent, ceaselessly active, it despised parliamentary institutions, it was militaristic and it glorified conflict and war … it provided a model and a parallel for the emerging Nazi party. Early Nazism … belonged firmly in this wider context of the rise of European fascism. For a long time, Hitler looked to Mussolini as an example to follow."[2] Fascism was style rather than substance, form rather than content. Il Duce himself praised fascism as "a doctrine of action." Fascism was indeed action, but it was action mixed with "a kind of political mysticism … a belief in the common bond of nationhood imbued in the personality of a charismatic leader."[3] That, and Mussolini's love for imperial trappings, was romantic stuff, but it was matched in city streets by the brutality of fascist thugs toward anyone on the political left. Yet to many Italians, Mussolini above all gave hope, that most elusive of emotions, as Hitler was to do a decade later to Germans. Perhaps the last word on Italian fascism may be left to the British historian A.J.P Taylor.

> Fascism never possessed the ruthless drive, let alone the material strength, of National Socialism [in Germany]. Morally it was just as corrupting – or perhaps more so from its very dishonesty. Everything about Fascism was a fraud. The social peril from which it saved Italy was a fraud; the revolution by which it seized power was a fraud; the ability and policy of Mussolini were fraudulent. Fascist rule was corrupt, incompetent, empty; Mussolini himself a vain, blundering boaster without either ideas or aims. Fascist Italy lived in a state of illegality, and Fascist foreign policy repudiated from the outset the principles of [the League of Nations in] Geneva.[4]

Mackenzie King, however, arrived in Rome well disposed to Mussolini. In his words, when one recognizes that he "came out with his Blackshirts to the King [Victor Emmanuel III in 1922], offered his services to clean up the Government and the House of Representatives [which was] filled with Communists, banished them all to an island, cleared the streets of beggars and the houses of harlots, one becomes filled with admiration. It is something I have never seen before ... I feel the deepest sympathy for the man."[5] Il Duce could hardly have expected better of a visitor.

At 10:30 on the morning of 26 September 1928, King called on Mussolini in his grand rooms at the Palazzo Venezia. The British ambassador had arranged the meeting at King's request since there was no Canadian diplomatic mission in Rome until 1947. Mussolini greeted King with a smile and a hand outstretched in a friendly way. Little is known about what they discussed (through an interpreter), but King opened with a less than scintillating topic: the constitution of Canada (as he would do again almost a decade later in an interview with Hitler). He pointed to Canada's membership in the League of Nations as evidence that the dominion was as "free" as the totalitarian state of Italy. While the subtleties of his exegesis on the constitution were lost on the blacksmith's son, who had been a socialist journalist before becoming the fascist leader, an evidently puzzled Mussolini asked the obvious question: what was the relationship of Canada to Britain? King was presumably more successful when he turned to praising Italy: "the fine appearance of the country, its evident progressiveness under his regime ... I wished him well and the necessary strength to carry on his work."[6] Surprisingly, neither Mussolini nor King appears to have referred to the Italian immigrants in Canada whose support, financial and otherwise, the fascist government was already pursuing.

King was much taken with Mussolini. Later, having had time to reflect on his visit, he became even more enthusiastic; "The impression on me was a very real and vivid one ... There were evidences of sadness and tenderness as well as great decision in his countenance ... I would not have missed the conference for anything ... [He] has won his way deservedly to his present position, a truly remarkable man of force, of genius, fine purpose, a great patriot,"[7] a fulsome description that King was to apply holus-bolus a decade later to Hitler. There certainly was no mistaking King's enthusiasm for Mussolini and his fascist regime: "the order of it all, the fine discipline, the evident regard for authority and [for] Mussolini himself."[8]

Vincent Massey, the affluent Canadian Liberal who had been minister of the legation in Washington, called on Mussolini three years later. His reaction was more mixed. On 6 April 1931 he recorded in his journal that during an audience (again arranged by the British ambassador), "I didn't see in Mussolini's face the evidence of power I had expected to see there … He showed plenty of force, however, and genuine intelligence. I made the obvious – and sincere – remark about having found a new Italy on returning after twenty odd years. He said, 'There are two factors in what has happened to make the new Italy … *war* and *revolution*.' Rather a disquieting observation."[9]

To be sure, in his praise for the imperial dictatorship of Il Duce King was far from alone. In much of Europe and the Americas in the 1920s, Mussolini was regarded as the saviour of Italy from communism and civil war. Fascism was seen by some as Europe's answer to communism. Italy's corporatist economy was welcomed by others as a model of how to save capitalism. Admiration for Mussolini's leadership was a commonplace, despite his ludicrous strutting about, eyes rolling and massive chin stuck out, in extravagant uniforms largely of his own devising. In France many regarded him as an authoritarian, anti-communist example to be followed. In Germany, more ominously, the agitator and would-be dictator Adolf Hitler had looked upon Mussolini, from his March on Rome of 1922, as his mentor on his own way to absolute power. From Rainer Maria Rilke to Mahatma Gandhi to Austen Chamberlain to Ezra Pound to King Faisal of Iraq to George Bernard Shaw to Franklin Roosevelt, a wide variety of observers saw Mussolini as just what a chaotic Italy and even Europe needed. In December 1922 Mussolini paid his sole visit to London, where the Italian community numbered about 20,000. He had come to attend a war reparations conference, but had soon become bored by it and cancelled one of several scheduled press conferences so that he could spend the afternoon in bed with a – presumably English – prostitute. (Mussolini's attention span was notoriously limited; the month before London he spent only two days at the lengthy Lausanne conference where Curzon eventually resolved the questions reflected in the Chanak incident.) The following year, 1923, Winston Churchill denounced Mussolini as a swine when he occupied the Adriatic port of Fiume against the wishes of the League of Nations, but by 1926, as chancellor of the exchequer, Churchill had reversed himself, speaking of Mussolini's "commanding leadership" against communism. He told journalists in London, after meeting Mussolini in Rome, that "If I had been an Italian … I should have been whole-heartedly with [him] from start to finish in [his] triumphal struggle against the bestial appetites and passions of Leninism." He added on a personal level, "I could not help being charmed."[10]

In Canada, Mussolini's regime received a mixed reception. Escott Reid, later the director of the Canadian Institute for International Affairs and a future diplomat but at the time a student in Oxford, attended an international conference in Rome ten months before the arrival of Mackenzie King. Skeptical about Mussolini's regime, Reid asked in a Canadian newspaper article several rhetorical questions that were the very reverse of what King was to say about Il Duce. "Is the Fascist party nothing more than the Ku Klux Klan with a black shirt instead of a white sheet, or is the black shirt rather a cloak behind which hides a capitalist feudalism? Mussolini, a theatrical ass in the lion's skin of Napoleonism, or the rightly worshipped '*Il Duce Magnifico*,' the saviour of his country? Does fascism rest upon the fervent assent of the Italian people or is it a dictatorship, abhorred by the majority?"[11] Historian Peter Waite has written that "Demagoguery was fashionable [even in Canada] … French-Canadian nationalism of the 1930s was also anti-Semitic. English Canadians had their anti-Semitism, too, but it was generally kept underground by the facts of business life. In French Canada anti-Semitism was much more open. Western democracies were, it seemed, governed by Jews, politicians, and the power of hard cash, in sharp contrast to Italy under Mussolini which was 'fort énergique, progressif, viril et discipliné.' Democracies appeared to be invertebrate, flaccid, and feeble." [12]

In Quebec, which had the largest number of Italian immigrants in Canada, Mussolini was a hero. He was given the credit for the economic revival of Italy, in part through grandiose public works dedicated to the greater glory of fascism (that he supposedly made the trains run on time is a late and unwarranted if amiable accolade). And in Quebec as well as wherever else the Roman Catholic Church was heard, Mussolini was extolled for the conclusion with the Holy See of the Lateran Accords of 1929. They recognized the Vatican as an independent secular state (which it had not been since 1870) and granted a host of other concessions, including financial, which won for Il Duce papal blessings. "A significant section of the Republic was indeed predisposed to view fascism in the Mediterranean setting not merely without alarm but with undisguised approval. The lofty sentiments of fascist doctrine elaborated by Mussolini's publicists, with the apotheosis of order, discipline, family, nation, their pseudo-syndicalist remedies for industrial unrest, gained powerful support among the elite of French Canada."[13]

Given the anti-communist enthusiasm with which the Roman Catholic Church and Quebec generally regarded fascist Italy, it was not until 1937 that the activities of the three Italian consulates in Canada began to be monitored by the Security Branch of the Royal Canadian Mounted Police – and then only lightly. For the previous decade or more, the Security Branch had devoted most of its time to watching closely the Communist Party, which was seen as threatening the capitalist system itself, during the unrest of the depression. Not until late in the 1930s were Italian – or even German – fascists accorded quite such close attention as communists. Italian immigrants were regarded as gratifyingly anti-communist and harmless supporters of a distant and slightly ridiculous dictator. Theirs was a coherent, concentrated community, mutually supportive, bound together by years of Mussolini's long reign. The Italian consulate general in Montreal, like Italian consulates across the world, channelled modest funds and extravagant propaganda to the local Italo-Canadian community, portraying Mussolini as the embodiment of all that was good and true in the heritage of the Roman Empire.*

To the Italo-Canadian community and beyond, the dramatic arrival in Montreal in July 1933 of a squadron of twenty-four Italian seaplanes under the command of the ebullient and appropriately named Italo Balbo, an associate of Mussolini since the March on Rome, confirmed the superiority of fascism over democracy, at least in Italy. Having made the hazardous crossing of the Atlantic by stages, the squadron continued on from Montreal to Chicago, evoking in Major Dwight Eisenhower, a military host for Balbo, the ambiguous compliment that his grand manner and sense of self-publicity made him almost more American than Italian. Certainly the Italian community in Quebec, some in black-shirt fascist uniform, regarded the successful transatlantic tour of the squadron as tangible evidence of the regeneration of Italy following a decade of Mussolini's rule. Thereafter, Canadian Nazis and Italo-Canadian fascists in Montreal held occasional joint meetings at the Casa d'Italia, endorsed by the Roman Catholic Church largely as a result of Mussolini's conclusion of the acclaimed 1929 Lateran Accords with the Holy See.

---

*In Montreal many in the Italo-Canadian community and its priests so revered Mussolini that he was given a prominent position in the murals of the new church of Notre Dame de la Défense on rue Henri Julien (where he can still be seen today).

7

The Advent of the Dictators: Hitler

When Prime Minister Mackenzie King had returned to Ottawa from Europe in the autumn of 1928, he was facing the prospect of an election in 1930 amid a damaging customs scandal, widespread economic discontents, and uncertainties – which he privately shared – about how to respond to the mounting economic depression. The year before, King had welcomed to Ottawa Charles Lindbergh, the solo transatlantic flier, with the diary observation that "a more beautiful character I have never seen … like a young god who had appeared from the skies in human form."[1] In the summer of 1929 both King and Borden listened to Churchill, again on an extensive North American tour, extol to the Canadian Club in Ottawa the magnificent splendours of the senior dominion, while decrying the pitfalls of Empire free trade.* Yet even such distinguished visitors could not enhance the Liberals' electoral chances. In the July 1930 election the Liberals were soundly defeated. Despite the assurance of a clairvoyant that the Liberals would win the election (clairvoyants invariably told King what he wanted to hear), the Conservatives won a solid majority of 126 seats to the Liberals' ninety-one. That was bad enough, but Liberal support in Quebec receded from sixty to an unprecedented forty seats. King was succeeded as prime minister by R.B. Bennett, first of New Brunswick and then of Alberta.

From the opposition front bench, King kept well away from foreign affairs. He said nothing about the rise in January 1933 to the German chancellorship of the anti-communist, anti- "non-Aryan," and anti-democratic Adolf Hitler and the extraordinary rapidity with which he had consolidated

---

*Churchill's irrelevant attack on the current British policy of withdrawal from direct rule in Egypt evoked the indirect response from King that Canada wanted no consultation on the subject (Dilks, *The Great Dominion*, 60–8).

his newly won power. As Churchill repeatedly warned, Hitler, once in office, accelerated the industrial and military resurgence of Germany and replaced Il Duce in the front rank of European dictators. The Führer brought to the chancellorship a decade or more of promises accompanied by hate-filled rhetoric. In his virtually unreadable *Mein Kampf* (written in 1923 when he had been jailed for a failed insurrection in Munich) and in later newspaper interviews, he deplored the postwar abasement of the German *Volk*, humiliated by the impossible demands of the victors at Versailles and the ensuing economic chaos, particularly the inflation that had so undermined the Weimar Republic. The Treaty of Versailles was unjust, grossly punitive, and unrealistic, especially in its exaggerated reparation demands. It had led to economic turmoil and near starvation, and the relocation of substantial ethnic minorities, including German, to new states, Czechoslovakia in particular. Hitler promised not only to bring together the *Volk*, but also to restore racial purity by purging the German nation of communists, international financiers, homosexuals, the mentally or physically handicapped, freemasons, Jews, blacks, and other so-called undesirables whom he blamed for Germany's humiliation at the hands of the Allies. He would join Mussolini as a bastion against the westward spread of Soviet communism. He would also rectify the artificial postwar boundaries of central Europe and reject once and for all the Allied charge of war guilt. In his platform for the 1933 elections in which the Nazis won the largest number of seats (although not a clear majority), Hitler promised, to wide acclaim, to repudiate the Versailles Treaty, including reparations, and have done with the Weimar Republic. As Führer, he would restore Germany to its rightful leadership in the comity of European nations and bring dignity as well as prosperity to the *Volk*, whether they lived in Germany itself or across the ridiculous frontiers imposed by the hated Versailles Treaty. He would, in short, restore the pride of the German people in their great nation.

With the failure of democracies, with the possible exception of Roosevelt's New Deal, to alleviate the hardships created by the Great Depression of 1929, many countries turned to dictatorships. In January 1933, Germany joined the ranks of the dictatorships which in Europe included Italy, the Soviet Union, Portugal, Romania, Bulgaria, Poland, and eventually Spain. Effective collective security had not emerged from the League of Nations: the United States had never joined and Japan withdrew in March 1933 and Germany in October. Accordingly, Britain and France pursued efforts to restore some sort of balance of power in Europe by attempting, for example, to discourage the southern European power of Italy from allying itself with the northern European power of Germany.

Mackenzie King had been leader of the opposition for more than two years when Hitler became chancellor. Abundant information about the new totalitarian regime was on offer to the dominions from both the Foreign Office and British intelligence, but there is no evidence that either Prime Minister Bennett or Leader of the Opposition Mackenzie King, in their different ways, availed themselves of very much (Bennett being content to leave the lead in foreign affairs to Britain, while King suspected that Foreign Office material was designed to advance its own imperial interests). King made no comment in his journal and asked no questions about the elimination of democratic government in Germany. He possibly hoped that any adverse comment that appeared in the *Ottawa Citizen* or *Journal* about Hitler – and it was very little – would prove to be exaggerated. There was almost nothing in the Canadian Press news service about Hitler's violence against communists and socialists at the time of the Reichstag fire in February 1933, one month after he became chancellor. The following month, the Nazis opened the first of their notorious concentration camps at Dachau, north of Munich, run by Heinrich Himmler's savage ss (*Schutzstaffel*). Sir Robert Vansittart, the permanent secretary at the Foreign Office and a committed customer of MI5 and MI6, knew from the beginning where Hitler's chancellorship would lead. Like Churchill, he was convinced that "the present regime in Germany will … loose off another European war just so soon as it feels strong enough … we are considering very crude people, who have few ideas … but brute force and militarism."[2]

Shortly before Hitler became chancellor, King told his diary that, although now only leader of the opposition, the Almighty had ordained him to play a central role in the maintenance of world peace, that God's dreams and work would be communicated to him from on High. King was certain that "I am being made the instrument of God."[3] He was confirmed in his certainty by his budding psychic experiences, finding occult solace in messages from the departed that came initially via table rapping sessions. Yet if he had read the *Toronto Star*, he would have been better informed about what was in fact happening in Germany. The *Star* sent its London correspondent, Matthew Halton, to Berlin in March 1933, a few weeks after Hitler came to power and immediately after the Reichstag fire. In a series of articles, Halton described the destructive power and the myriad prejudices unleashed by Hitler's arrival in office. On 16 September 1933, he wrote of Hitler at a rally in Berlin, "Using all the tricks of oratory with the most perfect disingenuousness, the little Austrian house-painter in his ugly brown uniform described the 'degradation' of Germany in searing phrases and a thundering voice that turned his hearers into maddening, moaning fanatics."[4] On 15 October Halton stated that during his last month in Germany, "I have seen and studied the most fanatical, thorough-going and savage philosophy of war ever imposed on any nation. It is this philosophy which gives the chief and fateful significance to Germany's tragic withdrawal from the League [of Nations] and the disarmament conference and the consequent destruction of fifteen years of the most difficult political reconstruction."[5] His articles, despite being published in a hitherto strongly anti-war newspaper, had surprisingly limited impact, especially among the isolationist-minded. Many in Western Europe and the United States regarded the new chancellor and a central Europe under German leadership as a sure bulwark against the feared spread of communism from Soviet Russia. The Liberal *Winnipeg Free Press* was notable for its endorsement of Halton's trenchant series on Nazi Germany. Two leading Toronto dailies, the *Globe* and the *Telegram*, were not so certain in their estimate of the new German chancellor, the *Globe* even publishing articles vaguely sympathetic to the discipline and good order of Hitler's *Reich*. The *Montreal Gazette* joined the *Globe* in its praise of the patriotic spirit of the new Germany.

Mackenzie King took little or no notice of the increasing number of ominous events in Germany, not even of the "Night of the Long Knives" of 30 June 1934. Shortly after his return from Venice, where he had his first and not entirely successful meeting with Mussolini, Hitler presided over the murder of one of his closest associates, Ernst Röhm, a fellow war veteran who had collaborated with him in his totalitarian ambitions as early as 1919. During the immediate postwar years, Röhm, as chief of staff of the Nazi Brown Shirts, the *Stürmabteilung* (SA) or Storm Troopers, had become the devoted, although not always uncritical, accomplice of Hitler. Egged on by his closest associates, Hermann Göring and Heinrich Himmler among them, Hitler convinced himself that Röhm was challenging his authority, even plotting to replace him following his return to Germany from several years as an advisor to the Bolivian army. In any event, the German army, the Wehrmacht, whose support Hitler coveted, was opposed to any such private armies as the Brown Shirts.

Röhm was murdered in Munich, along with General Kurt von Schleicher, Hitler's predecessor as chancellor, and an estimated eighty-five senior SA and other supporters, including twelve members of the Reichstag. The now doddering President Hindenburg congratulated the chancellor on his safe deliverance from traitors. The first secretary at the British Embassy in Berlin recorded that "after Hitler had flown ... to Munich to murder Röhm, he returned in the very highest spirits, mimicking to his secretary the gestures of fear which Röhm had made."[6] What remained of the notoriously violent SA soon all but disappeared into the ranks of the Wehrmacht, leaving in centre stage the Black Shirt SS of the sinister Himmler who, amid other nonsense, believed that he could summon up spirits of the dead.

The absence of any reference in King's diary to the darkening scene in Germany, despite the fact that he had said that he wanted to devise a foreign policy for Canada, suggests that he regarded the Reichstag fire and the terrible violence of the Night of the Long Knives as of no concern to anyone but the German people themselves. Domestic political developments, including violence, were Germany's business, internal matters not for comment or intervention by outsiders. But in the aftermath of the Night of the Long Knives, other observers were no longer so sure. For example, Beaverbrook, a frequent visitor to Germany, had in early 1933 adopted a wait-and-see attitude, eager to see Britain stand clear of conflicts in Europe and concentrate on building the Empire. But within a year he had become "solidly, fanatically, anti-Hitler; refers to him as Al Capone [a contemporary American criminal] and to the Nazis as gangsters!"[7] Certainly, the British ambassador in Berlin understood where things were going. On 8 August Sir Eric Phipps wrote to London, "foreign colleagues [are] very pessimistic as to the situation in Germany and as to what the future holds in store ... I see no reason to take a more cheerful view than they ... Violent, arrogant, fanatical, his [Hitler's] manner more than his actual language bodes ill for such of his unfortunate countrymen who venture to differ." The British military attaché was even more cryptic about the Nazi regime: "a mad-dog dictatorship."[8] King George V applied the same description to Mussolini and dismissed the Nazi leaders as simply "horrid fellows."

The fanaticism which Phipps and other diplomats and foreign journalists were readily identifying was displayed in an awesome form at a vast Nazi rally in Nuremburg in early September 1934, the first of such annual events. It is impossible now to say how much of the darkening German outlook Mackenzie King was aware of and how much he simply ignored. Newsreels around the world gave some idea of what was afoot, but King did not go to cinemas. What he made of press photographs he did not record. And he certainly did not seek comment from the British Foreign Office. If queried, King might have replied that none of the above was any of Canada's business. As leader of the opposition, he saw his role as opposing whatever Bennett's government proposed. And if he contemplated from the opposition front bench the formulation of a coherent foreign policy, it consisted of little more than sidestepping the uncertainties of Europe, concentrating on liberalized trade with the United States, and, *pace* Skelton, confidential reassurances to Britain that if it were seriously threatened, Canada would be at its side. On that fundamental commitment, King and Bennett tacitly agreed. They even agreed – then – on the need for Canada to support the League of Nations.

In London in June for the 1933 imperial conference, Bennett attended a dinner party of the pro-fascist society hostess Mrs Ronnie Greville, where from the even more pro-fascist Lord Londonderry and from the leading anti-fascist Winston Churchill he heard differing views of the recently ascendant Hitler. In Canada the leader of the opposition disregarded the wise – and Liberal – advice of Newton Rowell, the former president of the Privy Council in Borden's Union Government (and to be chief justice of Ontario from 1936), who recognized more clearly than most what was happening in Europe. Rowell saw the growing threat of the dictators and the mounting need to support the League of Nations as the only answer to them. Such advice also came to King from – among others – Robert Falconer, the Prince Edward Island-born president of the University of Toronto, and J.W. Dafoe, the editor of the *Winnipeg Free Press*, but most cogently from Rowell.

Following Laurier's death in 1919, Rowell, not King, might have been the next leader of the Liberal Party if it had not been for the insurmountable fact that in 1917 he had joined Borden's wartime union government, which introduced compulsory military service as the only answer to the rapidly increasing numbers of casualties on the Western Front and the need to keep faith with the volunteers who had gone before. The details of the ambiguous attitude of King himself during the conscription crisis of 1917 need not detain us here since what matters is that he was later able to convince Quebec Liberals that he, unlike Rowell or Thomas Crerar or the septuagenarian anglophile William Fielding, had been unalterably loyal to Laurier in his opposition to conscription. Rowell's support for Borden's Military Service Act ended any possibility that he would be acceptable to Quebec as leader of the Liberal Party, despite the fact that he understood more of Canada's evolving place in the British Commonwealth and in the world beyond than any Canadian, except perhaps Borden himself. As early as April 1933, three months after Hitler had become chancellor, Rowell's acute perception of what was happening in Europe was reflected in a letter to his daughter. "The tragedy of the situation is that the great powers, Great Britain and France and more particularly France, refused to meet Germany's just demands on reparations, disarmament, war guilt, etc., while Germany had a democratic Government in power and when much less than they are now prepared to concede might have been accepted. Their refusal gave the Hitlerites their appeal to the German people and now that democracy in Germany is overthrown, they are disposed to yield for fear of worse consequences."[9] King did not act on Rowell's enlightening analysis. It was Bennett who reflected his understanding. With Lester Pearson accompanying him, Bennett attended the League of Nations Assembly in Geneva in September 1934. There they heard in the corridors much about the new German chancellor that gave additional substance to the worst fears of observers like Rowell and Halton.

Fascist movements of various sorts continued to spring up in much of Europe. They had emerged in both France and Britain during the early 1920s. In France, Mussolini was acclaimed as a bulwark against communism and economic chaos, but any enthusiasm for Hitler was tempered with the fact that from 1870 Germany had been the latent if not active enemy of France. Although fascists in France, with a few exceptions, remained wary of appearing to be closely aligned with German fascists, they proliferated, spouting anti-communist and anti-Semitic hatred. Street fights and riots between communists and such right-wing organizations as the Croix de feu, La Ligue des jeunesses patriotes, and the royalist Action française spread to the point that in time they would be seen as threatening the stability of the republic itself. In the United Kingdom, the ambitions of local fascists advocating a strong, dictatorial government came to be centred on a would-be Führer, Oswald Mosley. Once a rising Conservative MP who in the late 1920s had crossed the floor to the Labour Party, he then swung his personal political pendulum all the way from socialism to fascism. By 1932, inspired in part by a visit to Mussolini and funding from him, Mosley founded the United Kingdom Fascist Party. He wrote that fascism in Italy "has produced not only a new system of government, but also a new type of man, who differs from politicians of the old world as men from another planet."[10] Strongly endorsed by Lord Rothermere's *Daily Mail*, the visibility and acceptability of the United Kingdom Fascist Party were enhanced when it became known, as the Beaverbrook journalist and former British agent in Russia Robert Bruce Lockhart recorded, that the Prince of Wales, the future King Edward VIII, "was quite pro-Hitler, [and] said it was no business of ours to interfere in Germany's internal affairs either *re* the Jews or anything else and added that dictatorships were very popular these days and that we might want one in England before long."[11]*

Fascism in Britain was largely homegrown, there being few Germans resident in the United Kingdom. By contrast, in the United States, as in Canada, there were many German immigrants or their descendants, often members of long-standing local, regional, or national German-American organizations. Rudolph Hess and Joseph Goebbels, two eminent members of Hitler's entourage, identified propaganda and other opportunities in the Western hemisphere, although Hitler himself exhibited little interest in transatlantic as opposed to European ventures. "By the fall of 1933, then, two alternative – though not necessarily contradictory – methods of approaching Americans of German ancestry had emerged … on the one hand … [Rudolph] Hess hoped to create a German bloc in America favourable to Nazi Germany by using a broadly based, German-sponsored party or Bund movement. On the other hand, Goebbels discounted the need for either a political party or a Bund movement and favoured a well-organized but camouflaged propaganda campaign directed at thousands of German-American organizations throughout the United States."[12] That tension between the two approaches was to be replicated in Canada on a smaller scale.

Deutscher Bund Canada's beginnings in 1933 were inauspicious. Before the designation of Hitler as chancellor in January, German-Americans had

---

*One of Mosley's lesser claims to fame was that King George V had attended his first wedding and Hitler his second – to the fanatical pro-fascist Mitford sister, Diana Mitford.

already formed the Friends of the New Germany. Amid the turmoil of the depression, it soon adopted as "its first purpose ... to provide the American public with an objective look at Hitler's Germany, to expose American Jewry as the tool of Moscow and to protect the German and German American community." By the late summer of 1933, the Friends of the New Germany had spread northward into Canada with a few embryonic branches established in Ontario. The new administration of Franklin Roosevelt, however, was strongly opposed to what it regarded as an alien organization controlled from abroad, "preaching anti-democratic and racist ideology" and the American Friends collapsed.[13] Within months, Friends of the New Germany was also gone from Canada, to be replaced almost immediately, on 1 January 1934, by Deutscher Bund Canada.

The four founders of Bund Canada all came from the small Ontario city of Kitchener, the former Berlin, the birthplace of Mackenzie King and, for the founders' purposes, the unpromising home for generations of pacifist Mennonites. In these circumstances, the Bund portrayed their organization as the Canadian flowering of a worldwide, pan-German social and cultural movement based in part on the *Volklich* romances of the nineteenth century. That such romantic antecedents had contributed to the rise in Germany of a malignant sport, the National Socialist – or Nazi – Party, was passed over lightly. Deutscher Bund Canada, the national organization of German Canadians, reflected enthusiasm, however erratic at times, for contemporary Germany and, more specifically, for its fascist government. In short, Bund Canada was for German Canadians, not for Canadian fascists as such.

The founders of the Bund were determined not to be identified as an emanation of the Nazi regime but rather as a pan-German organization committed, among other things, to countering both anti-German propaganda and the spread of communism. Given the emerging hostility abroad to the Nazi regime, Berlin soon came to regard at least the public appearance of independence as an important element in Bund activities across North America. "Directives from Germany ... – the most important from Hitler's deputy Rudolph Hess – forbade [Nazi] Party members resident in North America from introducing themselves into *Volklich* organizations."[14] Since the membership of Bund Canada was never large or affluent, the Bund was always in need of financial subsidies. Thus, whatever financial support – and it was limited – came from Berlin via the German consulates was welcome. Although it was estimated in the 1930s that as many as 500,000 Canadians were of German descent, Bund membership was no more than 1,200 to 2,000.[15] Further, less than 5 percent of the total Bund membership was thought to be also Nazi party members.

Mackenzie King at no time paid much heed to Bund Canada, confident as one born in Berlin, Ontario, that it was harmless and that any surveillance could be left to the minister of justice, Ernest Lapointe, and to the Security Branch of the Royal Canadian Mounted Police. He was aware that the majority of German Canadians, some of whose families had been in Canada for more than a century, knew little and cared less about the Third Reich. In any event, Bund Canada remained a confused and incoherent organization, never certain whether it wanted Berlin's approbation as a pro-Hitler organization or whether it should play down open support for the Nazi regime and concentrate more on its portrayal of the new Germany as of benefit to all humanity.

A principal reason for the uneven course pursued by Bund Canada was the uncertain leadership of its several Führers (the German title was consciously adopted). The first was Karl Gerhard, one of its original founders. He had arrived in Canada in 1930. After working as a farm labourer, he spent two years in residence at Huron College in the University of Western Ontario. Although later styling himself "professor," he took no degree. Gerhard, wearing the swastika symbol of the Nazi party, claimed to have been an early member of the party in Germany. He gave Bund Canada its initial form, discipline, and regional structure. But Gerhard did not last long. He was soon accused of embezzlement of the Bund's limited funds. Similar charges were also made against the next two Führers, who followed in quick succession. More effective was the fourth leader in six years, Bernard Bott of Winnipeg, who published the pro-Hitler *Courier* in Regina and later, with Berlin's indispensable financial and editorial assistance, the *Deutsche Zeitung für Canada* in Winnipeg, a racist and increasingly hate-filled newspaper estimated to have a national circulation of 6,000. It drew heavily on abundant material supplied by the German consulates, including Julius Streicher's notoriously anti-Semitic weekly *Der Stürmer*, which paraded a pathological view of Jews and their world conspiracy.

Such was Bund Canada in the 1930s. Parallel and separate were the pro-Nazi activities in Canada of non-Germans. Under a succession of names, what was in effect the Nazi party of Canada supported fascism both at home and abroad. Hitler had non-German admirers across the country throughout the 1930s, but they never numbered more than a few thousand. His single most active exponent was a talented but ne'er-do-well young French Canadian journalist, Adrien Arcand, who had worked for several Montreal newspapers in the 1920s. The son of an unsuccessful Labour candidate for parliament in the election of 1902, Arcand was paradoxically a bizarre mixture of an anti-separatist, pro-British junior militia officer (his brother had served with distinction as an infantry major in Flanders), an advocate of the poor, and a fascist. He had been a long-time admirer of Mussolini when Hitler became chancellor of Germany in 1933.

In August 1929, Arcand launched in Montreal the imaginatively named National Socialist Christian Party of Canada and an ill-funded but lively satirical weekly, *Le Goglu*, which extolled the authoritarian political models of Europe as offering a way out of the hardships of the economic depression. Arcand soon showed himself to be something of an anarchist, as well as anti-democratic, anti-liberal, and in favour of a "guided economy" purged of all Jews. As with fascists everywhere, it is easier to say what Arcand and his dedicated followers in Quebec were against than what they were for. They were clearly against liberals, socialists, communists, democrats, Jews, blacks, and big capital. Arcand himself defined "Fascism [as] … a doctrine of order, of justice, a doctrine that recognizes the duty of Christian charity."[16] *Le Goglu* became increasingly anti-Semitic, drawing in part on that long-standing element in Roman Catholic parish life; it argued that economic power in Quebec should be more concentrated in the hands of French Canadians, the only true route to recovery from the widespread hardships of the depression.

In Montreal in the autumn of 1932, Arcand received a visit from one Karl Ludecke of New York, who claimed that as a struggling businessman in Bavaria he had supported Hitler as early as 1922 and that he and his wife, Mildred, an American from Detroit, were among Hitler's personal friends. What role Ludecke in fact played in the early propagation of fascism in the United States and Canada and with what mandate, if any, from Hitler remains obscure. He initiated the dissemination in Canada of pro-Nazi material from Germany, which made its way into *Le Goglu* as well as into several other small publications. He eventually recanted his pro-Nazi enthusiasms. In his later book, *I Knew Hitler*, Ludecke describes how he and his wife "were in a happy mood when we drove [from New York City] to Montreal to keep an appointment with Adrien Arcand, the fiery leader of the 'Ordre patriotique des Goglus.' This was a violently anti-Jewish, in the main Catholic folkic [sic] movement which at the time was growing rapidly in French Canada, with three publications, all very demagogic and clever. I liked young Arcand at once, his vibrant, intelligent, fine-featured face, his genuine fighting spirit. He was greatly pleased when I gave him an autographed photograph of Hitler. We understood each other perfectly and agreed to co-operate in every way."[17]

Le Goglu was always close to bankruptcy, but the federal election of 1930, which brought Bennett's Conservatives into office, provided temporary relief. The speaker of the Senate, Pierre-Édouard Blondin, a major adviser about where to place Conservative Party advertising in Quebec, and a noted supporter of the right-wing *Jeune Canada*, readily recommended that the party buy advertising space in *Le Goglu*. Why Blondin sought to include Conservative advertising in *Le Goglu* is unclear. He must have been aware that *Le Goglu*'s pro-fascist readers (not specifically pro-Hitler, since he had not yet come to office) would vote Conservative if they voted at all (the Italian community in Montreal, with its many followers of Mussolini, could be dealt with separately). His recommendation was supported by three Montreal Conservative members of parliament: Samuel Gobeil, John Sullivan, and Leslie Bell. They were a mixed bag; Samuel Gobeil, who would become postmaster general at the end of Bennett's government, was especially outspoken in his anti-communist and anti-Semitic prejudices, which the other two MPs shared to a degree. At late as July 1939, two months before the Second World War, Gobeil "at a public meeting ... denounced to his devoutly Catholic audience that Lapointe was the kind of anti-clerical Liberal the papacy anathematized." He smeared him as "the friend and patron of communists ... to allow ... 2,000 Canadians to fight with the Spanish Reds" in the Spanish Civil War. In an anti-Semitic harangue, Gobeil also accused Lapointe and the Liberal government "of favouring Jewish immigration."[18] The records of the Security Branch of the RCMP do not, however, suggest that any of the three MPs was directly involved with Arcand or his public meetings. It was Blondin alone who continued to take the lead in attempting to channel Conservative advertising to *Le Goglu* and its small Sunday newspaper, *Le Miroir*, and it was he who, in parallel, observed that "young people to act will need the fiery sword wielded by our friend Arcand."[19]

During the 1930s, Arcand and his now renamed National Social Christian Party were the most shrill pro-Nazis in Canada, but small groups of Nazis, complete with swastika insignia, also emerged across the country. In Toronto, as in Montreal, anti-communism and anti-Semitism, frequently conflated, were already evident when Hitler came to office.* In the summer of 1933 in the Beaches district, groups of unemployed youth proclaiming their fascist convictions and displaying swastika symbols clashed with an all-Jewish baseball team (in itself a reflection of the degree of racism in Toronto). In response, the mayor banned the wearing of swastikas, but nevertheless a "Swastika Association of Canada" was launched on its uncertain and obscure course by a former British army sergeant major and Orangeman from Northern Ireland, Joseph Farr. He announced that his was "a purely Canadian organization to foster and encourage unselfishness, good fellowship, truth and loyalty to King and Country." It was not. It was a small pro-Nazi organization that paralleled the growth of yet smaller fascist gangs elsewhere in Canada. In Winnipeg in September 1933 another British army veteran, William Whittaker, launched the Canadian Nationalist Party.[20] His initiative was independent of Arcand and Farr (although the three small organizations were eventually to merge) and differed from them in calling for the abolition of provincial legislatures and their replacement by a single corporate state purged of all communists and Jews. That same month was marked by a brawl in Montreal involving undergraduates from l'Université de Montréal shouting anti-Jewish slogans.

In 1934, prompted by MI5 in London, which in May of that year had asked all chief constables to report on the membership of the British Union of Fascists in their areas, the RCMP began keeping an eye on the National Social Christian Party, but there really was not much upon which to keep its eye. As for the Bund, like its American version, it was seriously weakened by internal friction and accusations of financial improprieties. While the RCMP began to show some interest in the far right as well as the far left, it remained preoccupied with the Communist Party in particular and the Canadian left

---

*One example was André Laurendeau. He wrote that "Jews yearn … for the happy day when their race will dominate the world" (in Nadeau, *The Canadian Führer*, 99). Thirty years later, having become a noted journalist and editor of *Le Devoir*, he was appointed by Prime Minister Pearson co-chairman of the 1963 Royal Commission on Biculturalism and Bilingualism.

more generally. Perhaps this was not surprising since many unemployed and poor were seeking salvation from the hardships of the depression in a domestic order other than what they saw as the failure of democracy, although certainly more in communism than in fascism. The first inter-departmental meeting "to discuss a number of questions arising out of the activities of fascist agencies" was held in Ottawa in March 1936, but as late as September 1937, the RCMP informed King and Lapointe that they had concluded that there were "no Nazi activities nor any Nazi movement in Canada."[21]

8

King and Abyssinia: The Muddle

Such was the domestic fascist scene that Mackenzie King left behind as he made his way in the autumn of 1934 on one of his all but annual sojourns in Europe. Still leader of the opposition, he travelled as a private citizen, but that hardly explains how he could spend a week in Italy without referring in his diary to Mussolini's ill-concealed plans to invade Abyssinia or how he could ignore the growing concerns in London and Paris about the new chancellor of Germany. If Italy concocted a spurious reason to invade a fellow member of the League of Nations, as now appeared certain, Canada could be confronted with the question of what sanctions it would apply jointly with other League members against the aggressor. If asked, King might have evaded that awkward but basic question since any answer necessarily rested with Bennett as prime minister. King, as leader of the opposition, did have to decide whether to support the Conservative government in its understanding of Mussolini's grandiose plans for his homeland or ignore the whole issue of the dictators and collective security. King chose the latter, so there is no word of criticism in his journal for 1934 about the obvious preparations that Mussolini was making to demonstrate to an increasingly uneasy world the virility of the new Roman Empire. With some satisfaction King recorded in his diary that he had begun his visit to Rome by calling on the British ambassador, Sir Eric Drummond (later the sixteenth Earl of Perth), who had until the year before been secretary-general of the League of Nations. Drummond expressed great admiration for Mussolini, and assured King that Il Duce would never make war.

Mussolini's attitude to what he saw as Anglo-French manipulation of the League of Nations to counter Italian ambitions can be briefly told. In the secret London Treaty of 1915, Britain and France had brought Italy into the war on the Allied side by promising it territories in southern Europe and Asia Minor. When Lloyd George and Clemenceau failed to deliver on these promises in 1919, the Italian foreign minister walked out of the Paris Peace Conference. A fascist Italy vowed that never again would it be so cheated by Britain and France. In this perilous diplomatic game, Italy had one card to play, but it was a significant one. France was desperate to secure allies against a resurgent Germany. Italy appeared to be just such an ally in 1934 when it acted to prevent what it saw as a threatening merger of Austria with Germany.

The Italian-Ethiopian Treaty of 1928 had established the border between Ethiopia and Italian Somaliland. In 1930, Italy built a fort at Welwel, inside Ethiopian territory. When an Anglo-Ethiopian border commission arrived in 1934 to investigate, fighting broke out. Italy then engaged in a military build-up in Eritrea and Italian Somaliland, a clear sign of its expansionary plans. On 3 October 1935, Italy invaded Ethiopia.

Many French and some British statesmen regarded Abyssinia as an unknown backwater in Africa not worth risking the loss of Italy as a French ally. Even the League of Nations could not be given precedence over the demands of *Realpolitik*. Accordingly, Foreign Minister Pierre Laval strove unceasingly to retain both Britain and Italy as allies. If that meant jettisoning a fellow member of the League, and even fatally undermining the League, so be it.

Nearing his sixtieth birthday, Mackenzie King gave himself a long European holiday in the autumn of 1934, knowing that 1935, an election year, would be particularly demanding. After London and Paris in early November, he visited Rome. In 1921 he had commissioned sculptor Giuseppe Guastalla to create a bust of his mother. King, entirely satisfied with that sculpture, now travelled to Rome to view Guastalla's progress on marble busts of both his father and himself. (King had first viewed the work of Guastalla at the Panama-Pacific International Exposition in San Francisco in 1911.) The sculptor had had to work from photographs, but King was pleased with "the nobility of dear father's face – his pure life" (such praise for his kindly but ineffective lawyer father was nothing compared to his earlier admiration for the bust of his mother).

King's several sittings at the sculptor's studio were much enhanced by the presence of Giorgia Borra de Cousandier, the twenty-four-year-old wife of a neighbour. Guastalla spoke no English and King no Italian. Cousandier had at least a rudimentary knowledge of English and acted as interpreter, but being an ardent fascist she refrained from disclosing to King Guastalla's hatred for Mussolini. During the sittings, King became enamoured of her to the degree that he ever became enamoured of any woman. As Charlotte Gray wrote in her biography of Isabel, "to the outside world he might seem a commonplace, drab little figure ... but inside himself, he continued to nurse the fantasy he had shared with Isabel that he was a fairy-tale hero ... [His] pathological obsession with his mother's memory prevented him from ever committing himself to another woman."[1] Within the limits set by that pathological obsession, he confided to his diary that Cousandier "is one of the most charming persons I have ever met, and one of the most beautiful, a truly lovely nature."[2]

Soon after his return to Canada (appropriately on the Italian liner *Conte de Savoie*), King began a long if intermittent correspondence with Cousandier, who was unhappy in her marriage. It was to continue until 1950 (an unfinished letter to her was on his death bed), but he was always careful in what he said to her, even to the point of misleading her. For example, in December 1934 in a speech to the National Liberal Federation, headed by Vincent Massey, King had made clear his commitment to the League of Nations. "It is not sufficient that we, as Liberals, should express by words and resolutions our support of the League of Nations. We must become militant in our advocacy of those policies which may serve to strengthen the League in its work ... is [there] any reason why in a matter of so great importance to the world, Canada should wait for any other nation to take the lead? ... This country should definitely declare ... that it will give to any nation which wantonly disrupts the world's peace neither arms nor foodstuff nor credits."[3] Yet King wrote to Cousandier on 13 April 1935 that he regretted that he had been unable to write earlier; he had been so overwhelmed by pre-election demands on his time. He did not refer to the fact that Mussolini had met in friendship with Hitler two months before or that Italy's intention to invade its fellow League of Nations member, Abyssinia, was becoming unmistakable. He also refrained from explaining to her the role of the League in the event of such Italian aggression.

In 1935 elections were held in Canada in October and in the United Kingdom in November. In the months before the Canadian election, King's various evasions, procrastinations, and insecurities became ever more pronounced. He knew that he had to win the 1935 election to retain the

William Lyon Mackenzie King in 1899, aged twenty-five. He was about to embark on a winter tour in Europe thanks to a travel grant from Harvard University. Source: LAC, C–014191

US president Theodore Roosevelt (at right), pictured aboard a warship of his "Great White Fleet" – the popular name for the American battle fleet that toured the globe between 1907 and 1909. Roosevelt deployed the fleet to put pressure on Tokyo to reduce or eliminate Japanese migration to the United States. Source: Theodore Roosevelt Collection, Houghton Library, Harvard College, Roosevelt Class No. 560.52 1909

Mackenzie King, with his beloved mother, Isabel, and his father, John. The picture was taken sometime between 1909 and 1911, when King was minister of labour in the government of Sir Wilfrid Laurier. Source: Toronto Star Archives

The Canadian participants at the October 1926 imperial conference in London. From left to right: Ernest Lapointe, minister of justice; Prime Minister Mackenzie King; Vincent Massey, the minister designate at the Canadian legation in Washington; and Peter Larkin, high commissioner to the United Kingdom and principal financial benefactor of King.
Source: LAC, 1964-087 NPC

A jovial Mackenzie King strolling with British prime minister Stanley Baldwin along a London street on their way to – or from – a British Empire memorial service at Westminster Abbey in October 1926, honouring the million Empire dead in the First World War. Source: LAC, C–013263

The Canadian delegation to the 1928 Assembly of the League of Nations in Geneva. From left to right: O.D. Skelton, undersecretary of state for external affairs; Philippe Roy, agent general for Canada in Paris; Raoul Dandurand, government leader in the Senate; Prime Minister Mackenzie King; Charles Dunning, minister of finance; and Walter Riddell, Canadian advisory officer at the League of Nations. Source: LAC, 1964–087 NPC

King with Winston Churchill at King's bucolic retreat at Kingsmere, Quebec, on 14 August 1929. Churchill and his son, Randolph, spent several days in Ottawa while on a transcontinental trip across Canada and the United States. Also in the photograph is King's adored Irish terrier, Pat, who he came to believe embodied the spirit of his late mother. Source: LAC, PA-126203

King shaking hands with Ramsay MacDonald, Britain's Labour leader and sometime prime minister, presumably in Ottawa. The photograph from the National Portrait Gallery in London is undated, but MacDonald, as prime minister, visited Washington and Ottawa in 1929.
Source: NPG London, x194134

R.B. Bennett, the Conservative prime minister of Canada from 1930 to 1935, was more consistently supportive of the League of Nations than Mackenzie King. He recognized the obligations of membership, although cognizant of the limited influence Canada could have at Geneva. Source: NPG London, x165031

Unveiling of Canada's National Memorial at Vimy Ridge in July 1936. King Edward VIII (second from left) prepares to inspect the veterans. Mackenzie King's Quebec lieutenant, Ernest Lapointe, is the unhappy-looking figure third from the left; Mackenzie King himself was too "fatigued" to attend. Philippe Roy, far right, was since late 1928 minister of legation in Paris. Source: LAC PA–183543

US president Franklin Roosevelt (third from left) on 31 July 1936 at the Citadel in Quebec City, with Lord Tweedsmuir, governor general of Canada (second from left), who as head of state was his host. King is in the light-coloured suit to the right. Source: LAC, 1987–054 NPC

A London studio portrait of Mackenzie King in November 1936. Source: NPG London, x83687

Adolf Hitler, who met Mackenzie King in Berlin in 1937. At the end of their meeting, Hitler gave King this silver-framed autographed picture of himself. In translation, Hitler's inscription reads: "His Excellency the Canadian Premier Dr W.L. Mackenzie King in friendly memory of his visit, 29 June 1937." In thanking Hitler for the memento "of the day for which I was born," King wrote that it "is a gift of which I am very proud, and of the friendship of which it is so generous an expression, I shall ever cherish. May I again thank you for it and for all that it will always mean to me." Source: LAC, C–011452

Two days before meeting Hitler, King (far left) attended the opening ceremony of the All-German Sports Competition in Berlin. The colossal stadium had been built for the Olympic Games in 1936, and King was gratified to be seated in the same chair from which Hitler had viewed the proceedings. Source: LAC, PA–119007

Mackenzie King (second from left), seated with German officials to watch the tennis competition at the All-German Sports Competition in Berlin. Source: LAC, PA–119010

King and the German foreign minister, Konstantin von Neurath (who was soon to be replaced by Joachim von Ribbentrop). This photograph from June 1937 in Berlin is apparently the only one showing King with a German cabinet minister. None is available of King with Hitler.
Source: LAC, C–016776

Mackenzie King with German officials and admiring crowds in Berlin. Source: LAC, PA–119013

Adrien Arcand of Montreal. As the fiery leader of the National Unity Party, which brought together the pro-Nazi movements in Quebec, Ontario, and Manitoba, he was the most prominent fascist in Canada. Source: Canadian Jewish Archives, Fonds no. P0005, file PC1–3–77

The foreign minister of Germany, Joachim von Ribbentrop, welcomed British prime minister Neville Chamberlain upon his arrival at Bad Godesberg on 22 September 1938 for his second meeting with Hitler. Sir Nevile Henderson, the British ambassador to Germany, stands beside Chamberlain with his hand raised. Source: Bundesarchiv, Image no. 183–H12702

Vincent Massey, the Canadian high commissioner in London (far right, front row), was, along with his Australian and South African colleagues, among those at Heston aerodrome on 29 September 1938 to wish Neville Chamberlain Godspeed as he left for Munich on the third and final flight in a futile attempt to appease Hitler over Czechoslovakia and avoid a world war. Source: *Illustrated London News*, 8 October 1938.

British prime minister Neville Chamberlain, arriving in Munich for the last of his meetings with the German dictator. King saw himself as having played a key role in bringing Chamberlain and Hitler together. "I have been used as an instrument to help towards that great end … unseen forces have unquestionably been working together in using me." Source: Bundesarchiv, Image no. 183–H12967

King and his minister of justice, Ernest Lapointe, in full Windsor uniform (which the prime minister regarded as de rigueur, even if the British themselves did not) on 17 May 1939, at the beginning of a highly successful royal tour of Canada. King George VI and Queen Elizabeth disembarked in Quebec City from the CPR liner *Empress of Australia*. Source: LAC, C–035115

From left to right, Hermann Göring, Benito Mussolini, Adolf Hitler, and Gian Galeazzo Ciano, Mussolini's son-in-law and Italy's foreign minister from 1936 to 1943. Source: LAC PA–114781

leadership of the Liberal Party; he could not survive two successive electoral defeats. The decade of the 1930s had begun badly with his defeat by the Conservative R.B. Bennett. But more fundamentally, the scourge of economic depression following the Wall Street crash of 1929 still lay heavily on Western democracies. At one end of the political spectrum, the communists were convinced that they possessed the eternal verities. At the other end, the fascists were no less certain that they embodied the truth. Each decried the other extreme and all liberal democracies in between. In Canada no one – certainly neither King nor Bennett – knew what to do about the depression. Only Franklin Roosevelt in the United States with his New Deal of 1933 – parts of which King in his laissez-faire convictions privately dismissed as crazy – appeared to be groping his way toward solutions or at least amelioration. As late as the 1935 election, King was still dismissing all talk of deficit financing and anything like an interventionist New Deal, decrying Bennett's sudden "so-called reform of the capitalist system [as] … a further step towards the establishment of a fascist regime in Canada."[4]

King found the remaining months before the October election a time of mounting uncertainty. Fortunately, at the same time, voices from the Great Beyond (spelled with capitals G and B) were increasingly present to bolster his courage and to comfort him amid his myriad fears and self-doubts. Whoever or whatever the medium, he was at least certain of the ultimate provenance of the bracing messages. Laurier (d. 1919) offered the practical political advice (which King had himself already been mulling over) to stop being a "recluse" if he hoped to win the election. Far more numerous than Laurier's messages were those of King's mother. In his dreams and visions, her guidance was always central to his political as well as to his personal life. At a celebratory séance on his sixtieth birthday on 17 December 1934, following his return from Europe, King received more "words of love" from Lord Grey of Fallodon (d. 1933), the British foreign secretary before and at the beginning of the First World War whom King had known in London; William Gladstone (d. 1898), the long-serving British Liberal prime minister who was to reappear frequently in séances; the later Liberal prime minister, Sir Henry Campbell-Bannerman (d. 1908); and Laurier and Peter Larkin (d. 1930). They and other Liberal voices were categorical that King was doing just fine. None offered any criticisms, new thoughts, or political strategies, only direct reassurances, a most satisfactory beginning to the new year for a deeply worried leader of the opposition.

King, in his search for reassurance, became an even more pronounced spiritualist. He recognized what he needed, even if later observers failed to see what was abundantly clear to him. "Were it not for the assurances I have from Beyond … my confidence in my capacity and power would fail me."[5] As he progressed with the close friendship and assistance of Joan Patteson, the wife of an Ottawa bank manager, and in time the guidance of various spiritualists in Detroit, New York, and London, it had become evident by 1934 that God had chosen him, the leader of the opposition, "to help work out His will 'on earth as it is in heaven.'"[6] The voices from the Other World were fortunately all liberal, settling any doubts that he was on the right track, including his secret ambitions to play a leading international role, despite being still in opposition. His spiritualist progress moved from table rapping to a need for a medium to act as interlocutor to full, language-free "cosmic consciousness" with those in the Great Beyond, who never failed to provide him with the reassurances that he constantly sought.

In direct communications with the Beyond, the new year, 1935, began exceptionally well for the profoundly lonely leader of the opposition. On New Year's Day, he received reassuring greetings from Leonardo da Vinci (d. 1519) and Lorenzo de Medici (d. 1492) who, he recorded, stated that he would, in no particular order, win the election in October 1935; make a great name for himself in history; be a peacemaker; make many people happy; and teach nations the ways of peace.[7] In the next fortnight, two more séances followed. At them the former Liberal prime minister of Britain H.H. Asquith (d. 1928) joined Laurier in informing a receptive King that he had been chosen "to draw England and Canada closer together." He again rejoiced in the paradox that "The grandson of the one whom the Tories said was 'disloyal' [was] seeking to save and secure the British Empire as the greatest agency of peace and good will."[8] This was a timely political message for King to receive. He had for some time been thinking of trimming his isolationist-like sails. He had spent the decade of the 1920s proclaiming to Quebec, the Progressive Party, and to anyone else who cared to listen that he stood against imperial centralists and was for either an autonomist foreign policy, or no foreign policy at all. At the same time, however, in looking over his shoulder at English-Canada, he wondered whether he had gone too far in presenting himself in Quebec as an anti-imperialist isolationist.

In his spiritualist meanderings King was in a sense talking to himself. That way lay his desperately needed reassurances. But when the contents of his diary became public after his death, they gave rise to the "Weird Willie" fascinations of later generations. To dismiss revelations of his pre-occupation with the Great Beyond as irrelevant to an understanding of the man is to overlook the insight that they provide into his complex character. Worse, such an approach ignores the truism that all democratically elected leaders should be held to account for their character, their honesty, and their effect on their nations.

In his domestic political balancing act, King was reassured by voices from Beyond counselling that, as leader of the opposition, he should stand clear of attempts – if there were any – to influence what the United Kingdom might do about collective security at the League of Nations and Italy's threatened invasion of Abyssinia. British prime ministers Ramsay MacDonald and Stanley Baldwin (who headed the new National but largely Conservative government from June 1935) were swayed by, among other considerations, France's preoccupation with securing Italy as an ally; repeated negative assessments of British naval strength in the Mediterranean, the imperial route to the east; estimates of the cost of sanctions to the British economy; and, above all, evidence that Germany and Italy were drawing closer together. As early as the summer of 1933, Prime Minister Ramsay MacDonald had told Walter Riddell, the Canadian advisory officer at the League, on "motoring back to Geneva ... from a luncheon [together]... that he and Sir John Simon [the foreign secretary] were leaving [Geneva] the next day for Rome to talk the situation over with Mussolini. He said he was disturbed at the possibility of Italy being drawn into an alliance with Germany. He hoped that it might be possible to arrive at a satisfactory understanding, but he seemed very much concerned."[9]

Even more fundamentally, there were those in public life in Britain and especially in France who saw no merit in white men killing each other so that a ramshackle state of black men could continue in quasi-independence. Churchill spoke for many when, in recognizing Abyssinia as a "sphere of influence" of Italy, he questioned how anyone could pretend that it was "a fit, worthy, and equal member of a league of civilised nations."[10] There was, moreover, no reason to believe that members of the League, including Canada and the other dominions, would in the name of collective security be quick to support Britain in an active sanctions policy, including even the closure of the Suez Canal to Italy. Petroleum sanctions might be especially problematic, given that the United States, then a major international source for oil, was not a member of the League. It was clear, at least to Baldwin, that oil sanctions "ought not to be undertaken unless we were assured that they would be effective ... until we know what America was going to do, we should hold our hand."[11] Riddell reported from Geneva on 16 January 1935 that Anthony Eden had told him that the "Abyssinian–Italian situation does not seem to have cleared up to any extent ... The Italians have so far refused to settle the question outside the League and now object strongly to having it brought before the [League] Council ... The attitude of Rome ... is rather uncompromising and there is a feeling that Rome thinks that both the French and the British should be out of North Africa."[12]

Why Mussolini coveted the arid, impoverished land of Abyssinia, which could only be a further charge on the already beleaguered Italian exchequer, is part of his visceral romanticism. Italian taxpayers would pay heavily for his fulfillment of the "lure of Africa," he being convinced that only an imperial power could be a great power, emulating the triumphs of ancient Rome and avenging the humiliating Italian defeat by Abyssinian warriors at Adowa in 1896. Italy had been a late entrant in the scramble for Africa (Libya, Eritrea, and Somaliland had been international last prizes), but even poverty-stricken Abyssinia was better in Mussolini's eyes than no fascist addition at all to the struggling Italian colonies. In Geneva the consensus was that Mussolini saw a war with Abyssinia as a means of extending Italy's empire, strengthening national life, and relieving unemployment, and that he expected little effective opposition from League members. A border clash between rag-tag Abyssinian warriors and Italian mechanized units on 5 December 1934 gave a clear indication of what was to come in ten months.

Both in opposition in Ottawa and during his visit to Rome in 1934, Mackenzie King had had ample time to ponder what an Italian invasion of a fellow member state would mean for the League of Nations and the collective security provisions of its Covenant, but there is no evidence in his diaries that he gave the matter much thought. Newton Rowell, on the other hand, joined Walter Riddell in understanding very well that an effective League of Nations was humanity's last best hope to avoid a second world war. He had earlier deplored the failure of the League to confront Japanese aggression in China – and Cahan's support for the aggressor. He now wrote to Lester Pearson, then secretary at Canada House in London but soon to be sent on temporary duty to the League in Geneva, that "If Italy goes to war there could be no more flagrant violation of the Covenant ... and unless the sanctions of the League are applied … collective security must be … a complete failure."[13]

The British government for its part recognized the unwelcome implications of an Italian invasion of Abyssinia. In a cabinet document of 13 May, the dilemma confronting it was clearly stated. "His Majesty's Government are likely to be faced with an exceedingly difficult decision. If they support against Italy a practical application of League principles, their action is bound greatly to compromise Anglo-Italian relations and perhaps even to break the close association at present existing between France, Italy, and the United Kingdom … it would be hard to imagine a state of affairs which would be more welcome to Germany."[14] At the same time, the British government issued a white paper on defence which, despite strident Labour opposition, forecast substantial increased spending. To complicate matters further, Germany introduced conscription, new levels of armaments, and the re-creation of an air force denied it by the Treaty of Versailles, but since this was basically a violation of the Treaty and not of the League Covenant, France, Britain, and Italy protested, but did nothing more. The foreign secretary, Sir Samuel Hoare, went to Berlin in early April for talks with Hitler, but on his return to Geneva he told Riddell that the "situation that they had found in Berlin was much more serious than they had thought. Rearmament had gone a great deal further than they had anticipated and the attitude of Hitler and the German people had created a most serious state of affairs … Hitler had merely talked at them, telling them what Germany wanted without giving them an opportunity to say what they thought would be acceptable or not."[15]

With Italy making no secret of its intention to seize Abyssinia, Prime Minister Bennett recognized that the ultimate challenge to the League was rapidly approaching. In June, when he was in London for the silver jubilee celebrations of the reign of King George V, Riddell came from Geneva for two meetings to discuss the threat of an Italian invasion of Abyssinia. Bennett approved Canada's representation – in the person of Riddell – on a League "Committee of Thirteen" to define "the economic and financial measures which might be applied, should in the future a State … endanger the peace by the unilateral repudiation of its international obligations."[16] The former Conservative prime minister, Arthur Meighen, now government leader in the Senate, defined well the Bennett government's decision to accept Canada's participation in the sanctions committee. "Only in the definite knowledge that every country is ready to live up to its whole responsibility for the enforcement of compliance with Covenants can the League ever attain its end ... when we sought to reduce, abbreviate and attenuate the meaning and force of the covenants, we applied the poison from which the League is suffering."[17] On 9 July, Riddell, back in Geneva from his meetings in London with Bennett, informed the sanctions committee that Canada "agreed that economic and financial measures should be applied and the withholding of key products and raw materials is an important method of applying them ... the list of such key products and raw materials ... should be comprehensive."

As Italy's threats to Abyssinia mounted, Bennett appointed Howard Ferguson, the high commissioner in London and former premier of Ontario, to become concurrently the chief delegate to the League (where with Bennett he had already represented Canada in 1933). Ferguson, a strong advocate of the League and collective security, was also an ardent Conservative and imperialist, hence in King's view a "skunk." On 26 July Bennett wired Ferguson clear instructions: "The Abyssinian situation has given us much concern. We realize dangerous repercussions on European situation of any conflict between Italy and other members of the League of Nations, but if Italy persists in threat to attack Abyssinia, we consider League cannot evade task of seeking to effect conciliation and of considering what further action may be taken under the Covenant if this fails."[18] Three days later, with this forward policy in mind, Ferguson attended his first meeting at the Foreign Office with Hoare and Eden and the other high commissioners to discuss the Abyssinian dispute. After several more such meetings in London, the venue shifted to Geneva where Ferguson, sometimes with Riddell and Pearson, met with Eden and the other dominion representatives from 9 September to 11 October, a total participation by Ferguson in League matters of two-and-one-half months before the Canadian election.

On 9 August, the British high commissioner in Ottawa reported by cypher telegram to London that Scott Macdonald of the Department of External Affairs had reflected the positive stance of the Bennett government when he said that "in the dispute between Italy and Ethiopia ... there was only one solution, namely to apply sanctions under the Covenant of the League in order to prevent war. This [Canadian] attitude would not be dependent on the United Kingdom's attitude."[19] On 23 August the high commissioner added that "(1) The Prime Minister [Bennett] is inclined to favour personally a policy of sanctions under the Covenant ... (2) Any decision is made more than usually difficult for the Government by the fact that Parliament had dissolved and that a general election is pending ... (4) Mackenzie King and Liberal leaders, while they would probably be loath to refuse support for sanctions by the League, have to consider Quebec."[20]

The next day Lapointe sought from King a statement that a Liberal government "would not send ... men to Abyssinia." King did not agree. "I told him that was all right so long as we were not obligated thereto under our adherence to the League of Nations. We must continue to support the League."[21] During the election campaign, Lapointe, "speaking for himself," stated that he was "unalterably opposed" to Canadian participation in any League military sanctions against Italy,[22] but King continued in his caution not to rule them out. Yet on 23 August, the day following the leader of the opposition's admonition to his Quebec lieutenant, the isolationist undersecretary of state for external affairs, Skelton, who in Pearson's words was "very much opposed to sanctions,"[23] wrote the Canadian minister in Washington (Bennett's brother-in-law), "Our own [economic] troubles have been sufficient to prevent Ethiopia being regarded as anything [other] than as a diversion – a new colour film in which Signor Mussolini struts his usual magnificent role ... The Prime Minister [Bennett] is definitely opposed to undertaking military sanctions, but leans to the imposition of economic sanctions ... if definite aggressive action is taken by Italy." Despite being a senior public servant supposedly committed to implementing his minister's policies, Skelton stated flatly that "My personal prejudices are against taking any action."[24] He was even more dismissive of the League in a letter to Newton Rowell a fortnight before the election – in which he anticipated a Liberal victory. His own narrow conviction was that "if the League was to survive and to advance the cause of peace, it must be [only] through its functions of publicity" and abandon the whole idea of collective security.[25] Skelton seems to have had difficulty differentiating between his opposition to collective security and his minister's support for it, a curiously ambiguous stance for a deputy minister to assume.

As if Italy's aggressive designs on its fellow League member were not enough, Germany and Britain further confused the international picture by entering into a naval limitations agreement on 15 June. It carried with it the optimistic implication that one could do business with Hitler, but worse, it led France to fear being jilted and Italy to anticipate a free hand. And it gave an ever-hopeful Mackenzie King a false sense that Germany was genuinely committed to disarmament (all "humbug" in Churchill's view). Leopold Amery, the prominent Conservative MP and a frequent correspondent with King, shared his optimistic view of Hitler. On returning from Berchtesgaden on 13 August, he noted, "I did not find the hypnotic charm [in Hitler] I had heard of … but liked his directness and eagerness to let his hearer know all his mind. Intellectually he has a grasp on economic essentials and on many political ones, too, even if it is crude at times and coloured by deep personal prejudice. A bigger man, on the whole, than I had expected … we got on well together … owing to the fundamental similarity of many of our ideas." (Amery's mother was Jewish, but curiously he made no reference to Hitler's flagrant anti-Semitism.)[26]

In June 1935, Mosley's British Union of Fascists (BUF), against the background of the British election and the Anglo-German naval agreement, reached a peak in popular support or at least curiosity, but descended thereafter. A BUF rally at the Olympia stadium in London attracted an estimated 15,000, a testimony to the desperation of many British to identify a way, however radical, to prevent a recurrence of the economic depression. But the brutality of Mosley's blackshirts toward hecklers at the rally – communist or otherwise – and in street fights alienated many who concluded that he was in fact a fanatical acolyte of Hitler, committed to ending all free political debate by the establishing a fascist dictatorship. Baldwin was convinced that the BUF would come to nothing, but in 1936 his government nevertheless passed a more restrictive Public Order Act. Thereafter the BUF gradually came to nothing, although in the autumn of 1938 some of Mosley's followers gathered in their black shirts at Piccadilly Circus to salute the *Anschluss*, the German seizure of Austria.

At the same time, King could have been in no doubt about the ascendancy of Hitler if he saw photographs or read accounts of the initial Nazi party rally in August 1935 at the huge parade ground and the projected massive congress hall in southeast Nuremberg. From as early as 1923, the followers of Hitler and the fanatically anti-Semitic Julius Streicher had held annual "German Days" there. Hitler and Goebbels denounced the threat of Jewish-controlled Soviet communism. The adulation of the dictator himself by hundreds of thousands of regimented supporters – at a later rally exceeding 1.6 million – clearly demonstrated the popular support for the course on which the Nazis had successfully set Germany. On 15 September 1935 the

Reichstag unanimously approved the notorious Nuremberg laws that, among other things, deprived Jews of German citizenship and banned marriage and sexual relations between Jews and non-Jews. But as far as King was concerned, those were internal German matters best left to Germany – or at least to the United Kingdom and France.

Of all these international developments, King, as leader of the opposition, took little notice in his journal. During the 1935 election campaign he disregarded Italy's slow but relentless moves against Abyssinia. In London, Ontario, on 15 August he repeated his familiar promise that no decision would be made by a Liberal government about Italian aggression in Abyssinia "until the voice of Parliament is heard." Three weeks later, he moved toward a commitment to Quebec not to participate in any war arising from League sanctions, but in such ambiguous terms (and in a geographic misstatement) that even ardent supporters of the League in English Canada might not be alienated. Sharing a platform with Lapointe in Quebec City on 9 September, King said (in English), "the people of Canada would be strongly opposed to war connected with economic interests in the Near East." In so saying, he was playing to the conviction in much of French Canada that the Abyssinian conflict was basically over imperial hegemony and economic exploitation in Africa. Lapointe followed with a much clearer commitment (in French): "No interest in Ethiopia … is worth the life of a single Canadian citizen. No consideration could justify Canada's participation, and I am unalterably opposed to it."[27] On the campaign trail, King followed Lapointe's statement with a more carefully worded and delicately balanced campaign promise. "You can trust the Liberal Party to see to it that … not a single life is unnecessarily sacrificed in regard to any matter beyond what affects the safeguarding and rights of our own country."[28]

In the same month that King and Lapointe opposed any prospect of the League calling on Canada to provide troops to fight Italy, Bennett deplored the thought of "poor old England" being forced "to lead the world." Britain had won the Great War, but at such a cost that London, especially in the midst of an unprecedented economic depression, was incapable of meeting the financial demands of maintaining order in an empire wider still and wider with the addition of former German colonies mandated to it by the League of Nations. The chiefs of staff were hard put to find the armed forces necessary in India and the Middle East, and the challenge of fighting a three-front war – against the Germans on the continent, the Italians in the

Mediterranean and North Africa, and the Japanese across Asia – was simply out of the question. All of this and more Bennett would have heard in London, leaving him convinced that only a collective response by the members of the League of Nations could save the British Empire from an unthinkable three-front war.

> We perhaps expect too much of poor old England. Four times she has saved the world … and now, with her army reduced to a skeleton, with her navy so weakened as not to be able to protect her trade routes, and a wholly insufficient air force, it is suggested that she might "lead the world." But where? Into war? Her moral leadership is still the hope of mankind. I am satisfied she will do everything that can be done, but I do not believe that alone she can enforce peace upon Italy …
>
> The purpose of the Covenant was to secure an organization every member of which would be pledged to take specified action under indicated circumstances. The fact that so many members of the League decline to live up to that obligation has placed countries like England in a false position. Certainly where the Covenant contemplates united action by all the members, it would be idle to expect two of the number [Britain and Canada] to discharge an obligation that rested upon all.[29]

With the Conservative cabinet caught up in the final month of a most unpromising electoral campaign, Herridge, the minister in Washington, sounding a little like Churchill and Birkenhead to Lloyd George in 1922, advised his brother-in-law Bennett to distract the electorate's attention from the economic depression at home by making a political issue of an international conflict. If Bennett could identify "some dynamic force, powerful [enough] … to pierce this dead wall of hostility, it is conceivable that you may still get through."[30] With Billy King's cautious mantra of parliament-will-decide in mind, Herridge urged Bennett to go flat out and declare that the League economic sanctions against Italy would mean war. Such a statement "would subordinate every other issue now before the electorate to this paramount issue," winning the support of sober and decent French and English Canadians alike.

Bennett rejected his brother-in-law's suggestion, choosing instead to stand by the League. He would not come out against collective security, including economic sanctions. On 4 September, more than a month before the Canadian election, the British high commissioner in Ottawa reported that the Bennett government "shares the desire of the United Kingdom Government to maintain obligations and proceedings of the League of Nations and will be prepared ... to discuss ... the question of the application of economic sanctions."[31] Bennett's concern with economic sanctions was simply "that so many member states decline to live up to that obligation." In any case, there was no point in thinking that if collective security of the League failed, Britain was capable of saving the world. Despite the evident opposition in Quebec to any Canadian involvement whatever and despite reservations about sanctions in the absence at the League of certain powerful nations (primarily the United States), Canada was ready to discuss sanctions against Italy and would strive to prevent the loss of League authority as a result of members failing to carry out their Covenant obligations.

Bennett asked Ferguson to state the Canadian position at the League in Geneva. In addition to Riddell, he was assisted by Lester Pearson from his small London staff. Pearson wrote a sympathetic account of Ferguson at the League. He was "a kind and unpretentious chief. He spoke his views frankly and clearly, without verbal camouflage, but his friendly personality usually made it possible for him to express disagreement without giving offence."[32] Unlike Skelton in Ottawa, who urged upon Bennett a do-nothing policy at the League, Ferguson was clear that collective security, that is, League protection of its members, had to be sustained, even if the League had failed to do so previously in the case of Japanese aggression in Manchuria, that early League failure which had not been lost on Mussolini. "Foxie Fergy" readily agreed with his old friend Bennett that the positive lead of Britain and France at the League should be actively supported. If economic sanctions were promptly and comprehensively applied, Mussolini would surely desist in his madcap idea of invading Abyssinia.

Bennett confirmed to Ferguson on 13 September that he was free to state that Canada "believes that the League of Nations is an indispensable agency for world peace ... Canada will join with the other Members of the League in considering how by unanimous action peace can be maintained."[33] Riddell, however, retained a caveat about the commitment of France, dating from his luncheon conversation two years before with Ramsay MacDonald, then British prime minister. During the weeks remaining before the Canadian election, the long-heralded Italian invasion of Abyssinia became imminent. In London it was generally believed that the United Kingdom and France still stood for the collective security and League economic sanctions. There were frequent popular protests against Italy, and therefore the government's re-election platform had endorsed the League and all sanctions short of war.

In Ottawa, Mackenzie King from the opposition front bench was fulsome in his praise for both the League and Britain's positive policy toward it (a view which Churchill also shared, although at the same time calling for rearmament, especially for the Royal Air Force). King was "truly glad the League of Nations is standing for collective security ... Britain has never been finer in her whole action for mankind than within this past year and the effort she has made to preserve the peace of Europe ... it is Canada's duty to stand four-square behind the League of Nations."[34] The supportive statements of both Bennett and King must have been welcome to the Foreign Office which advised that "it would be highly desirable that co-operation between the Dominions [all fellow members of the League] and His Majesty's Government should be arranged so far as possible; it may indeed be that some of the steps ... are such that [His Majesty's Government] could not take them without being assured of the co-operation ... of most of the Dominions."[35]

With Italy's invasion of Abyssinia imminent, the new government of Baldwin privately continued to explore with France and Italy whether a compromise might yet be crafted that would be acceptable to both Abyssinia and Italy. On 5 September the Foreign Office sent Ottawa an account by Eden of how, on passing through Paris on his way to Geneva, he had found Pierre Laval, the French foreign minister, "anxious to maintain his friendship with Italy without breaking the Anglo-French front; the dilemma which he wished to avoid was the choice between Italy and Britain. I replied that I did not think that this was at all the position. If Italy deliberately violated the Covenant, the choice lay between the survival of the League and acquiescence in Italy's breach of the Covenant. But M. Laval would not have this definition."[36] To this fundamental insight into what was happening behind the scenes, Ottawa made no reply other than to thank London briefly for its "elucidation" of the French position.

Within days, Laval met again in Geneva with Eden and this time also with the foreign secretary, Sir Samuel Hoare. "We at once agreed to avoid military sanctions, to adopt no measures of naval blockade, never to consider the closing of the Suez Canal, in a word to reject anything that might lead to war ... We set aside all military sanctions and those which could lead to

[war]." King George V expressed his horror of another European war. "I will not have another war. I will not … if there is another one … I will go to Trafalgar Square and wave a red flag myself, sooner than allow the country to be brought in." He added to Hoare, "If I am to go on, you must keep us out of one."[37] Leopold Amery spoke for many Conservative MPS when he opposed military sanctions against Italy so as not to jeopardize a possible united front of Italy, Britain, and France against German rearmament. He put the question starkly: "There is only one way in which we can stop the war in Abyssinia. That is by declaring war on Italy ourselves or by taking such measures, as for instance blockade or seizure of ships, as will force Italy in desperation to make war on us. Is that what we want? For myself … I can say that I am not prepared to send a single Birmingham lad to his death for the sake of Abyssinia."[38] In short, a conflict in distant Africa could not be allowed to undermine the Anglo-French efforts to appease Mussolini. Ironically, in light of his later policy of attempting to appease the dictators, it was Neville Chamberlain, the chancellor of the exchequer, who spoke against this approach. He warned his cabinet colleagues that "if the League were demonstrated to be incapable of effective intervention to stop this war it would be practically impossible to maintain the fiction that its existence was justified at all."[39]

At the end of July, Riddell reported to Bennett that a senior member of the League secretariat had arrived back in Geneva from Rome convinced that "Mussolini is determined to make war on Ethiopia, believing that such a war would not only extend the territorial possessions of Italy but strengthen the national morale. Mussolini, he thinks, has counted the costs and considers that the Members of the League will offer little effective opposition … it is useless to think that Mussolini wishes any settlement or piecemeal territorial arrangements which might be brought about by the Great Powers. He desires war and therefore nothing short of applying Article 16 [sanctions] will carry any weight with him."[40] Laval, according to Riddell, preferred to delay any League consideration of the Abyssinian problem for at least a month in the hope that Italy might move decisively in his favour in the meantime.

Notwithstanding the private Anglo-French exchanges "setting aside all military sanctions," on 11 September Hoare pledged in a widely quoted statement at the League Assembly the British government's "unwavering fidelity to the League and all it stands for … And the case before us [the Italian invasion of Abyssinia] is no exception … my country stands … for steady and collective resistance to all acts of unprovoked aggression. The United Kingdom intends to fulfill the obligations which the Covenant lays upon them ... my country stands ... for the collective maintenance of the Covenant in its entirety." He did add, however, with his eye on the wavering France, the qualification that "if the risks for peace are to be run, they must be run by all."[41] Two days later, Laval, in his speech to the Assembly, was at once more succinct and more ambiguous than Hoare. "Our obligations are written in the Covenant. France will not fail to discharge them."[42] Following Hoare and Laval, Ferguson, having already stated that "the League is no longer to be scoffed at, but that it means business," declared that Canada would join with other members in considering how peace could be maintained by unanimous action.[43] Riddell added at a meeting of representatives from the British Commonwealth on 26 September that "the refusal of certain raw materials [to Italy] would prove to be quite an effective weapon."[44]

All who saw collective security as the most promising route to permanent peace and economic recovery were euphoric at Hoare's pledge. The United Kingdom had clearly put itself on the side of international justice. Given the memories of the horrors of the First World War of less than twenty years before, the deeply felt public support in Britain for collective security, the League of Nations, and disarmament was hardly surprising. Here, finally, in Hoare's speech was an unambiguous commitment, as had been advocated by Eden among others. The statements of Hoare and Laval to the Assembly suddenly, if only fleetingly, revived the League. Neville Chamberlain, however, remained skeptical of the reality of the French commitment: "when it actually came to a decision Laval must come down on our side, though he would wiggle and jib up to the last moment. But the French have been as disloyal as they could. Their [news]papers ... have been steadily representing in Rome that they were all the time holding back a ferocious Britain, determined to destroy Fascism and humiliate the dictator."[45] In talking with Chamberlain at the time, Amery came away with the conviction that "his whole view, like Sam's [Hoare], was that we were bound to try out the League of Nations (in which he does not himself believe very much) for political reasons at home and that there was no question of our going beyond the mildest of economic sanctions such as an embargo on the purchase of Italian goods or of munitions to Italy. When I pointed out that ... [not stopping] Mussolini meant open failure [of the League] in the eyes of the world, he tried to ride off with the hope that Mussolini might find measures embarrassing and was getting into hopeless financial difficulties any way. If things got too serious the French would run out first!"[46] When the League Council considered the formal designation of Italy as the aggressor in Abyssinia, the Italian representative declared with a straight face that on the contrary it was Abyssinia that "had been long contemplating aggressive designs on Italy." The Abyssinian representative denied this, since his "was a weak and poor country" without any aggressive capacity. It was Rome that sought "to impose the domination of white races upon black races."[47] Churchill, in the House of Commons although not in the government, called on his colleagues to put their trust in a dual policy: the League of Nations and simultaneous rearmament. In proposing sanctions against Italian aggression in Abyssinia, the League had proved that it was "alive and in action … It was fighting for its life … [He] ended by urging the British Government to use the machinery of the Covenant … in order to challenge aggression … The League of Nations has passed from shadow into substance, from theory into practice, from rhetoric into reality … [and is] now being clothed with life and power, and endowed with coherent thought and concerted action."[48]

During those same weeks, Mackenzie King, although still leader of the opposition, was convinced that he had a special international affairs mission from God that was reassuringly confirmed at a séance on 6 October 1935, three days after Italian forces had invaded Abyssinia and a week before the Canadian election. From the Great Beyond, Canada's second prime minister, Alexander Mackenzie (d. 1892), informed King that he was gratified that soon another Mackenzie would be prime minister. Asquith and Lord Grey of Fallodon reappeared with confirmation that "Long ago God meant that you should shew [the anachronistic spelling of "show"] men and nations the way to peace." Two new interlocutors, who certainly should know, St Luke and St John, agreed word for word with Lord Grey: after sending their love to Mrs Patteson, they affirmed to King that "God had chosen you to shew men and nations how they should live."[49]

Asquith again spoke from Beyond reassuring King that he would "succeed in making peace among the nations of the world."[50] Lord Grey of Fallodon reappeared a third time to state that King would be a peacemaker, whereas he himself had regrettably failed during the years leading up to the First World War. But to King's especial gratification, it was his own mother who was definitive in her reassurances: "Long ago, I knew God had chosen you to be his instrument to make peace among Men and Nations."[51] With sudden insight, King deplored to his diary – but only to his diary – the Italian invasion of Abyssinia. "How sad and tragic is the whole business of Italy's position. The dictator Mussolini bringing his people into war, destroying his nation. They will turn on him and destroy him eventually. I am truly glad that the League of Nations is standing for collective security and police action."[52]

The Liberals, as Lorenzo il Magnifico and Wilfrid Laurier had both forecast, won the 14 October 1935 election with 171 seats to the Conservatives' forty. In Quebec the Liberals rebounded from forty to fifty-five seats (of the sixty-five total). This was all highly satisfactory to the now reassured Mackenzie King. He had played to Quebec and Quebec had responded. When news of the Liberal election victory reached Geneva, Ferguson, accompanied by Pearson, returned immediately to London to resign as high commissioner. A somewhat perplexed Walter Riddell was left in Geneva holding the bag until the incoming Liberal government should decide whether it would reaffirm King's support of the League when he was leader of the opposition or whether it would in effect do nothing, as Skelton, who remained undersecretary of state for external affairs, was prompt to urge. In defeat, Bennett told the British High Commission on 19 October that "despite the existence of other views in certain circles and possible French Canadian opposition, he felt that [a] wave of sentiment would carry Canada to the support of the United Kingdom" and that "personally he was strongly in favour of a policy of sanctions ... but that Skelton ... [who] felt that it would be unwise to go beyond an expression of moral condemnation, had met him with strong opposition."[53]

Skelton had anticipated the Liberal election victory – not much of a political insight in the circumstances – by having ready for Riddell on 15 October a do-nothing-until-you-hear-from-me telegram. "In view of results of general election of yesterday and of fact that new Government cannot take over for some days, it will not be possible for you to take position on any further proposals in the meantime."[54] The propriety of Skelton sending Riddell such an unhelpful message before King's government actually took office on 24 October is a debatable point now academic, but Riddell, pending instructions from the new government on "any further proposals" quite correctly replied the same day that "Unless advised to the contrary, I shall continue to express ... Canadian policy regarding sanctions as defined in your communication concerning Committee of Thirteen."[55] Among his other responsibilities, including at the ILO for the drafting of an international convention limiting hours of work and another on child labour, Riddell continued to lend support at the League to past proposals for economic sanctions against Italy. The subsequent muddles in both Ottawa and Geneva over League sanctions and who said what to whom and when and with what authority has ever since provided material for learned papers and partisan posturing. But what matters is that the League Council's condemnation of Italy as an aggressor opened the way for a committee to propose and to monitor the application of economic sanctions.

Despite having made a public, pre-election commitment to the League – or perhaps because he had made one – King back in office continued to eschew discussions of foreign affairs in parliament. He was convinced that no good could come from such debates, given the isolationism in Quebec and the contrasting pro-League sentiment in much of English-speaking Canada. Yet he was still privately supportive of the League of Nations. On 17 October he confided to his diary that he had rejected Lapointe's ambition to be appointed secretary of state for external affairs in the new government rather than continuing as minister of justice. King knew that whatever equilibrium he had been able to achieve in his dual foreign policy would be disturbed by such an appointment. "I said to Lapointe that I had better take on External Affairs myself ... because of the [Abyssinian] war situation ... English-speaking Canada would not welcome his having control of External Affairs while war is on, also, he himself has not stood up for the League of Nations as I think he should have."[56]

9

King and Abyssinia: The Domestic Scene

On resuming office as prime minister, Mackenzie King turned with relief to the one thing on which all Liberals and indeed all three political parties could agree: the completion of Bennett's trade negotiations with the United States. He had long believed that he had been ordained to bring the two major English-speaking nations closer together with Canada in a sort of latter-day transatlantic balance of power. He thought that trade liberalization, first bilateral then trilateral, would help all three nations recover from the ravages of the depression. On that initiative Skelton agreed with his minister, but he also saw an opportunity, contrary to the express wishes of his minister, to shift Canada into the United States' political and economic orbit and away from the British Commonwealth.

Well before the election, King had decided that whatever were his deep-seated, post-Theodore Roosevelt misgivings about the United States and his conviction that the secret aim of every president was "to possess the country," his foreign policy priority must be to conclude immediately Bennett's trade negotiations with Washington. The 1932 Ottawa Imperial Economic Conference had not delivered what Bennett had hoped. The mean-spirited tariff haggling, Beaverbrook said, was worthy of none too friendly foreign powers, and Chamberlain, the chancellor of the exchequer, found the Canadian prime minister devious and unreliable (and presumably disliked Canadian agents tapping British delegation telephones). With Canada still mired in economic depression and only minor progress made at the Ottawa conference, Bennett had turned to the negotiation of a bilateral trade agreement with the United States. Before the difficult negotiation was completed, however, the 1935 election loomed (with reason to believe that Washington stalled the negotiations until its outcome was known, convinced that more was to be gained from a Liberal than a Conservative government).

On the first day back in office, King pledged to complete a bilateral trade agreement before the end of the year. He picked up the negotiations where Bennett had had to leave off, although of course he never acknowledged that he was thereby the beneficiary of a substantial Conservative legacy. According to the minister of the United States legation in Ottawa, King had taken the most unusual step of calling on him on his first day back in office (protocol required the very opposite). Sounding like Skelton, King had described to him how, faced with a choice of two roads, British Commonwealth or American (he evidently could conceive of no third road), he would choose "the American road," apparently assuming that is what an American would want to hear. For this reason, he explained, friends called him "the American" (although there is no independent record of King being called "the American" by friends).[1] Further, he realized that the Franklin Roosevelt of the New Deal was widely admired in Canada, making him more popular than he was himself, perhaps one reason why he was so deferential to Roosevelt.

On 5 November King went to Washington with Bennett's expert trade negotiating team intact.[*] In diary entries about his dinner at the White House on 8 November, King makes no reference to the current and worrisome actions of Germany and Italy. And Roosevelt seems not to have raised pro-Nazi manifestations in the United State itself: the rants of Henry Ford; the scare-mongering of Charles Lindbergh; the admiration of Joseph Kennedy for the anti-communist German chancellor; and other displays of support, large and small, that were to be found across the forty-eight states. Although Roosevelt's appointee as ambassador to Germany, William Dodd, wrote repeatedly to him about the abundant evils of the Nazi regime, its extensive military preparations, and its fixed purpose of a general war, all as forecast in Hitler's *Mein Kampf*, King records no conversation with Roosevelt about the two dictators. He was to have discussed "the international situation … [and] Ethiopia was on the agenda of the meetings, but no record of the talks appears to exist … in either the National Archives or the Roosevelt Library at Hyde Park."[2] Perhaps the president saw no need to raise the turmoil in

---

[*]During his brief sojourn in Washington, King was gratified to receive a message of encouragement from General Ulysses S. Grant (d. 1885), the former president, during a "sitting" with Grant's granddaughter, Julia Grant, a friend of many years. After her marriage to a Russian nobleman in exile, she appears occasionally in King's diaries as the Princess Cantacuzene, but King continued to make no references to Theodore Roosevelt, extraterrestrial or otherwise.

Europe, convinced, as he once told Churchill that King would always do what he was told to do.

By 19 October, five days after the Canadian election, the League's committee recommended five classes of sanctions against Italy: (1) an embargo on the export of arms; (2) cancellation of financial transactions; (3) prohibition of imports; (4) embargo on certain exports, including aluminum, tin, and iron ore; and (5) mutual support of those member states whose exports had been adversely affected by the application of sanctions. In the absence of specific reference to derivatives, however, Riddell recognized that Canada and other exporters of raw materials would be called on to control their exports to Italy while other countries, such as neighbouring France, could continue to supply Italy with the same materials in more manufactured forms.

Newton Rowell wrote to Skelton on 12 October that "Canada is of age, and she is responsible for her obligations and for the discharge of them … I am old-fashioned enough to believe that an obligation is an obligation … I do not see how international relations can be carried on and world peace and stability secured unless these obligations are recognized as binding on the parties which solemnly enter into them."[3] From Geneva, Riddell optimistically reported to Rowell on 22 October, "the measure of unanimity has been striking, and seems to augur well for the successful application of sanctions."[4] The British government was less optimistic. Baldwin was certain that Laval had been bought off by Mussolini, "a fact reported by the Secretary of State [Hoare] that money had actually changed hands."[5] In any event, as Riddell later recounted, "Mussolini knew long before this that he could depend absolutely on Laval."[6] Chamberlain wrote to his sister on 22 September, "We shall have to be very firm with France to prevent Laval's agreeing" to Italy's demands.[7]

In Ottawa on 19 October, King told Lapointe and James Gardiner, his minister of agriculture from Saskatchewan, of his concern that the cabinet would split over any Italo-Abyssinian conflict. "Lapointe immediately said that there would be no going into war by Canada," to which King responded, "that was well enough to say, but we had in this room itself a divided view on the point."[8] In its continuing efforts both in London and Geneva to keep the dominions informed of developments, the British government on 24 October described to them its several orders-in-council to implement the economic sanctions decided upon by the League. King, having told his diary on 2 october that it was Canada's duty to stand four-square behind the

League of Nations, put to his cabinet on 25 October the question of the League's sanctions. Although the majority was supportive, a split between French- and English-speaking ministers became clear. "Ilsley could scarcely wait to say how emphatic he thought we should be in declaring for sanctions. Rogers, and some of the others, were also quite strong on backing the League, Lapointe, Power and Cardin were all in the other direction."[9] King concluded that Ilsley and Lapointe were ready to resign. The next day, with the drafting of a basic statement on the new government's stance at the League, Lapointe threatened "that he would resign at once" if the government supported military sanctions and presumably even those economic sanctions (i.e., oil) that could be seen as leading to military sanctions.[10] Lapointe's threat was in fact unnecessary. Unknown to him, to King, and to the other ministers, the foreign ministers of France and Britain – the only two member states capable of making a reality of sanctions – had agreed six weeks before that in no circumstances would they apply military sanctions in the Italo-Abyssinian "dispute."

On 29 October, a fortnight after the election, King approved a bald public statement (copied by telegram to Geneva), setting forth his new government's position on the issues raised at Geneva by the Italian aggression. He remained categorical in his support for the League. It was "the overwhelming conviction of the people of Canada in declaring its continued and firm adherence to the fundamental aims and ideals of the League of Nations, and its intention to make participation in the League the cornerstone of its foreign policy ... In the present instance ... there is no room for doubt as to where the responsibility rests for the outbreak of war ... [Canada is] prepared to co-operate fully in the application of the economic sanctions against Italy ... The Canadian Government at the same time desires to make it clear that it does not recognize any commitment binding Canada to adopt military sanctions, and that no such commitment could be made without the prior approval of the Canadian Parliament."[11] The pledge regarding military sanctions was designed to meet Lapointe's threat of resignation, but King included it only reluctantly. A few months before he had refused to exclude military sanctions: Lapointe, in now demanding such an exclusion, "was going, perhaps, a little more in the way of caution and reserve than the majority of the cabinet would have liked, but which Lapointe regarded as most important."[12] From his press statement of 29 October, King never subsequently departed. He was still basing himself publicly upon it eight months later. And Riddell in Geneva understandably continued to interpret King's statement of 29 october as the fundamental policy of the new government.

Hitherto Italy had appeared confident about its ability to evade or otherwise withstand economic sanctions, but Mussolini defined a petroleum embargo as "an act of war." A British document stated clearly on 27 November that "Oil is an essential need, and it is obvious that a complete embargo of petroleum supplies to Italy would cripple the Italian Government."[13] Hitler's valued interpreter, Paul Schmidt, was only one of several who later attested to Mussolini's fear of oil sanctions. Mussolini told Hitler that "If the League of Nations had followed Eden's advice in the Abyssinian dispute and had extended economic sanctions to oil, I would have had to withdraw from Abyssinia within a week. That would have been an incalculable disaster for me." Schmidt, sounding like Riddell, added, "How different history might have been had the League been able to successfully bring Mussolini to heel."[14]

On 2 November, after sending in vain several cypher telegrams to Ottawa seeking any new instructions beyond the public policy set out in King's statement of 29 October, Riddell suggested to the subcommittee that to make economic sanctions effective, petroleum, coal, iron, and steel and their derivatives should be added to the list of embargoed exports. On 4 November the subcommittee referred the proposal to the Committee of Eighteen. Later the same day King sent a telegram in effect reprimanding Riddell for taking action on "any question of importance ... without definite and positive instructions."[15] In response, Riddell wired that he had received "no instructions regarding attitude of Government ... my only guide to attitude and policy of the Government has been the [prime minister's] statement given to the press and summarized in your unnumbered telegram of October 29."[16]

The Committee of Eighteen adopted the subcommittee's recommendation to extend economic sanctions on 6 November. What little hesitation there had been among some members to recommend an oil sanction arose partly from continuing concerns about whether the United States, a non-member of the League, would do whatever it could to discourage its petroleum exporters from selling to Italy. Their misgivings were not misplaced. In the Spanish Civil War of the following year, Franco's fascist forces were receiving an estimated two-thirds of their petroleum needs from US sources. With regard to Abyssinia, however, Cordell Hull, the secretary of state, had told the British government as early as 8 October that the president intended to issue an early "embargo declaration" and a warning that American nationals who traded with Italy would do so at their own risk. When the US observer in Geneva also pledged that the United States would "co-operate," Chamberlain duly recorded in his diary on 29 November that the "U.S.A. has already gone a good deal further than usual. The President's discretionary powers do not cover oil, but he and Cordell Hull made it very clear that in their opinion oil should not be supplied to Italy." Chamberlain concluded that "this was really a critical point in the League's history. If we weakened now because of Mussolini's threats we should leave the Americans in the air and they would be unable to resist the argument of their oil producers ... It was inevitable that in such circumstances U.S.A. should decline in future to help us in any way, sanctions would crumble, the League would lose its coherence and our whole policy would be destroyed."[17]

Throughout that autumn of 1935, the frequent meetings of the British Commonwealth representatives in Geneva as well as the waves of messages between London and its missions in Washington and Geneva were informed by seemingly endless speculation about what Washington would actually do if an oil sanction were implemented by League members and whether continuing US shipments to Italy would undermine their collective actions. Mussolini knew from Laval that France and Britain together were seeking to avoid a European war over Abyssinia, so he naturally threatened war if sanctions were extended to include petroleum.

With the addition of an oil sanction now in early prospect, Italy embarked on a major diplomatic campaign intended to counter any petroleum sanction, a campaign supported, Riddell reported, by a special fund of one million pounds sterling. Italian posts and clubs abroad were instructed to promote local opposition by every means possible. The Italian consul general in Ottawa, Luigi Petrucci, was prompt to do so. He stated in a speech in Montreal on 1 March 1936, "after criticising very severely the League of Nations ... which has condemned the action of Italy ... I cannot refrain from expressing my sorrow that Canada is applying sanctions against Italy."[18] With that, R.B. Bennett had had enough of Petrucci. The next day he described to the House how, when still prime minister, he had received a delegation of Canadians of Italian descent from Montreal. "They claimed that with his [Petrucci's] connivance there was being built up a secret fascist organisation called 'The National Organisation for the Repression of Anti-Fascism.' They charged that officials of this organisation were paid by the

Italian Government notwithstanding that they were British subjects by naturalization. They charged that the Consul threatened bodily harm to Canadian citizens but also to relatives of Canadian citizens who were still in Italy." Bennett had turned the delegation's plea over to Skelton, but he had learned that the undersecretary had done nothing before the election. Prime Minister Mackenzie King rather flaccidly replied in the House that "if an incident of the kind should come up again the Government would certainly have no option but to make immediate representations to the government of the country concerned."[19] Undeterred by King's restrained wigging, Petrucci continued his activities, reporting to Mussolini that his soundings had led him to the not very surprising conclusion that "the non-Roman Catholic" (i.e., Protestant) ministers in the government of Canada were particularly anti-Italian, implying that the Roman Catholic ministers, almost entirely from Quebec, were uniformly pro-Italian.[20] The Italian vice consuls in Toronto and Montreal, both fascist adherents appointed earlier by Mussolini to organize the Italian immigrant communities under the direction of the Fasci all Estro in Rome, joined in a campaign to raise support, money, and even gold wedding rings from overseas communities to help pay for the invasion of Abyssinia.* In a diplomatic note of 11 November, Petrucci protested to Lapointe about the "injustice" of the League's sanctions when Italy had "taken all necessary measures to prevent the present situation from deteriorating."[21] He delivered the note to Lapointe, the acting secretary of state for external affairs in King's absence in Washington to sign the US-Canada bilateral trade agreement. Accompanied by Skelton, King had left Laurent Beaudry as acting undersecretary of state for external affairs, temporarily placing French Canadians and Roman Catholics in the two most senior posts at External Affairs, as some critics were soon to point out. Riddell later commented that "the Italian Consul-General and his Quebec friends must have thought that Providence had smiled upon them."[22]

Even amid the *douceurs* of Sea Island, Georgia, where King and Skelton spent a fortnight's holiday together after the successful conclusion of the trade negotiations in Washington, they could not free themselves from the domestic impact of the League of Nations and Abyssinia. What tele-

---

*At the time, Churchill wrote to his wife that the Italians "were throwing away their wealth and their poor wedding rings on an absolutely shameful adventure" (Gilbert, *The Wilderness Years*, 143).

phonic messages passed between King and Skelton at Sea Island and Lapointe and Beaudry in Ottawa about a draft reply to the Italian note is now unknown, but Skelton did send Beaudry a cypher telegram on 23 November: "Press reports indicate [imminent] meeting League Sanctions Committee to discuss Canadian proposal to extend embargo on exports [to Italy]. Please instruct Riddell not to take any initiative in making or advocating proposal, though he may vote for proposal if [it] meets with approval of other members generally" (this permissive phrase was included at the behest of King; Skelton opposed it).[23] In a letter three days later, written perhaps after further telephonic conversations with "good old Ernest" in Ottawa, Skelton began to shift his – and his minister's – position by requiring Riddell to take no action "on the question before reporting precisely what the proposal is and receiving definite instructions thereon." On a more personal note, Skelton added to Beaudry, "It is evident the question is going to be full of dynamite, and in view of Riddell's previous unfortunate actions, he must not be allowed to act at his own discretion or pull any more of Mr Anthony Eden's chestnuts out of the fire."[24] Skelton did not pause to identify what particular chestnuts he had in mind.

Three days passed between the despatch of Skelton's permission to vote with other delegations for the sanctions proposal and the flat prohibition on any such vote until definite instructions had been received from Ottawa. The criticism of Riddell had hitherto been focused on the fact that he had taken an initiative, not what the merits of that initiative were. He was now to be reined in from taking *any* action despite King's clear public statement of 29 October. Beaudry, however, reported that Lapointe from Geneva was still "disturbed by headlines in Press emphasizing initiative taken by Canada and is wondering whether some course of action could be adopted to counteract this effect."[25] Skelton replied that the prime minister did not agree, since "any counter action at this time also involves difficulties" in English Canada.[26] The prime minister would only reaffirm that his government's position on sanctions had been set out in his press statement of 29 October, a full month before. As for an embargo extension, the government had taken no initiative, the opinion of the advisory officer having been offered only on his personal initiative as a member of the League committee. Canada would, as he had said a month before, "consider changes in situation [i.e., additional sanctions] as they arose."[27] Accordingly, King instructed Skelton to tell Lapointe to restore his phrase "including any proposals for extension of economic sanctions," that same permissive phrase which neither Skelton nor "good old Ernest" had liked.[28] King confirmed yet again the distinction that he made between rejecting an unwarranted initiative (a stance intended to placate Quebec) and continuing support for the substance of the initiative (a stance intended to placate English Canada). Clearly it did not rule out future Canadian support for oil sanctions.

The next day, 27 November, King endorsed from Sea Island a reply to the Italian note. It too reverted to his press statement of 29 October, informing the consul general that the Canadian government had no alternative when confronted with the evidence but to assent to the League finding against Italy of aggression. The government was "confident that in so interpreting their obligations they are expressing the overwhelming conviction of the people of Canada that continued and firm adherence to the fundamental aims and ideals of the League of Nations must remain the cornerstone of their foreign policy."[29] With that unhelpful reply, the Italian consul general went to work urgently to attempt to change the Canadian public position on a petroleum sanction as such and not merely on an initiative by Riddell.

At the same time, Riddell's initiative evoked no particular reaction in London. Chamberlain had on 29 November commented, "Mussolini has been making violent threats and Laval has once again been wriggling ... S[am] H[oare] said he thought if others were prepared to enforce them [additional economic sanctions including oil] we could not refuse to do so but we need not take the initiative. I replied that if anyone else would give the lead, well and good, but in the last resort if necessary we ought to give the lead ourselves rather than let the question go by default ... we should press Laval to tell Mussolini that if he attacked us, France would at once come to our assistance ... we should make it clear that France, and not we, were [sic] blocking oil sanctions."[30] In Geneva, Hoare congratulated Riddell on his initiative, which was "both very effective and very well timed," although the permanent undersecretary at the Foreign Office thought that it had been premature, but what he found "galling was for Ottawa now to run away [from it which] is not helpful to the more exposed members of the League."[31] Another Foreign Office official added: "it was obvious that it was a composite effort and owed a great deal to the Secretariat of the League,"[32] a senior member of which told Riddell that "he was confident that in two or three weeks the Canadian Government would try to claim credit for having proposed the embargo on oil ... When the history of the whole dispute was written the most important place may be still given to the initiative of the Canadian representative."[33]

In Ottawa, the fine distinction between an initiative and a commitment eluded Beaudry who, in a memorandum to Lapointe of 29 November, became highly excited, arguing that "war may be imminent if the oil embargo is to be applied ... the attitude of Great Britain towards the application of the embargo remains firm ... Canada, through the unauthorized action of Dr Riddell, has initiated the proposal for the oil embargo, the responsibility assumed by Canada is very great, and the consequences for Canada herself may be still greater ... Canada might become directly involved in the armed conflict in spite of our previous reservation on the question of military sanctions. Canada, having initiated the proposal and being supported by Great Britain, would probably become directly entangled in the conflict."[34] Lapointe in turn sought King's agreement to issue a clarifying statement. In reply, King directed him to "arrange to be interviewed" to reaffirm Canada's basic position as set out in his press release of 29 October. Lapointe went further in a press statement by declaring that Riddell's initiative in Geneva "represented only his personal opinion, and not the views of the Canadian Government."[35] This was not what King had authorized, departing as it did from his basic position of 29 October. Accordingly, the prime minister "in response to [press] enquiry ... [explained] that [Lapointe's] statement had reference only to the origin of proposal and not to its merits."[36] The British high commissioner in Ottawa went to the heart of the matter when he reported to London on 1 December that the reason for King's press statement was that the government had "been embarrassed, particularly in Quebec, by the impression that war might result from alleged Canadian Government initiative on oil"[37] and that Riddell's "personal" initiative was seen in Ottawa as the result of a "misunderstanding." With regard to the future, "Canada will continue ... to consider any proposals for revision of economic sanctions."[38] The same day Lapointe confirmed to Riddell that the government had felt compelled to state to the press that its basic position on economic sanctions, which the prime minister had enunciated on 29 October, "has not been modified in any way." The view abroad that Canada had taken an initiative to extend further the scope of economic sanctions was "due to a misunderstanding." The initiative of the advisory officer was "only his own personal opinion" and not that of the government, which had not intended to take the initiative of proposing an extension of the export prohibitions already agreed.[39] In a separate telegram to Riddell of the same day, Beaudry attempted to explain away the government's "reluctant" public disavowal of his initiative: "It was not possible in present grave situation to accept responsibility for initiating a policy whose outcome was regarded with anxiety in many quarters in Canada."[40]

Separately, Lapointe proposed to King that Senator Dandurand, the government leader in the Senate, replace Riddell in Geneva "to survey situation and prevent further commitment."[41] King rejected any such idea. He knew very well how the idea of appointing a French Canadian collective security skeptic to replace Riddell, the League advocate, would go down in English Canada. On 29 November he told his diary, "With the European situation what it is, it is better our French Canadian Members appear in it as little as possible."[42] Later he added candidly, "as a Party we will have to carry the load of Fr[ench] and C[atholic] domination, and I am afraid our friends F[rench] and R[oman] C[atholic] won't help us in meeting the situation."[43]

Many in Quebec had from the beginning opposed Canada involving itself in the Abyssinian debate. The world war veteran but now isolationist Charles "Chubby" Power, minister of pensions and national health, described the continuing opposition in his province. His own reservations about obligations arising from collective security at the League of Nations were long-standing. He had even spoken against membership in the League during the special parliamentary session of 1919 on the grounds that the League was essentially a European institution. As early as 1923, he had proposed in the House of Commons a motion for Canada's withdrawal. He later recalled Quebec's opposition to the League's economic sanctions against Italy: "Had Canada … acquiesced in what looked like hostile action against any nation, Quebec would have immediately considered that it was being ruled by a government more interested in international and imperial affairs than in the affairs of Canada. Quebec's reluctance to embark upon any international adventure was so strongly developed … that any suspicion in the minds of the Quebecker that Canada was interested in Abyssinia … would have been looked upon with considerable disfavour."[44]

The popular mayor of Montreal, Camillien Houde, proclaimed flatly that "in the event of a war between Britain [in upholding the League] and Italy, French Canada sympathies would be with Italy." The leading Canadian Nazi, Adrien Arcand, lauded the Italian massacre of "uncivilized cannibals." It was a crime, he said, "to give weapons to the worst barbarians of the human race so that they can shoot white people."* But it was Lapointe who summed up succinctly the attitude of Quebec: "no interest in Abyssinia is worth the life of a Canadian citizen."[45] Quebec, in a variety of voices, had spoken, but none in support of collective security at the League.

Rome, with the help of the then influential ultramontane Roman Catholic Church in Quebec, urged Lapointe to persuade King to reverse his support for economic sanctions against Italy. The Holy See had long declared to its hierarchies everywhere its gratitude to Mussolini for the conclusion of the Lateran Accords of 1929 which, after much pulling and hauling, had finally settled the sovereignty and compensation issues that had left the Vatican in a secular limbo since the Italian *Risorgimento* of the mid-nineteenth century. As a result, "even if the Vatican itself maintained a formal neutrality [in the Italian invasion of Abyssinia], its tolerance of the chauvinistic speeches and behaviour of members of the Italian hierarchy and other prominent Italian ecclesiastics constituted a direct encouragement to the Fascist leaders and an implicit support of the Fascist cause."[46] In all this the stakes were high – or were so portrayed by the Roman Catholic Church. "If Mussolini fell or if the Fascist regime moved leftward, forces hostile to the Church would take control in Italy depriving the Church of its educational and religious privileges, repudiating financial agreements with the Government and possibly even denouncing the Lateran treaty."[47] Accordingly, Il Duce must not be criticized and Italy not subjected to League economic sanctions for such a distant incident as Abyssinia. "The Roman Catholic Church … [was] severely compromised by the crisis … Italian bishops and archbishops had begun to speak out in support of the war," culminating in the proclamation of Pope Pius XI "that the aspirations of a good and great people, which was also his own people, should be fulfilled insofar as was compatible with justice and peace." The Vatican accordingly warned the British mission in Rome that "economic sanctions would prolong the war and may result after years of misery in plunging Italy into Bolshevism and anarchy."[48] Not surprisingly, the Foreign Office responded to its chargé d'affaires to the Holy See that it

---

*Some Western observers, in addition to Adrien Arcand, were not unhappy about the Italian slaughter of Abyssinians. Evelyn Waugh, for example, wrote to Diana Cooper from Addis Ababa that "i have got to hate the ethiopians more each day goodness they are lousy and i hope the organmen [i.e., Italians] gas them to buggery" (*Times Literary Supplement*, 11 July 2014).

was finding it more and more difficult "to distinguish between the Vatican and the Italian Government."[49]

As part of the Vatican's worldwide efforts to counter hostility to Italy's aggression in Abyssinia, the Vatican secretary for ecclesiastical affairs instructed the apostolic delegate in Ottawa to confront "the hatred of the Church's enemies who, by striking at Italy, would like to strike a blow against the Catholic Church and Holy See." In reply, the apostolic delegate lumped together the opposition of Canadian Protestants and communists and informed the Vatican that Prime Minister King had received a letter "from a certain E. Pound in Rapallo," informing him that the League sanctions "are the work of an international Jewish clique ... to provoke a European war." The apostolic delegate added that the prime minister had told him that until then he had not given much thought to the question of Jewish influence, but with this new information, he would study the matter more carefully.* King had added "that Judaism has extremely powerful elements in England and the United States, both in government circles and in general in public opinion," but, for what it was worth, he gave no indication that he recognized that "a certain E. Pound in Rapallo" was the notoriously anti-Semitic and pro-fascist Ezra Pound.[50]

From Sea Island, Georgia, King wrote on 30 November to Cousandier in Rome; "It has broken my heart, as I know it has yours, to see your country involved in war and in the differences which have arisen out of relations with the League of Nations. I feel an interest and, I might say, an affection for your country second to none of any other country in the world."[51] King did not reveal what lesser ranking he gave to Britain, the United States, France, or even Canada itself, nor did he say when speaking of being "heart broken" about Italy being involved in war, whose fault the conflict was or whether it had contributed to the undermining of collective security and the League of Nations itself.

King received an enthusiastic reply from Cousandier dated 15 December. She was delighted at what she understood to be King's disavowal of Riddell,

---

*King may have been among those whose ambivalent attitudes Paul Fussell described in *The Great War and Modern Memory*: "No one can calculate the number of Jews who died in the Second World War because of the ridicule during the twenties and thirties of Allied propaganda about Belgian nuns violated and children sadistically used. In a climate of widespread skepticism about any further atrocity stories, most people refused fully to credit reports of the concentration camps until ocular evidence compelled belief and it was too late" (316).

not understanding, with so many others, King's distinction between an initiative for an oil sanction and an oil sanction itself. Believing that she had played a key part in influencing her "brilliant friend" to reject an oil sanction, she wrote:

> When Italy crossed her greatest distressed moments, and I read that Canada had proposed the "petroleum embargo" I felt very sad and my heart was real broken then. I lost a friend, but when I read you with your government were doing for us, you [?]fessed your Minister Riddell, so great was my joy, so happy I was, because you have contributed in the biggest way to have faith again in the [?] and to believe in the friendship of men. We Italians are terrible proud, extremely proud people … What Italy's sons do in these days is great. For him who does not live here it is not possible to have a real and whole picture of this. The enthusiasm is in every heart. You may see little children who give their toys as [?] in order to help in any way their loved country. You may see poor, very poor women who give their dearest souvenirs, their humble jewels, few gold that would make the richest countries laugh, but that is its meaning and in the acts of offer is the demonstration of the most vast civilization. Deeds upon deeds. Italy is reviving her passionate days of Italian 'Risorgimento,' like then, in an inhuman effort, this country, little for dimension and poor of gold, there are not riches greater than those of our High Spirit and High Ideal. I am sure that peoples who have condemned us will reflect upon this unhappy situation. Certainly a war in any way is an awful thing, but it is worse to see a good and generous people who suffers, mothers who could not feed their children … to inferior people of [?] sons, our civilization, … meanwhile to ourselves the rights of a superior people, giving ground and bread to his children … I trust your understanding as you have appreciate our country. I am a poor [?] woman, but I thank you hearty as every Italian do. I am sure you will continue to help us.[52]

Cousandier aside, what, all in all, had happened? The short answer is that in appearing to abandon Riddell over the inclusion of petroleum in the economic sanctions against Italy, King had abandoned the League of Nations. The whole brouhaha became part of his increasingly convoluted balancing act between English Canada and French Canada. Foreign policy was for him relative. One looks in vain for absolutes beyond a united Canada, governed by the Liberal Party. King's basic press statement of 29 October, repeated in the 27 November reply to the Italian diplomatic note, was supportive of League economic sanctions against the aggressor Italy. For one month there had been no suggestion from Ottawa that in advocating the addition of several products, including oil, to the list of economic sanctions, Riddell had taken an unwarranted initiative. But sufficient opposition to the League's economic sanctions had gradually been fostered in Quebec – by the Roman Catholic hierarchy in particular –that at least some observers had come to believe that Liberal standing in the province was threatened. On the other hand, the British high commissioner reported that "Lapointe ... is anxious that ... Canada should protest strongly but that the Prime Minister has ... withheld agreement."[53] As a result, Lapointe's influence and authority as King's lieutenant were being questioned if not undermined in Quebec by King's continued retention of Riddell in Geneva. It was widely held that the Liberal Party would lose votes in Quebec if it appeared committed to a strong pro-collective security policy (where the Liberal vote might otherwise go was a question left unanswered). Lapointe convinced King that he had to do something. Fortunately, although a full month had passed since his "personal initiative" at Geneva, Riddell was still at hand as a convenient sacrificial offering to national unity and to the consolidation of Lapointe's status as the spokesperson for Quebec in Ottawa.

The reaction in Italy to Ottawa's repudiation of its representative's initiative – although not of the oil sanctions proposal itself – was jubilant. A gratified Italian foreign minister, ignoring all evidence to the contrary, proclaimed, "As the oil embargo [itself] has been repudiated by the Government purported to have made it, we believe it must now be discarded."[54] On 3 December, Drummond, the British ambassador in Rome, reported to London, "In editorial comments and in messages from Italian correspondents at Geneva and elsewhere the apparent revision of official Canadian attitude towards the extension of sanctions occupied much space. Phrases such as 'rebellion of Canada' against further sanctions are frequently used. Messages from Geneva assert that it is being said there that Canadian proposal not being supported by Canadian Government must automatically drop. This result also suggested by official spokesman of the Press Ministry."[55]

The Italian Foreign Ministry persisted in portraying Riddell as a cat's paw for the British minister for League of Nations Affairs. Anthony Eden's recollections were quite different. "In [any] one session [of the League committee on sanctions], several raw materials might be proposed for examination, and no particular significance attached to the individual delegate who might suggest their consideration. We worked as a team. So it befell that one day the proposal to include oil products in the list for embargo was made by Dr Riddell, the representative of Canada. Though supplies of oil were regarded as important, they were not then considered so outstanding or decisive as they later became. Dr Riddell had in truth no more real responsibility than the rest of us for the proposal and the censure of his action, which he afterwards received from his Prime Minister, was unjust."[56]

At much the same time, Riddell recalled for Skelton how in the days leading up to his proposal of 2 November, the Canadian delegation "came to the conclusion that while they should not take any leading part in the debate, they should, if Canadian interests appeared to be affected, take the stand that if sanctions were to be imposed they should be comprehensive in order to be effective and … they should be spread as widely and equitably as possible among the participating countries … it was my conviction that once the State Members had declared Italy the aggressor … the only way to prevent the transition from economic to military sanctions was to render economic sanctions effective."[57] On the same day, 7 December, shortly before Riddell left Geneva for Chile, Joseph Avenol, Drummond's successor as secretary-general of the League, assumed that both Riddell and "the President of the [League] Commission should be pleased with the attention we were receiving from the Italian Press."[58] Riddell replied that King had said to the press the previous day that the Canadian government had not raised the merits of the oil sanction question but solely the origin of it. This struck Avenol as odd in view of the unanimous acceptance of the proposal by the members. He confirmed that Lapointe's demand to King to disavow Riddell "was probably done through pressure from the Papal See through the Church in Quebec."[59]

In Canada, the reaction in the French-language newspapers – with the notable exception of *La Presse* – was, as expected, supportive of what was interpreted as a repudiation by King of oil sanctions, not more simply a disavowal of Riddell for taking an initiative. By contrast, much of the English-language press, all four Toronto dailies (especially the Liberal *Star*), the *Winnipeg Free Press*, the *Victoria Daily Times*, the *Ottawa Journal*, and the *Montreal Star* disapproved in varying degrees of the whole confused affair.

The *Globe and Mail*, for example, called on the government to rectify its error in issuing a "mischief-making statement."

Privately, Newton Rowell wrote to Riddell that "Your friends in Canada feel that you have been sacrificed ... to political exigencies."[60] To Lapointe, Rowell expressed regret that Canada had not taken the credit for initiating an oil embargo that would have stopped Mussolini. Lapointe, sounding like King, replied for the ears of English Canada that Ottawa would continue to cooperate loyally in the application of economic and financial sanctions "which have the general support of the League against a Covenant-breaking state."[61]

King kept his diary informed of what he was convinced was happening at Geneva. After two years of reflection, he was still convinced in 1938 that the villain in the Abyssinian piece had not been Mussolini but Eden, who "has not been far-seeing enough, and has been too self-conscious, determined ... to bring Italy and Germany to their knees." The mischief had begun with the proposed oil sanction, which Eden "nearly succeeded in having Riddell get applied" (in fact, it could only be applied at the subsequent decision of individual member states). But they were not as blameworthy as that skunk Ferguson. He was "responsible – culpably so ... His policy and tactics would have brought Europe into war," a remarkable assertion about the international powers and influence of a retired, small-town Ontario premier.[62]

Not surprisingly, the press at the time interpreted the mass of inconsistencies, contradictions, and muddle in Ottawa to mean that, in brief, the government was opposed not only to Riddell having taken an initiative but also to an oil sanction as such. King, on his return to Ottawa from Sea Island, attempted again to make it clear that this was not so, but it was no easy task. He had placed himself in something of a box with his public statement of 29 October. Riddell had seen it as justifying his proposal to extend sanctions. And King had later reaffirmed it. The best that King could do now was to repeat on 2 November that Riddell had taken an unwarranted initiative, but that did not mean that Canada should be seen as abandoning economic sanctions as such. The press should understand that he had what was in effect a dual policy. In a press conference on 6 December, after eight weeks of continuing to support the initial economic sanctions, including by implementing them, King attempted to explain yet again what Skelton's statement of 2 November really meant. The problem was not that Riddell had supported an initiative to extend economic sanctions, but that it was he himself who had taken the initiative to propose the additions. The statement issued by Lapointe, which King assured Quebec that he backed, made "no reference to the *merits* of oil sanctions." In other words, an oil sanction if necessary, but not necessarily an oil sanction. It was the purblind press who had got it wrong in representing Canada as opposing an oil sanction. The press should recognize that Canada's position on an oil sanction was the same as it had been on other economic sanctions, i.e., it would be considered on its merits when the proper time arrived for member states to do so. As for the month-long delay in issuing the statement of 1 December, that too was the fault of the press, "due to the fact that the alleged Canadian sponsorship had only recently been emphasized [by the press]."[63]

In so blaming the press, King was following a tiresome tradition of politicians everywhere when they do not know whom else to blame or what else to say. It was a convenient dodge during his high wire act of attempting to please both Quebec and English Canada. To be certain that the British government understood the fine distinction that he was attempting to make, King had Vincent Massey, Ferguson's successor in London, inform a meeting of high commissioners at the Foreign Office, with both Hoare and Eden present, that "what had given rise to the recent statement of M. Lapointe had been the misrepresentation of Dr Riddell's action by the press … the attitude of the Canadian Government remained unchanged. They would loyally observe any sanctions approved by the members of the League, but they had felt it necessary to disabuse the public opinion in Canada of the idea that the Canadian Government had been ahead of the rest of the world in desiring the application of sanctions against Italy."[64] A week later, Massey added more specifically to the dominions secretary that "relating to proposal 4(a) [the oil sanction], the Canadian Government are prepared to participate with other Members … in the proposed extension of export embargoes."[65] To be certain that the commitment of the Canadian government was fully understood in London, as late as 21 February 1936 Massey repeated to a meeting of the high commissioners with the dominions secretary, "there was no likelihood of the Canadian Government not being ready to fall in with a recommendation of the [League] committee [to implement an oil sanction against Italy]. What they had been concerned about in the past was the fact that events had conspired to make it appear that they had taken the initiative."[66]

If King had waited another week or so into December, he could have avoided the confused wiggling and hair-splitting over an initiative for a sanction versus a sanction itself by sheltering behind the sudden public disclosure of an Anglo-French confidential accord to put pressure on Abyssinia to surrender a major part of its territory to Italy. Hoare visited Laval in Paris on 7–8 December. Immediately thereafter, leaks, intentional or otherwise, began to appear in the European press that the two foreign ministers had, in a further attempt to appease Italy and isolate Germany, concocted an ultimatum to what was left of the government of Abyssinia: either surrender directly to Italy two-thirds of your territory and recognize the remaining third as an Italian protectorate or face alone the inevitable total seizure of your country by Italy.* The British ambassador in Paris added that since the resulting negotiations would take time, oil sanctions would not be imposed immediately. Following Riddell's departure for Chile to chair a major ILO conference, Massey attended meetings in Geneva and London from 8 December 1935 to a final meeting in Geneva on 30 June 1936 (the day before he publicly announced Canada's termination of economic sanctions against Italy).

To be sure, the French government had never been happy with Hoare's more forward public policy during the League's earlier discussions of Abyssinia, eager as it had long been to appease Italy in the vain hope of keeping it from allying itself with Germany. Eden, in his *Facing the Dictators*, gives a detailed account of Laval's persistent efforts to reconcile British opposition to the Italian invasion of Abyssinia with the need that many British as well as French felt to remain on good terms with Mussolini. Schmidt, Hitler's interpreter, put it more bluntly. "It was owing to the opposition of the French Government … that oil sanctions were not applied."[67] Yet if France were to be forced into the unwelcome position of having to choose between Italy and Britain, *Realpolitik* would in the end dictate Britain as the indispensable ally against Germany. The French government was accordingly highly gratified with the Hoare-Laval pact since it in effect removed the potential awkwardness of having to choose between Italy and Britain. And British Conservatives were relieved of the fear that collective security under the League could possibly lead some day to British forces fighting alongside the Soviet Union against

---

*The full text of the Hoare-Laval ultimatum to Abyssinia is in British Document 356, 10 December 1935, p. 451.

Germany. "Although many Conservatives liked neither the Nazi nor the Communist system, on balance they preferred Nazism, which did not present any great threat to the existing social order."[68]

Before realizing the implications of the self-serving Hoare-Laval effort to appease Italy, King, now back in Ottawa, sent instructions on 11 December to the acting advisory officer in Geneva (Riddell having sailed for Chile) "that Canada is prepared to participate with other Members of the League in the extension of the export embargo to cover the products enumerated in the Proposal [i.e., oil]."[69] In other words, King was reconfirming that he did not oppose an oil embargo as such; he had opposed – to please Lapointe – only the initiative of Riddell in proposing it. At the end of the day, there were more votes in English than in French Canada.

When King began to recognize in the confidential Hoare-Laval agreement a reversal of the past, highly public Anglo-French commitment to collective security in the League, he said so only to his diary. For him the covert agreement came not as a betrayal of those League members, Canada included, that had striven to make a reality of collective security, but rather as an offer of relief in the midst of his precarious balancing act between English and French Canada. On 19 December, employing his habitual hyperbole, he described Hoare as the saviour of the world from the manifold and evident dangers of collective security. He complacently recorded in his diary that he did not "believe oil sanctions will be imposed … [instead] we shall see a break up of the League, and Italy left to fight out the situation with Ethiopia."[70] King was largely correct in his forecast. On the same day, the League Council announced that in view of the Hoare- Laval "suggestions," it did not consider that it was called upon to express an opinion in regard to them and would continue only those limited, and ineffective, economic sanctions already in force (i.e., *not* oil).

The British public, however, was decidedly not pleased with what they regarded as the blatant chicanery of their government. When news of the Hoare-Laval plan leaked out in London, "it detonated an explosion of moral indignation … of a violence and magnitude never before seen."[71] The outraged public had only recently expressed its overwhelming support for the League in the country-wide "Peace Ballot" and in the burgeoning pacifist Peace Pledge Union of the magnetic Dick Sheppard, a canon at St Paul's Cathedral. Two years before, the Labour Party, led by a confirmed pacifist George Lansbury, adopted a resolution at its annual meeting "calling for the total disarmament of all nations." Harold Nicolson, a former diplomat and now an MP, recorded in his diary on 10 December that he had found the House of Commons "seething because of the Abyssinian proposals ... great indignation that ... we should be giving Italy more for breaking the Covenant than we offered her for keeping it."[72] The public outrage forced the resignation on 19 December of Hoare and his replacement as foreign secretary by the pro-League Anthony Eden. Prime Minister Baldwin, although he had approved a pro-League stance in the recent electoral campaign and had accordingly endorsed Hoare's September speech in Geneva committing Britain to the League, remained at heart an appeaser, if not a crypto-pacifist. But his chancellor of the exchequer and early successor, Neville Chamberlain, recognized the damage done by the Hoare-Laval agreement: "nothing could be worse than our position. Our whole prestige in foreign affairs at home and abroad has tumbled to pieces like a house of cards. If we had to fight the election over again we should probably be beaten."[73]

On all of this, Massey informed the dominions secretary, Ottawa had expressed no view, although he did allow himself to say to a meeting of high commissioners on 10 December, two days after the leaks about the Hoare-Laval plan, that "he was very much afraid of the effect of the present proposal on public opinion in Canada" and, indeed, the disapproval of what the Foreign Office had poetically called "the Paris peace proposals."[74] However, when Riddell, on his return trip to Geneva from chairing the ILO governing body meeting in Chile, met in Ottawa with King, Lapointe, and Skelton, Lapointe was "cold, critical and overbearing"; but King, conscious that there were still many supporters of the League of Nations across English Canada, was "gracious."[75]

10

King and Abyssinia: The End

As the Abyssinian fiasco was playing itself out in Geneva, Hitler exploited that distraction by reoccupying the Rhineland, which had been demilitarized by the treaties of Versailles and Locarno, on 7 March 1936. Sir Eric Phipps, the British ambassador in Berlin, had months before learned what was coming and had so reported and it is difficult to believe that the MI5 agents in the German embassy in London or the MI6 agents in Germany itself had not signalled in advance Hitler's intentions. Yet many in London, including King Edward VIII, regarded the reoccupation of the Rhineland with indifference or even with understanding, as an expression of self-determination in the face of the folly of Versailles. After all, Germany was reoccupying its own territory, recovering its own backyard, as some said, so ill advisedly taken from it by the Treaty of Versailles. Publicly, the British and French governments acted as if they were surprised by the "reprehensible" German reoccupation, but they must have realized that Hitler had taken note of the undermining of the League of Nations, the souring of relations between Britain and France, and the general enmity toward Italy over Abyssinia. Albert Speer, one of Hitler's close collaborators, understood that "Hitler concluded that both England and France were loath to take any risks and anxious to avoid any danger."[1] Their governments had proved themselves weak and indecisive. For a variety of reasons, including doubts (which were unfounded) about the ability of the large French army to counter the smaller German units (who reportedly were intentionally sent into the Rhineland without ammunition), Britain failed to act, and a decidedly uneasy France, with a cabinet divided, would not act without Britain. Harold Nicolson was not alone in fearing that if Britain and France did push Germany back out of the Rhineland, Hitler might be replaced by a communist government. There was, in short, no inclination in either war-weary country to march against

Germany over the reoccupation of the Rhineland. The appeasement of Hitler was seen as a more promising route.

December 1935 had marked the end of Abyssinia and, except on paper, the effective end of the League of Nations. Nevertheless King saw the sudden German reoccupation of the Rhineland as basically a challenge for Britain and France to address, despite the fact that the dominions were signatories of the Treaty of Versailles. Abyssinia was a sideshow, a far away country inhabited by uncivilized blacks about which no one knew or cared very much. But the reoccupation of the Rhineland raised more troubling questions, carrying with it the seeds of a possible direct confrontation between the enemies of the First World War, only eighteen years past. If worse came to worst, Britain would have to support France. And to King's especial unease, if direct fighting did occur between Britain and Germany, the Canadian parliament would no doubt decide by a pronounced majority to join in. Even the arch isolationist Skelton reluctantly acknowledged this. But such a decision would be deeply opposed in much of Quebec, dividing the country along the familiar lines of those who would fight alongside Britain and those who wanted nothing to do with another European or second world war. King therefore concluded that it would be best for Britain and France to accept the Rhineland reoccupation and, in a favourite phrase of his, act conciliatorily rather than confrontationally. In those uncertain days, he had modestly recorded in his diary that he himself "would be happy beyond words were I called upon to intervene in the European situation. It would be the greatest joy of my life – but it seems too great a mission to expect."[2]

On 13 March 1936, six days after Hitler's reoccupation of the Rhineland, King made a rare foreign affairs statement to the House of Commons, a rotund declaration of doing nothing: "We [should] wait until we are more fully informed than we are ... before attempting to pronounce more definitely upon the position which we ... shall take with regard to European affairs."[3] Three days later Chamberlain shared with the House of Commons his belief that public opinion in Britain draws "a clear distinction between the action of Signor Mussolini in resorting to aggressive war and waging it beyond his frontiers and ... the actions of Herr Hitler ... [which] have taken place within the frontiers of the German Reich."[4]

The fact that King's government was not "fully informed" was largely of his own doing: he had neither spent the money necessary to build an effective foreign service nor would he accept proffered British information. His evasions and procrastination left Massey, among others, in a state of mounting frustration. A telegram from Ottawa of 1 May 1936 had forbidden Massey's participation in consultations with the Foreign Office or Dominions Office. Despite his undeniable past work as president of the Liberal Federation, King had come to envy his cosmopolitan and sophisticated character and mistrust what he regarded as his excessive anglophilia. In a bitter diary entry, Massey saw King as "condemning me unheard without any effort to ascertain the facts … Ottawa is apparently panic-stricken and seeks to protect itself by an ostrich-like policy of not even wanting to know what is going on. I agree with the principles of Dominion autonomy in all things as much as any other Canadian, but not in my experience has there been the slightest risk of its being violated."[5] King had, if anything, become even more opposed to any public or parliamentary discussion of external affairs. He replied to Thomas Vien, a Liberal MP from Quebec and future speaker of the Senate, who had sought a foreign affairs debate, that the public interest required as little discussion as possible. Not surprisingly, Hume Wrong, a senior foreign service officer in the Department of External Affairs, observed that King's instructions to his department amounted to "say nothing and do nothing."

On 9 May 1936, two days after the German reoccupation of the Rhineland, Italy formally annexed Abyssinia. King Victor Emmanuel thereupon became emperor of Abyssinia and Marshal Badoglio duke of Addis Ababa. By then the British cabinet had convinced itself that no good purpose was served by continuing economic sanctions against Italy, foreshadowing yet later failures at appeasement. For King, however, the universe was unfolding as it should. Since the domestic contretemps over Riddell's initiative regarding additional sanctions, he had come to wish that the League of Nations could simply be "gotten out of the way" for reasons of Canadian unity. Certainly public debate would lead nowhere; his policy remained to "keep Canada united, and avoid controversies."[6]

Any lingering idea that the League could provide collective security against an aggressor was now gone. The end result of the Abyssinian crisis was the worst possible. The League had not stopped the aggression and Mussolini was alienated from Britain and France, who had failed in their muddled attempts to appease him in the hope that he might join them rather than Germany in any foreseeable European conflict. Yet King considered the attempt to appease Italy through the Hoare-Laval agreement the right policy. Of the Italian seizure of Abyssinia and its many adverse if not fatal implications for collective security, King continued to say publicly as little as possible. At the time, Chamberlain, in a *requiescat*, got it right: the Hoare-Laval crisis demonstrated the League's inadequacies and destroyed its ability to be a force for good.

Riddell saw things equally clearly. In his 1947 memoir, *World Security by Conference*, he recalled his conclusion at the time. "Eight and one-half months after I had tried to give sanctions new life, they were declared officially dead. With the failure of sanctions, the last chance of averting World War II had gone forever."[7] Even more eloquently and trenchantly, Churchill in retrospect said the same thing. "Mussolini would never have dared to come to grips with a resolute British Government … Germany could as yet give no effective help. If ever there was an opportunity of striking a decisive blow in a generous cause with the minimum of risk, it was here and now. The fact that the nerve of the British Government was not equal to the occasion can only be excused in their sincere love of peace. Actually it played a part in leading to an infinitely more terrible war. Mussolini's bluff succeeded, and an important spectator drew far-reaching conclusions from the fact. Hitler had long resolved upon war for German aggrandizement … In Japan, also, there were pensive spectators."[8]

By July 1937 the Japanese warlords were no longer spectators; they began a full-scale invasion of China. A three-front war in Europe, the Mediterranean, and Asia, the worst possible prospect for Britain and France, appeared increasingly likely. But Mackenzie King in his diary appears disengaged. Despite his travels of three decades before, he seldom refers to Asia. At the Foreign Office, however, the worst was feared. The permanent undersecretary, Sir Alexander Cadogan, wrote in 1939, with something of traditional Foreign Office understatement, "We cannot … provide China with arms and munitions. It seems that the Americans are unlikely to join in economic action against Japan (which without U.S. co-operation, would be worse than useless). As regards active operations against Japan … these are ruled out, owing to the situation in Europe. If Germany, Italy and Japan attack us simultaneously, we should have to do what we can, but we should probably be rather on the defensive in the Far East."[9]

Following the sorry dénouement of the Abyssinian imbroglio came the death of King George V and the ascent to the throne in January 1936 of King Edward VIII. Although the new king of Britain was also monarch of Canada, and the Statute of Westminster stipulated that accession to the imperial throne required the consent of the dominions, the Canadian prime minister, with great satisfaction, left to his British counterpart the resolution – eventually by abdication – of the crisis arising from the extramarital affair between the new monarch and the American Wallis Simpson, who had been divorced from her first husband but not yet from her second. Wary of a constitutional wrangle that might be viewed differently in English and French Canada, King did not respond to Woodsworth's repeated questions about whether Canada did or did not have a say in the controversial matter of the succession to the throne. Nor did he respond, when in London in September, to the suggestion of Baldwin and Geoffrey Dawson (the editor of the *Times* and a friend of Chamberlain and Halifax), among others, that he, in his audience with Edward VIII, tell him that the people of Canada were deeply disturbed by his liaison with Mrs Simpson.*

In Berlin the accession of Edward VIII (who spoke German, his mother being German) was welcomed. From the funeral of George V, the visiting Duke von Sachsen-Coburg und Gotha, an old Etonian who was president of the German-English Society in Berlin, reported that the new king, his cousin, saw an Anglo-German alliance as an urgent necessity and a guiding principle for British foreign policy. Twenty-five years later, the then Duke of Windsor told the press that his cousin's 1936 account of his admiration for Nazi Germany gave "a generally false impression,"[10] but he offered no explanation why he felt the need to modify his phrase "false impression" by "generally."

Edward VIII, Sachsen–Coburg reported to Berlin, was ready to meet Hitler, whether Prime Minister Baldwin approved or not. Additionally, at the funeral of George V, Edward had told the Soviet foreign minister and the ambassador, "As to the League of Nations, [he] had some doubts; he was afraid that the League might spread war all over Europe as a result of its efforts. There was the sense that Edward regretted the failure of the Hoare-Laval plan." After the funeral, they went to see Fred Astaire and Ginger Rogers in the immensely cheerful *Top Hat*.[11] Edward VIII's attitude toward Nazi Germany, and that of his brother, the Duke of Kent ("who took drugs and was voraciously bisexual"[12]), was seen in Berlin as decidedly

---

*That same evening, Massey gave an after-theatre reception for the visiting prime minister. King shared a taxi to Massey's residence with a young woman who he learned the next day was "a famous young movie star," Ingrid Bergman.

positive. A senior official from the Foreign Ministry lamented to Mackenzie King during his visit to Berlin that George VI did not seem so well disposed toward Germany as his brothers.* Certainly the friendly attitude of Edward VIII had given more respectability to Chamberlain's policy of appeasement. Wallis Simpson, whom both the Federal Bureau of Investigation (FBI) and MI5 kept under discreet surveillance, appeared even better disposed toward Germany. Rumours began to spread that she was concurrently the paramour of Hitler's new ambassador in London, Joachim Ribbentrop, who sent her roses daily. The United States ambassador, in a letter to Roosevelt, added another rumour: "'Many people here suspected that Mrs Simpson was actually in German pay ... [but] I think this is unlikely.' But though not in German pay ... she was wittingly or unwittingly a tool of German policy."[13]

Amidst the Abyssinian imbroglio, Mackenzie King developed a sequence of four foreign policy steps. It was to be such a carefully balanced sequence of external affairs initiatives that it would, he hoped, foster support for the Liberal Party in both English and French Canada. The first step would be to schedule what could not be put off any longer – a foreign affairs debate in the House of Commons during the last days of the spring 1936 session (thereby helping to ensure its brevity). To the House, King would describe in broad terms his antagonism toward the collective security provisions of the League of Nations, arising from his long-standing rejection of any obligation that its members join in eventual military sanctions against an aggressor. That explicit rejection would please Quebec and isolationists, pacifists, and continentalists in a Canada distant from the turmoil of Europe.

The second step would be to go to London to consult the British government about foreign policy, despite his past rejections of such consultations. Then he would feel better equipped to continue on to Geneva to make much the

---

*The degree to which the Duke of Windsor and his brother the Duke of Kent were disposed to Hitler's regime remains unclear, the Royal Archives having been exempted from the British Freedom of Information Act of 2000. More specifically, information about the abdication crisis and about the visit of the Duke and Duchess of Windsor to Hitler in 1937 remains closed. However, stills from a home cinema film of the princesses Elizabeth and Margaret as young children and their mother, the future Queen Elizabeth, in a garden at Balmoral giving the stiff-armed Nazi salute following the example of their uncle, the future Edward VIII, have somehow become public (*Guardian*, 18 July, and *Daily Telegraph*, 19 July 2015).

same speech to the League Assembly that he had made to the House of Commons in Ottawa. As he explained in a letter to Giorgia de Cousandier, "I have felt the whole European situation was so critical and the position of the League so uncertain, that I ought not to leave exclusively to others the representation of our country."[14] If his speech to the League went well, no one in Quebec or elsewhere could then accuse him of being less candid with its membership than he had been with his fellow Canadians during the brief House of Commons debate.

The third step would be to be seen by all Canadians as doing everything possible to convince Hitler, face to face, that Germany's own interests lay in peace, not war. Believing that he had been divinely ordained to do so, he would continue on from Geneva to Berlin to point the Führer in the right direction, after clearing with London in advance what he would say. That would demonstrate to Canadian voters as nothing else would that their prime minister was a man of peace.

Only after achieving the above three stages would King embark on his fourth and final step: a degree of rearmament, however modest it might be compared to the current British initiative. With his denunciation of collective security through the League, he anticipated a restoration of some sort of balance of power in Europe. That should help to quiet those English-Canadian voters who were becoming so concerned with the alarums and excursions of the dictators that they were beginning to press strongly for the early refurbishment of the armed forces that were sorely depleted, particularly in the wake of Bennett's repeated cuts in government spending during the worst years of the depression.

Neither Bennett nor King had, during the long economic depression, done anything to reverse the disrepair that had been the lot of the armed forces from the immediate postwar years, but King, on coming to office in 1935, was well aware of the impact that newspaper editorials and especially articles by George Drew, an artillery veteran and a vocal Ontario Conservative advocate of rearmament, were having in English Canada. Drew's *Canada in the Great War*, a pamphlet decrying American claims to have won the war, was widely popular. A future premier of Ontario and later leader of the opposition in Ottawa, he was a great favourite of the publisher Colonel J.B. Maclean. Drew wrote in *Maclean's Magazine* on 5 May, "Canadian defence forces are inefficiently organized, are badly equipped, and have only little opportunity for carrying out training that could fit them for modern conditions of warfare." King mistrusted him as an outspoken partisan, but he also recognized that his repeated advocacy of rearmament in *Maclean's* and its sister publication the *Financial Post* was finding support among a growing number of influential English Canadian voters.

King, however, remained cautious about advocating rearmament. In planning the first step in his four-part progression, a foreign affairs debate in the House of Commons, he was keenly aware of Quebec's opposition to spending taxpayers' money on armaments at the cost of social programmes. Early in the 1936 parliamentary session there were brief exchanges in the House of Commons about the League, including the debilitating impact on it of Italy's seizure of Abyssinia. In these brief exchanges, Bennett from the opposition front bench appeared supportive of the League, but he tempered his remarks by the tacit recognition that if the Conservative Party hoped to form a government again it had to win at least a modicum of seats in Quebec. The third party in the House, the new socialist Co-operative Commonwealth Federation (ccf), had no expectation of making any headway in Quebec, but it was the party of arch-isolationists and pacifists who, if for different reasons from those of Quebec, had been even more opposed to military sanctions. Opposition to military sanctions was in fact one of the very few subjects on which all three parties agreed. The exchanges in the House, including King's statements, were nevertheless frequently contradictory and inconsequential, being centred, as the ccf's Tommy Douglas said, on "the confusing subject of sanctions."[15]

That Douglas and other members of parliament, not limited to the ccf, found the subject of League sanctions confusing is not to be wondered at. No one on the front benches of either the government or the opposition was wholly confident about what to say publicly about the League in light of Quebec's well-known rejection of any economic sanctions that could possibly lead to military sanctions. Lapointe had made it clear that for Quebec it was yes to the League of Nations and to the autonomous status of Canada reflected therein, but no to the sanctions envisaged in its Covenant. That being so, the House spent much of its time going over the so-called Riddell incident, further reviewing the precise hour of despatch and receipt of various transatlantic telegrams, many in cumbersome cypher, with King defending his repudiation of Riddell's initiative (although not its substance). By contrast, Bennett extolled Riddell. Perhaps recalling Riddell's responsible stance in the Cahan incident, he told the House of Commons, "I have known no one in all my experience who was more careful not to take action without having authority to do so."[16]

On 11 February, in the debate on the Speech from the Throne, King spoke for three hours about external affairs, revealing the degree to which, in the face of Quebec's discontents, he had reversed himself about the League of Nations. Three months earlier, he had stated that his government was ready to "take the necessary steps to secure the effective application of the economic sanctions against Italy … [and is] prepared to co-operate fully in the endeavour."[17] Now, sounding like Beaudry, he told the House of Commons that when the story became known "he would not be surprised if it was shown the whole of Europe would be aflame today were it not for the action taken by Canada."[18] As for the disavowal of Riddell's initiative, he piously explained that it was "only because we are most anxious not to take any step which might possibly embarrass the situation in Europe or which might appear even remotely to indicate an exception on the part of Canada to what was being done by other parts of the British Empire [i.e., the United Kingdom itself]." In short, English Canadians should understand that the disavowal of Riddell had in fact been for the benefit of the British Empire.

Lapointe, in defending his role in the whole sorry affair, summed up his position as no to a Canadian initiative and yes to League economic sanctions (which he knew were going nowhere in the wake of the Hoare-Laval agreement). "It was not properly the repudiation of any man: it was the repudiation of what was being stated everywhere in the world that it was Canada that was proposing this oil sanction, when so many countries were disquieted and did not know what to do about it. We merely said that we had not given any instructions to that effect, that this was not a Canadian proposal, that Canada was quite willing to have the same responsibility as the other countries to join in any collective action." Lapointe also took the occasion to deprecate unspecified attempts to pillory him because of his French Canadian race and Roman Catholic religion.[19]

What the press gallery made of all this and other exchanges in the House is reflected in two examples from Vancouver. The *Province* reported the prime minister's claim that by repudiating Riddell's initiative, he had prevented a European conflagration and had maintained the unity of the British Empire. The other Vancouver newspaper, the *Sun*, concentrated more favourably on Hitler. "Canadians who do not allow themselves to be swayed by a personal dislike of Hitler [recognize that] Canada is only a spectator. There are not enough moral principles at stake to induce her to become otherwise ... Whatever morality lies in the scales seems to be on Germany's side of the balance."[20]

Perhaps the last word can be left to Sir Robert Borden who on 5 May 1936 wrote, "The Italians have overrun Ethiopia ... all Italy is rapturously acclaiming victory; the Germans delighted; the British Government is disconcerted; the British people are exasperated. At first Japan, then Germany and now Italy have flouted the League of Nations; it is apparent that its usefulness has reached the vanishing point. In Great Britain there is a proposal that the League should continue, but under a Covenant that does not include punitive measures for disregard of its obligations. Lewd fellows of the base sort who have been delighted to deride the League will now rejoice in its failure and will sharpen their dull wits for still more derisive contempt." Borden, a year from his death, did not confirm whether he included King as one of the dull wits.[21]

Recognition that the League was all but finished had spread through all three parties in the House of Commons, although the pacifist Woodsworth of the CCF still hoped that something might be resurrected from the wreckage. "The whole of the Treaty of Versailles needs to be revised, and the control of the League and even perhaps the formation of the League needs to be fundamentally recast."[22] Presumably unknown to each other, Woodsworth and King, exact contemporaries, had both spent part of the summer of 1900 in Germany. Woodsworth recorded his impression that "a fine company of German soldiers ... gives a lively appearance to a crowd." By the 1930s, he had become the leading socialist thinker and the pre-eminent pacifist in the House of Commons. His patent integrity as well as intelligence was such that he became the most effective and frequent critic of King's several foreign policies – or lack of them – as the Second World War approached.

King had given to the House of Commons on 11 February what he considered his definitive statement on *l'affaire Riddell*. A long debate on the Department of External Affairs estimates on 18 June represented an additional step in his four-part foreign affairs progression, yet his performance was in the end little more than sanctimonious posturing, anything but a clear analysis of the challenge that now faced Canada as a member of what King, with heavy humour, began to call the "League of Notions." With Italy's annexation of Abyssinia, King felt ready in mid-June to share with the House of Commons at least indirectly what he intended to say to the League Assembly in September in Geneva. Less than a week before the end of the parliamentary session, he continued to base himself on his press statement of the previous 29 October. He first attempted to explain why external affairs debates in the House would have been premature and would have merely complicated a difficult, even dangerous, situation. He then offered a convoluted and wordy *finis* to Canada's career at the League and particularly his government's role after assuming office in October 1935, almost a year before. He made much – or tried to make much – of Canada's real or supposed support of the League in the past fifteen years (including, although he did not say so, the six Tory years of Meighen and Bennett).

Although King's long statement was infused with what Bennett had once called Skelton's "epigrammatic idiosyncrasies," he was clear about one thing: it was "imperative to correct this serious misapprehension" about a Canadian initiative in support of League sanctions – especially oil – against Italy. King attempted yet again to explain away his disavowal of Riddell's initiative. Canada had implemented the initial sanctions policy endorsed by the League (he did not mention that this had been done by Bennett in the first instance), and although an oil sanction could have led to war, Canada would nevertheless have joined in enforcing it if other members of the League had "generally supported it." Canada would not, however, take the initiative of proposing "such a pretentious question" when Britain and perhaps France would have to sustain it with arms if necessary. Having thereby reassured at the same time Quebec, pacifists, isolationists, continentalists, and, incidentally, pro-fascists, King simply denied that Italy's invasion of Abyssinia had left the League in tatters. After all, it should never be assumed that "all that can be done is to meet force by force," although he was himself notably thin on what else could be done to conciliate the two dictators. He nevertheless went on to describe the League as "that indispensable agency" where "the statesmen of great countries are forced to come in the open and defend in public, before a world forum, the policies of their governments." The fact that the League could in reality force no statesman from great countries or small, especially from non-member countries – Germany, Japan, the United States, Italy, Brazil, and, until 1934, Soviet Russia – to come to Geneva was a fact King simply ignored. And as for member states, the League had not required Britain and France to defend before it the perfidy of the Hoare-Laval proposal. The purple prose of King's peroration was equally meaningless: "We must utilize constructively the League of Nations."[23] What King meant by utilizing the League constructively he did not say. As someone who had become intent on "getting the League out of the way," he did not explain to the House why he at the same time described the League as "that indispensable agency." Perhaps he believed that even on such thin gruel he could retain the support of Dafoe and Rowell and other League advocates in English Canada without jeopardizing Liberal support in Quebec.

As in his statements to the House in February, King said no word in June against Mussolini's defiance of the League over Abyssinia. He did briefly regret Italy's use of modern weapons – which had included mustard gas dropped from aircraft – against Abyssinian warriors, some armed only with spears, but he did not mention Mussolini by name.

As King had intended, it being late in the session, there was no time for an extended debate. Woodsworth was scathingly accurate: "After waiting for months we have heard what our foreign policy is supposed to be and we find that we have not any. We are just going around in a circle; we have no foreign policy."[24] There was little public reaction to King's long speech, although Dafoe (a Liberal "because there are less sons of bitches in the Liberal Party than in the Tory") deplored in the *Winnipeg Free Press* King's attitude, which "amounts to the rejection by Canada of the League ... With assurances of the most distinguished consideration, [it] was ushered out into the darkness by Mr Mackenzie King."[25]

With the League rendered completely powerless, Bennett concluded that there remained only one route to the maintenance of peace: "the greatest assurance we have for the maintenance of our peace lies in the strengthening of every tie that binds the commonwealth of nations, the members of the British empire."[26] In fact, King was himself covertly, and as usual ambiguously, moving in that direction, the only direction that remained open to him, having turned his back on the isolationism of the United States and Quebec, the pacifism of the CCF, and the continentalism of Skelton and his ilk. He was not, however, yet ready to risk the Liberal predominance in Quebec with overt support for additional ties with the British Commonwealth of Nations.

Vincent Massey was now attending frequent meetings in London of the high commissioners with the Dominions Secretary to discuss the current status of the continuing but limited League economic sanctions against Italy. King asked him to go to Geneva on Dominion Day 1936 to join with representatives of other member states in terminating these sanctions.

Massey explained, "While deeply regretting the failure of the joint attempt to protect a weak fellow-member of the League, there appeared to be no practical alternative for Canada ... but to support the discontinuance of sanctions."[27] At the same time, President Roosevelt paid the first state visit to Canada of a president in office, in Quebec during the last days of July, but nothing is known about whether King discussed with Roosevelt any League matters. Roosevelt, as head of state, was the guest of the Canadian head of state, the governor general, but King was an active participant in a day of friendship, good will, peace, and the blessing of all.

While King was elaborating his approach to the all but defunct League of Nations during the summer and autumn of 1936, Berlin rather than Geneva became the focus of international attention. Reflecting the mounting prominence of Germany in Europe, the most spectacular event that summer was the Olympic Games in Berlin. The International Olympic Committee had awarded the games to Germany almost two years before Hitler became chancellor, and Joseph Goebbels, the Nazi propaganda minister, knew a good thing when he saw it. He easily convinced Hitler to make a supreme effort to exploit the games to show what the Nazis had achieved in a few short years in the regeneration of Germany and its industrial and military potential. In Canada as elsewhere protests were held against the Olympic Games being held in Nazi Germany at all, but they were dismissed as coming from socialists, communists, organized labour, Jews, and other troublemakers. The blatant and brutal racism of the Nazis, whitewashed as much as possible by German officials, was not much criticized; it was the protestors who were portrayed as the spoilsports. In the opening parade at the winter Olympics at Garmisch-Partenkirchen and again at the summer Olympics in Berlin, the Canadian teams, in their red and white maple leaf uniforms, left the impression with their stiff-armed salutes that they were uncertain whether they were giving the Nazi salute "as a gesture of friendship" or whether they were giving what some chose to call the "Olympic salute."

Hitler's pleasure at Germany winning the most gold medals at the games was palpable, but tempered by the triumphs of a non-Aryan, a superb black American athlete, Jesse Owens, who was even-handed in his criticism of the racism that he encountered both in Germany and in his native United States. The German performance was saluted by the *Toronto Globe*, which surprisingly attempted to explain away even Nazi press censorship. Matthew Halton of the *Toronto Star* had a different impression. He was appalled by the blind fanaticism reflected there. Whenever Hitler arrived at the Olympic stadium – which seated more than 100,000 spectators – "the world becomes for a few moments nothing but a sea of outstretched arms and a crashing roar of 'Heil! Heil! Heil!' and when you turn this way and that, examining men's eyes, you see in them something like mystic hysteria – a glazed, holy look as of men hearing voices."[28]

Toward the end of the Olympic Games in Berlin, weeks before King embarked for Europe, his minister of trade and commerce, William Euler, led a trade delegation to Germany, Switzerland, the Netherlands, and Britain. Euler, of German descent, was the former mayor of Kitchener and a newspaper publisher who had strongly opposed conscription in the First World War. He represented the German immigrant area where the Deutscher Bund Canada had been founded two years before. King may have known of Euler's request to the German consul general in Ottawa to arrange for him to call on the Führer during his visit to Germany (Euler, like King, did not want to be seen as using the good offices of the British ambassador in Berlin), but there is only one brief reference in King's diaries to his trade minister's enthusiastic visit to Hitler. King remained wary of Euler and his explanations of anti-Semitism in Germany: "Many Jews in Germany were newcomers and Marxists."* The German reaction to them was "no different than the Canadian to those of German heritage during the First World War."[29]

In his description to Canadian Press of his half-hour with the chancellor in Berlin on 6 August 1936, Euler described enthusiastically how "Hitler allowed me to ask numerous questions about the international situation. He answered me very carefully and with reasoned argument about the 'shackles of Versailles.' He expressed an earnest desire for peace and described his fear of Bolshevism."[30] Euler, although a minister of the crown, evidently felt enfranchised to discuss with Hitler "the international situation" and the freeing of Germany from the shackles of Versailles, although he may not have first cleared his visit to Hitler with the secretary of state for external affairs (i.e., Mackenzie King) or what he intended to say to him or, on his

---

*Pierre Berton, in *The Great Depression*, related that "In 1937 Euler was guest of honour on German Day in Kitchener. Euler agreed with other speakers who deprecated stories and articles critical of Germany and which instead of healing sores [tend] to keep up hatreds. The Minister declared that he sometimes thought that the publication of such propaganda should be made a criminal offence for newspapers" (464).

return, what he had said, although he must have known that his prime minister was sailing for Europe in a week or so after his own return to Ottawa. Dana Wilgress, a senior officer in the Department of Trade and Commerce who accompanied Euler, came away with a less optimistic impression of Nazi Germany. "We were driven in a government car to the Olympic Games … It was an impressive and at the same time a frightening sight. All that I saw in Berlin … convinced me that Germany was preparing to go to war."[31]

During his crossing to Europe in mid-September 1936, King had ample time, if so inclined, to reflect on Walter Allward's magnificent Vimy war memorial and its unveiling by the recently crowned King Edward VIII, before 8,000 veterans and their families. He did not record whether he regretted his decision to absent himself on 16 July, despite welcoming any occasion to be with his sovereign. But then King seldom recorded regret at any of his actions, relying if necessary on reassurances from the Great Beyond. He rationalized to his diary that he was right not to go to Vimy and to send a French Canadian (Lapointe) instead because he was "fatigued."[32] King was never comfortable at events with veterans and it is also possible that he may not have wanted to take a lead in the Vimy ceremonies celebrating victory over Germany only ten days before Euler's visit to the Führer and three months before his own. Paradoxically it was Hitler who visited the Vimy memorial in June 1940, not the fatigued Canadian prime minister in 1936.

On his voyage to Europe, King must have learned something from the ship's wireless news bulletins of a visit to Hitler by another Empire statesman, the former British prime minister David Lloyd George. Yet he makes no mention in his diary of the two meetings between Lloyd George and Hitler that preceded by only a few weeks what he assumed would be his own meeting.

Lloyd George was bowled over by Hitler: "We got on like a house on fire." Even before he met Hitler, he had told Ribbentrop (whom Hitler had appointed a few weeks before ambassador to the Court of St James), "it was most fortunate for Germany that she had found a leader in Hitler," then adding the ultimate blasphemy that he was "the resurrection and the life." On 4 September, after the first of two meetings, Lloyd George, having dismissed Edvard Beneš, the Czechoslovak president, as a jackal and a little swine, hailed Hitler "as a very great and wonderful leader … the Saviour of Germany."[33] Following a second meeting on 15 September, Lloyd George let himself go in an article in Beaverbrook's *Daily Express*. Hitler was "the greatest living German ... a born leader, yes, and statesman, a magnetic, dynamic personality with a single-minded purpose, the George Washington of his country." Britain's wartime prime minister summed up the conclusions of his visit in one sentence: "The Germans have definitely made up their minds never to quarrel with us again." In his praise of Hitler, he appears in fact to have himself in mind: "I only wish that we had a man of his supreme quality at the head of office in our own country today" (deeply frustrated at being long out of office, Lloyd George held Prime Minister Baldwin in open contempt.)[34]* According to Schmidt, Hitler's interpreter, Megan Lloyd George, who accompanied her father, had facetiously given an approximation of the Nazi stiff arm salute with a "*Heil Hitler!*" to which Lloyd George replied, "Certainly *Heil Hitler*! I say it too, for he is really a great man."[35] Churchill thought this was all nonsense. He later offered a different summation about the visit of his former cabinet colleague to Hitler: "All those Englishmen who visited the German Führer in those years were embarrassed or compromised. No one was more completely misled than Mr Lloyd George whose rapturous accounts of his conversations make odd reading ... Unless the terms are equal it is better to keep away."[36]

At the League of Nations Assembly in the summer of 1936, sanctions against the aggressor Italy were abandoned. Not knowing what else to do, the League invited member states to suggest how the Covenant might be revised to reflect what, if anything, they were in fact willing to do in the face of aggression. In response to a letter from Newton Rowell, King asked him what he thought. Rowell replied:

[The League] can never provide any real degree of security against aggression unless sanctions are maintained, and behind the obligation, there is the will to enforce the sanctions ... It is only by the due administration of justice, backed up by an adequate police force that the rule of law has been established and can be maintained in any country ... it is only by a similar process, although necessarily under very different conditions, that the rule of law in international affairs can be gradually established and international crime and anarchy suppressed. I therefore always have been and still am in favour of sanctions – universal, so far

---

*The dislike was reciprocal. Baldwin once described Lloyd George as having "no bowels, no principles, no heart and no friends."

as economic are concerned, necessarily regional as far as military operations are concerned, although recognizing the obligation of all to come to the defence of any member who is attacked by an aggressor state when carrying out a mandate of the League in imposing economic sanctions … I look upon the use of force to restrain an aggressor, not as war, but as a purely police measure and as the best possible means of avoiding war … had the members of the League lived up to their obligations under Article 16, Italy would not now be the conqueror of Abyssinia and Germany would have hesitated long before she re-occupied the Rhineland. Successful aggression breeds new aggression.[37]

Nothing that Rowell said was to King's liking. It contradicted directly the stand that he had taken in Quebec at Lapointe's adamant urging. He used none of it in his flaccid statements to the House of Commons and the League Assembly.

There is no evidence that King, before leaving Ottawa for Europe, had sought briefings from officials in the minute Department of External Affairs, other than perhaps from Skelton. But even he was beginning to be looked upon by King as too dogmatic in his isolationism. To help offset English Canadian misgivings, King would have benefited from reading an extensive memorandum that Burgon Bickersteth, the British-born warden of Hart House at the University of Toronto and something of a protégé of Vincent Massey, had prepared for British prime minister and family friend Stanley Baldwin, upon his return to Toronto from Europe. His lengthy report dwelt, *inter alia*, on the progress of Nazism, the sorry state of the churches, opposition of ordinary people to rearmament, military training, attitudes to recovery of the former German colonies, the opinions of the army, and feelings toward Britain.[38] There is no record that King ever read Bickersteth's report (which, if it had come via Massey, he would likely have dismissed as tainted), but en route to Geneva, he told Malcolm MacDonald, the dominions secretary, that many Canadians said that "we should keep out of the quarrel between Germany and France, wash our hands of it, and leave the Germans and French to kill each other if they want to."[39] On his arrival in Geneva, he invited the counsel of Eden, telling him that "Canada's wish … was that Great Britain would keep out of any European war altogether."[40] After all, as King told his journal, "It is what we prevent, rather than what we do, that counts most in Government."[41]

In his speech to the League of Nations Assembly on 29 September, King repeated much of what he had said in the House of Commons in June, although in even more elaborate and circumlocutory terms. He repeated his regret at the lack of universality in the membership of the League – as if the Assembly itself could do anything about that – and in light of the rejection of collective security, repeated that it should limit itself to conciliation. He piously advised the Assembly that its "emphasis should be placed on conciliation rather than coercion … automatic commitments to the application of force is not a practical policy." The League, he fondly hoped, was to be resuscitated by talk alone. He remained as convinced as he had been in 1918 when he had published his tediously verbose *Industry and Humanity* that talk could settle anything. As Lester Pearson said of King, "if he insisted on pushing his polices of caution and non-commitment at Geneva to the point of timid isolation, as he did, his abiding preoccupation with Canadian unity was behind every move – or, more accurately, every refusal to move … King's temperament and instinct preferred the process of consultation and conciliation to immediate decisions leading to decisive results. Collective talking was preferable to collective action."[42] Speaking over the heads of the League Assembly, King repeated yet again, mainly for Quebec voters, "We will not necessarily become involved in any war in other parts of the British Empire … Any decision on the part of Canada to participate in war will have to be taken by the Parliament or people of Canada."[43] That banality did not sound like what he had said in London, but different audiences got different messages. The Toronto press was not impressed with King's performance in Geneva. The *Globe* was clear that "No one can be accused of distortion of his text … who sees it as a step toward isolation … A direct assertion of Canada's determination to work with Britain and the rest of the Empire for the preservation of peace would have set the troublemaking nations thinking. The Prime Minister neglected a ready-made opportunity." The *Mail and Empire* was even more direct in its criticism. "Liberal coldness to Great Britain is again weakening the Empire and encouraging the Empire's enemies. This in spite of the fact that Canada depends for its defence almost entirely upon the British taxpayer. Is this course honourable? Is it remotely decent? Is it calculated to preserve peace?"[44]

Having told the "League of Notions" what he thought of it and having himself no constructive idea of what to do about it, King turned his mind to what he assumed would be his imminent trip from Geneva to Berlin. To reconfirm that the British government had no objection to his visit to Hitler, King spoke with Eden in Geneva, telling him that he had "for some time" been considering a visit to Germany (although not adding the corollary that at the same time he had been "divinely ordained" to bring peace to Europe). Having repeatedly eschewed in the past any idea of a common imperial foreign policy, he now informed Eden that he would speak to Hitler on behalf of the whole British Empire. He would let him know that some of his policies were costing him friends, hastily adding, however, "that was not so far as Canada, for example, and other parts of the Empire were concerned … [they had no] thought of continued enmity towards Germany but a desire to have friendly relations all around."[45] What if anything Eden made of King's claim to be expounding to Hitler a common foreign policy for the British Commonwealth is unknown, but he did offer to have the British Embassy in Berlin facilitate his visit. The ambassador was always ready to help those dominions without representation in Germany (only the independent-minded South Africa and the Irish Free State had legations). Eden himself had growing reservations about the course of aggression and violence that Hitler was following. The previous year he had recorded how on a visit to Berlin he had been "unfavourably impressed by Hitler's personality … He appeared negative to me, certainly not compelling … rather shifty."[46] But before Munich Eden was never clearly anti-appeasement; hence he told King that he supposed his visit could do no harm.

With that vaguely reassuring endorsement, King was ready to travel to Berlin from Geneva by the end of September 1936. But first he arranged to meet Giorgia de Cousandier in Milan. No doubt they discussed the League and Abyssinia and, perhaps, as he had said in his letter to her of two months before, the way in which goodwill could be restored "between the people of the British Empire [for whom King again saw himself as speaking] and Italy."* Upon returning to Geneva, however, King learned from the British embassy in Berlin, via London, that Hitler was unable to receive him during

---

*King did not see Cousandier again until Paris in August 1946, when he was immensely gratified that she had translated into Italian Emil Ludwig's recently published sycophantic *Mackenzie King: A Portrait Sketch*. Near destitute at the end of the war, she pleaded with him to arrange for her a much-coveted clerical appointment as a local employee at the proposed Canadian Legation in Rome. For whatever reason, the coveted job did not materialize. King was, however, still writing to her, and to Julia Grant in Washington, from his deathbed in Ottawa in 1950.

the autumn. He was disappointed but, in his own mind at least, he simply postponed his visit to the summer of the following year, 1937. He then spent a week in Paris where he saw Leon Blum, the Popular Front prime minister who was deeply uneasy at the unpredictability of Hitler's aggressive tendencies. King returned to London to consult with ministers about what, if anything, was to be done about the League and Hitler's reoccupation of the Rhineland and thereby his repudiation of the treaties of Versailles and Locarno. King did not differ from those who spoke placidly about Germany reoccupying its own backyard. He placed a special emphasis on doing nothing, justifying his inaction by insisting that Canada was simply a more difficult country to govern than most.

King rejected out of hand a suggestion from Massey in London that he use a planted question in the House of Commons in Ottawa to create an opportunity to set forth the government's attitude toward the reoccupation of the Rhineland. With some exasperation (Massey constantly annoyed him), King replied that a planted question "would only serve to provoke controversy from one end of Canada to the other."[47] Similarly, King told Grant Dexter of the *Winnipeg Free Press* that foreign affairs had to be downplayed since they were the principal threat to national unity.[48]

King remained consistent in his efforts to avoid public discussion of external affairs, both within parliament and without, convinced that amidst the deepening deterioration in Europe, "the least that is said means the least stirring up in the Commons and the Press and in the minds of the people." He continued to believe that foreign policy controversies were not for the minds of the people, at least not for the minds of a people preoccupied with the aftermath of the economic depression.[49] One neophyte backbencher, Paul Martin, who aspired to contribute to foreign policy debates, recalled that in the years leading up to the declaration of war in September 1939, "most Liberal MPs uncritically accepted King's every opinion on foreign affairs."[50] Martin, however, "saw clearly that the League of Nations was ... an ineffective operation not because the idea was wrong, but because of the failure of its members to live up to their obligations. And Canada was one of those that did not." But the prime minister, by limiting the opportunities for debate, was not going to have a young backbencher talking like that in the House of Commons. John Diefenbaker, the future Conservative prime minister, had it about right when he later said of King that he "considered foreign policy to be his own prerogative, and he did not like to have our external relations discussed in Parliament. Those debates that did take place … tended to be extremely general in context, and they were few and far between."[51] For King it was better to say nothing about the dictators and hope for the best.

Yet while still in London during the last fortnight of October, King must have heard something of the growing unease there about the dictators. Neville Chamberlain, who was to succeed Baldwin as prime minister in May 1937, described Hitler as half-mad and a lunatic and Goebbels as having a vulgar, common little mind. The Foreign Office, headed by Sir Robert Vansittart, had never been in any doubt that Hitler was "a half-mad, ridiculously dangerous demagogue."[52] Vansittart's brother-in-law, Sir Eric Phipps, the ambassador in Berlin, saw Hitler as a "psychopathic gangster." Others in London, however, regarded Hitler as not such a bad fellow. From the generally pro-fascist "Cliveden Set," Philip Kerr (as Lord Lothian, sent by Chamberlain as British ambassador to the United States on the eve of the Second World War) disagreed with Phipps. For him Hitler was "a visionary rather than a gangster." Lord Londonderry, the former secretary of the state for air, matched Lloyd George's admiration for the anti-communist Führer, a view which he freely expressed to anyone in either Britain or Germany who would listen to him or read his several pro-fascist tracts. But a parliamentary colleague characterized him "as not really equipped for thinking … Londonderry took himself very seriously and that was in a sense a tragedy, because others didn't take him at all seriously."[53] His writings, such as *Ourselves and Germany*, were dismissed by many as "Londonderry Herrs," but he and others in the upper reaches of British society did give a sort of spurious respectability to domestic pro-fascism. The German ambassador duly reported to Berlin that "the attitude of the City, in spite of Jewish influence, was against war-mongering." He also mentioned individual pro-Germans: "Lord Londonderry … as well as Lloyd George and Snowden, Lothian and the Anglo-German Fellowship [of Lord Mount Temple], and finally the wise and noble ruler of the British Empire [King Edward VIII]."[54] On 27 October, after an audience with Edward VIII, King recorded in his diary that "He … said to me that he meant to keep England out of war at all costs … I said that nothing could be worse than war; that to avoid it one should be prepared to incur almost any sacrifice."[55] This interview with his sovereign was for King further confirmation of what he had written in his diary four days before. "What has been told to me to-day has been a revelation as to how close one can be brought to the very summit of affairs ... There is no doubt that the voice of the Prime Minister of Canada is very far reaching in the affairs of the British Empire."[56]

His visit to Hitler postponed, King also called on Baldwin, whom he had met at imperial conferences as early as 1923. The exhausted and sickly prime minister had just seen Britain through the upheaval of the abdication of King Edward VIII and the unexpected succession to the throne of his brother as King George VI. Baldwin's limited view of the growing threat of Germany was based in part on his understanding of Hitler's ambition to win *Lebensraum* in Eastern Europe. "If there is any fighting in Europe to be done, I should like to see the Bolshies and the Nazis doing it."[57] King, a believer in the merits of personal diplomacy, joined others in London in urging Baldwin to visit Hitler as he himself proposed to do. Baldwin, although convinced that Mussolini and Hitler "were lunatics,"[58] declared himself not averse, but did not do so in the months that remained before Chamberlain succeeded him as prime minister.

From his conversations with Baldwin and others, although certainly not with Vincent Massey, who made him so uncomfortable, King would have been aware of the British government's decision – dangerously late in Churchill's view – to accelerate its programme of rearmament centred on the widespread fear that "the bomber always gets through." The year before, Hitler, again disregarding the Treaty of Versailles, had created a peacetime army of thirty-six divisions, introduced conscription, and confirmed the existence of a banned Luftwaffe. The British response to this and much else – the reoccupation of the Rhineland, the Berlin-Rome axis, the Spanish Civil War, and the German-Japanese anti-comintern agreement – first took the form of seemingly endless memoranda passing among committees of the cabinet and the chiefs of staff (who remained preoccupied by the dreaded possibility of a three-front war), but did eventually resolve into decisions to provide more funds for the renewal and expansion of the armed forces and yet more importantly of defence industries. The repeated delays in reaching these decisions, strongly opposed by Labour, were partly the result of fiscal constraints and partly of profound popular opposition to rearmament (the "Peace Ballot" of June having confirmed the degree of public fear of a second world war).

Chamberlain as chancellor of the exchequer, reluctant though he was to divert funds from social programmes, ensured that the increased defence spending was largely on the Royal Air Force (RAF), represented publicly as a defensive rather than an offensive arm. Baldwin added to King that Canada could play a vital part in the expansion of the RAF by the joint flying training over the vast empty skies of Canada and the supply of certain equipment. Chamberlain was not optimistic about Canada's response. Sounding like his late father, he had concluded at the 1936 imperial conference that "One of our greatest difficulties has been to keep the Dominions in step. Since the Statute of Westminster they have become extraordinarily touchy about their status and are always on the look out to see that we don't attempt to speak for them or assume that they will take the same view as we do. On this occasion we took immense pains to spare their susceptibilities and to keep them informed of the constant changes in the situation."[59]

Concurrently in Canada, the few Nazi supporters, having garnered little political support, came to the not very surprising conclusion that they would achieve greater status, visibility, and impact if they were to form one national organization. Adrien Arcand in Montreal and Joseph Farr in Toronto and, to a lesser extent, William Whittaker in Winnipeg began to collaborate, having identified synergies that a single national organization might achieve. Arcand, conscious of the benefits of fascist cooperation worldwide, was exchanging greetings with fascist parties in Britain, France, the United States, Belgium, Brazil, South Africa, Portugal, Australia, Southern Rhodesia (today's Zimbabwe), Sweden, Paraguay, the Netherlands, Spain, and Argentina (he praised the military dictatorship in Japan for being opposed to communists and Jews). In that long list of correspondents, he remained loyal to his first love, Mussolini's Italy, but his ties were especially strong with fascists in Britain, France, and the United States. Paradoxically, a surprisingly fervent supporter of the British Empire, Arcand never wavered in his necessarily distant attempts to help conciliate Britain and Germany. His admiration for Oswald Mosley never faltered. His cooperation with fascists in the United States had begun with Karl Ludecke's visit in 1932, the year before Hitler became chancellor. During Ludecke's second visit to Montreal in 1933, Arcand, supported by Senator Blondin, attempted in vain to arrange a meeting for Ludecke with Prime Minister Bennett. Perhaps Arcand's choice of words in praise of Bennett on the occasion of the Imperial Economic Conference in Ottawa the previous year had not helped. He had welcomed Bennett to the conference as part of the "fight against Jews and communists in the name of a vigorous British Empire."[60]

146   Mackenzie King in the Age of the Dictators

Arcand never succeeded in his attempts to win recognition from politicians of whatever level. His efforts were amateurish and futile. He flirted briefly with the isolationist, anti-British mayor of Montreal, Camillien Houde, and the premier of Quebec, Maurice Duplessis, who was too wily to be caught up in Arcand's extremism. And Senator Blondin remained primarily interested in how many, if any, votes Arcand could deliver to the Conservative Party. The resounding Liberal victory in the election of 1935 ended any truck, however slight, that fascists had through him with a mainstream political party.

Arcand was, however, encouraged by the visits to Montreal of Henry Beament, Mosley's chief operating officer in the British Union of Fascists, and from Céline, the *nom de plume* of the prominent French nihilistic and anti-Semitic physician, journalist, and novelist Louis-Ferdinand des Touches. He was especially gratified to receive an invitation to join the platform party of leading American Nazis at a mass rally at the New York Hippodrome on 30 October 1937, where the New York Police Band entertained the pro-Hitler, anti-Semitic audience estimated at 10,000. Later Arcand joined the other speakers and leading American Nazis at a dinner at the Harvard Club (where King and Roosevelt were both members). He pledged the collaboration of Canadian Nazis with American, resulting in coverage of Canadian Nazis in both the popular *Life* magazine and the more thoughtful *Foreign Affairs*.

In measured terms in *Foreign Affairs*, the anonymous author "S" (Frank Scott of McGill University) described for a mainly American audience how at a time when fascism was making notable progress in Latin America, it was also doing so in Quebec. "The most French and Catholic province in the Dominion ... has been the scene of a number of incidents which bear all the marks of fascist inspiration." Strongly anti-communist, anti-Semitic, and supporters of a corporate state though they were, the members of Arcand's National Socialist Christian Party were not so numerous as to present a threat to civil order, but they nevertheless represented a worrisome element in Quebec and, by extension, Canada.[61] *Life* magazine, as was to be expected, was more sensational, describing the founding rally of the National Unity Party at Massey Hall in Toronto as "a fine display of rabble rousing and Jew-baiting ... Arcand is something new in North America with his violent social prejudices and his militarized battalion of 3,000 men ... It is a sinister fact that by day Fascist Arcand, as press agent, edits the official paper of Quebec's premier Maurice Duplessis, a rabid Red baiter in his own right. By night Arcand is busy with his Fascism ... Yet for Canadians as a whole, Fascism is still a minor matter. Five times as many people attended an anti-Fascist rally in Toronto as listened to M. Arcand. Only in French-speaking Quebec, with one of the lowest standards of living in the Dominion, has it yet raised a commanding voice."[62] T.D. Bouchard, the long-time mayor of St- Hyacinthe and member of the Quebec legislature and later a senator, recorded both graphically and woefully the pro-Nazi and anti-Semitic agitation in his hometown.[63]

A cette époque, Hitler était au sommet de sa popularité et comptait, dans la métropole, des partisans. Ceux-ci avaient réussi à recruter, à Saint-Hyacinthe, des adeptes de l'hitlérisme. Ils étaient, naturellement, au nombre de mes ennemis. Je favorisais alors l'adoption d'un règlement accordant une subvention aux propriétaries d'une manufacture de vêtements, pour leur permettre d'agrandir leur établissement dans le but de donner du travail à un plus grand nombre d'ouvriers. Ces industriels étaient des Israélites. La nuit qui précéda la présentation de cette mesure au conseil, les Chemises brunes garnirent les glaces des vitrines de nos magasins situés en plein quartier commercial, de placards invitant les citoyens a s'insurger contre ce projet conçu par le maire pour "judaïser notre ville française." Ces appels à l'anti-sémitisme reçurent l'accueil qu'ils méritaient; il n'y eut que quatorze fanatiques, sur une population de quatorze mille âmes, qui désapprouverent notre règlement ...

Hitler était à l'apogée de sa puissance et ses adeptes au pays extériorisaient leur sentiment en faveur d'un régime dictatorial. Durant la nuit de Noël 1936, dans la chapelle du Collège des Frères du Sacré-Coeur, des fascistes de Saint-Hyacinthe, vêtus de leur uniforme de parade, s'étaient approches de la Sainte Table, au moment de la communion, en formation militaire. L'occasion était mal choisie pour s'affirmer de la sorte car, depuis quelques mois déjà des rumeurs de guerre nous parvenaient d'Europe.

Mackenzie King, intending to visit Hitler in 1936 as the third stage in his four-part external affairs project, had hoped to demonstrate thereby to the electorate that he had made every effort to promote permanent peace in Europe, but when Hitler indicated that the autumn of 1936 was inconvenient,

King decided not to delay his parallel fourth stage, modest rearmament, while rescheduling his visit to Hitler for the summer of 1937. Chamberlain, and possibly even King himself, increasingly took the position that a policy of appeasement would always fail in this imperfect world without military power to back it. The Soviet ambassador to the United Kingdom had put the point clearly in 1935: "By all means talk with Hitler and come to agreements and compromises. But talk to him with a rifle in your hand or he will pay no regard to your wishes."[64]

On New Year's Day 1937, King stood at attention in front of his radio as it played "God Save the King." Thus inspired, he pondered whether a strengthened Royal Canadian Air Force (RCAF) could be publicly presented as the leading element in an entirely defensive defence policy, a possible way around the problems inherent in the expansion of the Canadian army, which would be looked on with suspicion if not hostility in Quebec, where army divisions were seen as carrying in their knapsacks the possibility, sooner or later, of conscription. He concluded that the expansion of the RCAF, however modest, might do something to satisfy those English Canadians who were increasingly uneasy at the deplorable state of their armed forces, and might not wholly alienate Quebec. The rub was that the expansion of the air force and even the trifling support for the other two services cost money that could, in the eyes of the CCF as well, be better spent on social programmes.

From Quebec, Chubby Power, the minister of health, explained: "in 1937 the clouds of war, hovering over Europe and becoming daily more menacing ... the Minister of National Defence, Ian Mackenzie, felt that it was his duty to bring before the cabinet for support greatly increased estimates for national defence, especially to augment the infant air service. Immediately there was an outcry, both from Quebec and from a number of people strongly antagonistic to these estimates." Mackenzie responded, "There is no idea whatever of sending a single Canadian soldier overseas in any expeditionary force and there is not a single cent providing for that in the estimates. They are for the direct defence of Canada and for *the defence of Canadian neutrality*" (my italics). Lapointe added, "we are not committed. We shall decide when the time comes ... I trust the circumstances will justify Canada in remaining outside any conflict."[65] Mackenzie tabled estimates that were modestly increased from $15 million in fiscal year 1935–36 to $19 million in 1936–37. In hindsight it was a ludicrously small increase, but by doing little for the army and navy and favouring the air force, King could recommend the estimates to the House "as a Canadian defence policy for the direct defence of our Canadian shores and our Canadian homes." To include three "Canadians" in a single sentence would have led at least some members to infer rightly that King wanted them to recognize that there were no overseas commitments foreshadowed in the modestly augmented defence budget of December 1936. Skelton, ever the isolationist and even neutralist, argued with King against the small increase on the grounds that the Department of National Defence was covertly planning an overseas expeditionary force.

Even before the debate on the defence estimates in February 1937, the CCF had moved that "In the event of war, Canada should remain strictly neutral regardless of who [sic] the belligerents may be."[66] The debate was unusual in that no Conservative members participated, the partisan theory being that "Opposition speeches in favour of a Commonwealth defence policy would make it easier for the dissident Liberals [French Canadian members unhappy about the increased estimates] to support the Government's more limited Canadian defence policy. Silence might force the Liberal divisions into the open."[67] King knew very well the basic problem: "French Canada … thinks there is some conspiracy to have Canada drawn into Imperial wars."[68] Lapointe, who did not speak in the debate other than for one brief interjection, made certain that, for the ears of Quebec, Hansard included it. The increased estimates being for the defence of Canada only, "Canadian soldiers cannot be sent to the battlefields of Europe." A CCF amendment condemning the increased defence spending was readily defeated by a combination of Liberals and Conservatives. King was highly gratified. "One thing is certain. The right course has been steered, just enough has been done and not too much. We have kept the unity of the Party, and the unity of the country which, after all, is the important thing."[69] Thereafter King kept repeating that there was no overseas service foreseen for the marginally increased forces, only domestic defence. Many members, for whatever reasons, swallowed that sophistry. To be sure, there were from time to time a few growls and grumbles about even this modest defence spending, but since they were generally made in French (there were no interpreters either in the House of Commons or in the Liberal caucus), King was content with his Quebec lieutenant's reassurance that if the emphasis was kept on domestic defence (whatever exactly that was), the discontents of Quebec could be contained. Unlike Ian Mackenzie, King made no reference to "Canadian neutrality," but in a long statement to the House on 25 January 1937, he stressed yet again that any decision about going to war would be for parliament to decide.

In the debates of defence estimates on 18 February 1937, the CCF, not Quebec members, took the lead in arguing that government spending should not be on the armed forces but, as Canada was beginning to emerge from the depression, on social services. CCF member M.J. Coldwell suspected that the army was receiving more money than the government publicly acknowledged. "We are told by the Prime Minister that if war should come, Canada would decide. But, taking these estimates at face value, it seems to me that some sort of decision has already been made."[70] Mackenzie duly repeated that the forces "were entirely for the protection of Canadian shores." But no one appears to have questioned how a soldier or airman, once fully trained, was not as qualified for overseas service as domestic. Later, sounding as convoluted as his prime minister, Mackenzie elaborated: "In maintaining the essential principles of Canadian unity ... the prevailing sentiment of public opinion ... today would not be in favour of committing the Canadian people to automatic responsibilities in regard to any centralized or coordinated scheme or plan of defence."[71]

In the debates, the Conservatives, keeping their eye on their still depleted fortunes in Quebec, were careful in what they said in favour of increased defence spending. It was the anti-military, even pacifist, CCF that made an issue over the votes for cadet training, stores, bases, the Royal Military College, exchange of officers with the United Kingdom, ratio of officers to men, etc., etc., despite the fact that the total army permanent force was only a little over 4,000. Throughout the defence debates, no one, including the prime minister, ever suggested that the armed forces might do well to be more welcoming to and accommodating of French-speaking volunteers. And French-Canadian members of parliament took little direct part in the defence debates: that was an English-Canadian vocation and, in any case, there was no translation service. They relied, with good reason, on Lapointe to ensure that on fundamental issues their voice was heard loudly and clearly by the prime minister and the cabinet. The CCF took the occasion to include another broadside about how King had defined Canada's position on the Abyssinian crisis, this time by the pacifist Agnes Macphail (the first woman member of parliament): "If there were anything necessary to stop Italy in Abyssinia, it would be the application of oil sanctions. This

Government repudiated the suggestion supposed to have been made by Canada's representative at Geneva. Could there be anything more calculated to give assurance to Italy that Canada was not with the League than this attitude with respect to the application of sanctions? It was a matter of giving comfort to the enemy, and I say in doing so that Canada sabotaged the League." To this unrelenting broadside King contented himself by saying that an oil sanction was merely "a suggestion of a committee of the League." For some reason, he concluded the debate by reading to the House from *Hamlet* (a copy of which, he said, he happened to find in his pocket) the advice of Polonius to his son, Laertes, which includes "give thy thoughts no tongue, nor any unproportioned thought his act … give every man thine ear, but few thy voice" (act 1, scene 3).

With the adoption of the defence estimates, King now felt better equipped to proceed to London for almost two months to revel in the pageantry of the coronation of King George VI, to be followed by the 1937 imperial conference and by his postponed visit to Germany. But first, in early March, when parliament was still in session, he took another fortnight holiday in the United States, this time at Virginia Beach. Overnight at the White House was the high point of his holiday, although Cordell Hull, the secretary of state, and possibly others, regarded it as primarily an opportunity for the president to enlist "the American" as an advocate of tariff reductions, especially of imperial preferences, at the pending imperial conference.* Roosevelt and King also discussed King's vague idea of a reconstructed League of Nations, which at least Italy might be enticed to rejoin, as well as the president's equally vague idea of a universal conference for peace. (Churchill always regretted that Chamberlain had rejected this idea out of hand). On his return to Ottawa, King wrote to Roosevelt underscoring his "desire to co-operate in every way towards furthering the peace of the world"[72] and offering to promote the common interests of the British Empire and the United States.

That was King's message to Roosevelt. But with the British ambassador in Washington he had left a quite different impression. King incongruously

---

*The Canadian public certainly had no idea of what the visit was about. Typically in an Ottawa press conference King was obfuscation itself. "He told the assembled reporters he was off to Washington to see FDR. 'What is the purpose of your visit?' a Quebec scribe asked. 'To discuss the situation,' King replied. 'What situation?' the reporter inquired. 'Matters of mutual interest' King answered. And that was the extent of it" (Levin, *King*, 267).

employed terms that might be welcome to American interlocutors, but hardly to the British ambassador, who reported that he had said "that Canada was resolved to maintain neutrality in any war at any price, and that on no account would she be dragged into any hostilities ... [an] attitude that corresponded very closely to that generally adopted in America."[73] If King did say that – and it is highly unlikely that the ambassador would have misunderstood him – it remains a puzzling statement. If he really did say that his government was resolved to maintain neutrality in any war at any price, he was directly contradicting himself. From 1923 he had repeatedly affirmed to the British government that if "a great and clear call of duty comes, Canada will respond, whether or not the United States responds." Perhaps he had concluded that by presenting himself to the British ambassador as a neutralist, he could somehow enhance the chances of the United States and the United Kingdom each recognizing him as a valued interlocutor between them (they of course did not need him, being perfectly capable of speaking in the same tongue to each other). Intentionally or otherwise, King seems to have gotten his signals crossed.

While King was moving cautiously toward rebuilding Canada's armed forces, guerilla resistance continued in Ethiopia. In 1938, Britain and France recognized the king of Italy as the emperor of Abyssinia, and not until June 1940, when Mussolini declared war on France and Great Britain, did the Ethiopian Free Forces begin to receive the military assistance that enabled them to re-enter Addis Ababa in May 1941.

11

Appeasement

From the debacle of the Hoare-Laval pact in December 1935 to the Anglo-French recognition of the king of Italy as emperor of Abyssinia in November 1938, the Dominions Office was assiduous in keeping the dominions fully, even exhaustively, informed of British attempts to conclude with Italy a comprehensive agreement that would settle such disparate matters as the borders of Italian and British Somaliland, the status of Italian nationals in Palestine and Syria, the evacuation of foreign volunteers in the Spanish Civil War, the activities of Christian missionaries in Abyssinia, and the territorial integrity of Saudi Arabia and the Yemen.[1] The diligence of the Dominions Office and Foreign Office arose in part from a belief that it would prove useful to have the dominions, partners in the League, fully aware of how Anglo-French efforts to appease Mussolini and soon Hitler were progressing. But King showed no interest. In light of Lapointe's messages about the intransigence of Quebec against collective security under the League, he did not bother to read the long cypher messages from London. In his attempts to understand what was actually happening in Spain or Germany or Italy or elsewhere across Europe, he had handicapped himself by continuing to limit his sources of information, ignoring the almost daily telegrams from London describing at length the darkening developments in Europe. When General Andrew McNaughton became chief of staff in early 1929, he wrote to his minister, "Most of the [British Intelligence] information stops in the [Defence] Department ... I do not think we as a country are getting all the benefit out of it that we should. I think much of it should be of use to ... External Affairs."[2] King was not persuaded. He continued to doubt whether Canadian diplomats were capable of judging for themselves the quality and value of the freely offered "prints" of British despatches, telegrams, and intelligence reports. Still occasionally vocal about imperial centralists, whom he portrayed for Quebec as tireless in their schemes to return hapless Canada to a quasi-colonial status, he continued to decline offers of the Foreign Office to share yet more information and comment from a range of British sources. The proffered diplomatic and other reports might somehow be a British ploy to enmesh Ottawa in unwanted commitments or detract from Canada's autonomous place in the British Commonwealth of Nations, and hence might be suspected in Quebec as a commitment to the Empire.*

Equally, King did not welcome comment from the Canadian High Commission in London. As the prime minister of a dominion, he saw himself as dealing directly with his homologue, the British prime minister, or if necessary with the secretary of state for the dominions. In his several insecurities, King wanted no intermediary at Canada House advising him, certainly not Vincent Massey, whom he regarded as excessive in his admiration for all things British. He continued to forbid him from attending the weekly meetings between the several high commissioners and the secretary of state for the dominions, Malcolm MacDonald (the son of the former prime minister Ramsay MacDonald). Such weekly meetings might be misinterpreted, especially in Quebec, as an imperial council. Both Larkin and Massey (but not Ferguson) were accordingly put to the time-consuming awkwardness of having to request separate meetings – and even then to use a back door – to receive the same information made available to the other high commissioners at their weekly meetings. That King continued to oppose participation in such conversations led MacDonald to write to him on 22 May 1936 that Massey had told him of a telegram from Ottawa indicating that "there is some apprehension on the part of the Canadian Government lest an erroneous impression may be created in Canada as to the object of such meetings." MacDonald repeated to the British high commissioner in Ottawa

---

*The present author as a junior – very junior – foreign service officer in the Department of External Affairs during the late 1950s never sensed that his Canadian judgment or that of his fellows was eroded by reading regularly – with admiration as well as edification – the perceptive Foreign Office "prints" and other analytical material that London freely made available to the dominions (and Kim Philby et al. freely made available to the Russians). Especially useful were copies of reports from British missions in those many countries where Canada had no diplomatic representation. One of our senior colleagues, Charles Ritchie, had it right when he wrote in July 1939, "For a mixture of naiveté and cunning give me any British Ambassador – and their prose – the casual style, the careful avoidance of purple passages and fine phrases, every now and then the rather wry little joke" (Ritchie, *Siren Years*, 35).

that he had affirmed to Massey that prime minister-to-prime minister or minister-to-minister was the channel always to be followed on any matter of policy. His informal meetings with the high commissioners were to exchange background information and clearly not to reach any conclusions or commitments.[3] Massey thereafter simply ignored King's *ukase* against participation, bringing benefit to all concerned, including to King himself. Yet to Massey's repeated suggestion that Canada House could be more effective in providing information to Ottawa than occasional prime-minister-to-prime-minister exchanges, King replied, "I know this British crowd … they wanted watching." Massey concluded that King's "point of view … seemed to reflect an anti-British bias (one of the most powerful factors in his make-up), extreme egoism … and a very definite lack of confidence in my own ability to withstand … sinister British influences."[4]

Shortly before the month-long 1937 imperial conference which began on 14 May, MacDonald told a meeting of his fellow ministers and senior officials that at the conference he hoped to "state the foreign policy of the United Kingdom, to ask the Dominion Delegations to indicate the foreign policies of their Governments, and then to hope that these policies might so harmonize that, in effect, they would be one."[5] Cooperation in defence policy might then naturally follow from voluntary harmonization of foreign policy. The odds, however, were against MacDonald. A senior official saw clearly where things were going. "In so far as appeasement called for an attempt to come to an understanding with the Dictators, this was not a policy forced on the Dominions by Chamberlain, most of them expressed this general idea before the Conference started. Nor was the policy dictated to Chamberlain by the Dominions, though in yielding later to Hitler's demands over Czechoslovakia, Chamberlain may well have recalled the refusal of all the Dominions to be involved in British policy vis-à-vis Central and Eastern Europe."[6] As Middlemas has confirmed, "The Dominions were never united in an imperial foreign policy and were only rarely sympathetic to the European involvement of Britain, yet they represented liabilities which had to be defended … The Dominions … continued generally … to object to any further British commitment to Europe … and this pressure on London was used by the British Government at will to justify its profoundly mistrustful attitude towards continental involvement."[7]

King, although no longer terrified by imperial conferences, arrived in London in May 1937 with myriad reasons for still doing as little as possible, whatever might be the ambitions for a solid "British front" in the increasingly gloomy international scene. At earlier imperial conferences, Australia and New Zealand had often followed a divergent course from Canada, offering King and Skelton more evidence for questioning the possibility of a common imperial foreign or defence policy. A basic if unspoken assumption was that Canada could, if necessary, shelter under the umbrella of the United States, whereas Australia and New Zealand were dangerously exposed in the Pacific to possible Japanese aggression, with only a distant prospect of military assistance from a chronically overstretched United Kingdom caught up in European entanglements. An Australian historian accurately described King's unspoken attitude. "It cost him no effort to turn in upon Canada. For thus he could avoid the complications of Empire, of the League of Nations, and of foreign affairs outside North America, whilst taking advantage of the shield provided by the United States."[8]

During the 1937 imperial conference, the prime minister of New Zealand was blunt to King: Canada had evaded its international obligations and was joining in the destruction of the League of Nations of which it was a member. King hardly bothered to respond. He was content, with the support of South Africa, to see the end of collective security, New Zealand notwithstanding. But the Canadian historian James Eayrs had the final word on this fundamental difference between the two dominions. New Zealand "set an example of honesty in a singularly dishonest period ... the New Zealand Government did what one government could do to raise the standard of morality in an era that was setting new records for political degradation [and] ... expedient dishonesty. The proof that Canada should have been concerned is found in the fact that the failure of the League brought many thousands of Canadians to their death in another war. It is true that Canadian efforts would almost certainly have failed, as did those of the sister Dominion. But New Zealand at least tried."[9]

King continued to be wary of imperial conferences appearing as a council making decisions affecting all members. In the meetings, he told his peers that they had gathered as a pragmatic "Conference of Ministers to state our own position and see how far our policies could be brought toward some point of agreement." For the prime ministers of Canada and South Africa, as Eayrs observed, "the delicate balance of ethnic, regional and political interests on which the internal stability of their countries depended, remained the prime concern. The imperial conference could not be allowed to upset it."[10] Its function, King declared, "is not to formulate or declare policy. The value of this, as of other Imperial Conferences, lies mainly in the free exchange of information and opinion." There should be no resolutions, a practice alien to imperial conferences. Resolutions would be certain to precipitate an unsettling domestic debate on foreign affairs within Canada. Equally, public revelations of the differences between French and English Canada over foreign policy, defence collaboration, or guarantees of wartime supplies, even of foodstuffs and raw materials, must be avoided. With notable candour, King shared with the conference his satisfaction at how he "had endeavoured to prevent discussion on foreign affairs in Parliament by persuading Members in [the Liberal] caucus to leave the matter alone in the House of Commons."[11]

On the first day of the conference, Eden, as foreign secretary, began his detailed and articulate if largely inconclusive statement by sharing his misgivings about the Abyssinian debacle. "During Italy's campaign in Abyssinia the position in Europe was still further complicated by Germany's reoccupation of the Rhineland. This event made France … more than ever determined not to entangle itself in an African adventure. A distinct divergence of view really existed between France and ourselves in respect of the Abyssinian dispute. Some day history may be able to tell the true story of what passed between M. Laval and Signor Mussolini in January 1935. Was it true, as M. Laval had assured British Ministers, that he had only agreed to make certain economic concessions to Italy in Abyssinia, or was it true, as Signor Mussolini maintained, that he [Laval] had given Italy a free hand in Abyssinia?" Those questions led Eden to a more fundamental one. "If France had given whole-hearted support to the Oil Sanction … would the League have been successful, and would Italy have been restrained?" To which he added wryly, "one grim fact remained … that Italy was now enduring the severest sanction of all, namely, the possession of Abyssinia, while the League had failed." Eden continued, "In our view if the League had succeeded against Italy it would be stronger and better prepared to face any future aggressor. In the view of France, Italy must not be antagonised lest she should be driven into the German camp." The members of the League were then confronted with the fundamental question of what was to become of it. "There was a divergence of views between those who favoured the strengthening of the Covenant, the closer definition of obligations, and the making of those obligations more far-reaching and more automatic, and on the other hand the view of those" – perhaps at that point looking at

Mackenzie King – "who thought that everything possible be done to facilitate the return of non-members of the League, even to the extent of eliminating sanctions."[12]

Surprisingly, King began his initial statement to the conference by praising Eden for "the balanced judgement and the combination of idealistic principles and frank facing of realities which we have come to expect from Mr Eden" (presumably King had forgiven him for what he had seen as his unprincipled manipulation of Riddell and Ferguson and his efforts to bring Germany and Italy to their knees two years before). King, however, stayed well away from the thorny question of Anglo-French relations. Equally, there was no word of criticism of the dictators, of the evil of Hitler and the foul buffoonery of Mussolini. No word of what King himself might do at home to help open the eyes of English and French Canadians alike to the iniquitous ambitions of the two dictators. Instead, he spent a major part of his long, rambling, and largely sterile opening statement and subsequent interventions still decrying the collective security of the now near defunct League of Nations, as well as describing in great detail Canada's relations with the United States.

In the Abyssinian dispute public opinion supported giving the method of sanctions a fair trial in what appeared the most favourable conditions possible for the experiment. Disillusionment followed. There are still elements which favour a policy of collective sanctions, but they are in a minority; in some cases their support is based upon a desire to turn the League of Nations into an anti-fascist alliance. There is no question that public and parliamentary opinion at present is emphatically against any interpretation of League policy which would involve automatic sanctions.[13]*

*Perhaps coincidentally, Skelton was at the same time decrying the League of Nations to an audience in Missouri. Presumably having cleared the text with his minister – although that is not evident – he said, "With a universal and firm undertaking in advance to use force against any and every aggressor out of the question for the present ... alternative policies are being sought. The advocates of securing peace by force follow the old cul-de-sacs of individual rearmament and regional military alliances, or explore the newer proposals which would divide the world into two or three camps based on ideological sympathies. At the same time, less spectacular but more constructive efforts are being made to rebuild confidence and restore co-operation. Trade and currency agreements are sought in. the conviction that economic stability and prosperity will drive out the fear and unrest that are at the bottom of political tension and military arrogance" (*Our Generation*, 60).

In Canada the people had been much disillusioned by what had happened at the League. With this latest failure and with the United States remaining outside, it would be very difficult if sanctions were insisted upon, to keep Canada in the League. The neutrality law had given the people of the United States of America a feeling of great security. In Canada, people were saying that membership in the League constituted a real risk of their becoming involved in war.[14] ...

The League of Nations has failed and Ethiopia has perished.[15]

Chamberlain rather lamely proposed that advantage should be taken of the League's failure over Abyssinia and the recognition of the futility of sanctions by "emphasising strongly the bearing of these events on the importance of pressing forward with the examination of the future organisation of the League of Nations."[16] Quite how that might be done or what he expected to come of it he did not say. Nor was positive thinking about the League or how it might be successfully reshaped reflected in King's subsequent statements. He concluded "that the sanctions provisions of the Covenant have ceased to have effect ... and nothing should now be done which could facilitate their revival."[17]

The limited discussion of trade that did take place at the conference centred on it as the most promising route available to closer cooperation between the British Commonwealth and the United States, but when "confronted with the full details of the American [tariff] demands ... [even King's] enthusiasm for acting as a mediator failed." In short, "The Commonwealth no doubt was not yet prepared to pay the American bill for uncertain political gains."[18] In face of the American demands, King made little headway in fostering support in London for an early Anglo-American trade agreement that he believed would help to set the stage for wider "economic appeasement," seen by many in the City as helping to counter a second world war, which would erode British economic power. Liberalized trade and investment – across Europe and, even more important, across the Atlantic – would, the optimists hoped, emerge from a settlement of Germany's various grievances.

Having given up on the League of Nations and transatlantic trade liberalization, King might have been expected to hazard a word or two, however vague, in favour of greater Commonwealth collaboration, including in rearmament. He was coming to recognize the necessity of rearmament in Canada even in the face of continuing opposition in Quebec. Eden had emphasized in his unequivocal opening statement: "we must rearm." Any reform of the League of Nations would carry little conviction without parallel rearmament. King, with his eye on Quebec's many seats in the House of Commons, continued to reject imperial defence collaboration before a major conflict had actually begun. Canada would not issue – in one of Skelton's favourite clichés – blank cheques in advance. "In some sections of the country [i.e., Quebec]," King repeated, "public opinion is practically unanimous against any participation in either a League or a Commonwealth war." For Britain and the dominions to consult together on foreign or defence policy in the name of imperial unity could imperil Canadian unity. In any event, as King repeatedly stated, if the question of Canada's participation in a major war did arise, parliament would decide. The greatest contribution that Canada could make to the British Commonwealth was to keep itself united.[19]

Canada's defence minister, Ian Mackenzie, elaborated his prime minister's approach to the conference. "General Staffs would prefer centralisation, but centralisation was impossible. Centralisation inevitably meant disunity. A system of separate national defence policies might be unwieldy and costly, but the alternative would be more costly still. The best contribution that Canadians could make either to Canada or to the Commonwealth was to keep Canada united. That was the objective of their present policy." Mackenzie concluded that "Canadian public opinion would not, under present conditions, support any larger [defence] appropriations ... Canadian public opinion was definitely opposed to extraneous commitments ... The most important contribution they could render at this time ... was ... to preserve [national] unity."[20]

But speaking chiefly to Quebec was not in itself a viable, balanced policy, and no longer reflected King's own evolving and convoluted thinking. With the Hoare-Laval pact, *Realpolitik* had trumped collective security. King had now to face the question that Dafoe had seen as early as 1928: "If the League of Nations and all it stands for were to go by the board, there are questions of imperial relationships ... to which answers would have to be found. Chief among them would be the matter of to what degree one British nation could involve another in active war by pressing individual policy to the point of embarking upon hostilities."[21] That testing time had now arrived. Talk of League "renewal" was a waste of time, and any idea of Canadian dependence on the United States, locked in its isolationism, was, in King's view, equally fallacious. One close observer of the conference has deplored the effect of the Abyssinian crisis on whatever lingering support there had been for an imperial foreign policy. "By crippling the League of Nations … it had deprived the Commonwealth of its external forum for a common foreign policy, and the chance of a genuine imperial accord had finally slipped away."[22] Only Britain and its empire remained as the bastion of Canada's security. And Quebec would now have to be led to recognize that inescapable if, for itself, awkward fact.

In these circumstances King inched his way forward in appealing concurrently to both English Canada and Quebec. He concluded his major statement to the imperial conference by summarizing the elements that would initiate Canadian participation in a conflict in which Britain's interests were seriously at stake. "There would be the strong pull of kinship, the pride in common traditions, the desire to save democratic institutions, the admiration for the stability, the fairness, the independence that characterize English public life, the feeling that a world in which Britain was weakened would be a more chaotic and more dangerous world to live in."[23] That lyrical passage did not sound much like Skelton nor indeed like King himself. In fact he had lifted it almost verbatim from the August 1936 instructions for the Canadian delegation to the League Assembly, but for the imperial conference he intentionally omitted the anti-imperial words that Skelton had inserted immediately following.

King now attempted to appeal to English Canada through expressing great confidence in Chamberlain (who was to succeed Baldwin on 28 May as prime minister and hence chairman of the imperial conference until its adjournment on 15 June). King became enthusiastic in his embrace of the "realistic" policy of appeasement of the dictators as enunciated at the conference by Chamberlain. In its initial stages, appeasement attracted little of the derogatory vocabulary of pusillanimity, betrayal, and surrender that gradually gathered around it. A revived Germany, rendered content with practical revisions to the Treaty of Versailles, could be a strong barrier to Russian communism which, by subversion or otherwise, was seen as a major threat to the British Empire, its trade, and security. If that barrier had to be in central Europe, where Hitler had focused his ambitions for *Lebensraum* in *Mein Kampf*, there were many across the Empire who had no objection. In these circumstances, peace might be had not from conferences but from direct contact with Hitler and Mussolini. The Hoare-Laval pact had undermined the League of Nations, and with Britain inadequately armed and over-stretched in its imperial commitments, Chamberlain urged appeasement as the only way forward to European peace. Many in France doubted that such optimism was justified, but the alternative of another world war was as unthinkable in Paris as it was in London.

In light of the conscription crisis and devastation of the First World War and the threat that a second would present to Canadian unity, King became an enthusiast for appeasement, but he did declare to Malcolm MacDonald – for the ears of his cabinet colleagues only – that during his pending visit to Berlin, he would tell the Führer frankly that if Germany were to go in for any "destructive work" threatening the United Kingdom, then it would have to reckon with every one of the Dominions before she had finished." In that and other ways both within the imperial conference and without, King's statements and motives remained "a complex jumble of liberal rhetoric, naïve optimism and Canadian self-interest."[24]

When King had first met Neville Chamberlain almost fifteen years before, he was wary of the son of that imperial centralist par excellence, Joseph Chamberlain, but he now displayed unbounded admiration for the new prime minister. Chamberlain even had the special merit of having excluded Winston Churchill from his government.* King would have agreed – for once – with Alice Massey who later described Chamberlain as "the most extraordinary simple, honest and wonderful person."[25] Other contemporaries had, however, a decidedly lesser opinion of him. Noel Annan later wrote, "a dangerous opponent using every weapon to maim dissenters in his Party and to express his contempt for those outside it. He had neither humour nor imagination – sad deficiencies in a prime minister."[26] The long-serving Conservative minister, Lord Swinton, agreed: "He was always rather cold, aloof, withdrawn, somewhat superior and condescending in manner … when he ventured into foreign affairs for the first time … he became autocratic and intolerant of criticism … he became almost intolerably self-assertive."[27] Chamberlain had few more ardent supporters of his efforts to appease the dictators than his Canadian opposite number, despite King's earlier public

---

*From well before the First World War, King felt that Churchill was an unreliable, bellicose imperialist, not to be trusted and greatly wanting in judgment. Days before the Second World War, he described him as "the one dangerous factor" in the gathering gloom. During the 1926 General Strike in Britain he made an even more trenchant dismissal of him: "For Churchill I feel a scorn too great for words. He has been the evil genius in this" (King diary, 3 May 1926).

aversion to being seen as simply following British foreign policy. Chamberlain for his part remained skeptical of King. As early as 1922, from a train between Moose Jaw and Medicine Hat, he had written to his sister, "Loud and deep are the curses on Mackenzie King for his miserable and shameful hedging, but he is a weak man dependent for his continuance in office upon the French Canadian vote from Quebec."[28] Fifteen years later, as the 1937 imperial conference was ending, Chamberlain wrote to Tweedsmuir that King "seems to me to get more timid as he grows older, and timidity is not the quality most required in Canada to-day."[29]

King recorded in his diary on 10 May, four days before the imperial conference began (when Baldwin was still prime minister and Chamberlain chancellor of the exchequer) that at a state dinner at Buckingham Palace, "I had a long talk with Neville Chamberlain … about the speech that he had made on the League [in February]. I told him that speech had meant everything to me; that it had taken a tremendous burden off my mind; that I agreed with every word of it … Almost immediately after talking with Chamberlain, I was introduced to [Joachim] von Ribbentrop, the German Ambassador."[30] Hitler had recently appointed Ribbentrop ambassador to the United Kingdom (he had already appointed Ribbentrop's brother-in-law ambassador to the United States). Chamberlain held him in contempt. He was "so stupid, so shallow, so self-centred and self-satisfied, so totally devoid of intellectual capacity that he never seems to take in what is said to him."[31] Phipps from Berlin could not have agreed more: "he is a lightweight (I place him near the bottom of the handicap), irritating, ignorant, and boundlessly conceited."[32] David Low, the immensely popular London political cartoonist from New Zealand, depicted him more graphically as "von Brickendrop," but King had the opposite impression. He happily found Ribbentrop "very prepossessing, very natural, a man I could get along with quite easily."[33]

Ribbentrop was assiduous in inviting to Berlin anyone whom he thought might help to improve Anglo-German relations or who could be impressed – or intimidated – by Germany's rapid economic and military resurgence. The head of Reuters, Roderick Jones, was an obvious target, but that initiative came to nothing. Ribbentrop "was verbose. It soon became plain that he disliked interrogation or criticism … He was never again invited to our house. He was too unpleasant a contrast with Hoesch," his predecessor who was "completely out of sympathy with the Hitlerites … Throughout Ribbentrop's reign at the German Embassy I avoided him."[34] Nevertheless, Ribbentrop reported to Hitler and to Konstantin von Neurath, the foreign minister, on the progress that he imagined he was making in distributing invitations to visit Germany. "I have ... agreed with following influential Englishmen that they should visit Germany in the course of this summer and I would warmly recommend that every one of these people be received by the Führer: Baldwin ... Derby... the Minister of Defence Inskip, who seems very favourably disposed; Winston Churchill, whose transformation into a friend of Germany may perhaps yet come about ... the Canadian Prime Minister, Mackenzie King, who is very friendly towards Germany and whose visit I consider particularly important in view of the significance of the Dominions for British foreign policy."[35]*

In a letter of 3 May, Ribbentrop raised with King the possibility of an early visit to Berlin to replace the postponed visit of the year before. King was well disposed to accept not least because of Ribbentrop's prewar years at Molson's Bank in Montreal, as a logger on Vancouver Island, and as a wine salesman in Ottawa. A noted social climber, Ribbentrop probably also enumerated for King invitations in Ottawa from the governor general, the Duke of Connaught, brother of King Edward VII and uncle of Kaiser Wilhelm, who spoke English with a strong German accent. King may have responded by enumerating his own much-valued invitations from Earl Gray, Connaught's predecessor.[36] In return, King described for Ribbentrop his birthplace in Berlin (Ontario), the large number of his schoolmates who were of German descent, and the happy months that he had spent in Berlin (Germany) in 1900.

At the imperial conference itself, following a brief *tour d'horizon* of the international situation with Ribbentrop, King urged Chamberlain and Eden to collaborate with Ribbentrop in "economic appeasement," by which he seems to have envisaged, among other things, recruiting the support of the United States in reducing international trade barriers which were "preventing Germany ... from expanding her trade." To his diary King said that "the United States was of the view that on economic appeasement alone depends

---

*This same source notes that "No other documents on Mackenzie King's visit have been found" (footnote 2 in document 425, Ribbentrop to Berlin, 13 June 1937). In 1946 Ribbentrop was found guilty of war crimes by the International Military Tribunal sitting at Nuremburg. Before his execution at age fifty-three on 16 October, he mused in his diary how different his life would have been if he had remained in Canada in 1914 instead of returning to Germany to serve in the army in the First World War.

the peace of the World ... Canada was prepared to consider the whole question of economic readjustment in a big generous way." King asked Ribbentrop whether "America could be of any help ... [since] unless friendship is established in a real way between England and Germany, there will be war between them, and war to the death within the next two years."[37] King recorded no response from Ribbentrop.

After King introduced Charles Dunning, his minister of finance, who, with Lapointe, was attending the conference, he and Ribbentrop got down to practical business: "He asked me if I could not go to Germany and said that he would like to arrange for me to meet Hitler."[38] Eden joined them briefly, volunteering that King should "go to Berlin and talk with Hitler." Separately, Chamberlain, backed by the cabinet secretary Maurice Hankey (who had visited Canada three years before), was "quite emphatic" that King should accept Ribbentrop's invitation to "a quiet luncheon" at the embassy residence on 26 May to discuss details of the proposed early visit to Berlin. Later, King recalled that during his conversation with Ribbentrop, "[he had] beckoned to [him] to come over where [we] were. As the three of us talked ... people moved away and we seemed to be pretty much the centre of interest. [They] ... were looking in a rather surprised way at the cordiality of the conversation the three of us were having," leading King to the unwarranted conclusion that "Chamberlain and I and Hitler have figured in a relationship that has been exceedingly significant."[39]*

As the month-long imperial conference neared its close, King recorded in his diary on 2 June "my admiration for Chamberlain's knowledge of questions, his ability to present different subjects grows each time that I listen to him. He has too a much more conciliatory manner than one might have first supposed." Two days later, King added, "As I listened to Chamberlain, it seemed to me that what he was saying pretty closely approached what von Ribbentrop had indicated to me would serve to avoid enmity between Germany and Britain, and to meet the European situation without any sacrifice of Britain's friendship for France ... I felt a distinct lifting of some of the clouds that had been threatening."[40] Thus reassured on every side,

---

*Ribbentrop handed out invitations to leading British figures with such largesse that, if all were accepted, some said that Hitler would have done little else but meet with them. He twice invited Churchill but in vain. He had more luck with the Duke of Windsor, Lloyd George, Lord Lothian, and Lord Halifax, the president of the council, who upon arrival at Berchtesgaden in mid-November 1937, mistook Hitler for a footman and began to hand him his hat.

King confirmed to Ribbentrop on 4 June that he planned to arrive in Berlin on 27 June for a four-day visit (later reduced to three). A week later, on 11 June, King was immensely gratified to have an audience with King George VI at Buckingham Palace. Ever the royalist at heart, he was pleased to tell his sovereign that he would soon cross to Germany "to have a word with Hitler." To his delight, "The King said that he thought that was all to the good, that there was nothing like meeting men personally."[41]

Although he does not say so in his diary, Mackenzie King appears to have taken the occasion of his gratifying audience with his monarch to raise a quite different matter: a royal tour of Canada. Fully aware of the success of the Prince of Wales's postwar tour, especially in light of the refusal of George V, when king, to travel in the Empire, and the unfortunate impression left by the tawdry abdication of Edward VIII, Tweedsmuir, in initiating the idea the previous December (1936), had already enlisted the support of Chamberlain and Halifax in exploring the dimensions of a royal tour. The Canadian prime minister duly informed the British prime minister of his support, certain that a transcontinental rail trip by the royal couple – with him of course in constant attendance – would have the happy result of promoting Anglo-Canadian cooperation of all sorts, strengthening national unity, and consolidating his own position as the prime minister loyal to the rehabilitated crown in the election then foreseen for the autumn of 1939. Canada would be publicly affirmed as a brother-in-arms in any major war. As Tweedsmuir had suggested, the tour would also provide a base for a brief royal visit to the United States to underpin the closer ties for which both he and Mackenzie King were working.

Three days after his audience with his sovereign, King mailed what he called a personal letter to Ribbentrop thanking him for the arrangements that had been made for his visit to Berlin. "The fact that you spent part of your life in Canada ... leads me to feel that between us we should be able to do not a little to strengthen Anglo-German friendship."[42] Presumably MI5 was reading Ribbentrop's mail as Berlin was reading Henderson's, but in any event the next day Chamberlain took King aside at a dinner party, partly to be certain that he understood what he was attempting to accomplish with Hitler. He told him that "he felt there were two questions of concern in Germany's mind – one the [future of the former German] Colonies and the other, the possible expansion on the Eastern front ... That he, himself, felt that Germany was more or less entitled to certain economic precedences in

Eurpoe … I gave an account of my talk with von Ribbentrop … and what I had in mind saying to Hitler. Chamberlain and Eden both again strongly approved of my going to Germany … it would be a great help to them … When I said that I would make clear [to Hitler] … that if Germany became aggressive, he would find it impossible to hold back our country or any of the Dominions, he [Chamberlain] said a statement to that effect would help … to preserve the peace in Europe … I have come to have the greatest admiration and the greatest confidence in Chamberlain."[43]

King concluded his diary entry for 15 June by summarizing his satisfaction at his own performance at the imperial conference. He had "made clear to the British Ministers that in Canada, we could not and would not consider anything in the nature of an Expeditionary Force … any effort to have us drawn into European situation was like expecting us to jump into a bag of fighting cats … I stated, however," and here King came to the point, "that if it became evident that Germany … was guilty of aggression … the voluntary feeling in Canada would assert itself in a strong way, and that it would be difficult to hold back those who would be prepared to see that aggression was stayed." Three days later, on 18 June, Eden wrote to King,

> I carefully considered whether there was anything that I could usefully add to the outline [of what he intended to say to Hitler] which you were so good as to give Mr Chamberlain and me at dinner the other night. On reflection, my own conviction is that what you yourself propose to say could not be bettered. I by no means despair of coming to an eventual agreement with Germany nor, as you know, will I accept the inevitability of war. If, however, we are to have the best chance of success, Germany must be persuaded of two things. The first, that the world is truly anxious to meet and discuss with her legitimate grievances with a view to their peaceful adjustment. The second, that if she resorts to methods of aggression to secure these objectives, then she will have active opposition in many places and sympathy and support nowhere.[44]

For Chamberlain the imperial conference had "ended amidst general congratulations and satisfaction and I was pleased to hear … that the Premiers had not been backward in expressing their appreciation of my personal contribution. Mackenzie King, who was generally considered the weakest vessel in the team, declared that he had heard many speeches at Conferences but never any one which impressed him so much as that with which I concluded the proceedings. I was interested to hear that he is preparing to go to Germany and have an interview with Hitler at which among other things he intends to say that if he [Hitler] should ever aggress in any way to injure us, Canadians would swim the Atlantic rather than to be prevented from coming to our aid."[45]

When Malcolm MacDonald reported to Chamberlain and his cabinet colleagues after the conclusion of the imperial conference, he noted that "The Canadian Prime Minister had spoken in a slightly isolationist spirit … Mr Savage [the prime minister of New Zealand] would like a combined foreign policy of the Empire, though Canada and South Africa would not approach that." MacDonald added that "King was about to visit Germany, where he would see Herr Hitler … After expressing sympathy with Hitler's constructive work and telling him of the sympathy which was felt with Germany in England, he intended to add that if Germany should ever turn her mind from constructive to destructive efforts against the United Kingdom, all the Dominions would come to her aid and [repeating King's little jest to Chamberlain] that there would be great numbers of Canadians anxious to swim the Atlantic!"[46] By then, in the eyes of one Canadian historian, in a real if not public sense, "Canadian participation in the Second World War was a foregone conclusion."[47]

Fortified in his plans to visit Hitler by the approbation of the British prime minister, the foreign secretary, the cabinet secretary, and even by the monarch himself, King completed his month in Britain by going to Westminster Abbey to see whether he could collect any old stones for his beloved if awkwardly contrived ruins at Kingsmere, just north of Ottawa in Quebec. More immediately pleasing was a gift of silver-framed photographs of the princesses Elizabeth and Margaret. On the other hand, a friendly if cautionary comment about his planned visit to Hitler arrived from the Duchess of Athol, preceding a similar but more outspoken comment from Violet Markham, his old friend and financial benefactor: "Don't let him hypnotise you … he is the head of a detestable system of force and persecution and real horrors."[48] Confirmation came from Ribbentrop that Hitler would receive the "very friendly" Canadian prime minister in Berlin at noon on 28 June. During his three-day visit, he would also be received twice by Marshal Göring; have lunch with Konstantin von Neurath, the foreign minister; and meet Rudolph Hess, the deputy leader and confidant of Hitler.

While King was seeking final approbation in London for his visit to Germany, a Canadian army officer who had attended committees of the imperial conference travelled to Hamburg and Berlin to gain a first-hand if brief impression of the Nazi regime. Colonel H.D.G. Crerar, the director of military operations and intelligence and secretary to the Joint Staff Committee at Defence Headquarters (and a delegate with Pearson and Robertson to the 1932 disarmament conference in Geneva) departed Berlin on 21 June, six days before King's arrival. King does not mention the colonel's visit to Germany, but then King, that most unmilitary person, had no contacts with the deputy minister of national defence or with senior officers, leaving that to his underemployed minister of national defence or to Lapointe. Further, Skelton suspected senior officers to be closet imperial centralists, only too prompt to collaborate with their British counterparts (alongside whom they had served throughout the Great War) in defence planning, training, and equipment procurement, all initiatives that if known would be anathema to isolationists in Ottawa and Quebec. He strove to prevent them from discussing "even … the steps planned by the United Kingdom for the protection of Newfoundland,"[49] but given the minute size of the Canadian forces, senior officers depended on Britain for advice. Further, as Crerar's biographer has written, "Their conviction that public opinion would draw Canada into any major war in which Britain was involved and their assessment that Britain's foreign policy was returning to its more traditional balance of power and away from commitments to the League of Nations were far more accurate than E.A.'s [External Affairs'] assessments."[50] Crerar's estimates of German belligerency were different from those of the prime minister – but he had the benefit of meetings with, among others, the well-informed British military attaché in Berlin, while King kept himself away from any such contacts. Crerar accurately forecast to Defence Headquarters in Ottawa, "It will be one or perhaps two years before the [Nazi] military organisation … will be sufficiently ready for [a major European war]. At the same time, not even the 'Leader' is infallible and in his aggressive pursuit of external objectives, which appear to him to be obtainable by the means at his disposal, he may miscalculate. The step from international blackmail to international bloodshed is all too easily accomplished. The overriding impression that I took away with me … was that of a highly dynamic nation, determined before long to break its present bonds and consequently increasingly dangerous to Europe and indeed to world peace."[51]

On 23 June on the platform at Victoria Station to bid farewell to King on his departure for Berlin were the dominions secretary, Malcolm MacDonald, the high commissioner and Mrs Massey, Lord and Lady Cranborne (later Salisbury), and George and Pauline Vanier from the High Commission. Massey would have preferred to be on the train himself. He too had been invited to visit Germany by his diplomatic colleague Ribbentrop (whom he considered "very second rate"), but King keenly mistrusted what he regarded as the imperial centralist inclinations of his former colleague and always felt intimidated by him. King did not want to share his visit to Hitler with anyone, certainly not Massey. He told MacDonald of his satisfaction at the British government endorsement of his visit, seeing it as "the greatest possible service [I could do] ... by my visit to Germany if I would say to Hitler what I had talked about with ... Mr Chamberlain ... I told Malcolm that I hoped that no matter how driven they [the British Government] might be ... by no means to let the Empire into a War ... Not to allow War at any cost ... I felt in talking with Malcolm a sort of feeling as though this whole country [i.e., the United Kingdom] was actually looking to me to help it."[52]

12

A Berliner in Berlin

Four days later, on the morning of 27 June 1937, the British ambassador in Berlin, Sir Nevile Henderson, accompanied by an official of the Foreign Ministry, met Mackenzie King's train from Paris at the Berliner Hauptbahnhof. Henderson, who had succeeded Sir Eric Phipps only six weeks before, at the end of April 1937, was a career diplomat who had spent his thirty-five-year career entirely abroad (including in Turkey at the time of Chanak), but as his obituary in the *Times* later stated, he was never in the first rank of British heads of mission. After only one year as ambassador to Argentina, he had been promoted ambassador to Germany.* Why he should have been chosen for Berlin over more capable colleagues is nowhere explicit.† The Nazis had clearly expressed their dislike of Phipps (a sentiment warmly reciprocated), but the hand of Chamberlain, the prime minister designate, was everywhere seen in Henderson's unexpected appointment. Felix Gilbert, in *The Diplomats, 1919–1939*, says that Henderson's selection "had certainly been influenced by the fact that he was clearly untinged by anti-German or pro-French bias." Before his departure from London for Berlin, "he had had a long talk with Chamberlain, who explained the principles of his new policy. From that time on, Henderson considered himself less as a subordinate of the Foreign

---

*On a German liner from Buenos Aires to Hamburg, when he was not reading *Mein Kampf*, Henderson shared his thoughts about what British policy toward Hitler's Germany should be with Wilfrid Ashley, Lord Mount Temple, the president of the Anglo-German Fellowship. Lady Mount Temple was the only child of the Jewish financier Sir Ernest Cassel. Their two daughters were accordingly accounted half Jewish, yet Mount Temple did not resign the presidency of the Anglo-German Fellowship until November 1938, less than a year before the Second World War. His brother-in-law, Viscount Greenwood of Whitby, Ontario, was by contrast an anti-Nazi.

†Henderson himself later candidly acknowledged that he had doubted his fitness for a diplomatic career and that it had been a mistake to send him to Berlin.

Office than as a personal agent of the Prime Minister, whose policy he was charged to carry out. Thus, he remained in constant touch with Sir Horace Wilson [Chamberlain's personal *éminence grise*, whose primary experience was the private sector] and directed appeals to him whenever he disapproved of the instructions which he received from the Foreign Office."[1] During the month of April, while he was still in London, Henderson later recalled, Baldwin and Chamberlain (chancellor of the exchequer) "agreed that I should do my utmost to work with Hitler and the Nazi party as the existing government in Germany ... Mr Chamberlain outlined to me his views on general policy toward Germany ... I followed the general line which he set me, all the more easily and faithfully since it corresponded so closely with my private conception."[2]* Given their backgrounds in industry, Chamberlain and Horace Wilson shared the illusion that the "same arts of round-table negotiation which served with English employers and trade unionists would also serve with Adolf Hitler,"[3] a sentiment King shared.

Henderson's two predecessors in Berlin, Rumbold and Phipps, could not have disagreed more. Rumbold, who had informed London five months after Hitler became chancellor that "Many of us here feel as if we were living in a lunatic asylum," added with typical Foreign Office understatement, "the persons directing the policies of the Hitler Government are not normal." In his farewell despatch in mid-1933 upon his retirement, he further forecast that "the outlook for Europe is far from peaceful ... It would be misleading to base any hopes on a return to sanity or serious modification of the views of the [new] Chancellor and his entourage."[4] It took no time for Phipps, Rumbold's successor in Berlin, to conclude that Hitler (whose fulminations he had observed in Austria during his previous appointment as minister in Vienna) was a psychopathic gangster and Göring a baboon. Josef Goebbels, the propaganda chief for the Reich, was "a vulgar, unscrupulous, irresponsible demagogue ... and Hermann Göring a ruthless adventurer, reported to be a drug addict ... vain and ambitious ... a public danger."[5] Shortly after his arrival in Berlin, Phipps wrote to his receptive brother-in-law, Sir Robert

---

*The degree to which Henderson acted as the creature of Chamberlain and not of the Foreign Office may be gauged by the following diary entry of 20 October 1938 by Sir Alexander Cadogan, the permanent undersecretary: Henderson on a visit to London "told me privately ... that he had put Göring up to objecting to our guarantee of Czecho[slovakia]." Cadogan does not say whether in response he bothered to remonstrate with Henderson or even to caution him (Cadogan, *Diaries*, 122).

Vansittart, the permanent undersecretary at the Foreign Office, that Hitler was "violent, arrogant, fanatical ... his actual language bodes ill for such of his unfortunate countrymen who venture to differ from him."[6] Vansittart shared with Phipps, basing himself in part on MI6 reports, his conviction that "The present regime in Germany will loose off another European war just so soon as it feels strong enough ... We are considering very crude people who have few ideas ... but brute force and militarism."[7]

King heard none of that from Nevile Henderson, the antithesis of Rumbold, Phipps, and Vansittart. Henderson believed that his appointment "could only mean that I had been specially selected by Providence with the definite mission of ... helping to preserve the peace of the world,"[8] a belief that, unbeknownst to him, he shared with the prime minister of Canada, who regarded his own visit to Hitler as divinely ordained.* Henderson was convinced that he had been sent to Berlin "to do my utmost to work with Hitler and the Nazi Party as the existing government ... any public attempt to co-operate with the Nazi Government would constitute somewhat of an innovation [after Rumbold and Phipps]."[9] He capped this declaration of independence with an extraordinary salute to the two dictators in his later apologia, *Failure of a Mission*. "One cannot, just because he is a dictator, refuse to admit the great services which Signor Mussolini has rendered to Italy; nor would the world have failed to acclaim Hitler as a great German if he had known when and where to stop."[10] Others, however, came to view Henderson's term as British ambassador as a disaster. Eden concluded, "It was an international misfortune that we should have been represented in Berlin ... by a man who, so far from warning the Nazis, was constantly making excuses for them."[11] Others went even farther. Vansittart "says that Henderson is a complete Nazi and that the Foreign Office do not trust him to represent their real point of view ... Henderson is stupid and vain and has become almost hysterical in the Berlin atmosphere."[12]

King's first of his three days in Berlin began with visits to camps for girl and boys and then to the cavernous, swastika-festooned Sportpalast to see something of an All-German Sports Competition. To his gratification, he was given the seat that Hitler himself had occupied at the Olympic Games

---

*The hand of Providence was felt by Hitler as well as by *inter alia* King, Henderson, and Halifax. At the time of the German reoccupation of the Rhineland in March 1936, Hitler declared that he went the way Providence dictated.

the year before. That was the high point of his first day, which ended with a brief viewing of the house at 70 Kaiserin Augusta Strasse near the Tiergarten where at the age of twenty-five he had lived for two months in 1900 with Professor Anton Weber, his wife, and two daughters.

That evening King had a long meeting with Henderson. He had declined the ambassador's invitation to stay at the British residence rather than at the Hotel Adlon, still asserting that "there was always the danger of the Dominions feeling that they were being drawn into an Empire centralization scheme." For the same reason, he also declined Henderson's offer to accompany him to his meeting with Hitler. Despite having on two successive years sought approbation in London for his visit to Germany, King told Henderson that he did not want to be seen publicly as "under the wing of the British Government [or it to be thought] that Canada could not stand on her own feet in relation to Germany." Henderson gave King a *tour d'horizon* of Anglo-German relations, concluding that Germany "could not be expected indefinitely to keep aloof from countries which were populated largely by Germans." As he consistently urged upon the Foreign Office, "Austria was largely German. He could not see how [Hitler] could rightly prevent that union if the Austrians wished it … If the Germans [in Czechoslovakia] wished union with Germany … he thought that was something to be permitted. He believed Germany had her problems, her needs for expansion in Europe, and that if Britain tried to prevent this, it would be a great mistake." To King's satisfaction, Henderson spoke of the League of Nations "as a horror, and as a terrible institution; 'collective security' as something that was worse than meaningless, a real danger." He also recorded with pleasure that Henderson's understanding of Chamberlain "was much the same as myself; he thought Chamberlain had a better grasp of foreign policy than Baldwin had, and, in some ways, was stronger than Eden."[13]

The arch-appeaser Henderson made a highly favourable impression on King, reassuring him in his positive views of Nazi Germany, but King made no impression on Henderson. King's visit to Hitler goes unrecorded in his apologia *Failure of a Mission*, other than a passing reference to a luncheon he gave in honour of an unnamed visiting Canadian prime minister, but then only as a hook on which to record an unflattering anecdote about the contrasting *taille* of Marshal and Madame Göring. More specifically, Henderson records no notice of King's statement to him that "he must not judge … that we [in Canada] would be indifferent to acts of aggression which might threaten the liberty, the freedom which we enjoy as members of the British Empire; that we had gone into the last war not because we had to, but purely voluntarily ... and that natural feeling would express itself if there was aggression on the part of Germany."[14] King, in so speaking to Henderson, was telling him something that he had not yet confirmed with his cabinet colleagues or with his undersecretary of state for external affairs. Henderson appears to have disregarded King's statement as a mere platitude and seems not to have reported it to London.

Before his mid-day meeting with Hitler on 29 June, King met with Göring for an hour and a half at his grandiose office. On leaving the Hotel Adlon, King mulled over various Old and New Testament passages, sensing "the presence of God in all this, [my] guardian at every step ... the day for which I was born ... May God's blessing rest upon this day and the nations of the world – and His peace be theirs." Göring greeted him with thanks for a gift of Canadian bison to the Berlin Zoo.* "I said we were only too pleased to be able to supply some of these animals and would gladly let him have more at any time ... To get under way with friendly feeling, I spoke to him of being born in Berlin [Ontario]." When Göring, after briefly touching on the prospects for increased trade between Canada and Germany, asked King

---

*Göring was an aficionado of big game hunting and zoos as well as of bison (according to some wits as a result of sharing a girth). On 11 June 1934, Göring invited the ambassadors of Britain, France, Italy, and the United States, and several ministers of the Nazi government to view his shooting box and other paraphernalia at his new rural bison enclosure. The British ambassador, Sir Eric Phipps, recorded, "On the conclusion of General Göring's address, three or four cow bison were driven towards a large box containing a bull bison. A host of cinematograph operators and photographers aimed their machines at this box preparatory to the exit of the bull. Those who, like myself, have seen the mad charge of the Spanish bull out of his 'torril' looked forward to a similar sight on this occasion, but we were grievously disappointed for the bison emerged from his box with the utmost reluctance and, after eyeing the cows somewhat sadly, tried to return to it." Tactfully, Phipps did not record whether the non-performing bull bison was Canadian (*Our Man in Berlin*, 56).

The Canadian and other bison and elk reappeared on the international diplomatic scene when in November 1937, four months after King's visit to Berlin, Chamberlain sent Lord Halifax, then lord president of the council, to make direct contact with Hitler through Henderson, bypassing the increasingly troublesome foreign secretary, Anthony Eden. The ostensible reason for his visit, however, was to attend, as a former master of foxhounds, a gathering of the German Hunting Association which included among other gala events a visit to the hunting lodge and bison enclosure of *Reichsjägermeister* Göring.

The Canadian bison and other edible quadrupeds at the Berlin zoo came to a sorry end during the Second World War. Amid near starvation, they were slaughtered and eaten.

whether it was necessary in dealing with the dominions to go through London (as noted above, only South Africa and the Irish Free State had legations in Berlin), King referred to the visit the year before of the trade mission led by William Euler, his minister of trade and commerce, as evidence that Canada and Germany could deal directly with each other. This set him off on his favourite paradox: "It was the freedom we all enjoyed which kept the British Empire together. Every step we had taken toward independence and self-expression had really brought us closer together than would have been the case had there been any attempt at control or compulsion on the part of Britain." Having assured Göring that he was all for peace, he invited him to visit Canada. The Reichsmarschall readily accepted the invitation in principle, noting that Canada was the first country to invite him. He specified that he would go for "the big game," elk and bear, but he did not want to go anywhere near the United States. King replied that "we would be glad to see the necessary arrangements made." King repeated the favourable comment about Henderson made to him by King George VI, to which he added that he had himself found the ambassador well suited for his new post. But the burden of King's conversation with Göring was about the many merits of the new British prime minister, the peace-loving Neville Chamberlain, who stood for non-intervention in the internal affairs of other countries. Göring replied that he was pleased to hear it.[15]

Having mused on the cloud of witnesses from Berlin, Ontario, who were sanctioning with their unseen presence his visit to the original Berlin, King arrived for his mid-day conversation with Hitler convinced that it was an important diplomatic initiative. But in the words of Neatby, one of King's biographers, the visit "was for Hitler probably no more than a brief audience with a minor visiting dignitary."[16] Perhaps not even that, it being likely that Hitler, in his *Weltanschauung*, regarded Canada as little more than an ill-defined appendage of Britain. Accordingly, if Hitler had anything new to say about how he saw the world, it would not be to a prime minister of Canada. In the event, Hitler said nothing new, but he did it in "a friendly manner ... Hitler did not appear to be the least excited in anything he said ... He spoke with great calmness, moderation and logically, and in a convincing manner." Addressing King through his "exceedingly effective" interpreter Schmidt, Hitler described yet again the many injustices of the Treaty of Versailles and the looming threat of Soviet communism. But to King's satisfaction, he also emphasized the peaceful intentions of Germany, a country fully familiar with the horrors of modern warfare. As a result, King described the Führer in his diary as "an intense nationalist, resentful of the wrongs against Germany, but not a reckless or resentful man who would heedlessly provoke a war with Britain." In short, "he is really one who truly loves his fellow men."[17]

King began by volunteering to Hitler that the British foreign secretary, Anthony Eden, had endorsed his visit. Presumably in conveying this British approval to Hitler, King sought to establish his *bona fides* that he was speaking for the British Empire, notwithstanding his long-standing and public opposition to an imperial foreign policy and his incongruous statement to Hitler that his visit was " purely a personal one." He explained that "what Canada valued above everything else as one of the Nations of the British Commonwealth was the freedom which we all enjoyed … secured by our free association together and common allegiance to the common crown." By including this in his later memorandum to Chamberlain and Eden and not in his diary, he was underlining for them how committed he was to supporting British foreign policy. Also via his later memorandum, King reported that he had attempted to instruct Hitler on the finer points of the Canadian constitution (as he had done with Mussolini a decade earlier). He was unaccompanied by the British ambassador, he explained, because "Some foreign countries [or even some Canadians] might think that this was evidence of some tendency towards separation between Canada and Britain … it was evidence of something quite to the contrary … had the British ambassador accompanied me, they would have had in Canada a feeling of subordination as far as our Dominion was concerned. It was the fact that we were all so completely free to settle our own policies that would cause us at all costs to maintain the unity which we enjoyed in the Commonwealth of Nations."

King then elaborated a reference to defence expenditures. He told Hitler that increased expenditures were "occasioned by what was taking place in Germany in the way of increased outlays for war purposes." He had added, he said, that "if the time ever came when any part of the Empire felt that the freedom which we all enjoyed was being impacted through any act of aggression on the part of a foreign country, it would be seen that all would join together to protect the freedom which we were determined should not be imperilled." Seeing himself as speaking for the whole British Common-wealth, King described how he had assured Hitler that "there was no thought of aggression in the mind of any member." It was the "sense of freedom and security which we enjoyed in our British institution which was the real element of the Empire."

Hitler, in turn, said that all of Germany's difficulties grew out of the "enmity" of the Treaty of Versailles, which had imposed "indefinite subjection" on the German people. The complete disarmament of Germany had necessitated rapid rearmament "to defend herself" and to reclaim a position "where we will be respected." The choice was plain. "We were either to be held in permanent subjugation or to take a step which would preserve us in our own rights." In his diary account, King readily accepted this explanation, but was even more gratified by Hitler's flat statement that there would be no war as far as Germany was concerned: "My support comes from the people and the people don't want war," King adding that "this impressed me very much as a real note of humility."[18] In his memorandum to Chamberlain and Eden, he also records Hitler as stating that "nothing that can be said to me will ever cause me to commit Germany to go to war with regard to some situation that might arise in the future ... I am not like Stalin. I cannot shoot my Generals and Ministers when they will not do my will. I am dependent for any power on the people who are behind me. Without the people I am nothing."[19]

In his memorandum but not his diary, King at this point included a statement by the Führer about the British ambassador: "Herr Hitler said that Sir Nevile Henderson had not been in Germany very long, but they all liked him and felt that he had a good understanding of German problems."[20] Hitler concluded his conversation with King (who was gratified that it had lasted more than an hour instead of the mere thirty minutes scheduled) with an invitation to six students and undesignated "officers" to spend three weeks in Germany to see what had been accomplished since he had become chancellor five years before. For whatever reasons, King did not refer to this invitation in his later memorandum to Chamberlain and Eden, although Hitler repeated it two years later (on 21 July 1939, the result of prompting by King's friend, the German consul general in Ottawa).[21] King was careful to convey in his memorandum his belief in Hitler as a fellow mystic at the head of what had rapidly become again one of the most powerful countries in the world. In his diary, King described Hitler as a mystic who had told him "in a most positive emphatic way that there would be no war so far as Germany was concerned." Hitler's face was "not that of a fiery, over-strained nature, but of a calm, passive man, deeply and thoughtfully in earnest ... As I talked with him, I could not but think of Joan of Arc."* He added to Chamberlain that the Führer impressed him as "a man of deep sincerity and a genuine patriot."[22]

The following morning, King had his second meeting with Göring, tea with Rudolf Hess, and an hour with Foreign Minister Konstantin von Neurath. King told Chamberlain and Eden but not his diary that, during his second conversation with Göring, he went a good deal farther in indicating that Germany might expect to find "all parts of the British Empire" firmly united "in the event of the unity of the whole being threatened by any act on Germany's part." He was less categorical in response to a specific question from Göring about whether Canada would support Britain in the event of the "Germans of Germany and Austria wishing to become one people; would Canada go to the length of supporting Britain if she tried to prevent a step of the kind?" King replied rather lamely, "We would wish to take all circumstances into account and judge the question on its merits."[23]

---

*Mackenzie King's comparison of Hitler to Joan of Arc was not unique to him. George Bernard Shaw's *Saint Joan* had played in Berlin and Vienna after its opening in London in 1924 where King, although not a frequent theatregoer, may at some time have seen it. Sir John Simon, the British foreign secretary, wrote to King George V on 27 March 1935 and to Sir Eric Phipps on 5 April 1935 that Hitler was Saint Joan with a moustache (Cowling, *The Impact of Hitler*, 442). According to Walter Riddell's diary for 16 April 1935, Simon said to him over dinner in Geneva, following his return from Berlin, "as he watched [Hitler] hour after hour, he could not help thinking of him as a Joan of Arc." Riddell duly wrote to King in September 1936 that Simon had told him that Hitler "seemed to consider himself a kind of Joan of Arc, as a great deliverer whose mission was to free his people."

Shaw's plays were much admired in their German-language versions from the opening of *Pygmalion* in Berlin in October 1913. Shaw was in turn an enthusiast of both Mussolini and Hitler, strong men who had "the personality to change the world," and Oswald Mosley was "the only striking personality in British politics." Shaw's plays, including *Saint Joan*, which Hitler favoured, were presented across Germany in the 1930s. Goebbels attended the Berlin premiere of *The Millionairess* in 1936 and Hitler *Caesar and Cleopatra* in 1939. Karl Ludecke was not alone in seeing Hitler as the obvious model for Battler in Shaw's bizarre 1939 anti-League of Nations play, *Geneva*.

Shaw asked a German friend (Ribbentrop was a frequent interlocutor) to tell Göring "that I have backed his regime in England to the point of making myself unpopular." Beatrice Webb, however, found the attitude of her fellow socialist toward the dictators all nonsense. She asked him in early 1934 why he admired Mussolini and Hitler when they had "no philosophy, no notion of any kind of social organisation except their undisputed leadership instead of parliamentary self-government" (Holroyd, *Shaw*, 3: 113.)

King's meeting with Hess went unrecorded, despite the fact that King could have known from the Security Branch of the RCMP (who had it from the British) that Hess had long been urging the organization of a pro-Nazi Bund movement in North America and the supply of Nazi propaganda to it. Neurath, who had been ambassador in London from 1930 to 1932, assured King that as "long as he was at the Foreign Office, there would never be [a] possibility of war between Germany and England." King added with satisfaction that "the Baron von Neurath had a very great personal admiration for Mr Chamberlain ... and a strong belief in his desire and ability to find the solution of the problems existing between England and Germany."[24] King's programme ended with a night at the opera where, again to his gratification, he sat in the seat reserved for Hitler, which prompted him to acknowledge Hitler as a great music lover.

King summed up to his diary on 30 June 1937 – the night he left Berlin – his delight about it all: "It was as enjoyable, informative and inspiring as any visit that I have ever had anywhere." Even more importantly, he had discovered that Canadians were more like Germans than anyone else: "The German people seemed to me much easier to understand, and more like ourselves than either the French or the English." And everything in Nazi Germany, even the racial hatreds and political violence, was explicable: "the hatreds ... are mainly those which arise from position and privilege ... one does not like regimentation, but it is apparently the one way to make views prevail ... I have come away from Germany tremendously relieved. I believe there will not be war."[25]

Unfortunately, there is extant no German record or commentary on King's visit. There is, however, a brief and indirect record of his talks with Göring left by the British air attaché in Berlin. Göring had been a brave fighter pilot in the First World War and in his admiration for the courage of the British air attaché he often chatted with him candidly. On 28 July, four weeks after King's departure, Göring told Group Captain M.G. Christie that he was pleased by the understanding attitude of some – unnamed – dominion premiers toward German ambitions in central Europe, a region in which they had declared no interest. More specifically, Göring told Christie that he had had a good talk with the Canadian prime minister Mackenzie King which "had pleased him much. Christie retorted that Mackenzie King was the last man qualified to speak for the Canadian people in any question of the Dominions' backing the mother country's policy of opposition to aggression; during the first [world] war, after all, King had spent his time in complete safety in the USA, and the fact that he had not volunteered for service with Canadian troops abroad had been a subject of much criticism among Canadian voters."[26]

Although Göring thought the prospects for Anglo-German relations were rather better than he had previously imagined, he made no secret from Christie that Germany wanted to take Austria, Bohemia, and Moravia. In his conversation with Göring, King had in fact said that Canada was determined to preserve the freedom that membership of the Empire conferred and if at any time it felt this freedom imperilled by an aggressive act toward Britain "our people would almost certainly respond immediately to protect our common freedom." Göring asked whether Canada would necessarily follow Britain in everything; for example, if Germany and Austria wished to unite, would Canada support Britain in trying to prevent it? King gave the predictable and inevitable reply, Canada would wish to examine all the circumstances before coming to a decision. "I do not wish you to think," Göring hastily replied, "that there is going to be any attempt to take possession of Austria, but I am speaking of a development which might come in time."[27]

To return to King's diary, he noted that he left Berlin at 2122 on 30 June on the night train to Brussels where he arrived at 0815 on 1 July in time for an early audience with the king of the Belgians with whom he shared his good impressions of Hitler. He also sent a prompt thank-you letter "from his heart" to the Führer for the great privilege of meeting him, emphasizing that "you … can do more than any man living to-day to help keep your own and other countries along the path to peace and progress." He added that Hitler's gift of a silver-framed photograph of himself "is a gift of which I am very proud, and of the friendship of which it is so generous an expression, I shall ever cherish. May I again thank you for it and for all that it will always mean to me."[28]

King also recorded that he arrived in Paris by train on the same evening in time to speak with remarkable public candour the next day at the Canadian pavilion at the Paris exposition (where the largest national pavilion was the bombastic German, and the prize-winning film was Leni Riefenstahl's adulatory *Triumph of the Will*). As Malcolm MacDonald informed his cabinet colleagues, King declared there that "the British Commonwealth prized its great liberty and freedom: If the United Kingdom were imperilled from any source whatever … [the result would be to] bring us together

182 Mackenzie King in the Age of the Dictators

again in preservation of it."[29] Free from the presence of Skelton, King saw himself as able to make such public commitments not only for Canada but for the whole British Commonwealth, much to his deputy minister's subsequent consternation.

King continued his dialogue with Walter Riddell by inviting him to come to Paris from Geneva to discuss League of Nations and European affairs, discussions that would be welcomed by whomever remained of pro-League Canadians. He described his visit the week before to Hitler. To Riddell's surprise, "Mr King then seemed quite satisfied that Hitler was being misunderstood and that he did not constitute any danger to peace." When Riddell suggested to the contrary that Hitler's aggressive policies were bound to bring him into conflict with the United Kingdom and France, King recalled Hitler's own words during their meeting in which he had assured him that "he had no intention of making war."[30]*

Before embarking on the Canadian Pacific Railway's (CPR) new flagship *Empress of Britain* from Cherbourg on 3 July, King sent telegrams of thanks to Henderson and Ribbentrop. Henderson replied immediately that "I still believe that the people who fought in that war [the Great War] don't want war again … and that in consequence it will be avoided … I am grateful to you for the encouragement no less than the help you gave me. You put heart into me and I look back on our talks with great appreciation and sympathy."[31] In London before sailing for Montreal, King found awaiting him a letter from his University of Toronto classmate, Viscount Greenwood. "You must have had a most interesting time … in your visit to Hitler. I am sure that the prime minster here [Chamberlain] would be very glad if you would send him your impressions."[32] Within a fortnight, King had done so. With his memorandum of 6 July, addressed to both Chamberlain and Eden, King in effect left two accounts of his visit. The first is his diary account, compiled the same or on the following day. The second is a fourteen-page memorandum (and a two-page covering letter) that he dictated on 6 July for Chamberlain and Eden before sailing for Canada.[33] King's diary account, not surprisingly, has an air of spontaneity that the later and more formal memorandum lacks. The sequence of his conversation with Hitler also differs and even some of

---

*Lapointe wanted to dismiss Riddell from the diplomatic service, but King instead transferred him in 1937 to Washington as deputy head of mission and in 1940 to Wellington as Canada's first high commissioner to New Zealand.

the content varies substantially between the two accounts, but perhaps the most striking differences are the way in which he describes in the memorandum to Chamberlain and Eden his firm statement to Hitler about how unified the reaction of the British Commonwealth to German aggression would be and, second, the degree to which he extolled Chamberlain and Henderson as great advocates of peace between Germany and Britain, in whom Hitler could have every confidence.

A month after his arrival back in Ottawa on 11 July, King received from Chamberlain a five-page reply dated 28 July to his memorandum of 6 July. Given that there was only surface mail service (including for the British diplomatic bag that would have carried Chamberlain's letter), it could not have reached King before mid-August, six weeks after his visit to Berlin.* King was thus able to draw on its thinking before and following Chamberlain's three appeasement visits to Hitler in October. Chamberlain was profuse in his gratitude for King's account and the "very kind words" that he had said to Hitler about himself, but more important, he acknowledged King's commitment to the British Commonwealth by quoting back to him his words that all the countries of the Commonwealth would be alongside Britain if war were to come. Eden, in light of Chamberlain's five-page letter, sent hardly more than a paragraph recognizing Chamberlain's reply and contenting himself with the assurance that the Foreign Office had found his memorandum of "great use."[34]

In a rare CBC broadcast of 19 July 1937, King reported that "neither the government nor the peoples of any of the countries I have visited [Britain, France, Belgium, and Germany] desire war ... as other than likely to end in self-destruction and the destruction of European civilisation itself."[35]† However, if war did come, King was privately convinced that it would be the fault of the international press, which in his mind now matched the League of Nations as the prime international villain. "Through its misrepresentations and persistent propaganda, some incidents will arise which will occasion conflict. If that comes ... it will be ... because of the interests

---

*The ambitious plan to create an imperial network of airships, endorsed by the 1926 imperial conference, had suddenly ended with the crash of a prototype in northern France in October 1930.

†Perhaps inspired by the popular success of the broadcasts of King George V and the "fireside chats" of Roosevelt, King embarked hesitantly on occasional CBC broadcasts prior to the Second World War.

behind the press, not because it is the wish either of the Governments or of the peoples." King's ultimate conclusion about his visit with Hitler was remarkably self-serving; if Hitler held back, Mackenzie King's visit to Germany and talk with Hitler, more than any single factor, would be responsible.[36]

In a thank-you letter to Göring of 28 July (following the telegram he had sent him from France), King reviewed in detail possible arrangements for him to travel by rail across Canada, including on the Kettle Valley line in the East Kootenay district of the CPR. He enclosed travel pamphlets and brochures, but also included the text of his CBC broadcast, in which had said that if war did come it would be the fault of the international press.[37] A fortnight later, King sent Ribbentrop a three-page handwritten letter of warmest thanks, asking him to tell Hitler, Göring, von Neurath, and Hess "how deeply touched I was … and how deeply gratified I have felt at the visit as a whole."[38]

At a small dinner party at Laurier House soon after his return to Ottawa in mid-July, King told the journalist Bruce Hutchinson that he had found Hitler "'a simple sort of peasant' and not very bright, who wished only to possess the Sudetenland of Czechoslovakia. That insignificant prize would satisfy him and the theft of foreign property did not seem to distress King. No, he said, Hitler did not intend to risk war. And to those peaceful motives King undoubtedly felt that he had made his own valuable contribution.[39] Later, in October, the visiting British economist Lord Stamp recorded how King had given him "in full detail an account of his talk with Hitler … Apparently [he] talked with Hitler directly about the colonial demands which Hitler treated as not a matter of any consequence. Mackenzie King said that it might be difficult to stop the agitation if it grew very powerful and Hitler declared that he could always dampen it down at any moment when required" (this is the only known reference to any discussion between Hitler and King about the return of prewar colonies to Germany).[40] King had recorded none of this in his diary or in his memorandum to Chamberlain and Eden, but to the US chargé d'affaires in Ottawa on 23 July 1938, a year after his visit, he was still describing Hitler "as being … a very sincere man. He even described him as being 'sweet'… he had the face … of a good man, although he was clearly a dreamer and gave the impression of having an artistic temperament."[41] What Roosevelt, Hull, or the State Department made of this is unrecorded, but when Chamberlain flew to Germany for the first of his three meetings with Hitler, King was convinced that he had played the key role in bringing them together. "My last words with Hitler were that he would like Chamberlain, that he could trust him, that he was a man he could deal with, that he was truly anxious to bring about better relations between Germany and Britain."[42]* King was quite clear that he "was the first to give Hitler faith in Chamberlain, telling him that … Chamberlain could be relied upon to see what was fair and right was done."[43]

The Duke and Duchess of Windsor – at Germany's expense – visited Hitler from 11 to 23 October 1937 (four months after King, a year after Lloyd George, and a fortnight after Mussolini's visits in Munich and Berlin). With Ribbentrop dancing attendance, the duke and duchess inspected "workmen's settlements" before meeting with the Führer and his leading colleagues. The duke, who had as Prince of Wales been "vociferous in his oft-expressed admiration for Nazi Germany," repeated much of his earlier praise of the Nazi regime.[44] He recalled his controversial speech to the British Legion of the year before in which he had urged friendly relations between British and German ex-servicemen organizations. Some visionaries in Berlin continued to toy with the madcap idea that once Britain had been defeated, they would foster a movement in Britain to restore the duke to the throne, but details of the visit of the duke and duchess have not been released. The *New York Times* of 13 October did, however, report that the Duke had said in Berlin that "the British Ministers of to-day and their possible successors are no match for the German and Italian dictators."

---

*On 11 August 1944, at the height of the Second World War, King was even more expansive in the Canadian House of Commons about his statements of commitment to support Britain during his visit to Berlin seven years before. His visit, he now declared, "had as its objective to make it perfectly clear if there were a war of aggression, nothing in the world would keep the Canadian people from being at the side of Britain. That was known to the German Government at the time and my action was fully known to the British Government."

13

Appalling Mischief

In mid-July 1937 when Mackenzie King returned to Canada from his two months in Europe, he, like many politicians before and after him, gave no impression that he was pleased to be back in provincial Ottawa after his giddy excursion into international affairs. As he saw it, he had played a central, even divinely ordained, role in keeping peace in Europe. With reluctance, he took up the domestic political challenges that awaited him, dreading in particular controversies with Premier Duff Pattullo in British Columbia who promised something called "socialized capitalism"; with the newly elected Social Credit premier of Alberta, William Aberhart; with his brash nemesis in Ontario, the Liberal premier, Mitchell Hepburn; and in Quebec with the controversial nationalist premier, Maurice Duplessis. Canada, along with other developed countries, was gradually emerging from the economic depression that had, *inter alia*, overwhelmed Bennett's Conservative government, but continuing high levels of unemployment and widespread western drought compounded persistent fiscal differences among the provinces and between them and Ottawa. And to complicate further the sour federal-provincial relations, a national election loomed in the autumn of 1939 (held, in fact, in 1940).

Early in 1938 foreign and domestic affairs coincided briefly with a bizarre incident in Canadian-German relations that surfaced unexpectedly in the Gulf of St Lawrence. The *Montreal Gazette* reported on 2 December 1937 that a Dutch company was discussing with the Consolidated (later the Consolidated Bathurst) Paper Company the possibility of buying the whole of Anticosti Island – larger than Prince Edward Island – and building a sulphite pulp mill there. In fact, the Dutch company was soon found to be a front for unspecified German interests, which had a team of engineers and technicians already on the Quebec island. Stories began to appear in newspapers, prompting a question in the House of Commons on 14 February 1938 whether Canada was protecting its sovereignty over the island and in the Gulf of St Lawrence.[1] King returned a bland affirmative, but on 24 March Maxime Raymond warned the House that the German engineers on Anticosti had been sent "to secure raw materials or to establish a military base: one is as alarming as the other."[2] After King replied that he would look into the matter, the German consul general in Montreal provided reassurances to him and to the now concerned premier of Quebec, Maurice Duplessis. More importantly, Göring wrote to his friend King, confirming that the technical team's visit was "purely commercial," intended to develop a dependable source of pulpwood for Germany. In the House of Commons on 17 May, the CCF carried forward its questioning, but with no result.[3] Finally, on 24 June, six months after the first public reports, a long, rambling discussion in the House led by Bennett effectively ended the Anticosti incident, with King finally stating that Quebec and Ottawa had agreed that the island would not be sold to a foreign government.[4] The team thereupon returned to Germany and the "Dutch" option lapsed, but there remain questions about the incident that have not been answered. The ragged way in which the discussions in the House played out suggests that the prime minister may have offered the leaders of the two opposition parties information from the RCMP or other confidential sources on the agreed understanding that it would not be made public in the House or otherwise, a practice occasionally followed when it is believed that any such disclosure would be contrary to the public interest.

From troublesome domestic matters King could still find diversion in exhilarating foreign affairs, at least intermittently. In early 1938 Franklin Roosevelt proposed an international conference to which the major powers, including Germany and Italy but not Japan, would be invited to discuss their grievances. The strength of American isolationists meant that no such conference could be held in the United States itself or at Geneva; Roosevelt favoured the Azores. Chamberlain, however, replied to a preliminary enquiry with no enthusiasm wherever it was to be held, believing that he could achieve more by his personal diplomacy. "What a fool Roosevelt would have looked if he had launched his precious proposal. What would he have thought of us if we had encouraged him to publish it, as Anthony [Eden] was so eager to do? And how we too would have made ourselves the laughing stock of the world."[5] It appeared most unlikely at the time that Stalin, Mussolini, or Hitler would accept any such invitation, but as Churchill later speculated, Roosevelt's proposal, if it had been accepted, might at least have had the effect of involving the isolationist United States in the threatening scene of Europe and subjecting Germany and Italy, whether or not they attended, to closer international scrutiny. "That Mr Chamberlain, with his limited outlook and inexperience of the European scene, should have possessed the self-sufficiency to wave away the proffered hand stretched out across the Atlantic leaves one ... breathless with amazement. The lack of all sense of proportion, and even of self-preservation ... is appalling."[6] Churchill's rhetoric aside, Roosevelt's idea remains as one of the "what-ifs" of the interwar era.

In the spring of 1938, war in Europe appeared increasingly likely. Chamberlain told the House of Commons that "At the last election it was still possible to hope that the League might afford collective security. I believed it myself. I do not believe it now ... we must not try to delude ourselves and, still more, we must not try to delude small weak nations into thinking that they will be protected by the League against aggression ... when ... nothing of the kind can be expected."[7] Whether Chamberlain had Austria or Czechoslovakia or both in mind he of course did not say. In Ottawa King pursued his favourite theme of how difficult it was to govern Canada. It was almost always better to do nothing than to attempt to lead or to persuade. He cautioned his fellow Canadians against talk of war. As he told the House of Commons in one of his now more frequent references to external affairs, a war in Europe "would bring out deep, in some cases fundamental, differences in opinion, [it] would lead to a further strain upon the unity of a country already strained by economic depression and the consequences of the last war and its aftermath."[8] No word here of the horrors of war. King was as usual harping on the threat of internal discord, leading him to pursue the lowest common denominator in foreign policy. He told Lester Pearson that "in the course of human history, far more had been accomplished by preventing bad actions than by doing good ones."[9]

From the Spanish Civil War, which had begun in July 1936, King kept himself and Canada as far away as possible, but it was never absent as an element in continuing British post-Abyssinian efforts to conciliate Italy and wean it away from the embrace of Germany. Baldwin spoke of Chamberlain's government as being resolutely determined not to be distracted, not to be dragged into the conflict, not to antagonize Mussolini or Hitler by supporting the Spanish republic. King in his silence had an additional reason: national unity. He avoided speaking about the war publicly, knowing that French-Canadian and Roman Catholic sentiment, led in part by Cardinal Villeneuve of Quebec, was on the side of the fascist general Francisco Franco, the latest would-be dictator to arrive on the European scene, against the allegedly communist-dominated Republican government. In one of its many editorials on the Spanish Civil War, *L'Action catholique* forecast that "[Franco's] victory will be that of Christian civilization against Marxist savagery."[10] The papal delegate in Ottawa described Franco's forces as an "army of heroes justly called Christ's militia."[11] Quebec had many more votes than the small number of active pro-Republican Canadians, but King, when forced to say something about Spain, again pursued a dual policy. He shunned the Republicans for Quebec's satisfaction while attempting to placate English Canada by copying the same "keep out" domestic legislation that London and Paris had enacted. Britain had stood aside from the war partly from Chamberlain's ill-founded conviction that Spain would only be a distraction, however vicious, in his broader efforts at appeasement. In an attempt to appear even-handed, Britain made it illegal for its citizens to volunteer or to provide military assistance to either side. King was gratified and promptly introduced almost identical legislation in early 1937. The Foreign Enlistment Act and amendments to the Customs Act together militated against Canadian involvement before Franco, with the indispensible help of Italy and Germany, ended the three-year civil war in March 1939 by finally taking Madrid.

In Ottawa there was no real debate about either the restrictive legislation or the Spanish Civil War itself. Parliament, following the lead of the prime minister, stayed out of it, aside from the occasional comment from Quebec that Canada was well rid of communist and other volunteers who should not be allowed to return to their homeland. Maxime Raymond, the Quebec MP who in time was to become one of the most outspoken anti-conscriptionist nationalists, represented many of his colleagues when he welcomed Canadian volunteers going to Spain "to enlist in the Red Army ... it will rid us of those undesirable people provided that they do not return here."[12]

Italy had placed whole divisions of soldiers and Germany squadrons of aircraft at the disposal of Franco, partly to put pressure on France to remain more or less passive. For Germany, the Spanish Civil War also served as a testing ground for modern weapons. Soviet Russia's aid to the Republicans prolonged the civil war, but in the continuing absence of assistance from Britain and France the Republicans were ultimately doomed. About all of this, King said nothing. Yet even among isolationists the conflict had an inconvenient way of intruding on the government's time. Canadian volunteers, to a total of 1,200, some confirmed communists, some anti-fascist democratic idealists, had managed to make their way to Spain to fight in the Canadian Mackenzie-Papineau brigade as part of the larger pro-Republican International Brigade. The Canadian surgeon and communist Norman Bethune, who provided a much-needed blood transfusion mobile unit to the Republicans, was convinced that "democracy will survive or die" in Spain. For King, however, the Spanish Civil War was just that: a civil war for Spaniards alone. Certainly he did not take the occasion of his meeting with Hitler to recommend that everyone should, like Britain, France, and Canada, keep out. The civil war remained a problem for British-Italian relations, in which London spent what little influence it still had in Rome in attempting to induce Italy to remove its large forces from Spain, giving Hitler additional evidence that London would go to any length to avoid involvement in foreign disputes. Britain did, however, benefit in one way from the Spanish Civil War: the Government Code and Cypher School (later at Bletchley) began its successful reading of military operational code by breaking the Italian navy's use of a commercial version of Enigma.

On 6 February 1938, Mackenzie King wrote a letter of congratulation to Ribbentrop on his appointment as foreign minister, following his two energetic if erratic years as ambassador in London. King regretted that "very few will write him and that a note of congratulations, expressing faith in his purpose of good will. England and Germany might ... in the balance save a world war ... Henderson has been helping towards bringing both countries together."[13] A week later King set out his own claims for having played a central role in preventing a world war. He reflected complacently on "my own efforts for peace between classes and nations which, if followed, would have saved the world today," yet he offered parliament no account of those frustrated efforts at world salvation.[14] To a question from a CCF member about his visit to Hitler, he curtly replied, "The interchange of views and information which took place was of a nature which it is not the practice to disclose."[15] A Conservative member was not surprised at King's dusty response. "In the past it has been extremely difficult to get a discussion of foreign affairs ... It has been the practice to bring in the estimates of the Department of External Affairs near to the close of the session ... Year after year about the only opportunity that the House has had of discussing foreign or external affairs has been on the estimates, and they have come in very late."[16]

On 20 February 1938, King pondered again the continuing international turmoil after reading the leaves in his teacup. He told his diary that he was convinced that a major speech that Hitler was scheduled to make the same day "will be firm but conciliatory for peace and I believe that ultimately all will be well ... my letter to Von Ribbentrop ... may have [tipped] the balance ... I expressed faith in Hitler and his purpose being peace, with fearless assertion of what he believed to be justice to the German peoples. My letter would arrive just at the right moment." In the evening, King with great satisfaction duly described Hitler's "fine speech [as] indicating real leadership in an appalling European situation."[17]

As King reviewed what he regarded as his crucial role in promoting Anglo-German reconciliation, Joan Patteson telephoned him to say that she had heard on her husband's radio that Anthony Eden had resigned as foreign secretary, disagreeing with Chamberlain over, among many other things, Chamberlain's inept handling of Roosevelt's peace initiative and his continuing efforts to appease Mussolini. Public reaction in Britain toward Mussolini had become decidedly negative. It would presumably have been even more so if the unorthodox role of Austen Chamberlain's widow in Italian-British relations had been widely known. Temporarily resident in Rome, she wrote a private letter to Mussolini in an attempt to persuade him that her brother-in-law, Neville Chamberlain, was ready to put aside the Abyssinian imbroglio in the interest of greater mutual understanding. King, who had condemned Eden as the manipulator of Riddell and the League of Nations itself, welcomed his resignation: "Chamberlain and the cabinet are not favourable to League of Nations control ... [and] are looking to more direct relations with Germany and Italy, which ... is all to the good."[18] But King ignored the fact that Eden's departure contributed to the questions that gradually gathered round Chamberlain's premiership. Eden's less than clearly articulated reasons for resigning remained a handicap if he had ambitions to unseat Chamberlain. A.J.P. Taylor for one was not impressed. "Eden, the man of strong words, acquired retrospectively a mythical reputation as a man who favoured strong acts."

On 21 February, the prime minister appointed Lord Halifax, lord president of the council, as foreign secretary, although some cynics wondered why he had bothered since Chamberlain saw foreign policy as a one-man band and treated the cabinet like lap dogs. Halifax's qualification as foreign secretary, after a distinguished if occasionally controversial public career in India as well as in Britain, did not impress Duff Cooper, among others. The francophile first lord of the admiralty, wrote,

> I am afraid Halifax will be a bad Foreign Secretary. He knows very little about Europe, very little about foreigners, very little about men. He is a great friend of Geoffrey Dawson [the imperialist keep-out-of-Europe editor of the *Times*] whose influence is pernicious, and I think he is also a friend of Lothian's [sent by Chamberlain to Washington as ambassador on the eve of the war], who is always wrong. Nancy Astor [the American wife of Lord Astor] is to give a reception for him which is very foolish of him to allow her to do as she and her friends [the so-called Cliveden set] are justly suspected of being pro-German.[19]

Noel Annan, the lively chronicler of the 1930s, brought Nancy Astor (whom King had first met in London in 1923), Lord Halifax, and the Cliveden set together in a rather different way: "our generation thought her typical of the ruling class: numbed by the fear of communism and hypnotised like rabbits by the fascist stoat. For that was what Halifax appeared to be to the young – not a noble stag at bay but a bewildered, timorous rabbit … insight was not Halifax's strongest suit. When [in 1940] Churchill felt strong enough to sack him as Foreign Secretary and to persuade him to become ambassador in Washington, Halifax recorded his 'lively feeling of gratitude to Providence, operating through Churchill …' His wife, far more fly, knew exactly why Churchill offered him the job" – to get him out of the way.[20] Others, however, were not so certain of the shortcomings of the new foreign secretary when he gradually became more skeptical of the dictators than the prime minister. It was he who in 1939 stood up to Chamberlain on such a fundamental question as the guarantee to Poland.*

Amid the international turmoil of 1938, King remained certain of one thing: his favourable impression of Hitler. He wanted desperately to believe

---

*The measure of Halifax's success in demonstrating leadership and foreign policy understanding to many who remained wary of Churchill's adventurism was reflected in the fact that in May 1940 when Chamberlain resigned as prime minister he was seen as the only possible alternative to Churchill.

in him, the latter-day pilgrim who had become his guide. Nine months after his visit to Hitler, King was especially gratified that "it is no mere chance that I have met him … It is part of a mission … He is a pilgrim … his love of music, of Wagner Opera … strange this bringing together of Hitler and [John] Bunyan, both … meant to guide me at this time to the purpose of my life … which I believe to be to help men to know the secret of the path to peace."[21] He concluded yet again that his letter of congratulation to Ribbentrop of 6 February had somehow – he did not explain how – played a key part in the Führer committing himself to peace and justice for the German people. Equally, in commenting on what he saw as Chamberlain's wise policy of working for friendly relations with Italy and Germany, he had convinced himself that his visit to Berlin "was the beginning of drawing together … of [Britain and Germany]."[22] Chamberlain, however, in a letter of 13 March, reflected his belated and contrary conviction: it had become clear "that force is the only argument that Germany understands … a visible force of overwhelming strength backed by determination to use it."[23] A week later he added, "You have only to look at the map to see that nothing that France or we could do could possibly save Czecho-Slovakia from being overrun by the Germans if they wanted to do it … Czecho-Slovakia … would simply be a pretext for going to war … That we could not think of unless we had a reasonable prospect of being able to beat her [Germany] to her knees in a reasonable time and of that I see no sign. I have therefore abandoned any idea of giving guarantees to Czecho-Slovakia or to France in connection with her obligations to that country."[24] Of all this King sought no discussion. "The least that is said means the least being stirred up in the Commons and in the Press and in the minds of the people."[25]

At the same time, and with Quebec always in mind, King stayed as clear as he could of the League of Nations, the Spanish Civil War, and the persecution of Jews by the Nazis intent upon a "Jew-free" Germany. The Jewish Congress of Canada could be ignored, its membership being small, its influence still limited and most decidedly unwelcome to Quebec. On 29 March, King recorded in his diary a rare reference to the deteriorating plight of Jews in the Third Reich, a plight that had been briefly discussed in cabinet that same day. With Congressional elections, as always, pending in the United States, Roosevelt, at the urging of Jewish organizations and others, had invited twenty Latin American and nine European countries and Canada, New Zealand, and Australia to attend a conference on refugees at Evian on the

Swiss-French border (Switzerland had declined to be host). Its purpose was to encourage the invited governments to admit more – or any at all – German and Austrian (largely Jewish) refugees. Unknown to Ottawa, Washington privately described the initiative as intended "to have immigration laws liberalized."[26] In his diary King wrote,

A very difficult question has presented itself in Roosevelt's appeal to different countries to unite with the United States in admitting refugees from Austria, Germany, etc. That means, in a word, admitting numbers of Jews. My own feeling is that nothing is to be gained by creating an internal problem in an effort to meet an international one. That we must be careful not to seek to play the role of the dog in the manger so far as Canada is concerned, with our great open spaces and small population. We must nevertheless seek to keep this part of the Continent free from unrest and from too great an intermixture of foreign strains of blood, as much the same thing as lies at the basis of the Oriental [immigration] problem. I fear we would have riots if we agreed to a policy that admitted numbers of Jews. Also we would add to the difficulties between Provinces and the Dominion [i.e., between Quebec primarily and Ottawa].[27]

Little came of Roosevelt's initiative, other than he could now say during pending domestic elections that he had tried. The United States would not increase the numbers of refugees admitted annually, although it would allow those already in the United States on visitor visas – an estimated 15,000 – to remain (among them Thomas Mann and Albert Einstein). But Cordell Hull, the secretary of state, was convinced that "The more intelligent and thinking people in the country looked upon these racial and religious occurrences [in Germany] more as a matter of temporary abnormality."[28] On 6 June 1938, after Canada had reluctantly accepted Roosevelt's invitation of late April to Evian, Frederick Blair, the director of immigration, sent instructions to the advisory officer at the League of Nations in Geneva, Hume Wrong, who would represent Canada at the conference, along with the Canadian commissioner of European immigration based in London. Blair pointed out that Canada had in the previous six years accepted in proportion to its total population more Jewish refugees than the United States under its quota system.[29] He added, however, "speaking generally, refugee immigration has never been popular here and it presents problems beyond that of ordinary immigration." On 11 June the prime minister agreed, reviewing without comment much of the instructions to be sent to the permanent delegate, but he did add that the government "deeply and genuinely sympathizes with the victims of oppression and will be prepared to consider, as part of any general settlement, to apply its regulations in the most sympathetic and friendly fashion which may be practicable in the circumstance."[30] In other words, as in the case of oil sanctions at the League of Nations, Canada would not take an initiative but would go along with the majority. Skelton was even more wary than King of the Evian conference, since it could increase domestic pressures to do something for Jewish refugees. Both were aware from Lapointe as well as from Quebec newspapers, petitions, and other sources that the province was strongly opposed to any dilution of the stringent refugee policy – or the admission of refugees at all. Lapointe, fully aware of the electoral challenge facing the provincial Liberal Party from Duplessis's Union Nationale, saw yet another justification for opposing Jewish refugees

As early as September 1933, only nine months after Hitler had become chancellor, the Ligue d'action nationale had reflected the thinking of many Québécois still mired in economic depression. The Ligue, successor to L'Action canadienne française of which the controversial Abbé Groulx had been a director, sent a resolution to Bennett's government: "That the frontier of Canada should be completely closed … at this time of general unemploy ment … [and] that the Government of Canada should remain completely inflexible in the face of whatever Jewish pressure, national or worldwide … a group [i.e., Jews] which is accused by Germany of Marxism and communism … could not be a useful element for Canada, being on account of its faith, its customs and its unassimilable character, a source of division and dispute."[31]

The director of the Immigration Branch, housed unobtrusively in the Department of Mines and Resources, was one Frederick Blair, a long-serving official who "mirrored the increasingly anti-immigration spirit of his times. He believed, said one observer, 'that people should be kept out of Canada instead of being let in.'" Pressure on the part of Jewish people to get into Canada, he wrote, "has never been greater than it is now."[32] Whether Blair, in preparing the instructions for the delegation to the Evian conference in consultation with Skelton, was recommending what he believed the prime minister wanted to hear in light of the anti-Semitism primarily but certainly not exclusively in Quebec, or whether he was expressing his own deep-seated conviction that the prohibition against Jewish refugees was always the right policy to recommend to a particularly receptive prime minister can be left to those who have pursued with understanding that dolorous subject.[33] What is inconvertible is that King was ultimately responsible for Canada's pursuit of an anti-refugee immigration programme.

At the Evian conference, the chief American delegate – a steel tycoon – limited himself to the declaration that the United States would not increase its already filled German-Austrian quota, but aired Roosevelt's stillborn idea that a homeland for Jews might be found in one or more of the former German colonies in Africa or in the French colony of Madagascar. The Dominican Republic made a dramatic if self-serving offer of entry for 100,000 refugees, but only 757 had arrived by the beginning of the war. In the aftermath of the Kristallnacht, 9–10 November 1938, which drove many Jews to seek refuge abroad, Britain took many more children. Australia, however, said that it was free of "racial problems" and intended to remain so (although at the end of the year it reversed itself and announced its readiness to receive 15,000 refugees). Since, as had been widely anticipated, no "general settlement" emerged at Evian, King, fearing national divisions and even riots, did not elaborate on what if anything he intended to do. He felt no need to explain what he had meant by applying immigration regulations "in the most sympathetic and friendly fashion."[34]

On 20 February 1938, the same day that Eden resigned as foreign secretary, King welcomed news of Chamberlain's decision to discuss problems directly with Hitler, not through the League of Nations. This "is all to the good … The League of Nations is responsible for most of the situation as it is today. It is a second government trying to control the British and other governments."[35]* In the late 1930s, the dismissal of the League as a disaster had become a recurring leitmotif in his diary. Having made up his mind about its hopelessness, "the only real difference of opinion he had ever had with [Ernest] Lapointe was with regard to Canada's acceptance of the pres-

---

*Almost a decade after the Italian invasion of Abyssinia and the Hoare-Laval pact had in effect ended the League of Nations, King could still not leave it alone. In May 1944, when he went with Churchill to view the Normandy invasion fleet in the south of England, he said that "he did not believe there would have been a war if the League of Nations had never existed. He [Churchill] defended the League stoutly. He claimed that if action had been taken promptly when Hitler went to invade the Ruhr [sic], things would not have got any further" (King diary, 13 May 1944).

idency of the League Assembly." King had opposed it on the ground that "it would stimulate League thought in Canada, tend to lead us more deeply into League affairs and, possibly, foreign commitments."[36] In parallel, Chamberlain told his diary that "the League had failed to stop the [Abyssinian] war or to protect the victims and had thereby demonstrated the failure of collective security."[37] King could not have agreed more, but he never set out in any reasoned way his now unending opposition to the League or what he thought should replace it – if anything. In response to a comment of M.J. Coldwell of the CCF that "oil sanctions ought to have been agreed to," King responded briefly that they would have led to a war.

With regard to the crippled state of the League, King comforted himself with the thought that as far as communication between national leaders was concerned, there should be "an understanding between minds in different parts of the world without any exchange of correspondence. Certainly that has been the case between Roosevelt and myself … equally the case with Hitler and myself on what he, at heart, has mostly in mind. It relates itself also in a way to sharing in 'Cosmic Consciousness.'"[38] Why "Cosmic Consciousness" was superior to the League of Nations, King did not explain. Its unspecified shortcomings and failings he contrasted unfavourably with the superiority of his own undefined initiatives. The League became a ready scapegoat for his own misjudgments, frustrations, and insecurities. If he had not had the League at hand to castigate at the time of the Abyssinian and Sudetenland crises, he could not have escaped acknowledging that Hitler and Mussolini were much worse fellows than he ever admitted, at least until the beginning of the Second World War itself.

Despite Hitler's obvious designs on Austria, which Mussolini had earlier valued as a useful buffer state with Nazi Germany, Il Duce entered into a singularly ill-advised Rome-Berlin axis during Hitler's visit to Rome in May, leaving the French government even more uneasy. In central and Eastern Europe, the local dictatorships offered France no real military counterbalance to German aggression in the West, especially when Stalin's longer-term ambition was to replace such authoritarian regimes of the right by yet more authoritarian regimes of the left. Left- and right-wing street clashes in Paris and the provinces only increased France's uncertainties and sense of vulnerability. As King continued to fret about the League of Nations, the German army marched into Austria on 12 March 1938, triggering the *Anschluss* or merger that had been long and clearly forecast by Hitler. King recorded with astonishment, "The amazing fact of this whole situation is that it is all in complete accord with the book which Hitler himself has written, entitled *Mein Kampf*."[39]

In his diary King kept on grumbling about the League of Nations, instead of reflecting on what Hitler's ultimatum to the Austrian chancellor meant for the wider world. If the vicious Spanish Civil War was in his view no one's business but Spain's, it was no great jump to the conclusion that what was going on in Nazi Germany was no one's business but Germany's. King made no public and little private comment on the *Anschluss*, other than to record that he had felt all along that the annexation of Austria was inevitable. After all, Austrians spoke German, they were part of the *Volk*, and Hitler himself had been born in Austria. A plebiscite in Austria would, it was everywhere expected, reflect a widespread desire to join the now more prosperous Third Reich. But Lester Pearson, still secretary at Canada House in London, was at one with those such as Leopold Amery who were greatly concerned at the sudden and unilateral overturning of the balance of power in Europe. Pearson recalled, "Though I had for some years felt we should be patient and understanding about the Nazis because Germany would throw off this infection in due course, my views changed after the take-over of Austria. I became convinced that a showdown with Hitler was now inevitable and that if he did not back down (which he was unlikely to do), war could not be avoided. In Ottawa I was considered something of an alarmist."[40]

King was not alone in regarding the *Anschluss* as a natural development. "Only the wisdom of not attempting to meet force with force but yielding to an overpowering force has saved war between Austria and Germany to-day," a war in which Britain might well have become entangled and which would certainly have overturned the balance of power in Europe. King followed with a non sequitur. Sounding as if he were making a determined effort to convince himself, he dictated that "the sooner the League breaks up altogether as an instrument seeking peace through collective security, the better it will be for mankind. If it had never existed, we would not have had the situation we have in Europe today … it is just appalling the mischief that the League has wrought. It has been a millstone to bring down country after [unspecified] country who [*sic*] remains adhering with mere pretence to its Covenant … I have the satisfaction of knowing that I spoke out two years ago, at Geneva itself. Had a similar course been taken by Britain whose Ministers really felt as I did but were too frightened to speak for [domestic] political reasons ... even now the situation would be very different than it is." Undeterred he added, "a European war means the end of our present day civilisation in Europe ... the break-up of the British Empire ... That is too big a price to pay for any attempt to brook the actions of dictators in central Europe ... Better let freedom assert itself from within as is the rational way rather than to seek to impose it by force of arms ... That is where the League has made its appalling mistake; it was on a false basis from the start."[41] This from King who three years before had called on his fellow Canadians to stand four-square behind the League of Nations, the cornerstone of Canadian foreign policy.

The governor general, the novelist John Buchan, who had arrived in Ottawa at the end of 1935 as Lord Tweedsmuir, was soon convinced that "Canada has never yet thought out her position vis à vis the Empire and international affairs and is monopolised with her own domestic problems ... one of my chief tasks is to make Canada a little more conscious of her international obligations."[42] But to his sister in England he appeared more relaxed. "I do not myself quite see what there is to fuss about. Austria will be much more comfortable, economically, under Germany's wing. That should have been done long ago in the Versailles Treaty. The chief trouble will be if there is any real threat to Czechoslovakia; but there again, I think the frontier should be rectified. Surely the Versailles agreement was the most half-witted thing ever perpetrated."[43] Certainly the prime minister tacitly agreed with the governor general's detached views, as did many in London.

In the wake of the *Anschluss*, King recorded in his diary that "I am convinced he [Hitler] is a spiritualist – that he has a vision to which he is being true ... his devotion to his mother – that Mother's spirit is ... his guide and no one who does not understand this relationship – the worship of a highest purity in a mother – can understand the power to be derived therefrom or the guidance ... the world will yet come to see a very great man – a mystic, in Hitler." King again extolled the simplicity of the Führer's origins and tastes compared with the corruptions of the "smart set," repeating that he "will rank someday with Joan of Arc among the deliverers of his people, and ... the deliverer of Europe."[44] For Chamberlain's passive reaction to the *Anschluss*, King sent hyperbolic praise to Malcolm MacDonald: "I hope you will tell Mr Chamberlain that I cannot begin to express the admiration for the manner in which he has performed a task more difficult ... than any with which any Prime Minister of Great Britain has ever been faced. I approve wholeheartedly of the course he has adopted, particularly his determination to get in touch with Italy and Germany … and his exposure of the unreality, and worse, of the situation at Geneva."[45]

Following his successful *Anschluss* with Austria, Hitler next championed the discontented Sudeten German minority in Czechoslovakia, a further step in his hazardous *Drang nach Osten*. King, concerned that war might result from a Sudetenland confrontation, consoled himself with the thought that Britain was "doing all she can to bring Czechoslovakia to her senses."[46] But Czechoslovakia had still not come to her senses on 24 May – as Canada uniquely in the Empire celebrated Queen Victoria's birthday – when it rejected Hitler's aggressive claims. The subsequent months of 1938 were of dire uncertainty as Hitler pressed his extreme demands. Czechoslovakia sought the support of its 1924 treaty ally, France, while Britain attempted in vain to promote conciliation between Prague and the Sudeten Germans, Hitler's puppets. In these circumstances, Soviet Russia again sounded the wary British and French governments on how a common front against potential German armed aggression might be formed, given the fact that Poland and Romania had made it clear that they would not welcome Russian forces crossing their territories, any more than Chamberlain was enthusiastic about the Red Army establishing itself in Prague.

Mackenzie King believed that Britain was doing everything possible to avoid a war over the Sudeten Germans by putting pressure on Prague and by Henderson's appeasement efforts in Berlin. During a brief debate on foreign affairs in the House of Commons on 24 May, he declared, "There is no man in this Parliament who believes more strongly in the British Empire and the part it is playing in the world to-day than myself." If some Canadians saw that statement as some sort of commitment, King hastened to add for domestic political reasons, "There are no commitments of any kind on the part of this government with respect to any war in which the United Kingdom may be engaged. What may be done will be done as a result of the action of this Parliament."[47] In his two statements, he was satisfied that he had offered something for every Canadian.

King had been wary of Neville Chamberlain when he first met him, but now he looked upon him as the one person who could save humanity from another world war – and Canada from division. On becoming prime minister in May 1937, Chamberlain began to give substance to his fundamental conviction that appeasement in the form of "personal diplomacy" could result in restraining Hitler's vaulting ambitions. Churchill, and the troublesome young members of parliament who supported him, derided appeasement, especially when it was not backed by armed might, but it had few more ardent advocates than King. King set aside his real or assumed decade-old wariness of imperial centralists who in his view had been intent upon foisting upon the dominions a foreign policy of Whitehall's devising. Chamberlain, on the contrary, gave full expression to King's own conviction that anything was better than war. Hence King's praise for him throughout 1938 became almost endless. He compared him to Jesus Christ.

This was something of the background to King's reflections on the worrisome state of Europe in 1938, but in his diary there is little about the Spanish Civil War, the growing threat to the small states of central and Eastern Europe, and almost nothing about the mounting persecution in Germany of socialists, communists, outspoken church leaders, homosexuals, Jews, blacks, and other racial minorities. Other than his tirades against the now all but defunct League of Nations, King's priority through 1938 was to support Chamberlain's policy of conciliation of the two dictators without uttering a word of criticism of either.

Fifteen years before, at the 1923 imperial conference, King, making a show of opposing imperial centralists for domestic political reasons, had rejected any practical foreign policy collaboration among the dominions and Britain. But by 1938 he was, at least privately, in the vanguard of dominion supporters of Britain, even to the point of beginning to soft-pedal his mantra "parliament must decide," rightly confident that parliament, with its Liberal majority, would decide as he directed it. *Pace* Skelton, King was convinced that Canada should be at war when Britain was at war. Skelton had from the 1920s attempted to "stiffen" King in an isolationist stance, but in the end his almost two decades of "stiffening" were to no avail. Yet he persisted to the outbreak of war and even beyond in giving his minister the same basic advice that he had expounded since 1923. In so doing, he departed from the fundamental duty of a deputy minister to offer his minister his best advice (it was never then "her advice") and, if not accepted, to either loyally carry out the contrary policies of his minister or seek a transfer or resign. Skelton adopted none of these three options. He was throughout a most unorthodox deputy minister.

Jack Pickersgill, one of King's secretaries, was not surprised at his enthusiastic embrace of appeasement. "Over and over again he said that it was not what a leader accomplished but what he prevented that mattered most."[48] King was not, however, to escape the question so easily of what exactly his government was prepared to do if Britain became engaged in a major war. The question was indirectly but tangibly forced on him by queries from London about whether Canada would manufacture a Czech-designed light machine gun (the notably reliable Bren gun) for the British army and, if it chose, for the Canadian as well. A proposal for the training of Royal Air Force aircrew in Canada arrived at about the same time. King was unsettled by both. George Drew, the prominent Conservative, levelled ill-founded charges of corruption in the Bren manufacture. These were disproved by the prompt appointment of a review commission and the contract was eventually filled without arousing any real concerns in Quebec or elsewhere about Canada being drawn thereby into comprehensive defence cooperation with Britain. Yet the government's handling of the Bren gun project was marred by equivocation and delay. Even more so was the repeated query from London whether British airmen could be trained in Canada. King procrastinated and discussions about who was to be trained and who was to pay for what training and who was to serve where were strung out over three years, marked throughout by misunderstandings and frustration on both sides. Initially the plan was presented, at least to the naive, as an alternative to a Canadian army expeditionary force. King, at his equivocal worst, still pleaded national unity instead of devising ways in which both the British and Canadian air forces could be best trained to counter the undeniably formidable Luftwaffe. The agreement was finally concluded only upon the declaration of war itself. Once instituted, the British Commonwealth Air Training Plan proved to be a huge success.

Amidst these and other uncertainties, King was certain that only he could preserve the unity of Canada. Utterly unmilitary himself, he had long since condemned the use of armed force to settle international disputes. Talk offered a better way. If the League had been simply a place for talk, King might have remained supportive, but he eventually came to the remarkable conclusion that not Hitler but the League and its collective security provisions were responsible for the Second World War.

If King had been challenged in his proclaimed misgivings about the League and sanctions in particular, his candid answer might have included a regret that the League had destroyed the time-honoured "balance of power" that had served from the end of the Napoleonic wars in 1815 at least to the Franco-

Prussian War of 1870. That elusive concept had never been clearly delineated, but King appears to have concluded that the idealism of the League's founders had subtracted grievously from Britain's pre-eminent role in the world and had reduced France to seeking a spurious balance of power by alliances with a doubtful array of central and Eastern European states – including the Soviet Union – as a counterbalance to the menace of Germany's rapidly growing military and economic power. Italy's invasion of Abyssinia had effectively ended the League of Nations, although King, in his long speech to the House of Commons on 24 May 1938, repeated his statements that "the sanctions articles have ceased to have effect ... and cannot be revived by any state ... at all." Accordingly, King reasoned that it was time to line up behind Britain, supporting Chamberlain's dual policy of appeasement and rearmament. Sounding like Bennett, King concluded that "co-operation between all parts of the Empire and the democracies is in Canada's interest in the long run ... the only possible attitude to be assumed."[49]

Skelton finally recognized that his minister had wholly abandoned isolationism, in fact had never embraced it. King was clearly veering back toward the imperial fold, the only haven for Canada with the League all but gone. With Chamberlain embarking upon his ill-fated efforts to appease the two dictators, King became increasingly single-minded in his support of a British – or an imperial – foreign policy. To the isolationist Skelton's consternation, King had not in fact drawn away from the Empire as he had appeared to do in the early 1920s. He now spoke instead of the triumphs of British diplomacy (Skelton only of its failures) and began to send frequent and fulsome private messages to Chamberlain that Canada supported him to the hilt in his appeasement efforts, reflecting in an aberrant form Laurier's and Meighen's "Ready, aye Ready."

Chamberlain noted with satisfaction Canada's support, as expressed variously by King, Bennett, and Beaverbrook. He wrote to his sisters, "I had a letter from R.B. Bennett the other day and he says that Max Beaverbrook recently wrote to him, 'N.C. is the best P.M. we've had in half a century. He is dominating Parliament, but the country has not yet taken to him. If he gets Baldwin's popularity he will be P.M. for the rest of his life. At 69 he works harder than any of his colleagues. His efforts to separate the Italians from Germany will succeed, I think.' And I also heard from Tweedsmuir ... who says 'I am delighted to see that you have British opinion solidly behind you. You certainly have Canada's.'"[50] In King's view, Chamberlain "merits immortal memory if he saves – as he is doing – the world from a war."[51] Indulging in no false modesty, King saw himself as playing a central role in Chamberlain's pursuit of the appeasement since "I know of no man who has to the degree that I possess it the confidence of Chamberlain, Roosevelt, and Hitler, and I might add [Prime Minister of France Leon] Blum and also Mussolini and Japan."[52]

By May 1938, Czechoslovakia had obviously become Hitler's next and immediate target. Yet King remained hopeful. "If Hitler holds back I shall always believe that my visit to Germany and my talk with him – more than any other single factor – is responsible ... Also the friendship that I have maintained with von Ribbentrop. There is no doubt that there was the beginning of the rapprochement between England and Germany ... also that my attitude with Chamberlain helped in relations with Italy, etc."[53] He asked Tweedsmuir "whether it is not agreed that my little visit to Berlin, a year ago, was not helping to inspire a little more in the way of confidence?"[54] His unique perception of his own key role was only strengthened by his recollection that Hitler was a man "who is abstemious in his habits, and gets into the quiet atmosphere of his mountain retreat in reaching the great decisions which decide not only his own fate and that of his country but one might also say the fate of mankind. I still believe that he will hold to his decision not to permit a general war. His decision, however, may be set at nought should the Czechs become aggressive."[55] King added to Joan Patteson, who was helping to keep him informed of what was happening in Europe by listening to her husband's radio, that he was glad that Hitler "did not drink ... loved nature and the quiet ... Joan remarked ... on the curious circumstance [that while] Hitler was in his home in the country, I was at my retreat in the country, and said to send a thought to him" (presumably by "cosmic consciousness"). King prayed that God's guidance might be vouchsafed to Hitler. "I pray he may ... help the cause of world peace and European appeasement ... if he does he will come ere long to be loved as dearly as he is greatly feared ... This is his chance – a really great opportunity ... he will rise to it for I have faith in him. I have prayed for him in my prayers, for God's guidance."[56] Given these yearnings, it is not surprising that King found reassurance in a long letter from Tweedsmuir, on sick leave in Britain, in which he described how Chamberlain and Halifax were "pretty optimistic. They are finding difficulties with the Czecho-Slovakian Government which is pretty obstinate and they are speaking very candidly to it."[57]

In parallel with his support of appeasement, King instituted, however reluctantly, a small degree of rearmament, following Chamberlain's more extensive programme. For the first time King discussed briefly with cabinet colleagues the possibility that war might break out over the Sudeten issue. He finally said to a few of his ministers what he had already said to Hitler and to Chamberlain; that if Britain itself were threatened, Canada would not stand idly by. He had repeatedly proclaimed from the early 1920s that parliament would decide whether Canada should go to war, but now he acknowledged explicitly to his diary that the Liberal majority in parliament would do whatever he told it to do. This had not been clear to the British government at the time. Hoare later wrote "the fact remains that the Commonwealth governments were unwilling to go to war on the issue of Czechoslovakia. Dominion opinion … was overwhelmingly against a world war … As early as March 18, 1938, he had been told South Africa and Canada [and Ireland] would not join us in a war to prevent certain Germans from rejoining the Fatherland."[58]

By the end of May 1938, Chamberlain was uneasy about the increasingly aggressive noises that Hitler was making about the Sudetenland. Worse still, Chamberlain deplored an incident on the Czech border as showing "how utterly untrustworthy and dishonest the German Government is and it illuminates the difficulties in the way of the peacemaker."[59] But Lloyd George, from the parliamentary sidelines, spoke of Germany being "surrounded by a mob of small states, many of them consisting of peoples who have never previously set up a stable government for themselves, but each of them containing large masses of Germans."[60] As in the case of Austria, the *Volk* of the Sudetenland should again be one with other Germans. That distortion of the principle of self-determination, so central to the Versailles treaty, did not appear unreasonable to appeasers in a Britain intent above all upon avoiding war, an attitude that King fully shared.

In these worsening circumstances, Roosevelt in effect extended the Monroe doctrine to Canada. The president received an honorary doctorate from Queen's University in Kingston, Ontario on 8 August. (This was his second visit to Canada in two years.) He began his acceptance speech by recognizing that "The Dominion of Canada is part of the sisterhood of the British Empire." More pronounced Canadian isolationists, the former Queen's University dean Skelton among them, would not have put it quite that way, but they joined in welcoming Roosevelt's pledge: "I give to you assurance that the people of the United States will not stand idly by if the domination of Canadian soil is threatened by any other empire."[61] Even an isolationist United States could be counted on, for reasons of its own security, to protect Canada and to support the British Empire to whatever degree possible as a sort of first line of defence, Roosevelt speculating privately that the United States could be bombed by long range German or Japanese aircraft from bases in pro-fascist states in Latin America. In his gratification, King no doubt reflected the majority view across Canada, but in the privacy of his diary, "the American" recorded his reservations about whether the United States could always be trusted.

On 31 August 1938, in the wake of Roosevelt's visit, King took a rare initiative. He told two of his ministers, Chubby Power of Quebec and Ian Mackenzie of Vancouver, that if war came as a result of the mounting German pressure on Czechoslovakia, "I would stand for Canada doing all she possibly could to destroy those Powers [Germany and Italy] which are basing their action on *might* and not on *right*, and that I would not consider being neutral … for a moment." Power responded to King's unwonted candour that in such circumstances "some of the Quebec men [would consider] leaving the Party." King bluntly replied – no circumlocutions this time – that Quebec cabinet ministers should realize "that it would be the end of Quebec if any attitude of that kind were adopted by the French Canadians in a world conflict … They, as members of the Government [and not the prime minister himself], ought to lead the Province in seeing its obligation to participate, and making clear the real issue and what it involves."[62] Ironically, the same might have been said of King himself at the time of the Abyssinian crisis.

Publicly, King remained wholly committed to Chamberlain's policy of appeasement. It could appeal to both English and French Canada, Quebec supporting appeasement as a means of avoiding another devastating war – and possible conscription – while much of English Canada supported it since it would help to preserve the position of the British Empire in the world. The British economy and imperial trade and, more basically, domestic democratic traditions and institutions were not to be jeopardized for the sake of a small state in central Europe. For this and much else, King took some of the credit for Chamberlain's efforts. "I shall never cease to be grateful enough or to believe that it was other than providential that I was the first to give Hitler any faith in Chamberlain and telling him that

I believed Chamberlain could be relied upon to see that what was fair and right was done."[63]

On 6 September, King was able to send to Chamberlain a direct message of encouragement via Hamar Greenwood, his old classmate at the University of Toronto, rather than having to rely on transatlantic telegrams or surface mail. Viscount Greenwood, his wife, and two of their children called on him at Kingsmere, following the conferring of an honorary doctorate upon Greenwood by his alma mater. "We had been talking about my visit to Hitler and of what I had said to him about not destroying anything, not to be tempted to acts of destruction, but to carry on with his works for the people … I told him to tell Chamberlain by all means to keep on keeping the nations out of war; that he was adopting the Christian attitude of non-resistance in the face of great provocation. That that was appealing strongly to the people and that if action [i.e., fighting] were precipitated, the Empire might be torn into shreds."[64] King's message to Chamberlain via Greenwood was heartfelt.

On 8 September, two days after seeing Greenwood, King turned his mind to "the renewed unfortunate happenings in Czechoslovakia" ("unfortunate happenings," not German aggression). Again, King did not condemn Hitler, instead defining the Sudetenland seizure as "the sort of thing that Hitler had said so often might lead to a beginning of hostilities beyond his control … The only hope I see now is pretty much Chamberlain and Hitler being brought in as direct touch with each other as possible in a manner which will ensure solution of the larger German problems and cordial relations with Germany."[65] Although Chamberlain, unlike King, now regarded Hitler as "utterly untrustworthy and dishonest," he nevertheless pressed on with his additional attempts to appease him.[66]

King could not deny himself another unedifying broadside at the League of Nations, perhaps in an effort to convince himself of the correctness of the nonsense that he kept repeating to himself. "It was the League of Nations' policy which led to Britain's disarmament … the League of Nations had been responsible for the present world condition … The absurd way with which the League people talk of collective security always exasperates one." He concluded that Hitler "has made clear that if the problem of the Sudeten Germans is not settled, he will go to their assistance and solve it."[67] King had set out the correct route to peace in his long book on labour relations, published two decades before, with the basic theme that conciliation was better than coercion. Its turgid ambiguity, which opens it to almost any interpretation by King or anyone else, was in his mind as much an argument for international as for industrial conciliation and avoidance of conflict. "The more I think of the world's problems today ... the more I believe that in my *Industry and Humanity* will be found the fundamental truths with respect thereto ... I wish that I had spent part of my years preaching the Gospel; only a sort of sensitiveness ... in the way of publicity has prevented me from doing that."[68]

Skelton, in a long memorandum, again argued that Canada must be isolationist, sheltering under the umbrella of the United States. King rejected this, convinced that "our real self-interest lies in the strength of the British Empire as a whole, not in our geographical position."[69] On the same day in London, Massey, although once an appeaser himself, put his view of Hitler more succinctly in his diary. "It is a ghastly thing that our fate rests in the hands of a demented paperhanger,"[70] but from Paris there arrived a reassuring letter from Philippe Roy, the long-serving Canadian minister in France and sometime delegate to the League of Nations, reflecting the now desperate optimism in Paris that Hitler might yet be appeased. Sounding like King himself, Roy wrote to him, "The impression prevails in Europe that war is inevitable [but] as I hold Hitler for an intelligent man, my opinion is that peace can be preserved ... the German Chancellor will not take the risk of spoiling his wonderful achievements in Germany."[71]

Hitler, in King's sympathetic view, had good reason to deplore the rumoured intent of Britain and France to make a deal with Stalin, which Churchill was urging as a "Grand Alliance." Hitler "has made out a strong case in reference to democracies against dictatorships when he said that the chief ally of France and England was Russia, the worst of all dictatorships. Hitler has spoken out like a man. Exposed fearlessly some of the current hypocrisies. It looks as though pressure will be put on Czecho-Slovakia to have matters settled by a plebiscite."[72] Hitler himself was doing no wrong. It was the obstinate Czechs who were so difficult in supporting the intransigent Edvard Beneš. King wrote to Charles Dunning, the minister of finance, on 3 September that "My mind is wholly clear as to the course we should pursue ... I have tried to anticipate what might be necessary ... with regard to the summoning of Parliament, most important of all would, of course, be the question of our participation in the event of Britain going into the war."[73] King repeated his conviction to Norman Rogers, the minister of labour and, rare for King, something of a convivial protégé. Rogers agreed with him that "it was a self-evident national duty, if Britain entered the war, that Canada should regard herself as part of the British Empire, one of the nations of the sisterhood of nations, which should co-operate lending every assistance possible, in no way asserting neutrality."[74] King's timely if not belated elaboration of his pledge to the 1923 imperial conference was wormwood for Skelton, who had wasted more than a decade vainly attempting to wean his minister away from strengthening the British Commonwealth of Nations toward embracing North American isolationism and even neutrality.

The reaction of London and Paris to the Sudetenland crisis included variously confusion, anxiety, fortitude, and appeasement. As fear of another world war became more prevalent, massive Anglo-French pressure was put on Prague to accede to even the most extravagant German demands. For example, on the same day that King and Rogers spoke about Canada's self-evident national duty, Duff Cooper, first lord of the admiralty, recorded in his diary, "There were a lot of Foreign Office telegrams to read, including one admirable one instructing Henderson [the British ambassador in Berlin] to make it quite plain to the German Government where we should stand in the event of war [over the Sudetenland]. In reply to this there was a series of messages from Henderson which seemed to me almost hysterical, imploring the Government not to insist upon his carrying out their instructions, which he was sure would have the opposite effect to that desired. And the Government [despite Foreign Office advice to the contrary] had given way."[75]*

Chamberlain's efforts to appease Hitler, so welcomed by King, were not based on the simple proposition that Hitler might somehow be bought off. During 1937 and 1938 the British cabinet, with few exceptions, rightly feared that neither the army nor the air force was prepared for a major conflict on the continent, let alone across the Empire. At the end of 1937, the chiefs of staff had endorsed a fundamental consideration: "We cannot exaggerate

---

*One month before, the attorney general of Australia and future prime minister, Robert Menzies, on visiting Berlin, had a different impression of Henderson from that of Cooper. In addition to noting how highly Chamberlain and Halifax were thought of in Berlin, he wrote to his prime minister, "Henderson is an extremely clear-headed and sensible fellow with a frank and even breezy method of putting the British view to the Germans. The Czechoslovakian government, on the other hand, was being difficult over the Sudetenland and a very firm hand by the British will be required in Prague" (Menzies to Lyons, 6 August 1938, in Meany, *Australia and the World*, 438).

the importance ... of any political or international action that can be taken to reduce the numbers of our potential enemies and to gain support of political allies." Lord Halifax, the foreign secretary, put the case against France, Czechoslovakia's ally, going to that country's assistance; "it was hopeless if she chose to do so and it accordingly behoved us to take every step that we could and use every argument that we could think of to dissuade France from going to the aid of Czecho-Slovakia" (thereby triggering a continent-wide if not world war). Halifax then raised the central question: whether it was "justifiable to fight a certain war in order to forestall a possible war later." Duff Cooper, in referring to the Anglo-French idea of a plebiscite in the Sudetenland, correctly put Halifax's question on its head: "the choice was not between war and a plebiscite, but between war now or war later."[76] With the League of Nations undermined by the failure of Britain and France to act on Italy's invasion of Abyssinia, Chamberlain and Halifax, although agreeing that Hitler was "probably mad" or at least "half mad," continued to cast about for some peaceful way to avoid Nazi Germany's seizure of the Sudetenland by force, even if confronted by Czechoslovakia's exceptionally well trained and equipped army.

Chamberlain launched his personal diplomacy with a dramatic message to the German chancellor. "In view of the increasingly critical situation, I propose to come over at once to see you, with a view to finding a peaceful solution ... am ready to start tomorrow."[77] The next day, 14 September, the British high commissioner in Ottawa informed Skelton of Chamberlain's offer to fly to Germany to discuss "the Sudeten problem." On 15 September, the British prime minister landed in Munich on what was to be the first of three visits within a fortnight. King recorded his huge gratification at Chamberlain's sudden initiative. In a press statement he declared, "the whole of the Canadian people will warmly approve this striking and noble action on the part of Mr Chamberlain."[78] Privately to his diary he was both enthusiastic and certain that he had played a key part in bringing about Chamberlain's dramatic decision.

> What Chamberlain is doing is entirely the right thing ... I recall how my last words to Hitler were that he would like Chamberlain, that he could trust him, he was a man he could deal with, that he was truly anxious to bring about better relations between Germany and Britain. Hitler said to me that he was pleased to know this. That will be

remembered at this time … It is the most momentous meeting between two men that has ever been held in the history of the world. Each of them has peace at heart … It is well for Chamberlain that he was born into this world, and for the world that he was born into it. His name will go down in history as one of the greatest men that ever lived … I believe that his [late] father and brother have been at his side in every move and that they and all the forces above them have been directing his course … I know each of them, and I have talked to each of them about the other, and there is sufficient confidence between the three of us to cause me to feel pretty sure as to what the outcome will be … Chamberlain and I and Hitler have figured in a relationship that has been exceedingly significant … My life's efforts to further peace between classes and races and, in particular, between Germany and Britain are being answered to-day, and I have been used as an instrument to help toward that great end.[79]

To help toward that great end, King immediately sent a telegram to Ribbentrop in Berlin, asking him to tell Hitler "how thankful I am that he and Mr Chamberlain are to meet each other tomorrow … and how sincerely I believe their joint efforts may … further the peace of the world." In a separate *en clair* telegram to Henderson in Berlin, King asked him, if he thought it helpful, to convey a similar message to Hitler.[80] He cabled Chamberlain his "profound admiration for the vision and courage shown in your decision to have a personal interview with Herr Hitler."[81]

Following Chamberlain's arrival at the Munich airport on 15 September, a special train took him to the chancellor's beloved mountain retreat at Berchtesgaden in the Bavarian Alps. Hitler described the unendurable suffering of the Sudeten Germans under despotic Czechoslovak rule. If Prague did not immediately cede the Sudetenland to Germany, Hitler would seize it by military force. Chamberlain undertook to place Hitler's decision before his cabinet and the French government. Both London and Paris agreed in turn to put to Prague the stark choice of either accepting the outrageous German demands or being left to fight Germany alone.

Before his departure for Germany, Chamberlain had told one of his sisters that the chancellor was a lunatic, "entirely undistinguished. You would never notice him in a crowd and would take him for the house painter he once was."[82] According to the United States ambassador in London, Chamberlain returned from his first encounter with Hitler with an "intense dislike [of him] as cruel, over-bearing ... and thoroughly convinced ... that he would be completely ruthless." But Chamberlain recorded that he nevertheless wanted to believe well of Hitler and his intentions. "It was impossible not to be impressed with the power of this man. He was extremely determined; he had thought out what he wanted and he meant to get it." He also deluded himself into believing that " Hitler's objectives were strictly limited." Of course they were not. Chamberlain and the French prime minister, Édouard Daladier, despite French treaty obligations, acquiesced to Hitler's demand for the cessation of the Sudetenland, on the specious justification of self-determination for the *Volk* in the Sudetenland. "The alternatives are not between abject surrender and war. Acceptance of the principle of self-determination is not an abject surrender."[83] Several of Chamberlain's cabinet, however, saw the Berchtesgaden meeting as an abject surrender.

Chamberlain justified his efforts at appeasement at a second meeting with Hitler on 23 September at Bad Godesberg on the grounds that the dominions were opposed to any confrontation with Hitler, among other reasons. The British prime minister "may well have been influenced by the knowledge that the Dominions would not view a struggle to keep certain Germans under Czech control as a good and sufficient cause for which to launch a European war."[84]At best the Commonwealth, like British public opinion, would be divided. But Duff Cooper for one disagreed. "As for the Dominions, could we expect that they would even all be united on the prospect of coming into a European war? They were not necessary to us for the conduct of the war ... If we were now to desert the Czechs or even advise them to surrender, we should be guilty of one the basest betrayals in history."[85] But Chamberlain again gave way to Hitler. The British and French forced Prague to cede the territory – and with it Czechoslovakia's formidable border defences – to Germany.

In this King rejoiced. "Somehow I feel that at last a way out is going to open. Hitler might come to be thought of as one of the saviours of the world ... He was looking to Force, to Might and to Violence as means to achieving his ends, which were ... the well-being of his fellow-men ... Chamberlain will be known as much if the present conferences open a path to peace. He has thought nothing of himself and his life, not for the men of his own race alone, but for the world's peace. There has been nothing finer in the Christian era."[86] In one of his rare statements to the press, Mackenzie King stated that he regarded Chamberlain's decision to fly to Germany as a truly noble act.

Highly gratifying to King was the thought of the instrumental part he had played in bringing Chamberlain and Hitler together. "My message to Chamberlain will be helpful. It will be helpful to Chamberlain. It will be helpful to Hitler. I know each of them, and I have talked to each of them about the other, and there is sufficient confidence between the three of us to cause me to feel pretty sure as to what the outcome will be." After reviewing for his diary every step in his relationship with Ribbentrop, including his 1937 Christmas greeting "with a word direct to Hitler" and the steps he had taken to provide Göring with additional bison, King concluded, "I have been used as an instrument to help towards that great end ... unseen forces have unquestionably been working together in using me ... in the great purpose of the preservation of peace."[87] As he wrote to Tweedsmuir, "You may recall how strongly I urged those personal contacts. While it is not yet clear war will be avoided, it is altogether certain that but for Chamberlain's meeting with Hitler we should have been in the throes of a world war today."[88] From London, Churchill, still dismissed by some as a militarist warmonger, could not have disagreed more. In a press release of 21 September, he proclaimed, "The partition of Czechoslovakia under pressure from England and France amounts to the complete surrender of the Western Democracies to the Nazi threat of force. Such a collapse will bring peace or security neither to England nor to France. On the contrary, it will place these two nations in an ever weaker and more dangerous situation."[89]

In recording again his unbounded enthusiasm and gratitude for Chamberlain's efforts to appease Hitler, King reverted to his conviction that "If there is to be war ... and Canada is to be in it, it is much better that we should come in as a united country, and that we should not be hopelessly divided before war itself takes place. I am still hoping, and believe, that war will be avoided." In reviewing his role "as representing Canada as a really significant Dominion of the Empire," King dictated to his secretary his special gratification that a second Chamberlain-Hitler meeting would be "half way [between Berlin and London], Hitler suggested [Cologne] and the third meeting, would have Hitler himself coming to London."[90]

Ivone Kirkpatrick, the first secretary at the British Embassy in Berlin who accompanied the prime minister on all three visits to Hitler, saw clearly enough the man whom Chamberlain was attempting to conciliate. He told Harold Nicolson that to meet [Hitler] socially, and when he is host in his own house, he has a certain simple dignity, like a farmer entertaining neighbours. All very different from the showy vulgarity of Mussolini. But that once one begins to work with him, or sees him dealing with great affairs, one has such a sense of evil arrogance that one is almost nauseated ... Evil and treachery and malice dart in Hitler's mystic eyes. He has a maddening habit of laying down the law in sharp, syncopated sentences, accompanying the conclusion either with a short pat of the palm of his hand upon the table or by a half-swing sideways in his chair, a sudden Napoleonic crossing of his arms, and a gaze of detached but suffering mysticism towards the ceiling. His impatience is terrific.[91]

Yet Chamberlain recorded a positive impression of Hitler that at least for the moment approached King's conviction: "here was a man who could be relied upon when he had given his word."[92]

When Prague, with understandably the greatest reluctance and foreboding, agreed to the Anglo-French "advice" to cede the Sudetenland to Germany, Chamberlain made his second flight to Germany, to confirm to Hitler Prague's agreement. To his consternation, Hitler now demonstrated that he certainly could not be relied upon when he had given his word. At Bad Godesberg he raised the ante by telling a disconcerted Chamberlain that Prague's acceptance of the German demands as pressed on it by France and Britain would take too long and was no longer sufficient. German forces would immediately occupy the Sudetenland up to new borders to be drawn by Germany alone, not to be negotiated with Prague. He added that Poland and Hungary also demanded their pound of flesh: the cessation to them of certain areas of Czechoslovakia where their nationals formed a substantial minority. Acceptance of the Bad Godesburg demands would, in the apt words of the *Daily Telegraph*, render Czechoslovakia militarily indefensible, economically broken, and politically subjugated completely to German domination.[93] Skeptics regarded Chamberlain's effort at appeasement as "a clever plan of selling your friends in order to buy off your enemies."[94]

King concluded in a monumental understatement that the second meeting between Hitler and Chamberlain, who "has been fighting the battle of those who wish to avoid war at all costs, ... has not been too good."[95] He nevertheless had found time on 20 September to write to the governor general about Asia, imaginatively proposing that he himself lead an undefined mission to

Japan, which had invaded China a year before (he told his diary he would draw on his experiences of thirty years before to explore appeasement of Japan's various ambitions across Asia). Tweedsmuir's reply, if he made one, is unknown.[96]

In an extraordinary diary entry of 23 September, dictated in several stages, King concluded that the League of Nations and not Nazi Germany was responsible for the Sudeten crisis. The League, once the only hope for the world, had in his mind become "a curse to the world … unsettling nations in the direct management of their own affairs and substituting talk for reality, 'gibber' as Hitler calls it." King repeatedly reviewed whether "paganism or Christianity is to be the basis of civilisation … Whether might or right is to control. Whether materialism is to triumph over spiritualism."[97] In his diary dictation, he was reassuring himself that he was on the right course in developing phrases for a public statement advising Canadians to keep calm (although not yet to dig), to have confidence in their government, etc., etc. The isolationist Skelton was predictably "avert [*sic*] to anything of the sort," but King kept dictating phrases of commitment to Britain before calling a cabinet meeting in the late afternoon to which he candidly put as the essence of his position that if the United Kingdom were to be involved in war over Czechoslovakia, Canada would be as well. He would issue a public statement: "The world might as well know at once that Canada will not stand idly by and see modern civilization ruthlessly destroyed if we can by co-operation with others help save mankind from such a fate." With that, King finally abandoned his familiar mantra of parliament will decide.

J.L. Ilsley, the minister of national revenue, and Ian MacKenzie, the minister of national defence, were for making such a public statement immediately. In the absence of Lapointe, at the League of Nations in Geneva, Power assured his cabinet colleagues that Quebec was much less antagonistic than he had hitherto thought. Quebec's leaders were impressed by the "extent to which Britain and France had humiliated herself [*sic*] and … seemed to feel that Hitler could not be allowed to go farther." Cardin, the minister of public works, agreed with Power. On the other hand, Euler, the minister of trade and commerce, agreed with Lapointe's message from Geneva that no "statement should be issued and was not sure that a war would yet come about."[98] Lapointe had cabled – in King's words – that "he was very anxious nothing should be done till Parliament meets." With apparent strong feeling, Lapointe had concluded, "I do not see how I can advise any course of action that would not only be opposed to personal convictions and sacred pledges to my own people, but would destroy all their confidence and prevent me from carrying weight and influence with them for what might be essential future actions."[99]

King, regarding Lapointe's telegram as tantamount to a threat of resignation, reversed himself, deciding that no public statement need be issued immediately; better to wait to hear from London what exactly Chamberlain had concluded at Bad Godesberg. He felt like a "cad" for not issuing his original statement, but he did clarify, once and for all, how he proposed to proceed, opposition of Lapointe notwithstanding. "There never was a clearer issue or one that demanded that all who love peace should be prepared to sacrifice their lives … to see that it is maintained … if Germany goes too far, the struggle will not end until those who put their reliance on force are well-nigh exterminated."[100] On 27 September, King issued a watered down press statement to satisfy Lapointe, restoring "Parliament will decide." The government "is making preparations for any contingency and for the immediate summoning of Parliament if the efforts which are still being made to preserve the peace of Europe should fail. For our country to keep united is all-important. To this end, in whatever we say or do, we must seek to avoid creating controversies and divisions that might seriously impair effective and concerted action when Parliament meets."[101]

Chamberlain returned to London from his second meeting faced with the stark choice of war or acceptance of Hitler's additional demands. On 26 September Massey reported that after an hour-long meeting of the high commissioners with the prime minister – on this occasion King did not respond by likening the meeting to an imperial council – "My impression is that he and his Government feel that they have exhausted every means of avoiding catastrophe and they are none too confident that it can be averted."[102] The next evening Chamberlain began a BBC broadcast with a remarkable sentence that would plague him for the few years of life that remained to him: "How horrible, fantastic, incredible it is that we should be digging trenches and fitting gas-masks because of a quarrel in a far away country between peoples of whom we know nothing," adding, "I would not hesitate to pay even a third visit to Germany, if I thought it would do any good."[103] King promptly announced that he was in "complete accord with the statement Mr Chamberlain has made to the world to-day."[104] That same evening Chamberlain told a suddenly ecstatic House of Commons that Hitler had delayed his invasion of Czechoslovakia to allow time for a conference in Munich the next day. Chamberlain flew to Munich for his third confrontation with Hitler at a hastily cobbled together "last effort."

King was thrilled to receive word from London "that Hitler had agreed to meet Chamberlain, Daladier, and Mussolini at Munich tomorrow." No news could have been better, replete as it appeared with promise for a peaceful future. It also countered a wrong impression in Quebec left by King's statement of the day before. "It did not occur to me that the Province of Quebec might regard the [statement] as indicating a determination to participate [in a war] … I confess to a relief indescribable." But King was quite clear to Skelton that Canada would participate if war came. Parliament would decide "that if Britain was at war … we would have to accept the view that Canada was also at war … I do not agree with S[kelton]'s view that it would be sympathy for Britain that would be the determining factor for Canada going into war … the determining factor would be the determination not to permit the fear of Force to dominate the affairs of men and nations."[105] Skelton was left with a full year before the war to ponder the failure of his obstinate attempts to convince his minister that perfidious Albion would seek to drag Canada into a war which was European in essence and had nothing to do with Canada's interests, moral or otherwise: "This is not our war," Skelton continued to say, although to no avail. King had effectively sidelined him.

At Munich on 29 September Hitler, to his annoyance, did not gain all of Czechoslovakia at one fell swoop, but he did acquire the Sudetenland without firing a shot. Britain, France, and Italy endorsed his immediate occupation of the Sudetenland. Poland and Hungary took those areas of Czechoslovakia that they coveted. What then was left of Czechoslovakia was guaranteed – for the moment – against unprovoked aggression, a guarantee that proved meaningless when six months later Hitler seized the remainder of the country. The British historian A.J.P. Taylor analyzed Chamberlain's final meeting with Hitler in terms of *Realpolitik*. "Appeasement had begun as an impartial consideration of rival claims and the remedying of past faults. Then it had been justified by the French fear of war. Now its motive appeared to be fear on the part of the British themselves."[106] Chamberlain went to Munich not to seek justice for the Sudeten Germans or even to save the French from war; he went, or so it appeared, to save the British themselves from air-attack. Elsewhere Taylor added, "Munich sprung from a mixture of fear and good intentions. In retrospect, fear dominated."[107]

King rejoiced in the Munich agreement, as did huge crowds in London and Munich itself, freed from the fear of war. Lady Diana Cooper, Duff Cooper's wife, later described how "The Prime Minister called at the Palace to announce his so-called triumph to the King and Queen. They were photographed on the balcony on each side of him (a photograph that I saw the next day torn and burnt in the fireplace by a man of principle). The Mall and Whitehall I could imagine from the noise held millions of joy-mad people, swarming up the lampposts and railings, singing and crying with relief that it was peace ... Duff and I sat ... holding hands ... That evening he resigned."[108] The popular relief was hardly less pronounced in Canada. The *Toronto Star* on 30 September reported that "men and women ... [were] frozen in their tracks until news of the agreement had been digested. Their eyes alight, faces gleaming, arms around each other they danced happily off to celebrate the lifting of the curtain of death which hung like a black, heart-stopping pall over their lives."

As Mackenzie King was happily contemplating the post-Munich Hitler "as one of the saviours of the world," Chamberlain himself thought of the dictator quite otherwise. Duff Cooper recorded Chamberlain as telling the cabinet that at Munich, Hitler had struck him "as the commonest little dog he had ever seen, without one sign of distinction, nevertheless he [Chamberlain] was obviously pleased at the reports he had subsequently received of the good impression that he had himself made. He told us with obvious satisfaction how Hitler had said to someone that he had felt that he, Chamberlain, was 'a man.'" In fact, Hitler spoke of Chamberlain and Daladier as "small worms."[109] Göring did not come out of the crisis intact, as a result of urging upon a highly excited and impatient Hitler a delay in invading Czechoslovakia. Ribbentrop had been the hawk, and a violently anti-British one at that. But those were details. For people across the globe, Munich was seen as an unmitigated triumph of the will for Hitler.

On 29 September King wrote in his diary, "What a happy man Chamberlain must be, and what an example he has set the world in perseverance of a just cause ... I ... knelt down and thanked God with all my heart for the peace that has been preserved to the world."[110] The following day King did a most unusual thing for a head of government or even a secretary of state for external affairs. He called upon the heads of mission in Ottawa of three of the four countries represented at Munich (Germany, Italy, and France), but as the British high commissioner reported with some amusement to London, "his visits failed to include one to this office," King seeing himself as communicating directly only with the British prime minister, the dominions secretary, or the governor general.[111] With Hitler himself, King sought to share his exhilaration. He asked the German consul general to wire him "how relieved and delighted I was that the four-power agreement had been reached."[112]

Munich was later seen by some as having bought a valuable year for Britain to accelerate its rearmament, but that leaves unanswered the question of whether in the Anglo-German arms race the relative strengths of the two countries had in fact changed substantially in Britain's favour between Munich and the beginning of war. Churchill was certain that he knew the answer. "It is probable that in this last year before the outbreak, Germany munitions at least doubled, and possibly tripled, the munitions of Britain and France put together … They were, therefore, getting weapons at a far higher rate than we … the year's breathing-space said to be 'gained' by Munich left Britain and France in a much worse position compared to Hitler's Germany than they had been at the Munich crisis."[113]

What was indisputable was that Munich was a triumph for Hitler. Britain and France, the victors of the First World War, had kowtowed to the chancellor of the defeated Germany. The Sudetenland, with boundaries to be drawn by him alone, was to be Germany's by 10 October. Czechoslovakia as it had been created at Versailles would no longer exist. The only real democracy in central or Eastern Europe had been dismembered. Whatever the price, the relief in Western countries was palpable, a near hysterical outpouring of relief and thanksgiving. Too bad about Czechoslovakia, which in the eyes of some had in any case been awkwardly and artificially cobbled together twenty years before. A world war had been avoided, thanks to the tenacity of the blessed peacemaker Chamberlain. On 29 September King made public his message of gratitude to the British prime minister: "The heart of Canada is rejoicing tonight at the success which has crowned your unremitting efforts for peace. May I convey to you the warm congratulations of the Canadian people, and with them, an expression of their gratitude that is felt from one end of the Dominion to the other? My colleagues in the Government join me in unbounded admiration at the service you have rendered mankind. Your achievements in the past month alone will ensure you an abiding and illustrious place among the great conciliators which the United Kingdom, the British Commonwealth of Nations and the whole world will continue to honour."[114]

But Chamberlain's capitulation to Hitler's demands – still called appeasement – was soon seen by increasing numbers in Britain as a profound defeat, as Churchill, its most vocal opponent, characterized it. "The German dictator, instead of snatching his victuals from the table, has been content to have them served to him course by course."[115] Clement Attlee, the Labour leader of the opposition, in moving his party toward support for rearmament, spoke for many when he said to the House of Commons on 3 October, "The events of the last few days constitute one of the greatest diplomatic defeats this country and France have ever sustained ... it is a tremendous victory for Herr Hitler ... He has overturned the balance of power in Europe ... He has successfully defeated ... the forces that might have stood against the rule of violence." The next day Amery from the government backbenches denounced Munich in similar terms as "a triumph of sheer naked force, exercised in the most blatant and brutal fashion."[116]

Privately King was aware that not everyone agreed with his adulation of Chamberlain and his relief at the Munich agreement, but he spoke of him wholly sympathetically. "The storm against Chamberlain for having yielded to Hitler will be very great. Liberals and Labour will say he has again sold out the League and collective security. He can afford to let them say what they like. It is now clear that he has saved a world war, and nothing he or others could do could be comparable to that ... [There is a] beginning of bitter resentment at Chamberlain who was a brave man in facing it."[117] To the House of Commons, King praised at great length Chamberlain's performance at Munich. To his diary, he returned repeatedly to his admiration for him. "Chamberlain must be going through an agony like Christ in the Garden of Gethsemane, his own countrymen turning against him, public meetings being held, even in many of the Dominions; also America critical of his whole attitude."[118] Canadians generally shared in the widespread relief that greeted Munich, but at least in Winnipeg it never occurred to Dafoe to compare Chamberlain to Jesus. Having published far more of Churchill's warnings than any other Canadian newspaper, he wrote a scathing editorial, "What's the Cheering For?" with its memorable concluding paragraph: "The doctrine that Germany can intervene for racial reasons for the 'protection' of Germans on such grounds as she thinks proper in any country in the world which she is in a position to coerce, and without regard to any engagements she has made or guarantees she has given, has now not only been asserted but made good; and it has been approved, sanctioned, certified and validated by the governments of Great Britain and France, who have undertaken in this respect for the democracies of the world. This is the situation and those who think it is all right will cheer for it."[119] Ian Kershaw, in his biographer of Hitler, with advantage of hindsight, was even more succinct. "None but the most hopelessly naïve, incurably optimistic or irredeemably stupid could have imagined that the Sudetenland marked the limits of German ambitions to expand."[120]

King continued to hope against hope for peace, but he also began to phase out his repeated public statements of "no commitments" and "Parliament will decide." The now retired R.B. Bennett was, however, not alone in remaining skeptical of King's apparent change of heart. In his continuing ambiguities, King "seems to have gone to extra lengths to avoid committing himself in any way, even to the extent of leaving important cables from the British Government unopened for days, and of refusing to say whether Canada would permit the export of munitions to Britain in the time of war! He … would in the event of war have had a plebiscite as to whether Canada should take part, relying on the French and foreign votes to secure a satisfactory result."[121]*

King felt called upon to send a message of thanks to Roosevelt as well, although what he was thanking him for is unclear, the president not having been involved in the events of that momentous month except to exhort any and all to keep the peace. He did, however, send a post-Munich telegram to Chamberlain simply saying "Good man!" Perhaps by expressing publicly his gratitude to Roosevelt as well as to Chamberlain, King was attempting to foster the impression that Munich had the support of the whole English-speaking world, including the United States.

Chamberlain had consistently ignored or rejected the reports of MI6 about what to expect before and following Munich. King went even farther. He had long since declined to receive British intelligence reports. But Gladwyn Jebb, later a distinguished senior diplomat, recalled that MI6, although

---

*In a vain attempt to appeal to Quebec, Arthur Meighen, as leader of the Conservative Party, had in 1920 embraced the wholly impracticable idea of having an election before any declaration of war.

notoriously underfunded, "did warn us of the September [Munich] crisis, and they did not give any colour to the ridiculous optimism that prevailed up to the rape of Czechoslovakia, of which our official reports did not give us much warning."[122] More specifically, one MI6 agent in central Europe "supplied not only excellent information about Germany's order of battle and mobilisation plans ... but also advance notice of Germany's intervention in the Sudetenland from the summer of 1937, for action against Czechoslovakia from the spring of 1938, for the seizure of Prague in the spring of 1939 ... and for the attack on Poland ... Whitehall obtained during the Munich crisis the schedule of Germany's original mobilisation plans."[123]

None of this Ottawa accepted, King having rejected British reports, analyses, or intelligence, whatever the source. During the interwar years, London offered Ottawa a Special Monthly Secret Intelligence Summary, a monthly Confidential Intelligence Summary, a weekly Secret Intelligence Summary from India, and periodic reports from the other dominions and Singapore and Hong Kong and from military attachés at a range of British missions abroad. King had consistently refused to sanction the appointment of service attachés at Canada's few posts abroad. As the history of Canada's military intelligence records, "Unfortunately, Dr Skelton had such a deep and lively suspicion of British intentions that he was often reluctant to accept reports from [all] such sources."[124]

On the foreign policy attitudes of the dominions more generally, Malcolm Macdonald, echoing Asquith and Curzon before the First World War, wrote to cabinet colleagues that he "had never favoured our adopting a particular foreign policy merely in order to please the Dominions." Over a British commitment to Czechoslovakia, however, "the British Commonwealth might well break in pieces," especially since Canada and South Africa "would see no reason whatever why they should join in a war to prevent certain Germans from rejoining their Fatherland." [125] That was also the impression of Geoffrey Dawson, the imperialist and strongly pro-appeasement editor of the *Times*, who was indefatigable in urging the high commissioners to extol appeasement to their governments. He later wrote to Chamberlain, "No one who sat in this place, as I did during the autumn of '38, with almost daily visitations from eminent Canadians and Australians, could fail to realise that war with Germany at that time would have been misunderstood and resented from end to end of the Empire."[126] Dawson was given to over-simplification and his understanding of dominion attitudes was no exception, but Robert Self, a biographer of Chamberlain and editor of his voluminous diary-letters to his sisters, analyzed the situation accurately.

> Undeniably, Dominion attitudes were mentioned regularly in Cabinet, in negotiations with the French and even in Parliament, but for Chamberlain such references were essentially parenthetical additional justifications for a policy he had infinitely more compelling reasons to pursue. Rather than redirecting Chamberlain's policy or limiting his freedom of manoeuvre, Dominion alarm was exploited ... as one of several convenient battering rams with which to overcome opposition in his own Cabinet, in much the same way as he later used it in his isolated fight against the Cabinet's desire for negotiations with the Soviet Union during May 1939 and his resistance to widespread press clamour for Churchill's admission to the government. Conversely they were not consulted over issues where their known policy positions conflicted with Chamberlain's own, as over Roosevelt's peace overtures in January 1938 and the Polish guarantee in March 1939. Unquestionably, Chamberlain's unflagging efforts for peace helped to educate the Dominions away from isolationism and into support of Britain, but this was essentially a satisfactory by-product of his personal diplomacy rather than its principal purpose.[127]

That was not the way King saw it. Over tea at Laurier House in Ottawa, Burgon Bickersteff, the young warden of Hart House at the University of Toronto, listened as the prime minister went carefully through his reaction to the

> Czechoslovak crisis. He was convinced after Parliament had been summoned on the outbreak of war, this country would have responded without any serious dissentient voice. He of course informed Chamberlain as to his position in Canada ... He also described the preparations made to deal with the emergency created by an outbreak of war. We were far further on in our preparations than was generally supposed.
>
> He was very caustic about Australia's and New Zealand's widely published expressions of loyalty and readiness to support Great Britain during the crisis. Lyon Savage [prime minister of New Zealand], he said, made these speeches in public, while privately telephoning franti-

cally to their [*sic*] High Commissioner in London instructing him to urge the British Government to keep out of war at all costs.[128]

King had sensed that Chamberlain would face a storm in London. In the three-day parliamentary debate over Munich – during which Duff Cooper was the only minister in an increasingly uneasy cabinet to resign – Churchill, Chamberlain's *bête noire*, expressed in a single brief sentence what Munich really was: "We have sustained a total and unmitigated defeat." He was nevertheless fair about Chamberlain's good intentions: "No one has been a more resolute and uncompromising struggler for peace … Never has there been such intense and undaunted determination to maintain and secure peace … [but now] all is over. Silent, mournful, abandoned, broken, Czechoslovakia recedes into the darkness."[129] In the wake of Munich, Halifax finally recognized "the unwisdom of having a foreign policy with insufficient armed strength."[130] And with Munich went any lingering idea that, *pace* Skelton, Canada could attempt to stand aside from the darkening events in Europe. Pearson from London said so bluntly to Skelton: "would our complete isolation from European events (if such a thing were possible) save us from the effect of a British defeat; and, even if it did, could we stand by and watch the triumph of Nazism, with all it stands for, over a Britain which, with all her defects, is about the last abode of decency and liberty on this side of the water?"[131]

Amidst the uncertainties following Chamberlain's three meetings with Hitler, Mackenzie King was much gratified to learn of Roosevelt's positive response to the proposal that King George VI, Queen Elizabeth, and their daughters should visit New York and Washington during the four-week royal tour of Canada in the late spring of 1939. This visit would help cement ties among the United States, Britain, and Canada. The president wrote to the king inviting the royal family to the United States at some point during their tour of Canada. The invitation was at once accepted for the king and queen, but the princesses were deemed too young for such a demanding trip, the first by a reigning monarch to North America.

After all the alarums of Munich, King also felt able to absent himself on holiday from Ottawa. He sailed from Halifax on a three-week cruise to the Caribbean with his deputy minister. Skelton did not want to let King, whom he now described as "belligerent," out of his sight, and King wanted to keep his eye on the isolationist and self-centred Skelton. In Kingston,

Jamaica, on the 24 October 1938, King dismissed in his diary Skelton's repeated claims that an isolationist Canada would be secure under the umbrella of the United States. "I do not like to be dependent on the U.S. ... There was more real freedom in the British Commonwealth of Nations, and a richer inheritance."[132]

King had had enough of the endless efforts of his deputy minister to set government policy. After their return to Ottawa, he reflected on his Caribbean conversations with Skelton, condemning to his diary his "republican attitude ... his negative viewpoint and inferiority complex in so many things – a real antagonism toward monarchical institutions and Britain – a sort communist sympathy ... an isolated Canada which I cannot accept. It ... raised a sort of wall of separation between us. He seeks to dominate one's thoughts, is intellectually arrogant ... I must control policy and be the judge of my own conduct ... to lead and not be controlled."[133]*

For most ministers, recognition of such arrogance in a deputy minister would be more than enough reason to seek a new one. King, anxious at all times about public "misunderstandings" of his various manoeuvrings, kept Skelton on, but with "a sort of wall" between them. O.D. Skelton – called by some wags in Ottawa "Odious Skelton" – gradually faded away into isolated isolationism. With the declaration of war, King repeated his regrets that he had not proclaimed in earlier speeches, against the advice of his deputy, the "probability of war and of Canada's probable part in any conflict that related to aggression."[134]

Munich was the pinnacle of King's appeasement hopes. It was also the turning point in his prewar thinking. He continued to pray that Hitler had meant what he had said when he had declared that Czechoslovakia "is the last territorial claim which I have to make in Europe." Not surprisingly, many have since decried the policy of appeasement as illusory if not downright cowardly. A few, however, continued to see it not as an ignoble surrendering of the rights of small nations, but as an initiative to meet legitimate German complaints arising from the misguided Treaty of Versailles. "Far from carrying its later connotations of weakness, fear and retreat in the face of bluff, it suggested accommodation, conciliation, and the removal of just grievances."[135]

---

*King's surprising condemnation of Skelton as a communist sympathizer may have arisen from an oubliette of his memory, recalling that Lenin, writing from Zurich in 1917, had congratulated Skelton on his doctoral thesis, published as *Socialism: A Critical Analysis* (Crowley, *Marriage of Minds*, 39).

And as the *Guardian*, for example, concluded, "Chamberlain was not a weak and ineffectual leader, but a strong-willed, realistic and able politician who saw that Britain and France were in no position economically or militarily to keep order in the world and wanted Britain to retain its independent power and influence within the world power system, which he thought could be achieved only if a second world war could be avoided."[136]

Even in the months after Munich, King did not acknowledge publicly any disillusionment with appeasement or for that matter with Hitler. He still spoke occasionally about challenges to Canadian unity. But echoing his statements to the 1923 and 1926 imperial conferences, he now took the major step of making it clear to his colleagues that Canada had "a self-evident national duty" to join in any war against Hitler. Lapointe might assert that increased defence spending was greatly disliked in Quebec, but King disregarded that as an irrelevancy. In Jamaica he had declared to his diary, "I must control policy and be the judge of my own conduct." Thereafter he specified that "my business was to tell Canada of her dangers, not of theories that could not save the lives of the people."[137] Ministers from Quebec said that this attitude would "probably cost us many seats in Quebec," but sounding a little like R.B. Bennett in his support for the League of Nations, he pledged, "If it would cost the [Liberal] Party its whole existence, I would much rather pay that price for what I know to be right."[138] And he later added, "the Quebec ministers should realize that it would be the end of Quebec if any [isolationist or neutralist] attitude ... were adopted by the French Canadians in a world conflict such as this one would be. They ... ought to lead the province in seeing its obligations to participate, and making clear the real issue and what it involves." If they did not, they would be dropped from the cabinet. "It might be necessary for some of them to consider whether they could do better in the way of steadying people in their own parts [of the province] by being out of the cabinet, rather than in it."[139]

Soon after Mackenzie King's return to Ottawa from Jamaica, he went to Washington for trade talks arising in part from the near expiry of the Canada-US bilateral trade agreement of three years before. On 15 November 1938, King participated in the conclusion of two separate but related agreements, further liberalizing trade among Britain, Canada, and the United States. The eight months of negotiations had, as King had sought, protected Canadian preferential tariff rates in the British market, but had lowered tariffs among the three countries. Even more important in King's eyes, the successful negotiation had brought the three English-speaking countries closer together in the post-depression era. In rather flowery terms, King spoke at the signing ceremony in Washington of Canadian satisfaction "that in facing the problems of today, the two countries, with whose fortunes those of Canada are so closely linked, have effectively strengthened the friendly relations which have long prevailed between them ... The stability of the civilisation we cherish depends more than ever on the friendly association of the great English-speaking nations of the old world and the new."[140] The signing of the Canada-US text in November 1938 was for King one of the very few bright spots in a generally gloomy year, with Laurier assuring King from the Great Beyond that Roosevelt "is very fond of you." King agreed, knowing where the credit for the successful negotiation was due. He told his old British friend and financial benefactor Violet Markham, "I can honestly say that but for the stand which ... I took pretty courageously ... neither of these agreements would be in existence today."[141]

What the self-styled courageous King had not foreseen was that Roosevelt would take the occasion of the signing of the trade agreements to raise again the question of safe havens for refugees from Germany and Austria. King speculated to himself that only the existence of powerful Jewish influences surrounding Roosevelt could explain the president's frequent references to what other countries were doing – or not doing – for Jewish refugees, but he would have found it more difficult to ascribe to "powerful Jewish influences" the concurrent concerns of Chamberlain, who said, "I am horrified by the German behaviour to the Jews ... Nazi hatred will stick at nothing to find a pretext for their barbarities."[142] Before his departure for Washington, King, relying largely on news reports, had described to his diary that "The sorrows which the Jews have to bear at this time are almost beyond comprehension ... Something will have to be done by our country." It would be "difficult politically" (i.e., opposition mainly from Quebec), but additional Jewish refugees should be admitted. That would be "right and just, and Christian," but on the other hand it could not be allowed to jeopardize national unity.[143]

In Washington, King listened to Roosevelt and Cordell Hull, the secretary for state, discuss possible aid for refugees and the difficulties of providing any relief, but said little himself. Upon his return to Ottawa, he told Tweedsmuir that Canada must, with the example of Britain in mind, allow more refugees to enter than the handful currently being admitted. However, despite popular demand for more to be done, on 21 November the cabinet decided that a proposal to allow more refugees needed additional study. "The problem was that Lapointe, speaking for Quebec, was adamantly opposed to any increase, as were Cardin and Rinfret. Rogers, Gardiner and Thomas Crerar were in favour, revealing a split in cabinet that might in time contribute to national disunity."[144]

On 24 November, after King had met in Ottawa with representatives of Jewish organizations, he called on his cabinet to adopt a "liberal attitude ... to act as the conscience of the nation ... although it might not be 'politically most expedient.'" But some in the cabinet continued to fear domestic "political consequences of any help to the Jews." Lapointe again warned him that accepting Jewish refugees – as well as increased defence spending – posed electoral dangers in Quebec. King thereupon decided not to "press the matter any further."[145] King and certainly Lapointe may well have known in advance the stance that the Conservatives would take. Their leader, Robert Manion, was ready to do or say almost anything in attempts to recover lost ground in Quebec. Supported by his French-Canadian wife, Manion collaborated to a degree with the provincial Union Nationale, reassuring Quebec about the opposition of the Conservative Party to *any* immigration whatever as long as any Canadian remained unemployed.

On 15 November Massey had written to King from London, "The anti-Jewish orgy in Germany is not making Chamberlain's policy of 'appeasement' any easier." He was referring to the shock and disbelief that had followed the Kristallnacht in Germany and Austria the week before when Nazi thugs destroyed Jewish homes, shops, and synagogues and killed several score, injured thousands of others, and incarcerated an estimated thirty thousand in concentration camps. Massey continued, "Chamberlain will not [however] be deflected from the course which he has set himself to obtain a European settlement. In fact, the other day ... he told me that his determination to arrive at a stabilization of Europe was too deep-rooted to be affected by the disappointment of the last few weeks."[146] King agreed. He replied to Massey on 3 December, "the post-Munich developments have made appeasement difficult and positive friendship [with Hitler] for the moment out of the question. That is no reason, however, why the effort should be abandoned."[147]

Between 1937 and 1939 King had moved from his dual foreign policy to a single if ill-defined policy: the British policy of appeasement. Yet with Mussolini's seizure first of Abyssinia and later of Albania and with Hitler's *Anschluss* with Austria, his occupation of Czechoslovakia, and his mounting threats to Poland, any British policy of attempting to appease the two dictators was in effect at an end. At Westminster a young Conservative MP, Ronald Tree, who actively supported Eden and Churchill despite the unrelenting pressures of the whips, recorded the drama as seen from the backbenches. "It was not until those ... disasters occurred that the Government finally took the decision to rearm totally and introduce a Bill for Conscription. Although rearmament had been underway since 1935 and strides had been made in certain directions, the 'Pay-as-you-Go' policy on which it had been conducted to avoid interfering with our export trade had resulted in many serious deficiencies ... The rape of what remained of Czechoslovakia, followed by Mussolini's invasion of Albania, finally lifted the veil from Chamberlain's eyes and of those around him. At long last it was realized that the solemn promises of the Dictators were not worth the paper they were written on."[148]

King, however, persisted in his hope that appeasement might somehow still succeed. At the same time, Hume Wrong, who had exchanged his post as counsellor at the legation in Washington with Riddell as permanent delegate in Geneva, wrote a masterfully trenchant seven-page analysis of just how little foreign policy Canada had in the wake of the Abyssinian debacle and in the mounting evidence of the futility of appeasement. Wrong was right, convinced that whatever foreign policy Canada had was still, *faute de mieux*, shaped by British foreign policy. In these circumstances, he contended in his overview that "It is undoubtedly open to us to be more prolific in advice, and it is probable that Canada could exert a considerable influence at times on the foreign policy of the United Kingdom ... more frequent consultation ... is better than silence which may mean acquiescence." To enable Canada to analyse and formulate its own thinking on international affairs, the undramatic but essential enlargement and reorganization of the Department of External Affairs was essential. From the day in 1909 when the department had been established and especially after the First World War and the Balfour Declaration of 1926, an effective foreign service should have been recruited and organized. Such an expansion might have crowded King, jealous of his own self-appointed if not divinely ordained leading foreign policy role. And Skelton, for fourteen years a self-inflicted overworked deputy minister, chose to conduct what was close to being his own one-man band. Further, as Wrong contended, not only were additional missions required, but under Skelton "the existing offices abroad are not now utilised as fully as they ought to be, and that no plan of expansion will be effective which is concentrated only on additional Canadian representation in other countries." Even at headquarters in Ottawa, the few foreign service officers were not fully used.[149] That was acceptable to King who always sought to avoid any involvement in foreign ventures that might conflict with the highest good of all, not national leadership but national unity. In short, King and Skelton, if not for the same reasons, had prevented any real expression of an autonomist foreign policy partly by severely limiting the size of the Department of External Affairs. It was in these circumstances that Pearson was soon to sum up the department as simply being "in a mess."

14

The End of the Affair

Munich was not in fact Chamberlain's final act of appeasement. He still hoped to entice Mussolini away from Hitler and free the Mediterranean from a potentially hostile Italian navy. He flew to Rome in January 1939 but returned empty-handed, Mussolini having "behaved to me like a sneak and a cad."[1] That Mussolini was indeed a sneak and a cad became even more evident ten weeks later, almost at the same time that Germany acquired the largely German-speaking city of Memel in Lithuania. The "smash and grab" Italian army suddenly invaded Albania, quickly subdued the almost non-existent forces of King Zog, and turned the Italian protectorate into an outright acquisition. Italy was now on the border of its Adriatic neighbour, Yugoslavia, free to apply pressure there and elsewhere in the Balkans.

The year 1938 – culminating in Munich – was a good year for Hitler, but not for his followers in Canada. Both the Deutscher Bund and the fragmented Nazi party in Canada moved into an irreversible downward trend. From Montreal, Adrien Arcand continued to communicate with his many overseas contacts, especially throughout the British Commonwealth and in the United States, but at home public interest and membership in the several pro-Nazi organizations dwindled, despite increasing press coverage on both sides of the US-Canada border. Justice Minister Lapointe dismissed all domestic pro-Nazi organizations as being of no real danger, claiming that their membership constituted only a handful in Ontario, Manitoba, and Quebec. The small local fascist organizations struggled on until mid-1938 when Arcand and other Nazis recognized that a single national organization had become their last best hope. Joseph Farr in Ontario and William Whittaker in Manitoba (until his fatal illness in the autumn of 1938) also acknowledged that their small local organizations, the Canadian Union of Fascists and the Canadian Nationalist Party, were going nowhere. They supported Arcand in his plan to create a single National Unity Party (NUP) while maintaining their distance from Bund Canada. As the Security Branch of the RCMP reported to Lapointe, there was "little or no liaison or co-operation between the [new] National Unity Party and the long-standing German and Italian clubs and other organizations across Canada."[2]

The RCMP estimated that 1,500 supporters attended the founding convention of the NUP at Massey Hall in Toronto on 4 July 1938, following an organizational meeting in Kingston, Ontario. Blueshirts with swastika armbands kept order by forcibly ejecting all hecklers, especially suspected communists. The meeting was, however, no great success. The *Globe and Mail* and the *Toronto Star* provided somewhat different accounts, but it soon became evident that the NUP was on a downhill track from its inception. Poisonous articles from the notorious *Der Stürmer* and other anti-Semitic propaganda provided by the German Consulate General in Ottawa continued to appear in party publications, but only the most faithful – and the Security Branch of the RCMP – scrutinized them regularly. Lapointe, speaking in Quebec City on 25 November 1938, attacked the fascist movement in Canada. He "obviously took Adrien Arcand ... more seriously than he let on in the House of Commons. He was aware from reports of the RCMP ... that fascists were infiltrating factories and government bureaux – employees at the Customs Department in Montreal [headed by a unilingual anglophone] distributed hate propaganda and gave the Nazi salute quite openly."[3] *L'Action catholique* proclaimed that Hitler had to be given "credit for having snatched his country from the hands of the communists by laying his iron hand on the disorderly elements, many of whom, in Germany as in Russia, were Jews."[4] Arcand concurred, but explained that "we don't attack Jews, we simply defend our country against their conspiracy."[5]

On the same evening as the NUP founding convention at Massey Hall, 4 July 1938, a much larger public meeting (as many as ten thousand) was held at nearby Maple Leaf Gardens. Organized by the left-wing League for Peace and Democracy, it heard William Dodd, until recently Roosevelt's ambassador to Germany – who had been too outspoken for in the State Department – repeat to his receptive audience what he had been saying since his return home six months before. "Fascism is on the march today in America.

Millionaires are marching to the tune. It will come in this country unless a strong defence is set by all liberal and progressive forces."[6]

No doubt Dodd had in mind Henry Ford, among others, when he spoke of millionaires in America marching to Hitler's tune. In July 1938 the German consul general in Cleveland went to Detroit to bestow upon a gratified Ford the highest German civilian medal. King must have been aware of the strong anti-Semitic element in Ford's admiration for Hitler since he had been travelling to Detroit to consult a favourite psychic there since 1932. For the same reason, he must also have known about the pro-fascist extravagances of the Canadian Roman Catholic "radio priest," Father Charles Coughlin, whose weekly broadcasts from Detroit had at their peak an estimated forty million listeners. Born of Irish immigrant parents in Hamilton, Ontario, and ordained in Toronto, a close associate of Henry Ford and a collaborator with the America First movement, his broadcasts and his National Movement of Social Justice and its journal *Social Justice* spread virulent anti-Semitic, anti-Roosevelt, anti-communist, and anti-League of Nations prejudices. (At the time of Mussolini's invasion of Abyssinia, he had broadcast repeatedly that "The League of Nations and its sanctions exist but for one single purpose – to act only when British interests are at stake.")[7]

A second American recipient of Hitler's highest civilian decoration was the solo transatlantic aviator Charles Lindbergh, who was spreading pro-German misinformation everywhere he went in North America and Europe. For example, the British military attaché in Paris reported, "The Führer found a most convenient ambassador in Colonel Lindbergh, who appears to have given the French an impression of its [the Luftwaffe's] might and preparedness which they did not have before, and who at the same time confirmed the view that the Russian air force was worth almost exactly nothing."[8] The chief of the French Air Staff subsequently visited Germany in mid-August 1938, arriving with a defeatist conviction that his own air force would be wiped out within the first days of a war with Germany and returning with the same pessimistic conclusion: it would be folly for France or Britain to wage war against the Luftwaffe. Lindbergh, with the less simplistic support of the US military attaché in Germany, had been assuring anyone who would listen that both technically and numerically the Luftwaffe could overwhelm any opposition. Lindbergh matched Ford's racism with bigoted calls at America First rallies to build "white ramparts" against Asians. In

Readers' Digest magazine he fulminated against a pressing sea of Yellow, Black, and Brown.

Joseph Kennedy, the millionaire ambassador of the United States to the Court of St James, and father of a future president helped to spread across Britain the wrong-headed convictions of Lindbergh. At heart an isolationist and defeatist, Kennedy initiated and personally oversaw Lindbergh's extensive visit to London following a similar visit to Paris. Again mixing fact and fiction about the supposedly invincible Luftwaffe, Lindbergh spouted his pro-fascist misinformation to whomever Kennedy had arranged for him to see, within the British government or without. For example, Tom Jones, the influential confidant first of Prime Minister Lloyd George and then of Stanley Baldwin, testified to the impact of Lindbergh when on 29 September 1938, he wrote, "Since my talk with Lindbergh ... I've sided with those working for peace at any cost ... because of the picture of our relative unpreparedness in the air and on the ground which Lindbergh painted and because of his belief that the democracies would be crushed absolutely and finally ... put all that I had been learning to sb [Stanley Baldwin] ... and impressed on him that by speaking in the Lords to-day ... [he] could save the country from war. He was for peace at any price ... I ... sent Lindbergh to see Lloyd George so that he might learn at first hand what an air expert thought of our chances."[9]

By mid-October 1938, while "that damned fellow Kennedy" (Roosevelt's phrase)[10] was attempting to arrange to visit Hitler, Lindbergh's misinformation spread across the Atlantic. In Washington, Roosevelt told his cabinet that Germany was out-producing Britain and France combined in military aircraft. In the same week that Lindbergh was making his third visit in eighteen months to Berlin, he wrote to the US military attaché there, "I am seriously considering the possibility of making our home in Germany."[11] Göring, at the United States ambassador's residence, presented Lindbergh, by order of the Führer, with the same high civilian medal that Henry Ford had received three months before. Lindbergh, proudly wearing the decoration, assured Göring that "It is an honour which I shall always prize highly." But Eleanor Roosevelt, who had lobbied for the Republican side in the Spanish Civil War, was aghast; "This German Jewish business makes me sick ... How could Lindbergh take that Hitler decoration?"[12]

Mackenzie King gradually recognized that the moment "with all the odds against you" of which Churchill had spoken might soon come. The time had indeed arrived when in the words of Blair Neatby, King had to "take positive steps to convince Canadians that being at Britain's side in a major European war was the only alternative which was consistent with national unity."[13] Quebec would no longer drive the issue. And, like Chamberlain before him, King now had to carry his country into rearmament, if only hesitantly and on a minor scale compared to that of the United Kingdom. Although gradually revealing to the public basic policy questions that hitherto he had kept to himself or to a few colleagues, he continued to handicap himself by seeking no timely advice or comment from the High Commission in London. Pearson later recorded in his diary, "Mr King has been sending personal telegrams ... to the P.M. [Chamberlain] – a stupid procedure – ... But it suits his *amour propre* ... He would die before using this Office."[14]

On 13 November 1938 – almost to the day the twentieth anniversary of the end of the First World War – King described to his cabinet's defence committee how the "gangster nations" of Europe threatened a war against which Canada must now equip itself. On 2 December he finally told the full cabinet of "the necessity of Canada joining with the other nations in impressing dictators with the determination of the democracies to make themselves more powerful to resist aggression."[15] He recalled for his diary that "[I] made up my mind that I would not allow myself to take the one-sided view that I was crowded into ... the last session which ignored the possibility of Canada being at war when Britain was at war."[16] No more circumlocutions now for the sensibilities of isolationists or of Quebec. Quoting Laurier in the naval debates of 1910, he stated unequivocally to the House of Commons on 16 January 1939 that "if England is at war we are at war." If, as an agitated Skelton responded, his statement had "provoked profound alarm and anger not only in Quebec but among all nationalists," that was too bad for them. Isolationism was "not my position nor that of my Party."[17] King was surprised that Lapointe, a fortnight before, had objected to him quoting Laurier's words and opposed issuing such a statement until war was actually declared (Lapointe's reaction, *inter alia*, ignored King's need to pave the way for the royal tour). Lapointe again threatened resignation, even taking the wholly unacceptable step of attempting as a minister to enlist King's deputy minister (Skelton) to prevent his own minister (King) from saying that Canada would support the United Kingdom, but in the event Lapointe did not resign. And Power told King that he "did not think there would be the opposition in Quebec that Lapointe feared." In any event, King flatly rejected any idea – including from Skelton

– that Canada could remain neutral in a major war involving Britain without triggering "a civil war in Canada."[18]

Lapointe and Skelton, while still concerting together against their prime minister, were dismayed by the degree of King's increasing public candour about his commitment to stand by Britain. For King there were two good reasons for doing so in early 1939, before the arrival of the royal couple on their transcontinental tour. First, much of English Canada simply expected no less a commitment. And, second, if he made such a pledge only after the pending royal visit, French Canada might infer that King George VI had forced it from him. He was not about to alter or retract his commitment that Canada would stand by Britain in the event of a major war, but he told Lapointe bluntly that he hoped "to get our views so accommodated that there could be no need for anyone to go out" of the cabinet.[19] King knew that although some "accommodation" with Lapointe was pressing, it would now be on his own terms. Even with an election pending, there could be no question that Canada had to stand with Britain. The majority of voters across Canada would settle for nothing less. The accommodation, or pact as some called it, that emerged by late March was quite simple: Lapointe would support Canada's entry into any major war involving Britain. In return, King would pledge that no government that he headed would impose conscription for overseas military service. Accordingly, on 31 March Lapointe assured his fellow Québécois that he would oppose any government that would enforce conscription.

While all this was happening, there was a concurrent controversy in Ottawa about whether the Canadian survivors of the Spanish Civil War – still condemned by some as dangerous communists – should be allowed to return home, as recommended by among others Massey in London. The answer was a curt negative, thereby avoiding criticism from Quebec. The hapless volunteers in the Spanish Civil War could face a jail sentence of two years for their enlistment in the Mackenzie-Papineau brigade.

At the same time, King wrote yet another letter to the Führer. On the first day of February 1939, two months after Kristallnacht and the month following Chamberlain's futile visit to Mussolini, he addressed New Year's greetings to "My dear Herr Hitler." His letter was delivered by the German consul general in Ottawa, who was going to Berlin on leave. In it, King recalled for Hitler his visit to Berlin in the summer of 1937, which "left an indelible impression on my mind." Again sending him thanks "for the many courtesies extended to me," King wrote that no one could do more than Hitler could "to help your own and other countries along the path of peace and progress." He was especially comforted by the thought of Hitler "being at your mountain retreat … knowing, as I do, how greatly the quiet and companionship of Nature helps to restore to the mind its largest and clearest vision." King's peroration was "I hope that you will think not only of the good you can do for your own country, but … the good that you can do for the entire world. You will, I know, accept this letter in the spirit in which it is written – an expression of the faith I have in the purpose you have at heart, and of the friendship with yourself which you have been so kind as to permit me to share."[20] Hitler did not reply for six months and then only briefly and formally at the repeated prompting of the German consul general in Ottawa.

By contrast, a now most disillusioned Lord Halifax, who in the wake of Kristallnacht had finally lost faith in Henderson and agreed with his Foreign Office officials that Hitler was a criminal lunatic, urged Chamberlain to demonstrate that Britain was not "decadent and spineless and could not with impunity be kicked about," and pressed him to accelerate rearmament to march in step with appeasement.[21] The ultimate disillusionment for whatever appeasers were left in London came on 15 March 1939 when the German army occupied Prague – just weeks before Mussolini nullified the Munich agreement by seizing Albania (over which it had declared a protectorate in 1926). Hitler, also disregarding the Munich settlement, now took what remained of Bohemia and Moravia after Poland and Hungary had joined in the final dismemberment of their neighbour (Slovakia broke away to become in effect a fascist puppet state of Germany). That was the end of any effort to appease Hitler. Two days later Chamberlain proclaimed, "I am convinced that after Munich the great majority of the British people shared my hope and ardently desired that that policy [of appeasement] should be carried further. But to-day I share their disappointment, their indignation, that those hopes have been so wantonly shattered."[22]

With the German occupation of the whole of what once was Czechoslovakia, Chamberlain not only stated his indignation: urged on by Halifax, he acted on it. On 31 March, he suddenly responded to Hitler's seizure of what remained of Czechoslovakia and to the Italo-German "Pact of Steel" by proclaiming that Britain would go to the assistance of Poland if its independence were threatened. In the weeks ahead, he laid down similar guarantees for Romania and Greece (and contemplated one with Turkey). The practicability of Britain and France effectively aiding any one of the countries, Churchill and others – including Chamberlain himself – knew was nil. Having passed up far more promising opportunities to stop Hitler or Mussolini in the past, there had now arrived, in Churchill's words, "the moment when you will have to fight with all the odds against you and only a precarious chance of survival."[23]

In these untoward circumstances, however, Britain and France never quite made up their minds about central and Eastern Europe, and especially communist Russia, until it was too late. France, with British backing, might have successfully countered Hitler's aggression in Czechoslovakia, the pivotal state in France's "little entente" of central Europe, but neither Baldwin nor Chamberlain viewed Hitler's *Drang nach Osten* with the fundamental misgivings of Churchill. There were those in British public life who, in acknowledging Germany's many discontents with the Treaty of Versailles, regarded Eastern Europe as a possible escape valve for Hitler's various frustrations. Given a free hand in the East, he might not menace the West. On 15 March 1939, Charles Ritchie, the first secretary at Canada House, recorded a reaction abroad in London: "My neighbour said at lunch, 'It may seem cynical, but I really cannot get excited over this. I do dislike all this sentimentality about the Czechs – as long as the Germans are going towards the east.'"[24]

France had long seen its little entente of Czechoslovakia, Poland, and Romania as a means of forcing Hitler to recognize that if he invaded Czechoslovakia he would risk a two-front war. But France also knew that Poland and Romania were ill equipped to draw away any significant part of the Wehrmacht from a Western front. The kingpin to effective resistance to Germany in the east remained the Soviet Union. Throughout Europe, however, that communist behemoth remained much feared. Churchill captured the stark dilemma: "Poland, Romania, Finland and the Baltic States did not know whether it was German aggression or Russian rescue that they dreaded more. It was this hideous choice that paralysed British and French policy."[25]

Massey wrote to King from London, following Hitler's seizure of the whole of Czechoslovakia, "I have just come back from the House [of Commons] where Chamberlain made his momentous statement giving the promise of assistance to Poland if she were attacked. I don't believe that any government could remain in power in this country and say less. All classes, all parties and all ages are now united in a grim determination not to allow the liberties of Europe, and indeed of the world, to be further threatened by stark force."[26]

King, however, was deeply unsettled by the British guarantee to Poland and any idea, however vague, of an alliance with the Soviet Union. He told his diary on 21 March that he "shuddered at the thought of great powers being brought into wars over wretched little states in the Balkans." Three days later he deplored to the British high commissioner that an alliance between the United Kingdom and Eastern European countries would cause "grave embarrassment and in particular expressed regret that it should apparently have been necessary for the United Kingdom to associate itself with the U.S.S.R."[27] Ten days later on 3 April, King added, "it is terrible that Britain has committed itself to fight for Poland, Romania and Greece, and to ally herself with Russia ... which would mean that she would be drawn into European wars through the actions of others with which she should have nothing to do."[28] He knew all too well how any Anglo-French alliance with the atheistic Soviet Union would be viewed in Quebec.

Following Munich, fascist meetings continued to be held in Montreal and Toronto under the banner of the new National Unity Party, replete with swastika flags, Nazi salutes, and questionable financial practices, but in light of increasing adverse coverage in newspapers and magazines of Nazi aggression and brutality, attendance at NUP meetings dropped eventually to a few score faithful. In mid-1938, the Security Branch of the RCMP in its weekly report recorded that "many members are said to have left the Party and attendance at meetings has fallen off considerably ... some officials of the Party have become somewhat apathetic and are not giving the fullest co-operation to the movement." At a membership rally at Marché Maisonneuve in Montreal in February 1939, RCMP agents reported that "no particular enthusiasm was evinced by the audience and no marked increase in the Party membership resulted."[29] A final membership promotion rally was held in Toronto in mid-1939, again at Massey Hall, but was even more sparsely attended.

With Hitler's seizure of what remained of Czechoslovakia on 15 March and his threats against Poland, King described at great length to the House of Commons on 30 March what Laurier had meant when he had proclaimed that "If England is at war we are at war." Following that exegesis, he added almost casually, "The present Government believes that conscription of men for overseas service would not be ... necessary ... or effective ... so long as this Government may be in power, no such measure will be enacted."[30] It remained for Lapointe to clarify publicly King's position the following day. When he did so, there was no mistaking where he stood. Drawing on his pact with King, his pledge against conscription dominated his speech. "I shall always fight against this policy; I would not be a member of a Government that would enact it ... I would oppose any Government that would enforce it."[31] In making this pledge to Quebec, Lapointe was on safe ground. Not only did he have King's word, but a few days before the Liberal commitment, the Conservative leader, Robert Manion, had already taken the initiative to oppose compulsory overseas service. King was miffed that Lapointe's statement received more press coverage than his had, but on the other hand he was gratified that his Quebec lieutenant had observed the other half of the pact by going "much further than I did in making clear Canada could not be neutral in a war in which Britain might be engaged."[32]

In these circumstances, King decided that he had to spend more of the taxpayers' money on rearmament, but publicly justified it as being "for domestic protection only." With only one or two modern aircraft on loan from the RAF, the depleted Royal Canadian Air Force, still described as a defensive arm, would receive the largest amount of the modest increase. The army would receive the least in terms of its needs, reflecting King's lingering hope that the day of the overseas expeditionary force, so opposed in Quebec, had passed. And the Royal Canadian Navy, "long the Cinderella of the nation's defence services, may be said to have remained so."[33] The National Defence estimates for the fiscal year 1936–37 had reached the diminutive total of $30 million and for 1937–38 $36 million. The estimates for 1938–39 were much the same. For 1939–40 they were doubled to $73 million, but cabinet discussions led King to reduce even that small amount to $65 million. It was not much in light of pressing needs, but it was all that he believed he could get through parliament, given the opposition to increased defence spending of both the CCF and most Quebec Liberal members – and equally of Euler, his minister of trade and commerce.

King was determined to leave no public impression that an overseas expeditionary force was in the cards (whatever the backroom planning in the Department of National Defence might be). Such a force could conceivably lead to conscription. The increased defence estimates were repeatedly described as for the defence of Canada only. It followed that industrial cooperation with Britain as well as military should be avoided. James Eayrs has pointed out the illogicality of King's stance. "In defence affairs what was most needed was co-operation, not non-co-operation, compliance in a common cause, not a stubborn reassertion of autonomists' rights. Canada's response to the menace of the Axis was to voice with unaccustomed fervour her approval of appeasement, while resisting improvements in imperial defence. It brought the worst of both worlds."[34]

A basic problem with the increases in the armed forces was not only that they were limited but that they were late. It takes a long time to equip and train armoured or artillery regiments, or to build even small warships, or to establish flying schools. And no effort was made to create more French-speaking units. A Defence Purchasing Board was belatedly established, but military and industrial cooperation having been earlier rebuffed, the result was that, as a volume (*The Control of Raw Materials*) of the British official history of the war deplored, "virtually no preparations had been made for the war-time purchase of raw materials in North America."[35] Despite British – and French – gold being shipped to Canada for safekeeping and munitions orders growing, Defence Minister Ian Mackenzie, presumably with opposition in Quebec in mind, denied any knowledge of such contracts. The unseemly haggling over the terms of a British Commonwealth Air Training Plan resulted in recriminations and above all delays, which continued until Massey's covert intervention on the eve of the Second World War. When the First Canadian Division went overseas in December 1939 (despite King's earlier opposition), it was at best half-trained and ill equipped. As the military historian C.P. Stacey rightly observed, the preparations "were utterly inadequate to the scale of the coming emergency." Only reluctantly and belatedly did Canada make "the preparations which she ought to have made long before."[36]

The year 1939 was for Mackenzie King an anticlimax, an end to his four years of divinely ordained direct excursion into the exciting world of international affairs. Baldwin visited the universities of Toronto and McGill in April 1939 – his third visit to Canada in twelve years. When he spoke about the possibility that Armageddon might yet be avoided, King was gratified, but his conclusion was in effect a warning to Hitler: Britain was ready if necessary to fight Nazism.

The only bright light in the rapidly gathering gloom – and for King it was very bright indeed – was the projected month-long visit of King George VI and Queen Elizabeth to Canada, in which he ensured that he played throughout a leading role. Like everything else that year, however, King measured the pageantry and romanticism of the royal tour in terms of what it could do to boost Liberal fortunes in the election planned for the autumn of 1939. As war approached, he saw the royal tour as helping to strengthen the unity of Canada under a Liberal government and to a lesser degree the collective security of the British Commonwealth of Nations. His interwar progress from near-isolationism to liberal imperialism reached its peak with the royal visit, an integral part of his policy of drawing nearer to Britain as the menace of the dictators increased. A life-long royalist, he had since the imperial conference of 1937 been exploring with London a visit by the royal couple, which the late King George V signalled to him from Beyond was "due to their affection for you."[37] With the apparent imminence of a second world war, he pressed hard with the assistance of Tweedsmuir (but excluding the support of Massey, at the High Commission in London) for a final royal commitment. The dates chosen in May-June proved to be just in time. War was declared only nine weeks after the king and queen returned to the United Kingdom.*

King, who now declared himself "a thorough-going monarchist," regarded the royal visit as a personal triumph. He so arranged matters that he and not the governor general would have the honour of welcoming the monarch to an autonomous dominion within the British Commonwealth of equal member states. Everywhere the royal couple went would also demonstrate for all to see that the Tories had no monopoly on loyalty to the crown and that he, Mackenzie King, the grandson of the leading rebel in 1837 in Upper Canada, could deliver the monarch to his dominion – or the dominion to its monarch.

King went to extraordinary lengths in personally vetting every detail for the cross-country royal tour, attracting the wry comment of many insiders and journalists. Two instances will suffice here. John Stevenson, the *Times* correspondent in Canada, wrote to his editor, Geoffrey Dawson, "King regards this royal tour as the crowning glory of his career and thinks of nothing else. He is personally supervising all the arrangements down to the last detail and doing the sort of work that a butler should. He has his entourage almost crazy and Government House is in despair … [at his] trying to make political capital out of the royal visit."[38] Dafoe shared with Howard Ferguson a similar perception: King would not spend any time reading despatches about the perilous state of Europe because "his mind is running on really important

---

*Air raid shelters were then being urgently built in Britain, but Skelton would not authorize any structural reinforcements to protect the Canada House staff. Massey finally paid himself.

things such as – well, let's say the kind of pillow the Queen will rest her head on."[39] King was shocked to learn that the flowers for the reception of the royal couple upon disembarkation on 19 May at Quebec City were to be blue, the colour of the Conservative Party. He saw it as a Tory plot and had the colour scheme changed to Liberal red, repeating to his journal, "in politics it is what we prevent even more than what we accomplish that tells in the end."[40] He also detected a Tory plot at the King's Plate in Toronto when the winning horse was owned by the arch Conservative proprietor of the *Globe and Mail*, but there was nothing that he could do to prevent that.

Butler-like or otherwise, King had accurately foreseen the enthusiastic reception that the king and queen would receive across Canada from the moment of their arrival, coincidentally three days before the ominous announcement of the Pact of Steel between Italy and Germany. From the royal train and in open cars and always accompanied by an attentive Mackenzie King as "Minister in Attendance," they visited dozens of cities and towns across the country. In Ottawa, the king gave royal approval for parliamentary bills and unveiled the national war memorial (just in time for the beginning of the Second World War). In addition to consolidating pre-election support for the Liberal Party – an essential element for King – the tour helped to ensure that Canada, as he had forecast, would without question be at Britain's side if war did come. At Laurier House, where he hosted a luncheon, he told the king and queen that "I was prepared to lay down my life at their feet in helping to further great causes which they had at heart."[41] With much satisfaction, he shared with the governor general on 26 August his conviction that "the King's visit had helped immensely in uniting Canada."[42] Pearson had already written from London on 9 June 1939 that the British public had gained "the conviction that all this talk of Canadian isolation and neutrality is academic eye-wash and that the reception given by Canada to the King has proved, if it needed proving, that 'the great heart of Canada is sound.'"[43]

The royal visit, which concluded in Halifax on 22 June, also helped to solidify Anglo-American relations in a way that nothing else could have done. In 1937, when Tweedsmuir had first mooted in London the idea of a transcontinental tour by the royal couple, he included as a desirable element a side visit to the United States. Roosevelt duly invited them (but against protocol he pointedly excluded Joseph Kennedy). Washington, Hyde Park, and the World's Fair in New York were in the eventual agreed itinerary of five days (7–12 June). It was a remarkably successful side trip, although an unsettling note was struck when at luncheon at the White House on 8 June the plight of Jewish refugees was raised without resulting in any new approach by Roosevelt or Mackenzie King.[44] For the evident success of their visit to the United States, the king and queen gave much of the credit to Mackenzie King, who accompanied them and who saw it as a dramatic way to further his goal of closer relations among the United States, Canada, and Britain.*

On many journal pages King described almost breathlessly the triumph of the royal tour "in which the voices of goodwill have guided me, used me as an instrument," but his friend Violet Markham knew where the credit lay. She wrote to Tweedsmuir, "To have engineered the visit to the President was a real stroke of genius on your part."[45]

The triumph of the royal tour aside, King's other diary entries in 1939 become decidedly more pessimistic. By then he had faced up to what he had always tried to avoid: a choice, as he saw it, between French Canadian isolationism and English Canadian commitment to the British Commonwealth. He had gradually revealed to his colleagues his unalterable choice, but he remained wary about having to make it public. Policy initiatives were now less reflected in his diary entries as the focus began to shift away from him to the military. Once he had committed to rearmament, decisions moved to the chiefs of staff and to all others who could take a part in preparing the forces and the country more generally for another world war.

In his developing political realism and commitment, King continued to have no help from his deputy minister. Skelton deplored the absence of prior consultation by London with the dominions over a range of issues, despite the fact that he had himself for more than fourteen years opposed foreign policy consultations between the United Kingdom and the dominions. He had a peculiar idea of the role of a deputy minister in a parliamentary democracy. It had now become evident that his minister was convinced that Canada could not remain aloof from any major war in which Britain itself was threatened (something that he had been hinting at or even saying in various convoluted ways since 1923). Instead of assisting his minister, the

---

*Sixty-one years later, in June 2000, the present author and his wife were invited to the Queen Mother's hundredth birthday party at the Guildhall in London. Upon her arrival, the Queen Mother bypassed most other guests and came directly to me to say, without any preliminaries, "High Commissioner, Mr Mackenzie King was very helpful to His Majesty and me in preparing us for our short visit to the United States in 1939. We knew little about the United States, but Mr King knew it well. And he went everywhere with us. Thank you, High Commissioner."

elected representative of his constituents, in implementing his polices after discussion, as all good deputy heads must finally do, he continued to oppose and hinder them, even as war was obviously approaching, making it more difficult for his minister to implement his policies. By 1939, still carping, Skelton had dealt himself out of his part. King lamented, "I feel more and more that I have ... made a mistake in letting myself be too controlled by the isolationist attitude of External Affairs [i.e., Skelton]."[46] He accurately recognized that he had "fourteen years effort here wasted,"[47] perhaps regretting that in 1930 he had not accepted the offer of the principalship of Queen's University where he might have made a more constructive contribution to public life.

A chill began to inform the exchanges and debates about foreign policy – or the absence thereof – in the House of Commons. Canada's recognition of the king of Italy as emperor of Ethiopia passed almost unnoticed, but international affairs debates, prompted chiefly by the CCF, took place on 15 and 20 March when in a speech in Birmingham, in effect abandoning appeasement, Chamberlain sounded almost Churchillian, warning the dictators that "no greater mistake could be made than to suppose that ... this nation has so lost its fibre that it will not take part to the utmost of its power in resisting ... a challenge."[48] By contrast, King's major foreign policy speech to the House a fortnight later, on 30 March, like so many of his speeches, obscured more than it revealed. Beforehand, he had reassured himself that he was following the correct course by consulting voices from Beyond. The late Peter Larkin offered King one simple word of cosmic advice: "preparedness." By coincidence, that was what King had decided to pursue. He did not on this occasion need to be reassured by saints Luke and John or others that a policy of modest rearmament was the right, if belated, post-Munich policy for Canada.

According to Jack Pickersgill, the secretary on loan from the Department of External Affairs, King's wordy contributions to the more frequent foreign affairs debates reflected his full realization that if Britain was involved in a European war, many Canadians would want to join in immediately. King, instead of deploring the undeniable diplomatic shortcomings of Britain and France, as Skelton was wont to do, pledged that "If there was a prospect of an aggressor launching an attack on Britain, with bombers raining death on London," Canada would be there. But at the same time, King stressed to the House his past efforts at peace, so much so that Woodsworth wryly drew attention to the fact that King's speech on 30 March contained "some crumbs of comfort … to the Canadian nationalist, the imperialist, the League of Nations collectivist, the North American [isolationist], the belligerent militarist." The dominion secretary Malcolm MacDonald was clear by this time that beyond all else, King "With deep sincerity … expressed affection for the British people, loyalty to the British Crown, and zeal for an abiding close partnership between Britain and Canada."[49]

Lapointe again sought to be appointed secretary of state for external affairs, but King, as at the time of the Abyssinian debacle, would not entertain the idea of a French Canadian presiding over foreign affairs. Only he himself could hold this portfolio, as the royal tour had demonstrated. The royal visit was for King a time of fleeting optimism. But his optimism turned to foreboding when he learned that Chamberlain would likely invite Churchill to join his gravely weakened government, opening the way for him to succeed as prime minister. As King had repeated over several decades, certainly since the Chanak fiasco, "Winston Churchill is one of the most dangerous men I have ever known."[50] Yet at the same time, he carefully avoided saying anything derogatory about the two dictators, still hoping to demonstrate to voters that he, with Chamberlain, missed no occasion to attempt to conciliate them.

During the uncertainties of the 1935 election and the virtual demise of the League of Nations over Abyssinia, King had sought to an unprecedented degree counsel from the Great Beyond. Once safely back in office in mid-1935 and with the League satisfactorily cast aside, he did not need as many reassurances from the Other World. But in 1939 the challenge of attempting to think well of the blatantly aggressive Hitler propelled him back into that world. A medium in London had already directed him in his search for the Holy Grail to a hitherto unknown Germanic priest-king and knight-templar, Johannes. But revelations of a more profound nature now came to him via Richard Wagner (d. 1883). Divine guidance had directed his random reading to a hitherto neglected Christmas present, a flowery biography of Wagner, *Richard Wagner: The Story of an Artist*, by Guy de Pourtales. A highly excited King instantly recognized from its lush prose that he would be guided by "the *Parsifal* motive from today on, more certain and clear than ever. How I recall going with dear Mother to see *Parsifal* [in New York in 1922] and how like her white head one of the characters in the play. She is guiding me, I know … like the highest and noblest influence in *Parsifal*." He added the next day, "the Wagner book has come by divine aid … it will help me in my inner life – in my political life … the understanding of Hitler and Germany and the world situation … This is the very thing that I have been thirsting for." In his excitement, King was convinced that he had been guided by his mother to Wagner as the ultimate key to understanding the Führer: "one should become saturated with Wagner … Hitler loves his music … and doubtless has imbibed his [Wagner's] philosophy."[51]

King could not have been more mistaken. William Shirer, the American foreign correspondent in Berlin, noted in his diary, "Though he [Hitler] is supposed to have a passion for Wagnerian opera, he almost never attends the Opera." What he loved were Hollywood films.* His denunciation of them as decadent Semitic trash was for public consumption; privately he was a devotee. In presenting the Führer with a Christmas 1937 gift of a dozen Mickey Mouse films – Goebbells and Hitler marked the birth of Jesus with exchanges of gifts – Goebbells had told his diary, "He will be very pleased and happy about this treasure."[52] Shirer agreed. Hitler "likes American films and many never publicly exhibited in Germany are shown him. A few years ago he insisted on having *It Happened One Night* run several times."

On 10 July, Charles Ritchie, then serving as secretary at Canada House, was in the House of Commons "when Chamberlain made his statement of support for Poland over Danzig. It was in so tepid a tone, delivered in such a mechanical manner and received in such silence that one felt chilled."[53] Certainly King felt chilled by this further iteration of the British guarantee to Poland, but on 21 July he sought reassurance from the German consul general in Ottawa, whom he regarded as a close friend. Upon his return from Berlin, the consul general delivered Hitler's reply to King's letter of six months before. It briefly recalled their 1937 "sincere endeavour at mutual understanding" and Hitler's invitation to send six students and six unspecified officers for a three-week visit to see for themselves the "impressive picture of Germany's newly won strength and its will to peaceable constructive work." King was elated to receive such a reply, however tardy, from the Führer – "on a day of Destiny" – since it clarified the "part I was intended to play in the relations with Germany… Hitler [by his letter] was opening a door

---

*Given Hitler's admiration for the British Empire, it is not surprising that he arranged to see frequently, and arranged for the ss to see, Gary Cooper in *Lives of a Bengal Lancer*, an imperial adventure story. *It Happened One Night*, however, is a light-hearted romantic comedy starring Claudette Colbert and Clark Gable. Greta Garbo was another perennial favourite (Shirer, *Berlin Diary*, 244, and Gilbert and Gott, *The Appeasers*).

to permit good relations being restored." Amidst his ruins at Kingsmere, King shared Hitler's message with Joan Patteson. Before doing so, however, he asked her to "take off her shoes for the place whereon she stood was holy ground," having been suddenly rendered so by Hitler's message.[54]

King was convinced that Hitler's positive if brief reply reflected Berlin's recognition of the triumph of the royal tour to Canada one month before. His message "certainly came as a result of the visit of the King and Queen to Canada and my position ... as a result of that visit ... above all ... 'forces unseen'... were working out the plans ... all part of a plan in which God using man to effect his will."[55] An excited King urged Chamberlain to have the king and queen make a broadcast appealing for peace on behalf of women and children everywhere, and he briefly contemplated promoting a royal visit to Hitler, only six weeks after their return to the United Kingdom and six weeks before the beginning of the Second World War. They, with himself in attendance, "would visit Hitler ... I could go to Germany and ... make possible a visit of the King and Queen, going with them [to Germany] as I did to the United States."

That same evening, King described to his diary how the German consul general and he had agreed "to work together for all we were worth ... to bring together into friendly relationship and understanding the German and British." King took some comfort from his quixotic conviction that the rapidly deteriorating situation in Europe was not entirely or even substantially the fault of Germany. "The British and French Governments had been wholly in the wrong in not seizing the moment to come to a real settlement with Germany. What Hitler said to me in 1937 I have every reason to believe that conferences even at that date would have led with very slight concessions (based on justice) to disarmament and peace in Europe. I keep coming back and back to the failure of England to try to make friends with Germany – postponing and postponing conferences."[56] Unfortunately for King's ambitions, his idea of himself leading twelve young Canadians to Germany for three weeks in November, after a Liberal re-election, suddenly came to naught when Ribbentrop signed an unexpected non-aggression pact with Hitler's hitherto arch-enemy, Stalin, in Moscow on 23 August. Chamberlain, who had consistently opposed such an accord between the United Kingdom and the USSR, only reluctantly agreed to begin negotiations in mid-1939, but he missed the bus. Without much hyperbole, A.J.P. Taylor later described the failure to move resolutely and promptly with the Soviet Union "as the greatest set-back for British diplomacy in the twentieth century."[57] The pact with Stalin rendered Hitler immune from fear of Russian intervention, leaving him free to invade the courageous but ill-armed Poland in the next week or so.* It made the Second World War certain.

On 24 August, the day after the signing of the German-Soviet pact, King took the unusual if again belated step of polling his cabinet on what the government should do in the face of the disintegrating situation. His diary records a unanimous agreement of the cabinet (including Lapointe): "In the event of war we had now decided that Canada would participate. We had further decided that we would summon Parliament at the moment war was declared ... At the same time we would announce our policy with respect to Canada being at war ... Parliament would decide details."[58] English-speaking ministers favoured an immediate statement of support for Britain. Euler, however, joined Quebec ministers in opposing any statement committing Canada to participation overseas.† These divided cabinet discussions were of course not made public, but King did inform the British high commissioner and, incongruously, the German consul general of them in confidence. In a public statement, he now declared that parliament would decide only the *details* of military participation. "We regard it of supreme importance at this critical hour that the country should remain united and this can best be met by proceeding with caution with respect to every step taken as the situation may develop."[59]

The next day, 25 August, as German threats to Poland continued to mount despite the Anglo-French guarantee, King sent telegrams to Hitler, Mussolini, and even to the president of Poland, urging a peaceful settlement of all differences. Chamberlain somehow remained cautiously optimistic. "We are not through the jungle, on the contrary the issue is still doubtful.

---

*A surprising number of young Canadians, however, continued to visit Germany on their own initiative or that of various youth groups (e.g., school children sent by the Overseas Education League of Canada). One young Canadian, Franklin Wegenast, recorded his impressions in a journal. See Wegenast, *Liberty Is Dead*, edited by Margaret Derry.

†Euler was increasingly seen as too much of an apologist for Germany. King, uncomfortable at having him any longer in his wartime cabinet, made him a senator in May 1940. That same month, the *Globe and Mail* ran a story that Canada's newest senator had been photographed the year before at a meeting of Canadians of German descent at the Concordia Club in Kitchener, standing in front of a swastika flag. Euler assured the newspaper that that was all nonsense, and the paper retracted the statement, but the photograph does include the Nazi flag among other "decorations."

250 Mackenzie King in the Age of the Dictators

But ... remember that the tide turns at the low as well as at the high level!"[60] Although only one week remained before Germany's invasion of Poland, King continued to hope that Hitler would pursue peace, recalling that during his 1937 visit to Berlin, he had "left Hitler not with a curse but with a blessing ... may God's blessing guide you."[61] Two days later, he added, accurately, "I never let myself declare ... against Hitler."[62] As an overt royalist, King rejoiced in sharing with Tweedsmuir his conviction that "the King's visit had helped immensely in uniting Canada ... that last September I would not have had a united Cabinet, that Lapointe, Cardin and Power (I might also have added Rinfret) would probably have resigned and there would have been difficulty besides in fighting for Czecho-Slovakia. Today I had all united on our participation if there were an act of aggression which brought England and France into a war with Germany."[63] King also sent a message to Chamberlain to urge King George VI to appeal directly to Hitler to allow more time for negotiation. He did so because he was convinced, as he recorded in his diary the next day, that Hitler believed "in compassion, pity as the thing to aim at, also ultimate perfection in purity of living ... [He] is a mystic ... a spiritualist ... and thus his life becomes intelligible. It is that which makes this appeal to his good, his spiritual side, important. Hitler will feel compassion for mankind, pity is holding the sword for today ... That I truly believe."[64]

Although having covertly indicated to cabinet colleagues as well as to the British and German governments his decision (not parliament's) that Canada would be at Britain's side if war came, King continued publicly his habitual ambiguities. In a public speech in Toronto in August, he was still denying that he had made any commitments whatever: "One thing I will not do ... is to say what Canada will do in regard to a situation that may arise at some future time and under circumstances of which we now know nothing."[65] That he would make such a declaration in Toronto would play well in Quebec, but King did not explain who was to blame for Canada knowing nothing. The day before Britain and France declared war, he wrote somewhat incoherently of his gratification that Hitler believed that "he is a reincarnated spirit and dwelling with the gods on the highest, obliged to come into humble circumstances into the world and win his way ... to [the] greatest heights of mankind ... It is the supernatural, the spiritual that counts."[66]

By then the Nazi movement in Canada – such as it was – had all but faded away. For many months previously, the RCMP, employing informers, intercepting mail and telephone messages, and drawing on information supplied by both MI5 in London and the FBI in Washington, had complied lists of pro-Nazi Canadians deemed a security risk in the event of war. The lists were not long. Lapointe assured the House of Commons that "the Government is keeping itself well informed as to what is going on … as regards Nazi or fascist or communist activities in Canada. I am happy to say neither the genuine imported articles nor the spurious local imitations are in any sense a serious political factor in any part of Canada."[67]

On the morning of 1 September, King's manservant awoke him with the news that the Wehrmacht had crossed into Poland. Confirmation came during the day from several sources, and in the evening Joan Patteson strolled through the woods at Kingsmere from her nearby summer house to report that she had just heard on her husband's radio that Britain and France had lived up to their guarantee to Poland by declaring war on Germany. The next day, while shaving, King remarked upon the shaving soap lather resembling "a perfect swan with a figure like that of [Wagner's] Siegfried … a guide to Hitler … like Siegfried [he] has gone out to court death, hoping for the Valhalla, an immortality to be joined by death … Wagner's emphasis on death to be aimed at." In the afternoon, the voice of King's father (d. 1916) told him that a Pole had just assassinated Hitler. Unfortunately, that message from the Great Beyond soon proved as incorrect as an accompanying one from Asquith that world war would be averted, despite Germany's invasion of Poland.[68] The Second World War had begun, and within ten days parliament would decide (with one dissenting vote) that an ill-prepared Canada would be part of it.

15

A Good Bit of Wool

On the surface at least it is difficult to say at any time what foreign policy – or foreign policies, if indeed any – Mackenzie King was pursuing in his decade-long personal aspiration to attain a leading role for himself in international affairs. But there is one consistent element in his foreign policy gyrations that dates back to his first days in Europe in 1899. That consistent element is his "ragbag of emotions towards Britain and the British."[1] He took pride in Canada's place in the Empire (he never readily adopted the later designation "British Commonwealth of Nations"). In London during the South African War he had been deeply moved upon seeing the Grenadier and Coldstream Guards marching to embarkation. He was no less moved by his own triumph forty years later in arranging – although not initiating – the first visit by a reigning monarch to Canada.

From his initial term as prime minister in 1921–26, King was careful to pursue privately at first but later publicly a policy of loyalty to the crown that might just pass muster in isolationist Quebec and at the same time leave little room for critics elsewhere to accuse him of disloyalty to the Empire. To be sure, he was always conscious that he was the grandson of a leader of the rebellion against the self-serving Anglo establishment in Upper Canada in 1837. But he saw his grandfather, William Lyon Mackenzie, as embodying the true British values of liberty and justice, not the self-serving preoccupations of a local Tory clique. A century later, King saw himself as true to both the legacy of his maternal grandfather and his public pledges to Quebec by working to loosen the anachronistic formal ties of the Empire and replacing them with the freely given allegiance of equal and autonomous nations within the Commonwealth. Throughout his life, King relished the paradox that the looser the formal ties, the stronger the Empire. In this he was assisted by the Conservative Party presenting itself – at least in the eyes of an alienated

Quebec – as more directly imperialistic, without the caution and ambiguities that the Liberal Party under King was careful to display. Left with no alternative, Quebec could be counted on to vote Liberal.

In this sometimes-precarious balancing act, King's first challenge was the Chanak incident. Once he realized that "the whole business [was] an 'election scheme'" (which Meighen never did) and once Churchill had fortuitously made it public, he could portray himself to Quebec (via Lapointe) as an opponent of imperial centralists, while recognizing at the same time – as he pledged to the 1923 imperial conference – that "there are great common interests in which all of us have an equal concern and are equally ready to share." From the 1923 imperial conference on, King's purpose in foreign affairs was to do whatever was necessary to retain a clear Liberal majority in the House of Commons. This required that the Liberals win most of the sixty-five seats in Quebec. If Canada was to remain unified, the Liberal Party, not the Conservative, must form the government. Although he never learned to know Quebec, he was acutely aware of its long-standing opposition to Canada's involvement in what it saw as Britain's imperialist wars; its aversion to financial support for the Royal Navy; and, above all, its hatred of compulsory military service overseas. But on such issues the unilingual King would take no direct leadership in Quebec. He relied almost exclusively on Lapointe to tell him what Quebec would accept or reject.

Twist as King might, sooner or later events would demand that someone make decisions in Canada's foreign relations, however cautious or limited those decisions might be. King repeatedly contended that a prime minister should be judged at least as much on what he did not do as what he did do. But there were times when a do-nothing stance was not enough. There is indeterminate evidence that King offered his services to Borden's pro-conscriptionist Union Government of 1917. If he did, he subsequently covered his trail effectively, cautiously presenting himself as an anti-conscriptionist. Italian aggression in Abyssinia, with its fatal repercussions for the League of Nations, was another such event, inherited from the Conservative government of Bennett. As we have seen, King transformed himself almost overnight from an ardent supporter of the League to an outspoken opponent, upon being warned by Lapointe that Quebec was unalterably opposed to the League imposing sanctions against Italy, convinced that economic sanctions could in time lead to military sanctions and even the overthrow of the dictator Mussolini, the true friend of the Vatican. As was often the case, King would have preferred to do nothing, but the Quebec seats were not to be trifled with. In any event, active, articulate, or influential exponents of the League and of collective security were few in number, however intelligent, perceptive, and far-seeing they might be individually. Happily for King, he was also able in the 1920s to take shelter behind the parallel rejection by the Conservatives, in their forlorn search for Quebec votes, of any automatic requirement that League members join in a military sanction against an aggressor.

Thus, when in 1935 Lapointe confirmed for King that Quebec would not accept any "collective security" under the League of Nations that could possibly lead to military obligations, King ended any role for himself as an advocate of the League. It is a cliché to say that foreign policy is an extension of domestic policy. King's domestic policy was for the Liberal Party to remain in office in a more or less united Canada and if that had foreign affairs implications, so be it. Abandoning collective security under the League, from May 1937 when Chamberlain became prime minister until the day that the Second World War began in September 1939, King followed enthusiastically the British policy of attempting to appease Hitler and Mussolini. But he carefully kept foreign affairs off the parliamentary agenda and away from public debate for as long as he could. Better to say and do nothing publicly about international events than to risk alienating either English or French Canada. And by extension, better to say nothing about the dictators. Better to be seen as appeasing, not confronting. If war did come, no one could then fault him for not having tried hard and long to help conciliate them.

King's deputy minister disagreed. Skelton would have had an isolationist Canada shelter behind an isolationist United States in an extension of the Monroe doctrine to Canada. Roosevelt's 1938 pledge of protection in a darkening world was enough for Skelton and some Canadians, but for King and a majority of English-speaking Canadians it was not enough, not by a long shot. Whatever the legal quibbles about the time-honoured proposition that if Britain-is-at-war-Canada-is-at-war, King knew perfectly well that if Britain and Germany were again at war, a great majority of English-speaking Canadians would want to be there – via the Conservative Party if necessary.

Woodsworth saw clearly what the prime minister was doing when he spoke in the House about King's "crumbs for everyone." But King's all-embracing, amorphous, and equivocal public stances could only be sustained so long as appeasement was seen as still having any chance of success. After the German seizure of Prague and the balance of Czechoslovakia in the spring of 1939, appeasement as a policy became as moribund as the League of Nations had become over Abyssinia. English Canada became increasingly worried – and vocal. Conservative political fortunes were accordingly on the rise in much of English Canada as the Conservatives pursued their more overt anti-Nazi policy. Whether he liked it or not, King would have to choose between openly pledging Canada to go to war alongside other members of the British Commonwealth or likely losing the election that he foresaw for the autumn of 1939. Privately at first but later publicly and in a convoluted way, he chose English Canada, but only after first giving his solemn word to Quebec that no government he headed would introduce compulsory military service overseas, a flat promise that the Conservative leader, Robert Manion, had already made publicly to a skeptical Quebec. It was a policy with its risks, but King saw his repeated assurances as the best way to remain in office.

All this and much else did not satisfy those Canadians who – at least in retrospect – have questioned why King did not contribute whatever he could to opposing the two dictators. One of his secretaries, Jack Pickersgill, concluded that "there was almost nothing really original in his attitudes or his policies, and his conduct was certainly not directed by any comprehensive political philosophy."[2] Lester Pearson put the question of whether Canada, under a more vigorous and decisive leader than King, could have made any difference in international affairs in the prewar years.

> My complaint with our foreign policy … was that we were too worried or timid to take any responsibility in any effort to avoid the war … we could have done positive things … even if they had no very important results. We could have taken a lead in Geneva … government policy, though it may well have reflected the general view of the country at the time, did not permit those representing Canada abroad … to take a lead, or indeed any initiative … The idealists who believed that international commitments should be taken in order to prevent war were at least realistic enough to know that there was no question of Canada staying out if war came; and no question of anything but full and bloody participation, especially … when it was not an old-fashioned war of balance of power and European ambitions, but one against Hitler, and Nazism, and fascism … The horror and danger of Nazism had gone deep into public opinion in Canada and other countries by 1939, and made it

possible, for countries like Canada, to participate wholeheartedly in such a war – without division and disunity.[3]

With the benefit of hindsight, Pearson analyzed accurately the nature of Canada's irresolute entry into the Second World War. What he did not include, not having read King's diaries, are two additional cogent facts. In King's voluminous prewar diaries and correspondence there are manifold references to the two dictators, but, in a self-congratulatory way, he permitted himself no derogatory comments about them. From the beginning, Mussolini was a danger to domestic opponents, but at the time of King's visit to Rome in 1928 he was not yet seen as a threat to anyone abroad. King did briefly write in late 1935 at the time of the Abyssinian crisis, "The Dictator Mussolini [was] bringing his people into war, destroying his nation." That, however, was a rare condemnation and essentially for domestic purposes. For years prior to that near unique statement, his favourable impression of the anti-communist Mussolini did not involve any threats to Canadian unity, however overdrawn they were. In Rome in 1928, he contented himself with regarding Mussolini's dictatorship as limiting itself to the continuing eradication of communists, harlots, and other lick-spittal. In any event, those were questions for the Italian people themselves (King, unlike more recent political leaders, did not court diasporas). But quite why he was so enthusiastic about Mussolini when he did not share the Mediterranean strategic imperatives of Chamberlain, Churchill, Halifax, and Laval, remains a question.

That Hitler was even more evil than Mussolini did not provoke a greater adverse reaction from King. His eagerness to believe the best of the Führer was not uncommon in the interwar years, certainly more common than the anti-Hitler tirades of the out-of-office Churchill. Lloyd George and others were even more gullible observers. As late as 27 August 1939, one week before the beginning of the war and after almost six years of Hitler as chancellor, King was still writing optimistically about him as the mystic, the spiritualist, someone whom he had "never let [himself] declare against." Why? King, chronically insecure, sought to avoid acknowledging that he had been wrong about Hitler all along. In his commitment to national unity, he desperately continued, against all evidence, to believe the best of him. King had turned his back on the League, that "international War Office," but he hoped to the very last moment that his fellow mystic in Berlin would avoid war, which in his view would divide Canada and threaten the Liberal Party as the chosen instrument to govern a united country. Better to say nothing derogatory about the dictator and hope for the best. As Violet Markham, King's longtime friend and financial benefactor, wrote succinctly to Tweedsmuir a month before the declaration of war, "Hitler I fear pulled a good bit of wool over our friend Rex's eyes."[4]

King's frequent repetition of "parliament will decide" appears for a time to have satisfied Quebec and isolationists elsewhere, who could hardly challenge such an apparent commitment to parliamentary democracy. In fact, however, as King himself knew as well as anyone, parliament with its Liberal majority, would decide as he directed it. Worse, parliament would be called upon to decide without having had adequate time set aside for debate of events and issues leading up to the declaration of war. King was convinced that no good could come from such debates, whether in cabinet or in parliament itself. His actions made a mockery of his own slogan. Richard Veatch, the historian of Canada at the League of Nations, was not fooled. "King's insistence that 'Parliament will decide' became little more than another way of enunciating the 'no commitments' policy which characterized his conduct of foreign affairs, and which left him an almost completely free hand in their conduct."[5] The historian Kenneth McNaught held King in contempt for such practices: "it was not the divisions in the House of Commons, or in the nation that most threatened Canadian unity – it was the attitude of the [King's] Government toward Parliament. The refusal to declare its support of Chamberlain *as a Canadian policy*, the refusal to accept … [a] resolution on the *right* of neutrality, the refusal to declare its decision to plan defence jointly with Britain, in fact its refusal to take Parliament into its confidence – these were the things that constituted a real threat to Canadian unity … Refusal to do this made utter nonsense of the doctrine of parliamentary supremacy, [and] was itself a cause of considerable disunity, and certainly debased Parliament."[6] By August 1939, even King could no longer keep repeating his mantra: he changed it to parliament will decide *the details*.

The second major factor revealed in King's diaries is his silence on the horrors of war. He never – at least as far as the present author has been able to discover – deplored, as Chamberlain and other appeasers repeatedly did, the deaths, the suffering, the torment, and the terror that warfare inflicts on combatants and innocents alike. King never served in any military capacity. Throughout his long term in office, he kept well away from the military, although there was on every side evidence of the pervasive impact of modern warfare: Italians gassing Abyssinians armed only with spears, or Stukas of the Condor Legion obliterating the undefended Guernica in Spain were only the more evident horrific examples. Yet King kept repeating that war must be avoided, although certainly not through collective security at the League of Nations if Quebec felt so strongly against it. With a curious coldness, he avoided speaking of how people's lives might be saved and their freedoms protected by collective security, but dwelled instead on the preservation of Canadian unity under the Liberals.

What if King had displayed intellectual integrity throughout? What if he had publicly derided the dictators? What if he had publicly deplored their lethal prejudices? Would Canada have made any difference to the wider world? Would more evident and resolute leadership have made any difference to Canada itself? What if King had resolutely joined in supporting collective security or other international commitments to prevent war? Would Canada have split, with Quebec somehow isolating itself in a second world war in an obscure corner of North America? Would a lead by Canada, joined by New Zealand and any other like-minded Commonwealth members, have garnered support for collective security, especially by Britain? The answer to such questions today can only be conjecture.

John Munro, an editor of documents relating to Canada's external relations in the 1930s, has written with the benefit of hindsight,

Canadian policy often seemed deliberately cloaked in confusion and decidedly negative in substance. Confrontation in international policies was an evil; collective security, an anathema. International appeasement and conciliation, if not vigorously pursued, were at least to be applauded and encouraged. No commitments, the avoidance of consultation (of course, we were offended when we were not consulted on questions that affected us) and a minimum of public examination and debate were the means adopted in achieving the "safety" of a back-seat position in international affairs. At all costs, Canada must avoid encouraging Britain in any course that might lead to war and thus expose the Anglo-Canadian relationship and threaten the partisan balance of domestic politics.[7]

Lester Pearson agreed, but took Munro's musing another step. "No doubt, Professor Munro's view is right that it was unlikely that we could have materially altered for the better the course of events in the 1930s ... However, the fact that it is unlikely that you may be able to make an important contribution to formulating a better policy surely is no reason why you shouldn't try ... we were too worried or timid to take any responsibility in any effort to avoid the war ... We could have taken a lead at Geneva ... [but] government policy ... did not permit those representing Canada abroad ... to take a lead, or indeed any initiative ... We very nearly became ... an observer."[8]

To be sure, the answers today must be hypothetical, but what had become possible in Canada in 1939 in the way of accelerated rearmament should with firm leadership also have been possible in 1937 or 1938 – as it was in Britain – despite fiscal constraints and grumbles from Quebec. For example, it is difficult today to see why the British Commonwealth Air Training Plan could not have gone forward in 1937 or 1938 without either bankrupting the country or fatally straining its unity. Army units, even if publicly still designated for home defence, could have been better expanded, trained, and equipped and additional French-speaking units promoted if King had been willing to take a lead, including in finding the necessary funding.

But that and much else must now be left to conjecture or debate. To be sure, Canada under King did enter the Second World War at least minimally united. But a basic question – however hypothetical today – abides. Could Canada, with more effective, realistic, and determined leadership instead of convoluted caution, have done more to help counter the menace of the dictators? One element in an answer must be that Canadian armed forces were in a deplorable state when war came in September 1939. Fortunately, the first year of the conflict was a "phoney war," leaving a little time for the more advanced training of a First Division in the United Kingdom and the raising of additional units at home. And fortuitously there was just time enough for training schools for aircrew to be hastily constructed and staffed across the country. The navy had to put to sea in a few ships none of which was equipped with the latest Royal Navy technology, leaving it incapable for two years or more of playing a significant role in the Battle of the Atlantic.

But what in the end did it matter if King variously abandoned the League of Nations and collective security; eschewed Commonwealth defence collaboration; remained deeply suspicious of the United States; and was parsimonious about both external affairs and defence spending? Canada was a small nation, remote from Europe, often with a dual, and always a passive, foreign policy of neither commitments nor isolationism that was somehow intended to satisfy both French- and English-speaking Canadians at the same time, thereby keeping the country more or less united. But no one in the chancelleries of continental Europe really cared what Ottawa thought or whether Canada was united or not. Very likely nothing that Ottawa could have said or done could have countered the Italian intimidation that led to the Hoare-Laval agreement and the end of the League of Nations. And certainly nothing that Canada could have said or done would have influenced the German reoccupation of the Rhineland; the *Anschluss* with Austria; the piecemeal seizure of Czechoslovakia; the German-Soviet pact; or earlier recognition in the United Kingdom that attempts at appeasement would go nowhere. King had by his drift, procrastination, prevarication, caution, platitudes, evasions, indecision, and banalities kept Canada from dividing – or so he assured himself.

But would Canada have divided fatally if King had been capable of urging Britain to display resolute defiance in the face of the dictators? Students of his long career as prime minister generally salute him in his exaltation of national unity as the highest good, exhibiting great agility in offering Quebec a no-commitments foreign policy while assuring English Canada, in somewhat obscure terms, that Canada would support Britain in any major war. Certainly at no time did he address the whole nation or even parliament with a ringing rejection of the claptrap of the dictators. As little as one week before the war began he was still congratulating himself for never having said anything derogatory about the dictators: "I never let myself say one word … against Hitler."

Was Canada in fact such a fragile country that two largely contradictory foreign policies needed to be pursued simultaneously? If from the end of 1938, if not before, King had presented an articulate case against the dictators, would he have divided the country irreparably? In any case, was national unity the highest good or was there something else of even greater value then and subsequently? Such matters must now be left to speculation, but even more fundamental questions remain. What did King's dual policies or lack of policy lead us then and now to think of ourselves? In sovereign nations, are international affairs in fact nothing more than an extension of domestic affairs? Cannot there be somewhere in international affairs a degree of morality and not merely of expediency?

Only when Hitler refused to be appeased by Britain and France at Munich did King gradually reveal that he had, in fact, a single foreign policy and that was to support Britain. Behind the closed doors of the 1923 imperial conference he had made a vague such pledge, repeated it privately at the conferences of 1926 and 1936, confirmed it to Chamberlain and Eden in his confidential account of his visit to Hitler and publicly at the Paris exposition of 1937 – of all places – before later proclaiming it at home to individual ministers, his full cabinet, and finally to parliament and hence to the public. There was never anything inspiring in King's habitual evasion of public leadership, but his endless manoeuvrings, foreshadowed in his *Industry and Humanity* of 1918, appear to have expressed his conviction that anything is better than war, in turn contributing substantially to his surprising political longevity. And certainly some observers, speculating to no real purpose on whether someone else might have achieved more or less, continue to stress his contribution to bringing Canada into the Second World War apparently unified, if grossly unprepared. He declared to the emergency session of parliament that took Canada into the war, "I have made it … the supreme endeavour of my leadership … to let no hasty or premature threat or pronouncement create mistrust and divisions between the different elements that compose the population of our vast dominion."[9] No word here about the iniquitous dictators.

In reviewing King's long career, efforts are frequently made to close the abundant loops, to square the abundant circles. But such efforts are generally in vain. At any given time King readily convinced himself of the clarity and the righteousness of what he was doing. Later observers, conscious of the contradictions, have not always found it so easy. Perhaps a final few words on why King failed so signally to provide clear public leadership and display convincing intellectual integrity can best be left to one who observed him more closely over a longer period than anyone else: Norman Robertson, the wise, perceptive, and kindly career foreign service officer who joined the Department of External Affairs in 1929 and was undersecretary of state from Skelton's death in January 1941 to September 1946 and again from 1958 to 1963. He twice became high commissioner to the United Kingdom, as well as ambassador to the United States and later secretary to the cabinet. In 1923 he found King "hopelessly undistinguished." By 1950, after almost twenty-five years of close observation, he had not changed his mind, especially with regard to Mackenzie King's handling of foreign affairs. Douglas Le Pan, himself a senior member of the department, recalled that on learning of King's death on 22 July 1950, he had made to the astute Robertson "the kind of anodyne remark about the late Prime Minister that the circumstances seemed to require. I will never forget his reply. He said quite simply: 'I never saw a touch of greatness in him.'"[10]

Notes

CHAPTER ONE

1 Lower, *Colony to Nation*, 541.
2 Holmes, *The Better Part of Valour*, 21.
3 King, public statement, "Liberalism and Reconstruction," August 1919, MG26–J5, LAC.
4 Pickersgill, "Mackenzie King's Political Attitudes and Public Policies," 18.
5 King, public statement, "Liberalism and Reconstruction."
6 British High Commissioner, Ottawa, to London, 16 January 1936, in Hillmer, *O.D. Skelton*, 43n158.
7 English, *Shadow of Heaven*, 189.
8 Pearson to Massey, 16 July 1939, in Massey, *What's Past Is Prologue*, 295.
9 Pearson, *Mike*, 1: 109.
10 Feiling, *The Life of Neville Chamberlain*, 320.
11 Dumitt, *Unbuttoned*, 216.
12 King diary, 2 January 1899.
13 Ibid., 4 September 1900.
14 Ibid., 2 September 1901.
15 Armstrong and Stagg, "William Lyon Mackenzie," *Dictionary of Canadian Biography*, 9: 508.
16 Pickersgill, "Mackenzie King's Political Attitudes and Public Policies," 16.
17 King to Amery, 2 April 1907, MG26–J1, LAC.

CHAPTER TWO

1 Offer, *The First World War*, 173.
2 Ibid., 191.

264   Notes to pages 14-29

3 Larmour, *Canada's Opportunity*, 28.

4 Macpherson to Laurier, 20 August 1907, MG26–G, LAC.

5 Laurier to the Liberal MP for Vancouver City, Robert Macpherson, 27 August 1907, MG26–G, LAC.

6 Greenwood to the Empire Club, Toronto, 13 September 1907, *Empire Club of Canada Speeches, 1907–1908*, 15.

7 Borden, *The Question of Oriental Immigration*, 9.

8 *Toronto Globe*, 14 September 1907.

9 Order-in-Council, 12 October 1907, LAC.

10 Dawson, *William Lyon Mackenzie King*, 148.

11 King diary, 31 January 1908.

12 Ibid., 25 January 1908.

13 Ibid.

14 Ibid., 24 February 1908.

15 Ibid., 25 February 1908.

16 Grey to Elgin, 17 February 1908, in Dawson, *William Lyon Mackenzie King*, 157.

17 Offer, *The First World War*, 193

18 Ibid., drawing on King diary of 28 January 1908.

19 Ibid.

20 Ibid., 160.

21 King diary, 9 March 1908.

22 Ibid., 27 February 1908.

23 Ibid., 8 April 1908.

24 Ibid., 20 March 1908.

25 Ibid., 4 March 1909.

26 Ibid., 17 March 1908.

27 Ibid., 28 March 1908.

28 Ward, *White Canada Forever*, 91.

29 Borden to Perley, 17 July 1914, DCER, 1: 649.

30 Isabel King to King, 6 November 1905, in Dawson, *William Lyon Mackenzie King*, 181.

31 King diary, 6 March 1909.

32 Ibid., 24 May 1909.

33 King diary, 6 March 1909.

34 King diary, 31 October 1911.

Notes to pages 32–43   265

CHAPTER THREE

1 King to Lewis, 25 August 1919, MG25–J1, LAC.
2 Sir Frederick Borden to 1907 Imperial Defence Committee, in Stacey, "Laurier, King and External Affairs," 86.
3 Borden to Christie, 16 April 1926, in Eayrs, *In Defence of Canada*, 1: 24.
4 Bliss, *Right Honourable Men*, 145.
5 Great Britain, Parliament, House of Lords, Debates, 22 July 1870.
6 Ibid., 2 August 1904.
7 Ibid., 12 August, 1911.
8 Dugdale, in *Arthur James Balfour*, 2: 378.
9 Asquith, Minutes of Imperial Conference, 25 May 1911, 71, and 23 May, 22.
10 Speech by Sir George Perley to the National Liberal Club (London), 6 April 1916, *Canadian Annual Review*, 1916, 449.
11 Canada, Parliament, House of Commons Debates, 2 September 1919.
12 Kerr to Grigg, 15 April 1920, in Butler, *Lord Lothian*, 79.
13 King diary, 19 November 1941.
14 Ibid., 20 May 1943.
15 Neatby, "Mackenzie King and the Historians," 8.
16 Hillmer, "Anglo-Canadian Neurosis," 67.
17 Massey, *What's Past Is Prologue*, 135.
18 Glazebrook to Dove, 24 August 1923, Bodleian Library, Oxford, mss, English History, c. 819, folio 177.
19 Robertson to his mother, 22 October 1923, in Granatstein, *A Man of Influence*, 10.
20 King diary, 25 August 1900.
21 Pickersgill, "Mackenzie King's Political Attitudes and Pubic Policies," 19.
22 King diary, 5 December 1922.

CHAPTER FOUR

1 Riddell, *The Riddell Diaries*, 385.
2 Ronaldshay, *The Life of Lord Curzon*, 3: 300.
3 Middlemas and Barnes, *Baldwin*, 110.
4 Colonial Secretary to Governor General, 15 September 1922, DCER, 3: 74.

266 Notes to pages 43–52

5 Walder, *The Chanak Affair*, 216; Beaverbrook, *The Decline and Fall of Lloyd George*, 160.
6 Campbell, *F.E. Smith*, 605.
7 Curzon to King, 8 October 1923, DCER, 3: 247.
8 King diary, 17 and 18 September 1922.
9 Beaverbrook, *The Decline and Fall of Lloyd George*, 160; Colonial Secretary to Governor General, 18 September 1922, DCER, 3: 76.
10 *Globe*, 19 September 1922.
11 Beaverbrook, *The Decline and Fall of Lloyd George*, 187.
12 King diary, 20 October 1923.
13 Gilbert, *Portrait of a Diplomat*, 275.
14 Campbell, *F.E. Smith*, 605.
15 Greenwood to King, King diary, 19 May 1944.
16 Ibid., 26 January 1923.
17 Ronaldshay, *The Life of Lord Curzon*, 3: 302.
18 Mosley, *Curzon*, 233.
19 Ronaldshay, *The Life of Lord Curzon*, 3: 302.
20 Sir Frederick Borden to the 1907 Imperial Defence Committee, in Stacey, "Laurier, King and External Affairs," 88.
21 Minister of Marine and Fisheries (Lapointe) to Prime Minister, 20 September 1922, DCER, 3: 79.
22 Meighen speech, 22 September 1922, to the Toronto Liberal-Conservative Business Men's Club, *Mail and Empire*, 23 September 1922, in Graham, *Arthur Meighen*, 2: 210.
23 King diary, 19 October 1922.
24 King to the 1923 Imperial Conference, 8 October 1923, DCER, 3: 246.
25 Cook, "J.W. Dafoe at the Imperial Conference," 31.
26 King to the 1923 Imperial Conference, 8 October 1923, DCER, 3: 245.
27 Ibid., 3: 248.
28 Wigley, *Canada and the Transition to Commonwealth*, 144.
29 King to the 1923 Imperial Conference, 8 October 1923, DCER, 3: 244.
30 MacLaren, *Commissions High*, 252.
31 Ibid.
32 Stacey, *Canada and the Age of Conflict*, 2: 67.
33 King diary, 2 April 1924.
34 MacLaren, *Commissions High*, 251.
35 King diary, 18 November 1923.

36 Curzon to his wife, 8 November 1923, in Marchioness Curzon, *Reminiscences*, 181.

37 Curzon to his wife, 18 November 1923, ibid., 192.

38 King speech, Quebec City, October 1926; Canada, Parliament, House of Commons Debates, 13 December 1926.

39 King to 1926 Imperial Conference, 4 November 1926, DCER, 4: 136.

40 Ibid., 110.

41 Balfour Declaration of 1926, *Documents on Canadian Foreign Policy*, ed. Riddell, 130; Statute of Westminster, in *Historical Documents of Canada*, ed. Stacey, 485.

42 King diary, 3 February 1927.

43 Ibid., 29 December 1926.

44 Betcherman, *Ernest Lapointe*, 129.

45 MacRae to Dafoe, 21 November 1926, in "A Canadian Account," ed. Cook, 61.

46 Betcherman, *Ernest Lapointe*, 124.

47 King diary, 11 September 1929.

CHAPTER FIVE

1 Rowell to the first League of Nations Assembly 1920, in Prang, *N.W. Rowell*, 361.

2 King diary, 9 April 1923.

3 Canada, Parliament, House of Commons Debates, Government Resolution, 21 June 1926.

4 Dawson, *William Lyon Mackenzie King*, vol.1.

5 Canada, Parliament, House of Commons Debates, 12 February 1929.

6 Ibid.

7 Ibid., 18 October 1932.

CHAPTER SIX

1 Hughes, "The Early Diplomacy of Italian Fascism in 1922–1932," 1: 230.

2 Evans, *The Coming of the Third Reich*, 22.

3 Brendon, *The Dark Valley*, 25.

4 Taylor, *The Origins of the Second World War*, 85.

268 Notes to pages 64-80

5 King diary, 26 September 1928.
6 Ibid.
7 Ibid., 26–27 September 1928.
8 Ibid., 24 September 1928.
9 Massey diary, 6 April 1931, University of Toronto Archives.
10 Gilbert, *Winston Churchill*, 5: 226; Edwards, "The Foreign Office and Fascism," 157.
11 *Toronto Star Weekly*, 21 January 1928.
12 Waite, "French-Canadian Isolationism and English Canada," 134.
13 Eayrs, "A Low Dishonest Decade," 69.

CHAPTER SEVEN

1 King diary, 3 July 1927.
2 Vansittart memorandum, 6 May 1933, in "Robert Gilbert Vansittart," *Dictionary of National Biography*, vol. 20.
3 King diary, 16 July 1933.
4 Halton, *Toronto Daily Star*, 16 September 1933, in David Halton, *Dispatches from the Front*, 79.
5 *Toronto Star*, 16 October 1933.
6 Nicolson, *Diaries and Letters*, 30 August 1939, 1: 415.
7 Lockhart, *The Diaries of Sir Robert Bruce Lockhart*, 1: 299.
8 Phipps to Simon, 8 August 1934, *Documents on British Foreign Policy, 1919–1939*, Second Series, 12: 4
9 Rowell to his daughter, 14 April 1933, in Prang, *N.W. Rowell*, 475.
10 Eksteins, *The Rites of Spring*, 303.
11 Lockhart, *The Diaries of Sir Robert Bruce Lockhart*, 263.
12 Diamond, *The Nazi Movement in the United States*, 127.
13 Wagner, "The Deutscher Bund Canada," 176.
14 Ibid., 140.
15 Wagner, "The Deutscher Bund Canada," 179.
16 *Le Patriote*, 12 January 1934, in Nadeau, *The Canadian Führer*, 101.
17 Ludecke, *I Knew Hitler*, 541.
18 Betcherman, *Ernest Lapointe*, 273.
19 Nadeau, *The Canadian Führer*, 94.
20 Fine, "Anti-Semitism in Manitoba in the 1930s and 40s," 41.

Notes to pages 81-93   269

21 Whitaker, Kealey, and Parnaby, *Secret Service*, 144; Wagner, "The Deutscher Bund Canada," 176.

CHAPTER EIGHT

1 Gray, *Mrs. King*, 363.
2 King diary, 9 November 1934.
3 Veatch, *Canada and the League of Nations*, 134.
4 King to Garson, 11 January 1935, MG25–J1, LAC.
5 King diary, 9 January 1935.
6 Ibid., 27 January 1934.
7 Ibid., 1 January 1935.
8 Ibid., 17 December 1934.
9 Riddell, *World Security by Conference*, 88.
10 Macleod, *Neville Chamberlain*, 185.
11 Baldwin, in Barnett, *The Collapse of British Power*, 375.
12 Riddell diary, 16 January 1935, York University Archives.
13 Rowell to Pearson, 19 August 1935, in Prang, *N.W. Rowell*, 479.
14 CAB 24 /255, CP 98 (35), 13 May 1935, UKNA.
15 Riddell diary, 16 April 1935, York University Archives.
16 Veatch, *Canada and the League of Nations*, 136.
17 Ibid., 132.
18 Bennett to Ferguson, 26 July 1935, DCER, 5: 377; Carter, "Canada and Sanctions."
19 British High Commissioner, Ottawa, to London, 9 August 1935, DO 6109/A/159, UKNA.
20 Ibid., 23 August 1935.
21 King diary, 22 August 1935.
22 Lapointe speech, 9 September 1935, in Stacey, *Canada and the Age of Conflict*, 2: 180.
23 Riddell diary, 9 May 1935, York University Archives.
24 Skelton to Herridge, 23 August 1935, DCER, 5: 379.
25 Skelton to Rowell, 2 October 1935, in Prang, *N.W. Rowell*, 480.
26 Amery, *The Empire at Bay*, 13 August 1935, 2: 396.
27 *Ottawa Morning Citizen*, 9 September 1935.
28 In Stacey, *Canada and the Age of Conflict*, 2: 180.

270 Notes to pages 94–100

29 Eayrs, *In Defence of Canada*, 2: 6.
30 Herridge to Finlayson, 3 August 1935, in Stacey, *Canada and the Age of Conflict*, 2: 190.
31 Bennett to Dominions Secretary, 3 September 1935, DCER, 5: 381; British High Commissioner, Ottawa, to London, 4 September 1935, DO 6109 A 270, UKNA.
32 Pearson, *Mike*, 1: 93.
33 Ferguson to League of Nations Assembly, 14 September 1935, in *Documents on Canadian Foreign Policy*, ed. Riddell, 535.
34 King diary, 11 October 1935.
35 CAB 24/ 256, CP 167(35), 20 August 1935, UKNA.
36 Foreign Office to British High Commissioner, Ottawa, 5 September 1935, DO 114/67, 6109, A 270, UKNA.
37 Cannadine, *George V*, 93.
38 Amery, *My Political Life*, 2: 175.
39 Chamberlain to Cabinet, 2 July 1935, in Macleod, *Neville Chamberlain*, 185.
40 Riddell diary, 26 July 1935, York University Archives.
41 Hoare speech to the League of Nations, 9 September 1935, in Riddell, *World Security by Conference*, 101.
42 Laval speech to the League of Nations, ibid.
43 Ferguson to the League Committee of Eighteen, 11 October 1935, in Pearson, *Mike*, 1: 96.
44 Note of a meeting at Geneva on 26 September 1935 of British Commonwealth Representatives, DO 114/ 68, 6109 A 403 S, UKNA.
45 Chamberlain to his sister, 19 October 1935, *Diary Letters*, 4: 157.
46 Amery, *The Empire at Bay*, 2 October 1935, 2: 237.
47 Eden to Hoare, 7 October 1935, *Documents on British Foreign Policy*, Second Series, vol. 15, no. 40.
48 Gilbert, *Winston Churchill: The Wilderness Years*, 139.
49 King diary, 6 October 1935.
50 Ibid.
51 Ibid.
52 Ibid.
53 British High Commissioner, Ottawa, to London, 19 October 1935, DO 114/67, 6109 A 3/2, UKNA.

54 Secretary of State for External Affairs to Advisory Officer, Geneva, 15 October 1935, *DCER*, 5: 393.

55 Advisory Officer, Geneva, to Undersecretary of State for External Affairs, ibid.

56 King diary, 17 October 1935.

CHAPTER NINE

1 Buckner, *Canada and the End of Empire*, 100; Bothwell, *Your Country, My Country*, *passim*.

2 Bothwell and English, "Dirty Work," 285n83.

3 Rowell to Skelton, 12 October, 1935, in Prang, *N.W. Rowell*, 481.

4 Riddell to Rowell, 22 October 1935, York University Archives.

5 Middlemas and Barnes, *Baldwin*, 877; James, *Memoirs of a Conservative*, 409.

6 Riddell, *World Security by Conference*, 131.

7 Chamberlain to his sister, 22 September 1935, *Diary Letters*, 4: 153.

8 King diary, 19 October 1935.

9 Ibid., 25 October 1935.

10 Ibid., 26 October 1935.

11 King press statement 29 October 1935, *DCER*, 5: 403; British High Commissioner, Ottawa, to London, 30 October 1935, DO 114/ 67, UKNA.

12 King diary, 29 October 1935.

13 Enclosure to Hoare and Eden Memorandum on Embargo of Oil Supplies for Italy, 27 November 1935, *Documents on British Foreign Policy 1919–1939*, Second Series, vol. 15, doc. 270.

14 Schmidt, *Hitler's Interpreter*, 60.

15 King to Riddell, 4 November 1935, *DCER*, 5: 406.

16 Riddell to King, 5 November 1935, ibid., 407.

17 Chamberlain diary, 29 November 1935, in Macleod, *Neville Chamberlain*, 187–8.

18 *Montreal Gazette*, 2 March 1936.

19 Mackenzie King, Canada, Parliament, House of Commons Debates, 2 March 1936.

20 Petrucci to Rome, 6 November 1935, *Documents on Canadian Foreign Policy*, ed. Riddell, 522.

21 Italian *aide-mémoire*, Ottawa, 11 November 1935, *Documents on Canadian Foreign Policy*, ed. Riddell, 552n3.

22 Riddell, *World Security by Conference*, 129.

23 Skelton to Beaudry, 26 November 1935, DCER, 5: 410.

24 Ibid.

25 Beaudry to Skelton, 28 November 1935, DCER, 5: 411.

26 Skelton to Beaudry, ibid., 413.

27 Ibid.

28 Undersecretary of State for External Affairs to Secretary of State for External Affairs, ibid., 414.

29 Reply to the Italian *aide-mémoire*, 27 November 1935, *Documents on Canadian Foreign Policy*, ed. Riddell, 552.

30 Chamberlain diary, 29 November 1935, in Macleod, *Neville Chamberlain*, 188.

31 Vansittart minute, *Documents on British Foreign Policy*, Second Series, vol. 15, doc. 294, p. 371.

32 Ibid.

33 Ibid.

34 Beaudry to Lapointe, 29 November 1935, DCER, 5: 414.

35 Lapointe to Riddell, 1 December 1935, DCER, 5:415.

36 King to Riddell, 6 December 1935, DCER, 5: 417.

37 *Documents on British Foreign Policy*, Second Series, vol. 15, 294, p. 370.

38 British High Commissioner, Ottawa, to London, I December 1935, DO 114/67, 6109/A/3/22, UKNA.

39 Lapointe to Riddell, 1 December 1935, DCER, 5: 415.

40 Beaudry to Riddell, ibid.

41 Lapointe to Skelton, 29 November 1935, ibid, 5: 413.

42 King diary, 29 November 1935.

43 Ibid., 6 February 1936.

44 Power, *A Party Politician*, 121.

45 Quebec *Chronicle Telegraph*, 9 September 1935.

46 Binchy, *Church and State*, 643; Baer, *The Coming of the Italo-Ethiopian War*, 258.

47 Baer, *The Coming of the Italo-Ethiopian War*, 139.

48 Montgomery to Hoare, October 9, 1935, *British Documents*, Second Series, vol. 15, 52, p. 62.

Notes to pages 114–22   273

49 Kent, *Between Rome and London*, 262.

50 Kertzer, *The Pope and Mussolini*, 460.

51 King to Cousandier, 13 April 1935, Beaverbrook Papers, Parliamentary Archives, London, BBK/A/243.

52 Cousandier to King, 15 December, 1935, ibid.

53 British High Commissioner, Ottawa, to London, 13 December l935, DO 114/67, UKNA.

54 Eayrs, *In Defence of Canada*, 2: 25

55 Drummond to Hoare, 3 December 1935, *Documents on British Foreign Policy*, Second Series, vol. 15, doc. 299, p. 375.

56 Eden, *Facing the Dictators*, 287.

57 Riddell to Skelton, 7 December 1935, DCER, 5: 423.

58 Avenol to Riddell, 7 December 1935, Riddell diary, York University Archives.

59 Baer, *Test Case*, 139.

60 Rowell to Riddell, 3 December 1935, in Prang, *N.W. Rowell*, 482.

61 Betcherman, *Ernest Lapointe*, 207.

62 King diary, 24 February 1938.

63 Ibid., 6 December 1935.

64 Note of a Meeting at the Foreign Office, 5 December 1935, DO 114/66, UKNA.

65 Massey to MacDonald, 12 December 1935, ibid.

66 Note of a Meeting at the Foreign Office, 29 February 1936, *Documents on British Foreign Policy*, Second Series, vol. 15, doc. 710.

67 Schmidt, *Hitler's Interpreter*, 60.

68 Thompson, *The Anti-Appeasers*, 38.

69 Secretary of State for External Affairs, to Acting Advisory Officer, Geneva, 11 December 1935, DCER, 5: 425.

70 King diary, 19 December 1935.

71 Barnett, *The Collapse of British Power*, 375.

72 Nicolson diary, 10 December 1935, Nicolson, *Diaries and Letters*, 1: 230.

73 Chamberlain to his sister, 15 December 1935, Chamberlain, *Diary Letters*, 4: 166.

74 Note of a Meeting of High Commissioners, 20 December 1935, DO 114/66, 6109, A/22/3, UKNA.

75 Riddell, *World Security by Conference*, 140.

274 Notes to pages 123–36

CHAPTER TEN

1 Speer, *Inside the Third Reich*, 72.
2 King diary, 5 January 1936.
3 Canada, Parliament, House of Commons Debates, 13 March 1936.
4 Great Britain, House of Commons, 26 March 1936.
5 Massey diary, 11 May 1936, in Massey, *What's Past Is Prologue*, 239.
6 King diary, 23 March 1936.
7 Riddell, *World Security by Conference*, 145.
8 Churchill, *The Gathering Storm*, 177.
9 Cadogan minute, 1 March 1939, *The Diaries of Sir Alexander Cadogan*, 153.
10 *New York Herald*, 22 May 1936.
11 Maisky diary, 29 January 1936, *The Maisky Diaries*, 64.
12 Cannadine, *George V*, 98.
13 Zeigler, *King Edward VIII*, 269.
14 King to Cousandier, 16 April 1935, Beaverbrook Papers, Parliamentary Archives, London.
15 Canada, Parliament, House of Commons Debates, 2 March 1936.
16 Ibid., 10 February 1936.
17 King press statement, Ottawa, 29 October 1935.
18 Canada, Parliament, House of Commons Debates, 11 February 1936.
19 Ibid.
20 *Vancouver Daily Province, Vancouver Sun*, 16 March 1936.
21 Borden, 5 May 1936, *Letters to Limbo*, 269.
22 Canada, Parliament, House of Commons Debates, 28 May 1936.
23 Ibid., 18 June 1936.
24 Canada, Parliament, House of Commons Debates, 7 June 1936.
25 *Winnipeg Free Press*, 18 June 1936.
26 Bennett, Canada, Parliament, House of Commons Debates, 18 June 1936.
27 Massey to the League of Nations Assembly, 1 July 1936, in *Documents on Canadian Foreign Policy*, ed. Riddell, 587.
28 *Toronto Star*, 25 August 1936.
29 English and McLaughlin, *Kitchener*, 165.
30 *Winnipeg Free Press*, 7 August 1936.

31 Wilgress, *Memoirs*, 105.

32 King diary, 26 May 1936; Canada, Parliament, House of Commons Debates, 23 June 1936.

33 Owen, *Tempestuous Journey*, 736; Gilbert, *The Roots of Appeasement*, appendix 2.

34 Letter from Lloyd George to Conwell-Evans 27 December 1937, in Owen, *Tempestuous Journey*, 737; Williamson and Baldwin, *Baldwin Papers*, 125.

35 Lentin, *Lloyd George*, 94; Gilbert, *The Roots of Appeasement*, appendix 2.

36 Churchill, *The Gathering Storm*, 250.

37 Rowell to King, 9 July 1936, in Prang, *N.W. Rowell*, 484.

38 Middlemas and Barnes, *Baldwin*, 957.

39 Record by Secretary of State for Dominion Affairs of interview with Mackenzie King in Geneva, 20 September 1936, *Documents on British Foreign Policy 1919–1939*, Second Series, vol. 17, 212; Hillmer, "The Pursuit of Peace," 149.

40 King diary, 26 September 1936.

41 Ibid., 27 September 1936.

42 Pearson, *Mike*, 70–1.

43 King diary, 29 September 1936.

44 Ibid., 30 September 1936.

45 Ibid., 25 September 1936.

46 Eden, *Facing the Dictators*, 133.

47 King to Massey, 8 June 1936, DCER, 5: 960.

48 Brennan, *Reporting the Nation's Business*, 72.

49 King diary, 14 March 1938.

50 Martin statement, 2 May 1970, quoted in Bothwell and English, "Dirty Work at the Crossroads," 284n81.

51 Diefenbaker, *One Canada*, 1: 232.

52 Colvin, *Vansittart in Office*, 19.

53 James, *Memoirs of a Conservative*, 405.

54 Middlemas and Barnes, *Baldwin*, 923.

55 King diary, 27 October 1936.

56 Ibid., 23 October 1936.

57 Baldwin, 24 July 1936, quoted in Gilbert, *Churchill*, 5: 777.

58 Cowling, *The Impact of Hitler*, 147.
59 Chamberlain to his sister, 13 December 1936, Chamberlain, *Diary Letters*, 4: 228.
60 Nadeau, *The Canadian Führer*, 88.
61 "S," "Embryo Fascism in Quebec," *Foreign Affairs*, April 1938.
62 *Life*, 18 July 1938, 9.
63 Bouchard, *Memoires*, 95 and 110.
64 Maisky, *The Maisky Diaries*, 35n6.
65 Power, *Party Politician*, 121.
66 Canada, Parliament, House of Commons Debates, 15 February 1937.
67 Neatby, *Mackenzie King*, 193.
68 King diary, 10 February 1937.
69 Ibid., 19 February 1937.
70 Canada, Parliament, House of Commons Debates, 15 February 1937.
71 Ibid.
72 King diary, 6 March 1938.
73 British Ambassador, Washington, to London, 8 March 1937, *Documents of British Foreign Policy*, vol. 18.

CHAPTER ELEVEN

1 Copies of these telegrams are in RG25–D1, vol. 817, LAC.
2 Elliott, *Scarlet to Green*, 63.
3 MacDonald to King, 22 May 1936, DO 114/68, 6109/A/3/54 UKNA.
4 Massey diary, 17 June 1937, in Massey, *What's Past Is Prologue*, 242.
5 Hillmer, "The Pursuit of Peace," 156.
6 Garner, *The Commonwealth Office*, 87.
7 Middlemas, *Diplomacy of Illusion*, 10 and 17.
8 Hall, *Commonwealth*, 509.
9 Keenleyside, introduction to *The Growth of Canadian Policies in External Affairs*,12.
10 Ibid.
11 King diary, 7 June 1937.
12 Eden to the 1937 Imperial Conference, 19 May 1937, *Documents on British Foreign Policy*, Second Series, vol. 18.
13 King to the 1937 Imperial Conference, DCER, 6: 162.
14 King to the 1937 Imperial Conference, 21 May, DCER, 6: 915.

Notes to pages 159-67 277

15 Ibid., 914.
16 Chamberlain to the Principal Delegates at the Imperial Conference, 22 May 1937, in Tamchina, "In Search of Common Causes," 83.
17 King to MacDonald, 18 August 1938, DCER, 6: 935.
18 Ibid., 92.
19 Mackenzie to Imperial Conference, 24 May 1937, DCER, 6, 202.
20 Ibid., 201.
21 Dafoe, *Great Britain and the Dominions*, 51.
22 Tamchina, "In Search of Common Causes," 82.
23 King to the Imperial Conference, 21 May 1937, DCER, 6: 164.
24 Hillmer, "The Pursuit of Peace," 163.
25 Alice Massey to her sister, October 1938, in Massey, *What's Past Is Prologue*, 266.
26 Annan, *Our Age*, 266.
27 Swinton, *Sixty Years of Power*, 110.
28 Chamberlain to his sister, 24 September 1922, Chamberlain, *Diary Letters*, 2:125.
29 Buchan Papers, Queen's University.
30 King diary, 10 May 1937.
31 Chamberlain to his sister, 13 March 1938, Chamberlain, *Diary Letters*, 4: 304.
32 Phipps diary, 21 October 1936, in *Our Man in Berlin*, 182.
33 King diary, 26 May 1937.
34 Jones, *A Life in Reuters*, 394.
35 Ribbentrop to Hitler, 18 May 1937, *Documents on German Foreign Policy*, Series C, 370, 757.)
36 After King was defeated in the election of 1911, he retained a residence in Ottawa although working for the Rockefeller Foundation in the United States; Ribbentrop arrived in Ottawa in late 1913.
37 King diary, 26 May 1937.
38 Ibid., 10 May 1937.
39 Ibid., 14 September 1938.
40 Ibid., 2 and 4 June 1937.
41 Ibid., 11 June 1937.
42 King to Ribbentrop, 14 June 1937, MG26–J3, LAC.
43 King diary, 15 June 1937.
44 Eden to King, 18 June 1937, MG26–J1, LAC.

278   Notes to pages 168-73

45 Chamberlain to his sister, 20 June 1937, Chamberlain, *Diary Letters*, 4: 255.
46 MacDonald to the cabinet, 16 June 1937, Cab 23/ 88, 610, 92, UKNA; Hillmer, "The Anglo-Canadian Neurosis," in *Britain and Canada*, appendix D.
47 McNaught, "Canadian Foreign Policy," 54.
48 Markham to King, 15 June 1937, MG26–J1, LAC.
49 Dickson, *A Thoroughly Canadian General*, 107.
50 Ibid., 104.
51 Ibid.
52 King diary, 23 June 1937.

CHAPTER TWELVE

1 Gilbert, "Two British Ambassadors," 2: 551.
2 Henderson, *Failure of a Mission*, 7.
3 Barnett, *The Collapse of British Power*, 460.
4 Gilbert, *Portrait of a Diplomat*, 383.
5 *British Documents*, 4 and 431.
6 Phipps, *Our Man in Berlin*, 14.
7 Vansittart entry in *Dictionary of National Biography*, vol. 20; Andrew, *Defence of the Realm*, 195,
8 Henderson, *Failure of a Mission*, 13.
9 Ibid., 7.
10 Ibid., 12.
11 Eden, *Facing the Dictators*, 511.
12 Nicolson, *Diaries and Letters*, 1: 334.
13 King diary, 27 June 1937.
14 Ibid.
15 King diary, 29 June 1937.
16 Neatby, *Mackenzie King*, 223.
17 King diary, 29 June 1937.
18 Ibid.
19 King Memorandum to Chamberlain and Eden, 6 July 1937, FO 954/4A, UKNA.
20 Ibid.
21 King diary, 21 July 1939.

Notes to pages 179-87 279

22 King Memorandum to Chamberlain and Eden, 6 July 1937, FO 954 /4A, UKNA.
23 Ibid.
24 King diary, 30 June 1937.
25 Ibid.
26 Christie Papers, I/5, Churchill College, Cambridge.
27 Dilks, *Britain and Canada*, 17.
28 King to Hitler, 1 July 1937, MG26-J 1, LAC.
29 King diary, 1 July 1937.
30 *Documents on Canadian Foreign Policy*, ed. Riddell, 158.
31 Henderson to King, 4 July 1937, MG26-J1, LAC.
32 Greenwood to King, 2 July 1937, ibid.
33 *Documents on British Foreign Policy*, FO 954/4A, UKNA.
34 Chamberlain to King and Eden to King, 28 July 1937, MG26-J1, LAC.
35 King CBC broadcast, 19 July 1937.
36 After rereading his interviews with von Ribbentrop and Hitler, King recorded in his diary, "it is clear to me beyond all doubt that in this way I am being made fully aware of the forces that are working behind the scenes to have good will prevail over ill will in international relations. The interview seemed to be more significant than ever in the light of the developments of the last few days" (22 February 1938).
37 King to Göring, 28 July 1937, MG26-J1, LAC.
38 King to Ribbentrop, 18 August 1937, ibid.
39 Huttchison, *The Far Side of the Street*, 110; *The Incredible Canadian*, 226.
40 Amery, *The Empire at Bay*, 5 November 1937, 450
41 United States chargé d'affaires, Ottawa, to Washington, 23 July 1938, quoted in Abella and Toper, *None Is Too Many*, 36.
42 Ibid., 14 September 1937.
43 King diary, 1 September 1937.
44 Cannadine, *George V*, 97.

CHAPTER THIRTEEN

1 Canada, Parliament, House of Commons Debates, 14 February 1938.
2 Ibid., 27 March 1938.
3 Ibid., 17 May 1938.

280   Notes to pages 187-96

4 Ibid., 24 June 1938.

5 Chamberlain to his sister, 12 March 1938, Chamberlain, *Diary Letters*, 4: 305.

6 Churchill, *The Gathering Storm*, 255.

7 Great Britain, Parliament, House of Commons Debates, 22 February 1938.

8 Canada, Parliament, House of Commons Debates, 24 May 1938.

9 Pearson, "Reflections," 39.

10 Thompson and Seager, *Canada 1922–1939*, 317.

11 *Le Devoir*, 14 July 1938.

12 Canada, Parliament, House of Commons Debates, 15 February 1938.

13 King diary, 6 February 1938.

14 Ibid., 13 February 1938.

15 Canada, Parliament, House of Commons Debates, 14 February 1938.

16 Ibid., 2 March 1938.

17 King diary, 20 February 1938.

18 Ibid.

19 Cooper diary, 3 April 1938, *Duff Cooper Diaries*, 245.

20 Annan, *Our Age*, 267.

21 King diary, 27 March 1938.

22 Ibid.

23 Chamberlain to his sister, 13 March 1938, Chamberlain, *Diary Letters*, 4: 305.

24 Ibid., 20 March 1938, 4: 307.

25 King diary, 14 March 1938.

26 Abella and Troper, *None Is Too Many*, 16.

27 King diary, 29 March 1938.

28 Gilbert, *The Appeasers*, 33.

29 Director of Immigration, Department of Mines and Resources, Ottawa, to Commissioner of European Immigration, London, 6 June 1938, DCER, 6: 796.

30 King diary, 11 June 1938.

31 *La Ligue d'action nationale* to Sir George Perley, 5 June 1933, in Stacey, *Historical Documents*, 195

32 Abella and Troper, *None Is Too Many*, 13.

33 Ibid., 7.

34 King diary, 11 June 1938.

35 Ibid., 20 February 1938.

36 Dexter to Dafoe, 17 December 1935, quoted in Eayrs, "A Low, Dishonest Decade," 68.

37 Chamberlain, *Diary Letters*, 19 March 1939, 393n51.

38 King diary, 29 March 1938.

39 Ibid., 11 March 1938.

40 Pearson, *Words and Occasions*, 29.

41 King diary, 11 March 1938.

42 Tweedsmuir to Eden, 23 March 1936, in Lownie, *John Buchan*, 253.

43 Tweedsmuir to his sister, 14 March 1938, in Smith, *John Buchan*, 443.

44 King diary, 27 March 1938.

45 King to MacDonald, 2 April 1938, *Documents on Canadian Foreign Policy*, ed. Riddell, 159.

46 King diary, 23 May 1938.

47 Canada, Parliament, House of Commons Debates, 14 May 1938.

48 Pickersgill, "Mackenzie King's Political Attitudes and Public Policies," 25.

49 Canada, Parliament, House of Commons Debates, 24 May 1938.

50 Chamberlain to his sister, 9 April 1938, Chamberlain, *Diary Letters*, 4: 312.

51 King diary, 19 April 1938.

52 Ibid., 10 April 1938.

53 Ibid., 21 May 1938.

54 King to Tweedsmuir, 23 July 1938, MG25–J1, LAC.

55 King diary, 22 May 1938.

56 Ibid.

57 Tweedsmuir to King, 15 July 1938, MG25–J1, LAC.

58 Templewood, *Nine Troubled Years*, 323.

59 Chamberlain to his sister, 28 May 1938, Chamberlain, *Diary Letters*, 4: 325.

60 Macleod, *Neville Chamberlain*, 208.

61 Roosevelt speech at Queen's University, 8 August 1938.

62 King diary 31 August 1938.

63 Ibid., 1 September 1938.

64 Ibid., 6 September 1938.

65 Ibid., 8 September 1938.

66 Rock, *British Appeasement in the 1930s*, 8.

282   Notes to pages 207-15

67 King diary, 12 September 1938.

68 Ibid.

69 Ibid.

70 Massey diary, 12 September 1938, in Massey, *What's Past Is Prologue*, 257.

71 Roy to King, 9 September 1938, DCER, 6: 1089.

72 King diary, 14 September 1938.

73 King to Dunning, MG26–J1 LAC.

74 Ibid., 13 September 1938.

75 Cooper diary, 13 September 1938, in Cooper, *Old Men Forget*, 226.

76 Cooper, *Old Men Forget*, 226.

77 Chamberlain to Hitler, 13 September 1938, Chamberlain, *Diary Letters*, 4: 345.

78 Secretary of State for External Affairs to Secretary of State for Dominion Affairs, 14 September 1938, MG26–J1, LAC.

79 King diary, 14–16 September 1938.

80 King to Henderson, 16 September 1938, ibid.

81 King to Chamberlain, ibid.

82 Chamberlain to his sister, 12 September 1938, Chamberlain, *Diary Letters*, 4: 129.

83 Parkinson, *Peace for Our Time*, 29.

84 Amery, *The Empire at Bay*, editors' note 2, 470.

85 Cooper diary, 27 September 1938, in Cooper, *Old Men Forget*, 239.

86 King diary, 15 September 1938.

87 Ibid., 14 September 1938.

88 King to Tweedsmuir, 20 September 1938, MG26–J1, LAC.

89 Churchill, *The Gathering Storm*, 303.

90 King diary, 17 September 1938.

91 Nicolson diary, 30 August 1939, Nicolson, *Diaries and Letters*, 14–15.

92 Chamberlain to his sister, 19 September 1938, Chamberlain, *Diary Letters*, 4: 348.

93 *Daily Telegraph*, 24 September 1938.

94 *Manchester Guardian*, 25 February 1939.

95 King diary, 23 September 1938.

96 King to Tweedsmuir, 20 September 1938, Buchan Papers, Queen's University Archives.

97 King diary, 23 September 1938.

98 Ibid.

99 Lapointe to King, 24 September 1938, Lapointe Papers, LAC; Neatby, *Mackenzie King*, 3: 291.

100 King diary, 23 September 1938.

101 King press statement, 27 September 1938, DCER, 6: 1097.

102 Massey to King, 26 September 1938, DCER, 6: 1096.

103 Chamberlain BBC broadcast, 27 September 1938.

104 King diary, 24 September 1938.

105 Ibid., 28 September 1938.

106 Taylor, *The Origins of the Second World War*, 228.

107 Taylor, *English History, 1914–1945*, 441.

108 Cooper, *The Light of Common Day*, 246.

109 Cooper, *Old Men Forget*, 299.

110 King diary, 29 September 1938.

111 British High Commissioner, Ottawa, to London, 7 October 1938.

112 King diary, 30 September 1938.

113 Churchill, *The Gathering Storm*, 339.

114 King to Chamberlain, 29 September 1938, DCER, 6: 1099.

115 Churchill, Great Britain, House of Commons, 5 October 1938.

116 Great Britain, Parliament, House of Commons Debates, 4 October 1938.

117 King diary, 30 September 1938.

118 Ibid.

119 *Winnipeg Free Press*, 30 September 1938.

120 Kershaw, *Hitler*, 2: 157.

121 Amery, *The Empire at Bay*, 19 October 1938, 531.

122 Hastings, *The Secret War*, 15

123 Hinsley, *British Intelligence*, 1: 58.

124 Elliot, *Scarlet to Green*, 64.

125 MacDonald to British Cabinet, 1938.

126 Dawson to Chamberlain, quoted in Macleod, *Neville Chamberlain*, 269.

127 Self, preface, Chamberlain, *Diary Letters*, 4: 15–16.

128 Bickersteff to his parents, 27 January 1939, Bickersteff Papers, University of Toronto Archives.

129 *Times*, 4 October 1938.

130 Charmley, *Chamberlain and the Lost Peace*, 144.

284 Notes to pages 224-34

131 Pearson to Skelton, October 1938, Pearson, *Mike*, 1: 130.
132 King diary, 24 October 1938.
133 Ibid.
134 Stacey, *Mackenzie King and the Atlantic Triangle*, 65.
135 Thompson, *The Anti-Appeasers*, 27.
136 McDonough, *Neville Chamberlain*, 4.
137 King diary, 31 August 1938.
138 Ibid., 28 September 1938.
139 Ibid., 27 January 1939.
140 King statement in Washington, 17 November 1938, *Documents on Canadian Foreign Policy*, ed. Riddell, 638.
141 King to Markham, 3 January 1939, MG26–J1, LAC.
142 Chamberlain to his sister, 13 November 1938, Chamberlain, *Diary Letters*, 4: 363.
143 King diary, 13 November 1938.
144 Ibid., 21 November 1938 (Rinfret was secretary of state).
145 Ibid.
146 Massey to King, 15 November 1938, in Massey, *What's Past Is Prologue*, 271.
147 King to Massey, 3 December, ibid.
148 Tree, *When the Moon Was High*, 83.
149 Wrong to King, 2 December 1938, DCER, 6: 1104.

CHAPTER FOURTEEN

1 Feiling, *The Life of Neville Chamberlain*, 407.
2 RCMP *Security Bulletins*, 391.
3 Betcherman, *Ernest Lapointe*, 256.
4 *L'Action catholique*, 17 February 1938.
5 *Maclean's Magazine*, 15 April 1938.
6 Wallace, *The American Axis*, 218.
7 Mussolini, in Kertzer, *The Pope and Mussolini*, 111.
8 Adamthwaites, *The Making of the Second World War*, 241.
9 Jones 29 September 1938, Jones, *A Diary with Letters*, 411.
10 MacDonald, "King: The View from London," 48.
11 Lindbergh to US Military Attaché in Berlin, 9 May 1938, quoted in Baldwin, *Henry Ford and the Jews*, 213.

Notes to pages 234-44   285

12 Eleanor Roosevelt, in Wallace, *The American Axis*, 193.
13 Neatby, *Mackenzie King*, 3: 296.
14 Pearson diary, 13 October 1938, quoted in English, *Shadow of Heaven*, 214.
15 King diary, 2 December 1938.
16 Ibid.
17 Ibid., 27 January 1939.
18 Ibid.
19 Ibid.
20 King to Hitler, 1 February 1939, DCER, 6: 1122.
21 Halifax to Chamberlain, in McDonough, *Neville Chamberlain*, 76.
22 Macleod, *Neville Chamberlain*, 274.
23 Churchill, *The Gathering Storm*, 362.
24 Ritchie, *The Siren Years*, 31.
25 Churchill, *The Gathering Storm*, 362.
26 Massey to King, 31 March 1939, quoted in Massey, *What's Past Is Prologue*, 276.
27 British High Commissioner, Ottawa, to London, 24 March 1939.
28 King diary, 3 April 1939.
29 RCMP *Security Bulletins*, 390.
30 Canada, Parliament, House of Commons Debates, 30 March 1939.
31 Ibid., 31 March 1939.
32 King diary, 31 March 1939.
33 Stacey, *Arms, Men and Governments*, 4.
34 Eayrs, *In Defence of Canada*, 1: 81.
35 Ibid., 1: 131.
36 Stacey, *Arms, Men and Governments*, 6.
37 King diary, 13 November 1938.
38 Stevenson to Dawson, 28 April 1939, *Times* Archives, London.
39 Dafoe to Ferguson, 19 March 1939, in Brennan, *Reporting the Nation's Business*.
40 King diary, 25 April 1939.
41 Ibid., 20 May 1939.
42 King to Tweedsmuir, 26 August 1939, quoted in Stacey, *Arms, Men and Governments*, 7.
43 Pearson to Skelton, 9 June 1939, in English, *Shadow of Heaven*, 370.
44 Levine, *King*, 291.

286 Notes to pages 245-56

45 Markham to Tweedsmuir, 17 January 1939, quoted in Lownie, *John Buchan*, 272.
46 Ibid., 28 April 1939.
47 Hillmer, *O.D. Skelton*, 41.
48 Chamberlain to his sister, 19 March 1939, Chamberlain, *Diary Letters*, 4: 393n51.
49 MacDonald, "King: The View from London," 41.
50 King diary, 10 June 1939.
51 King diary, 21, 22, and 23 June 1939.
52 Wegenast, "Germany in Nazi Times," in Bendazzi, *Animation: A World History*, 1: 148.
53 Ritchie diary, 10 July 1939, Ritchie, *The Siren Years*, 36.
54 King diary, 21 July 1939.
55 Ibid.
56 Ibid.
57 Taylor, *Englishmen and Others*, 157.
58 King diary, 24 August 1939.
59 Mackenzie King, in Reardon, *Winston Church and Mackenzie King*, 92.
60 Chamberlain to his sister, 27 August 1939, Chamberlain, *Diary Letters*, 4: 442.
61 King diary, 26 August 1939.
62 Ibid., 28 August 1939.
63 Ibid., 26 August 1939.
64 Ibid., 27 August 1939.
65 King speech in Toronto, August 1939, quoted in Soward, *Canada in World Affairs*, 148.
66 King diary, 30 August 1939.
67 Canada, Parliament, House of Commons Debates, 30 May 1939.
68 King diary, 2 September 1939.

CHAPTER FIFTEEN

1 Hillmer, *Britain and Canada*, 6.
2 Pickersgill, "Mackenzie King's Political Attitudes and Public Policies," 15.
3 Pearson, "Reflections," 40.

4 Markham to Tweedsmuir, 20 August 1939, Buchan Papers, Queen's University Archives.
5 Veatch, *Canada and the League of Nations*, 33.
6 McNaught, "Canadian Foreign Policy," 54.
7 Munro, Preface, DCER, 6: xiii.
8 Pearson, "Reflections," 40.
9 Canada, Parliament, House of Commons, Debates, 8 September 1939.
10 LePan, "The Spare Deputy," 4.

Bibliography

MANUSCRIPT COLLECTIONS

Library and Archives Canada, Ottawa (LAC)
  Wilfrid Laurier Fonds
  William Lyon Mackenzie King Diaries
Queen's University, Kingston
  Buchan Papers
United Kingdom National Archives (UKNA)
University of Toronto Archives
  Massey Family Fonds
York University Archives
  Walter Alexander Riddell Fonds

SECONDARY SOURCES

Abella, Irving, and Harold Troper. *None Is Too Many: Canada and the Jews of Europe, 1933–1948*. Toronto: Lester and Orpen Dennys, 1982.

Adamthwaite, A. *The Making of the Second World War*. Abingdon: Unwin Hyman, 1977.

Amery, Leopold. *The Empire at Bay: The Leopold Amery Diaries, 1929–1945*. Edited by John Barnes and David Nicholson. London: Hutchison, 1988.

– *My Political Life: The Unforgiving Years, 1929–1940*. London: Hutchison, 1955.

Andrew, Christopher. *The Defence of the Realm: The Authorized History of MI5*. London: Allen Lane, 2009.

Annan, Noel. *Our Age: English Intellectuals between the World Wars: A Group Portrait*. New York: Random House, 1990.

Armstrong, Frederick H., and Ronald J. Stagg. "Mackenzie, William Lyon." In *Dictionary of Canadian Biography*, vol. 9. Toronto and Quebec: University of Toronto Press/Université Laval, 2003.

Aster, Sidney. *1939: The Making of the Second World War*. New York: Simon and Schuster, 1973.

Avery, D., and P. Neary. "Laurier, Borden and a White British Columbia." *Journal of Canadian Studies* 12, no. 4 (1977): 24–34.

Baer, George W. *The Coming of the Italo-Ethiopian War*. Cambridge: Harvard University Press, 1967.

– *Test Case: Italy, Ethiopia, and the League of Nations*. California: Hoover Institution Press, 1976.

Baldwin, Robert. *Baldwin Papers: A Conservative Statesman, 1908–1947*. Edited by Philip Williamson and Edward Baldwin. Cambridge: Cambridge University Press, 2004.

Baldwin, Neil. *Henry Ford and the Jews: The Mass Production of Hate*. New York: Public Affairs, 2001.

Bartrop, Paul R. *The Evian Conference of 1938 and the Jewish Refugee Crisis*. London: Palgrave Macmillan, 2018.

Barnett, Correlli. *The Collapse of British Power*. London: Eyre Methuen, 1972.

Beale, Howard. *Theodore Roosevelt and the Rise of America to World Power*. Baltimore: Johns Hopkins Press, 1966.

Beaverbrook, Lord. *The Decline and Fall of Lloyd George*. London: Collins, 1963.

Bendazzi, G. *Animation: A World History*. 3 vols. London: Routledge, 2015.

Berton, Pierre. *The Great Depression 1929–1939*. Toronto: Doubleday Canada, [1990] 2001.

Betcherman, Lita Rose. *Ernest Lapointe, Mackenzie King's Great Quebec Lieutenant*. Toronto: University of Toronto Press, 2002.

– *The Swastika and the Maple Leaf: Fascist Movements in Canada in the Thirties*. Toronto: Fitzhenry and Whiteside, 1975.

Binchy, Daniel A. *Church and State in Fascist Italy*. Oxford: Oxford University Press, 1970.

Bissell, Claude. *The Imperial Canadian: Vincent Massey in Office*. Toronto: University of Toronto Press, 1986.

Bliss, Michael. *Right Honourable Men: The Descent of Politics from MacDonald to Chrétien*. Toronto: HarperCollins, 1994.

Borden, Robert Laird. *Letters to Limbo*. Edited by Henry Borden. Toronto: University of Toronto Press, 1971.

– *The Question of Oriental Immigration, Speeches (in Part) Delivered by R.L. Borden in 1907 and 1908*. n.p., n.d.

Bothwell, Robert. *Your Country, My Country: A Unified History of the United States and Canada*. Toronto: Oxford University Press, 2015.

Bothwell, Robert, and John English. "'Dirty Work at the Crossroads': New Perspectives on the Riddell Incident." *Historical Papers* 7, no. 1 (1972): 263–85.

Bothwell, Robert, and Norman Hillmer. *The In-Between Time: Canadian Foreign Policy in the 1930s*. Toronto: Copp Clark, 1975.

Bouchard, T.D. *Memoires de T.D. Bouchard*. Vol. 3. Montreal: Beauchemin, 1960.

Brault, Lucien, et al. *A Century of Reporting*. Toronto: Clarke, Irwin & Co., 1967.

Breitman, Richard, and Allen Lichtman. *FDR and the Jews*. Cambridge: Harvard University Press, 2013.

Brendon, Piers. *The Dark Valley: A Panorama of the 1930s*. New York: Knopf, 2000.

Brennan, Patrick. *Reporting the Nations's Business: Press-Government Relations during the Liberal Years, 1935–1957*. Toronto: University of Toronto Press, 1994.

Bruchési, Jean. "A French Canadian View of Canadian Foreign Policy." In *Canada: The Empire and the League*. Toronto: Canadian Institute on Economics and Politics, 1936.

Buckner, Phillip. *Canada and the End of Empire*. Vancouver: University of British Columbia Press, 2005.

Butler, J.R. *Lord Lothian*. London: Macmillan, 1960.

Cadogan, Alexander. *The Diaries of Sir Alexander Cadogan, 1938–1945*. Edited by David Dilks. London: Cassell, 1971.

Cannadine, David. *George V: The Unexpected King*. London: Penguin, 2014.

Campbell, John. *F.E. Smith: First Earl of Birkenhead*. London: Cape, 1983.

Carr, E.H. *International Relations between the Two World Wars, 1919–1939*. London: Macmillan, 1963.

– *The Twenty Years' Crisis, 1919–1939: An Introduction to the Study of International Relations*. London: Macmillan, 1939.

Carter, Gwendolen. *The British Commonwealth and International Security: The Role of the Dominions, 1919–1939*. Toronto: Ryerson, 1947.

– "Canada and Sanctions in the Italo-Ethiopian Conflict." *Report of the Annual Meeting of the Canadian Historical Association* 191 (1940): 74–84.

Chamberlain, Neville. *The Neville Chamberlain Diary Letters*, vol. 4, *The Downing Street Years, 1934–1940*. Edited by Robert Self. Aldershot: Ashgate, 2005.

Charmley, John. *Chamberlain and the Lost Peace*. London: Hodder and Stoughton, 1989.

– *Duff Cooper: The Authorised Biography*. London: Weidenfeld and Nicolson, 1986.

Checkland, Sidney. "Innocence and Anxiety: Canada between the Wars." *Bulletin of Canadian Studies* 5, no. 2 (October 1981): 25–37.

Chisholm, Anne, and Michael Davie. *Beaverbrook: A Life*. London: Hutchison, 1992.

Churchill, Winston. *The Gathering Storm*. London: Cassel, 1948.

Colvin, Ian. *Vansittart in Office*. London: Gollancz, 1965.

Cook, Ramsay. "J.W. Dafoe at the Imperial Conference, 1923." *Canadian Historical Review* 41, no. 1 (March 1960): 19–40.

Cook, Ramsay, and D.B. Macrae. "A Canadian Account of the 1926 Imperial Conference." *Journal of Commonwealth Political Studies* 3, no. 1 (1968): 50–63.

Cook, Tim. *Vimy: The Battle and the Legend*. Toronto: Allen Lane, 2017.

– *Warlords: Borden, Mackenzie King, and Canada's World Wars*. Toronto: Allen Lane, 2012.

Cooper, Diana. *The Light of Common Day*. London: Rupert Hart-Davis, 1959.

Cooper, Duff. *Duff Cooper Diaries*. Edited by John Julius Norwich. London: Weidenfeld and Nicolson, 2005.

– *Old Men Forget*. London: Rupert Hart-Davis, 1953.

Cowling, Maurice. *The Impact of Hitler*. London: Cambridge University Press, 1977.

Craig, Gordon, and Felix Gilbert, eds. *The Diplomats 1919–1939*. Princeton: Princeton University Press, 1953.

Crerar, H.D.G. "Colonel H.D.G. Crerar's Visit to Nazi Germany, 1937." *Canadian Military History* 5, no. 2 (Autumn 1996): 121–6.

Crowley, Terry. *Marriage of Minds: Isabel and Oscar Skelton Reinventing Canada*. Toronto: University of Toronto Press, 2003.

Curzon of Kedleston, Marchioness. *Reminiscences*. London: Hutchinson, 1955.

Dafoe, J.W. "The Imperial Conference of 1937." *University of Toronto Quarterly* 17, no. 1 (1937): 1–17.

– "The Problems of Canada." In *Great Britain and the Dominions*. Chicago: University of Chicago Press, 1928.

– *The Voice of Dafoe:A Selection of Editorials on Collective Security 1931–1944*. Edited by W.L. Morton. Toronto: Macmillan, 1945.

Davis, Richard. *Anglo-French Relations before the Second World War: Appeasement and Crisis*. Basingstoke: Palgrave, 2001.

Dawson, MacGregor. *William Lyon Mackenzie King: A Political Biography, 1874–1921*. Toronto: University of Toronto Press, 1958.

Department of External Affairs. *Documents on Canadian External Relations* (DCER), vols 3, 4, 5. Ottawa.

Diamond, Sander. *The Nazi Movement in the United States, 1924–1941*. Ithaca: Cornell University Press, 1974.

Dickson, Paul. *A Thoroughly Canadian General: A Biography of General H.D.G. Crerar*. Toronto: University of Toronto Press, 2007.

Diefenbaker, John G. *One Canada: Memoirs of the Right Honourable John G. Diefenbaker*. 3 vols. Toronto: MacMillan Company of Canada, 1975, 1976, 1977.

Dilks, David. *Britain and Canada in the Age of Mackenzie King*, Part 2, *Canada and the Wider World*. London: Canadian High Commission, 1978.

– *The Great Dominion: Winston Churchill in Canada 1900–1954*. Toronto: Thomas Allen, 2005.

Documents on British Foreign Policy, 1919–1939. Edited by E.L. Woodward and Rohan Butler. London: Her Majesty's Stationery Office, 1953.

Documents Relating to the Italo-Ehtopian Conflict. Ottawa: King's Printer.

Documents Relating to the Outbreak of War, September 1939. Ottawa: Secretary of State for External Affairs.

Dodd, Martha. *My Years in Germany*. London: Gollancz, 1941.

Dorril, Stephen. *Blackshirt: Sir Oswald Mosley and British Fascists*. London: Penguin, 2006.

Douglas, Roy. *The Advent of War, 1939–40*. London: Macmillan, 1980.

Drummond, Ian. *Imperial Economic Policy, 1917–1939*. London: Allen and Unwin, 1974.

Dugdale, Blanche. *Arthur James Balfour, First Earl of Balfour, K.G., O.M., F.R.S., etc.* Westport, CT: Greenwood Press, [1936] 1970.

Dummitt, Christopher. *Unbuttoned: A History of Mackenzie King's Secret Life*. Montreal & Kingston: McGill-Queen's University Press, 2017.

Duroselle, Jean-Baptiste. *France and the Nazi Threat: The Collapse of French Diplomacy, 1932–1939*. New York: Enigma, 2004.

Eastman, Mack. *Canada at Geneva: A Historical Survey and Its Lessons*. Toronto: Ryerson, 1946.

Eayrs, James. *In Defence of Canada*, vol. 2, *Appeasement and Rearmament*. Toronto: University of Toronto Press, 1965.

– "'A Low Dishonest Decade': Aspects of Canadian External Policy 1931–1939." In Hugh Keenleyside, ed., *The Growth of Canadian Policies in External Affairs*, 59–80. Durham: Duke University Press, 1960.

Eden, Anthony. *Facing the Dictators*. London: Cassell, 1962.

Edwards, Frederick. "Fascism in Canada." *Maclean's Magazine*, 15 April and 1 May 1938.

Edwards, P.G. "The Foreign Office and Fascism 1924–1929." *Journal of Contemporary History* 5, no. 2 (1970): 153–61.

Eksteins, Modris. *The Rites of Spring: The Great War and the Birth of the Modern Age*. Toronto: Vintage Canada, 2012.

Elliot, S.R. *Scarlet to Green: A History of Intelligence in the Canadian Army 1903–1963*. Canadian Intelligence and Security Association, 1981.

Empire Club of Canada Speeches, 1907–1908.

English, John. *Shadow of Heaven: The Life of Lester Pearson*, vol. 1, 1897–1948. Toronto: Lester and Orpen Dennys, 1989.

English, John, and Kenneth McLaughlin. *Kitchener: An Illustrated History*. Waterloo: Wilfrid Laurier University Press, 1983.

English, John, Kenneth McLaughlin, and Whitney Lackenbauer, eds. *Mackenzie King: Citizenship and Community*. Toronto: Robin Brass, 2002.

English, John, and J.O. Stubbs, eds. *Mackenzie King: Widening the Debate*. Toronto: Macmillan, 1978.

Esberey, Joy. *Knight of the Holy Spirit: A Study of William Lyon Mackenzie King*. Toronto: University of Toronto Press, 1980.

Evans, Richard. *The Coming of the Third Reich*. London: Penguin, 2003.

Feiling, Keith. *The Life of Neville Chamberlain*. London: Macmillan, 1970.

Ferns, H.S. "Mackenzie King: Foreign Policy." *Ottawa Citizen*, 4 August 1944.

Fine, Jonathan. "Anti-Semitism in Manitoba in the 1930s and 40s." *Manitoba History* 32 (autumn 1996): 26–33.

François-Poncet, André. *The Fateful Years: Memoirs of a French Ambassador in Berlin, 1931–1938*. New York: Fertig, 1972.

Fuchser, L.W. *Neville Chamberlain and Appeasement: A Study in the Politics of History*. New York: Norton, 1982.

Fussell, Paul. *The Great War and Modern Memory*. Oxford: Oxford University Press, 2000.

Gannon, F.R. *The British Press and Germany, 1936–1939*. Oxford: Clarendon Press, 1971.

Garner, Saville. *The Commonwealth Office, 1925–68*. London: Heinemann, 1978.

George, Margaret. *The Hollow Men: An Examination of British Foreign Policy between the Years 1933 and 1939*. London: Frewin, 1967.

Gilbert, Martin. *Britain and Germany between the Wars*. London: Longmans, 1964.

– *Portrait of a Diplomat: Sir Horace Rumbold, 1869–1941*. London: Heinemann, 1973.

– *The Roots of Appeasement*. London: Weidenfeld and Nicolson, 1966.

– "Two British Ambassadors: Perth and Henderson," in Craig and Gilbert, *The Diplomats*, 2: 537–54.

– *Winston Churchill: The Wilderness Years*. London: Macmillan, 1981.

– *Winston S. Churchill*, vol. 5, 1922–1939. London: Heinemann, 1976.

Gilbert, Martin, and Richard Gott. *The Appeasers*. London: Phoenix, 1963.

Gilmour, David. *Curzon, Imperial Statesman*. New York: Farrar, Straus, and Giroux, 1994.

Gilmour, Julie. *Trouble on Main Street: Mackenzie King, Reason, Race and the 1907 Vancouver Riots*. Toronto: Penguin, 2014.

Glazebrook, George. *A History of Canadian External Relations*. London: Oxford University Press, 1950.

Graham, Roger. *Arthur Meighen*. 3 vols. Toronto: Clarke, Irwin and Company Ltd, 1965.

Granatstein, J.L. "King and Country." *International Journal* 24, no. 2 (Spring 1969): 374–7.

– *A Man of Influence: Norman A. Robertson and Canadian Statecraft, 1919–1968*. Ottawa: Deneau Publishers, 1981.

Granatstein, J.L., and R. Bothwell, "'A Self-Evident National Duty':
Canadian Foreign Policy 1935–1939." *Journal of Imperial and Commonwealth History* 3, no. 2 (January 1975): 212–33.

Gray, Charlotte. *Mrs. King: The Life and Times of Isabel Mackenzie King.*
Toronto: Penguin Canada, 2008.

Griffiths, Richard. *Fellow Travellers of the Right: British Enthusiasts for
Nazi Germany, 1933–39.* London: Oxford University Press, 1983.

Hall, H. Duncan. *Commonwealth: A History of the British Commonwealth
of Nations.* London, New York: Van Nostrand Reinhold, 1971.

– "The Genesis of the Balfour Declaration of 1926." *Journal of Commonwealth Political Studies* 1, no. 3 (1962): 164–93.

Halton, David. *Dispatches from the Front: Matthew Halton, Canada's Voice
at War.* Toronto: McClelland & Stewart, 2015.

Hastings, Max. *The Secret War: Spies, Cyphers and Guerillas 1939–1945.*
New York: HarperCollins, 2015.

Heeney, Arnold. *The Things That Are Caesar's: Memoirs of a Canadian
Public Servant.* Toronto: University of Toronto Press, 1972.

Heere, Cornelis. "Japan and the British World, 1904–14." PhD thesis,
London School of Economics, 2016.

Henderson, George. *W.L. Mackenzie King: A Bibliography and Research
Guide.* Toronto: University of Toronto Press, 1998.

Henderson, Nevile. *Failure of a Mission.* London: Hodder and Stoughton,
1940.

– *Water Under the Bridges.* London: Hodder and Stoughton, 1945.

Henig, Ruth. *Canada and the League of Nations.* Edinburgh: Oliver and
Boyd, 1973.

Hilliker, John. *Canada's Department of External Affairs,* vol.1., *The Early
Years, 1909–1945.* Montreal & Kingston: McGill-Queen's University
Press, 1990.

Hillmer, Norman. "The Anglo-Canadian Neurosis: The Case of O.D.
Skelton." In Lyon, *Britain and Canada,* 61–84.

– *Britain and Canada in the Age of Mackenzie King,* Part 1, *"The Outstanding Imperialist": Mackenzie King and the British.* London: Canadian
High Commission, 1978.

– "The Foreign Policy That Never Was: 1926–1937." In S. Bernier and J.
MacFarlane, eds, *Canada 1900–1950: Un Pays Prend Sa Place/A Country*

Comes of Age, 141–53. Ottawa: Organization for the History of Canada, 2003.

– *O.D. Skelton: A Portrait of Canadian Ambition*. Toronto: University of Toronto Press, 2015.

– "The Pursuit of Peace: Mackenzie King and the 1937 Imperial Conference." In English and Stubbs, *Mackenzie King*, 149–72.

– ed. *O.D Skelton: The Work of the World, 1923–1941*. Montreal & Kingston: McGill-Queen's University Press, 2013.

Hilmes, Oliver. *Berlin 1936: Sixteen Days in August*. London: Bodley Head, 2018.

Hinsley, F.H. *British Intelligence in the Second World War*, vol. 1, *Its Influence on Strategy and Operations*. London: Stationery Office Books, 1979.

Holmes, John. *The Better Part of Valour: Essays on Canadian Diplomacy*. Toronto: McClelland and Stewart, 1970.

Holroyd, Michael. *Bernard Shaw*. 4 vols. London: Chatto and Windus, 1988.

Hoogenraad, Maureen, "Mackenzie King in Berlin." *The Archivist* 20 (1994): 19–21.

Hughes, H. Stuart. "The Early Diplomacy of Italian Fascism in 1922–1932," in Craig and Gilbert, *The Diplomats*, 1: 210–34.

Hutchison, Bruce. *The Far Side of the Street*. Toronto: Macmillan and Company, 1976.

– *The Incredible Canadian: A Candid Portrait of Mackenzie King*. Toronto: Longmans, Green, 1952.

Imperial Conference 1937: Summary of Proceedings. Ottawa: King's Printer, 1937.

The International Situation and Canada's Attitude towards Present Day World Problems. 30 March 1939. Ottawa: King's Printer, 1939.

James, Robert Rhodes. *Memoirs of a Conservative: J.C.C's Memoirs and Papers, 1910–37*. London: Macmillan, 1969.

Jones, Roderick. *A Life in Reuters*. London: Hodder and Stoughton, 1951.

Jones, Thomas. *A Diary with Letters*. London: Oxford University Press, 1969.

Keenleyside, Hugh, ed. *The Growth of Canadian Policies in External Affairs*. Durham: Duke University Press, 1960.

Kent, Peter. "Between Rome and London: Pius XI, the Catholic Church, and the Abyssinian Crisis of 1935–1936." *The International History Review* 1I, no. 2 (May 1980): 252–71.

– "The Catholic Church in the Italian Empire, 1936–1938." *Historical Papers* 19, no. 1 (1984): 138–50."

Kershaw, Ian. *Hitler*. London: Penguin, 2010.

– *The "Hitler Myth": Image and Reality in the Third Reich*. Oxford: Oxford University Press, 1989.

Kertzer, David. *The Pope and Mussolini: The Secret History of Pius XI and the Rise of Fascism in Europe*. New York: Random, 2014.

Keyserlingk, R.H. "Mackenzie King's Spiritualism and His View of Hitler in 1939." *Journal of Canadian Studies* 20, no. 4 (Winter 1985): 26–44.

Kimball, Warren. *The Juggler: Franklin Roosevelt as Wartime Statesman*. Princeton: Princeton University Press, 1991.

King, William Lyon Mackenzie. *Canadian Foreign Policy*. Ottawa: King's Printer, 1938.

– *Crown and Commonwealth*. Ottawa: King's Printer, 1937.

– *The International Situation*. Ottawa: King's Printer, 1939.

– *The Italo-Ethiopian Conflict and the League of Nations*. Ottawa: King's Printer, 1936.

– *King to the Canadian People*. Ottawa: King's Printer, 1935.

– *The Message of the Carillon*. Toronto: Macmillan, 1927

Larmour, Robert. *Canada's Opportunity: A Review of Butler's "Great Lone Land" in Relation to Present Day Conditions and Future Prospects*. Toronto: W. Briggs, 1907.

Larson, Erik. *In the Garden of Beasts: Love, Terror, and an American Family in Hitler's Berlin*. New York: Random, 2011.

Laurens, Franklin D. *France and the Italo-Ethiopian Crisis, 1935–1936*. The Hague: Martin, 1967.

Lawson, Robert. "Joachim von Ribbentrop in Canada, 1910–1914: A Note." *International History Review* 29, 4 (December 2007): 821–32.

Lentin, Antony. *Lloyd George and the Lost Peace*. New York: Palgrave, 2001.

LePan, Douglas. "The Spare Deputy: Portrait of Norman Robertson." *International Perspectives*, Ottawa (July/August 1978): 3–8.

Levine, Allan. *King: William Lyon Mackenzie King, A Life Guided by Destiny*. Vancouver:

Douglas and McIntyre, 2011.

Lockhart, Robert Bruce. *The Diaries of Sir Robert Bruce Lockhart*, vol. 1, 1915–38. Edited by Kenneth Young. London: St Martin's Press, 1973.

Lower, A.R.M. *Colony to Nation: A History of Canada*. Toronto: Longmans, 1946.

Lownie, Andrew. *John Buchan: The Presbyterian Cavalier*. London: Constable, 1995.

Lubrich, Oliver, ed. *Travels in the Reich, 1933–1945; Foreign Authors Report from Germany*. Chicago: University of Chicago Press, 2010.

Ludecke, Kurt G.W. *I Knew Hitler: The Story of a Nazi Who Escaped the Blood Purge*. New York: Charles Scribner's Sons, 1938.

Lyon, Peter, ed. *Britain and Canada: Survey of a Changing Relationship*. London: Frank Cass, 1976.

MacDonald, Malcolm. "King: The View from London." In English and Stubbs, *Mackenzie King*, 40–54.

MacFarlane, John. "Double Vision: Ernest Lapointe, Mackenzie King and the Quebec Voice in Canadian Foreign Policy, 1935–1939." *Journal of Canadian Studies* 34, no. 1 (Spring 1999): 93–111.

– *Ernest Lapointe and Quebec's Influence on Canadian Foreign Policy*. Toronto: University of Toronto Press, 1999.

Mackay, R.A., and E.B. Rogers. *Canada Looks Abroad*. London: Oxford University Press, 1938.

MacLaren, Roy. *Commissions High*. Montreal & Kingston: McGill-Queen's University Press, 2006.

Macleod, Iain. *Neville Chamberlain*. London: Muller, 1961.

Maisky, Ivan. *The Maisky Diaries: The Wartime Revelations of Stalin's Ambassador in London*. Edited by Gabriel Gorodetsky. New Haven: Yale University Press, 2016.

Martin, A.W. *Robert Menzies: A Life*. 2 vols. Carlton, Victoria: Melbourne University Press, 1993–99.

Martin, David. "Adrien Arcand." *The Nation*, 26 February 1938.

Massey, Vincent. *What's Past Is Prologue: The Memoirs of Vincent Massey*. Toronto: Macmillan, 1963.

McDonough, Frank. *Neville Chamberlain: Appeasement and the British Road to War*. Manchester: Manchester University Press, 1998.

McGregor, F.A. *The Fall and Rise of Mackenzie King: 1911–1919*. Toronto: Macmillan, 1962.

McNaught, Kenneth. "Canadian Foreign Policy and the Whig Interpretation: 1936–1939." *Report of the Annual Meeting of the Canadian Historical Association* 36, no. 1 (1957): 43–54.

300   Bibliography

– *A Prophet in Politics: A Biography of J.S. Woodsworth*. Toronto: University of Toronto Press, 1959.

Meany, Neville. *Australia and the World*. Melbourne: Longman Cheshire, 1985.

Menkis, Richard, and Harold Troper. *More than Just Games: Canada and the 1936 Olympics*. Toronto: University of Toronto Press, 2015.

Micoud, Charles. *The French Right and Nazi Germany, 1930–1939: A Study of Public Opinion*. New York: Octagon, 1964.

Middlemas, Keith. *Diplomacy of Illusion: The British Government and Germany*. London: Weidenfeld and Nicolson, 1972.

– "The Effect of Dominion Opinion on British Foreign Policy, 1937–1938." In *The Dominions between the Wars*, no. 13. London: Institute of Commonwealth Studies, 1972.

– *The Strategy of Appeasement: The British Government and Germany, 1937–39*. Chicago: Quadrangle, 1972.

Middlemas, Keith, and J. Barnes. *Baldwin: A Biography*. London: Weidenfeld and Nicolson, 1969.

Millman, Brock. "Canada, Sanctions and the Abyssinian Crisis of 1935." *The Historical Journal* 40, no. 1 (1997): 143–68.

Moher, Mark. "The 'Biography' in Politics: Mackenzie King in 1935." *Canadian Historical Review* 55, no. 2 (June 1974): 239–49.

Mommsen, W.J., and L. Kettenacker. *The Fascist Challenge and the Policy of Appeasement*. London: Allen and Unwin, 1983.

Morris, Edmund. *Theodore Rex: The Rise of Theodore Roosevelt*. New York: Random House, 2001.

Mosley, Leonard. *Curzon: The End of an Epoch*. London: Longmans, 1961.

Mowat, Charles. *Britain between the Wars, 1918–1940*. London: Methuen, 1955.

Munro, John. "The Riddell Affair Reconsidered." *External Affairs* 21, no. 10 (October 1969): 366–75.

Nadeau, Jean-François. *The Canadian Führer: The Life of Adrien Arcand*. Toronto: Lorimer, 2010.

Nagorski, Andrew. *Hitlerland: American Eyewitnesses to the Nazis Rise to Power*. New York: Simon and Shuster, 2012.

Neatby, Blair. "Mackenzie King and French Canada." *Journal of Canadian Studies* 11, no. 1 (1976): 3–13.

– "Mackenzie King and the Historians." In English and Stubbs, *Mackenzie King*, 1–14.

– *Mackenzie King, The Lonely Heights, 1924–1932*, vol. 2, 1963 and *Mackenzie King, The Prism of Unity, 1932–1939*, vol. 3, 1976. Toronto: University of Toronto Press.

– "William Lyon Mackenzie King." In R.L. McDougall, ed., *Canada's Past and Present*, 1–20. Toronto: University of Toronto Press, 1965.

Neville, Peter. *Appeasing Hitler: The Diplomacy of Sir Nevile Henderson*. London: Macmillan, 2000.

– *Hitler and Appeasement: The British Attempt to Prevent the Second World War*. London: Hambledon, 2006.

Nicolson, Harold. *Curzon: The Last Phase 1919–1925, A Study in Post-War Diplomacy*. London: Constable, 1934.

– *Diaries and Letters*. 3 vols. London: Collins, 1968.

Nossall, Kim, ed. *An Acceptance of Paradox*. Toronto: Canadian Institute of International Affairs, 1982.

Offer, Avner. *The First World War: An Agrarian Interpretation*. Oxford: Clarendon, 1989.

O'Leary, Grattan. *Recollection of People, Press and Politics*. Toronto: Macmillan, 1977.

Oliver, Peter. *G. Howard Ferguson: Ontario Tory*. Toronto: University of Toronto Press, 1977.

Ollivier, Maurice. *The Colonial and Imperial Conferences from 1887 to 1937*. 3 vols. Ottawa: Queen's Printer, 1954

Olson, Lynne. *Those Angry Days: Lindbergh and America's Fight over World War Two*. New York: Random House, 2013.

– *Troublesome Young Men: The Rebels Who Brought Churchill to Power and Helped Save England*. Toronto: Anchor Canada, 2008.

Ovendale, Ritchie. *Appeasement and the English-Speaking World*. Cardiff: University of Wales Press, 1975.

Overy, Richard. *The Morbid Age: Britain and the Crisis of Civilization, 1919–1939*. London: Penguin, 2000.

Owen, Frank. *Tempestuous Journey: Lloyd George His Life and Times*. London: Hutchinson, 1954.

Parker, R.A.C. *Chamberlain and Appeasement: British Policy and the Coming of the Second World War*. London: Macmillan, 1993.

302 Bibliography

Parkinson, R. *Peace for Our Time: Munich to Dunkirk: The Inside Story*. London: Hart Davis, 1971.

Pearson, Lester. *Mike: The Memoirs of the Rt. Hon. Lester B. Pearson*, vol. 1. Toronto: University of Toronto Press, 1972.

– "Reflections on Inter-War Canadian Foreign Policy." *Journal of Canadian Studies* 7, no. 2 (May 1972): 36–42.

– *Words and Occasions*. Toronto: University of Toronto Press, 1970.

Phipps, Sir Eric. *Our Man in Berlin: The Diary of Sir Eric Phipps, 1933–1937*. Edited by Gaynor Johnson. London: Palgrave Macmillan, 2008.

Pickersgill, J.W. "Mackenzie King's Political Attitudes and Public Policies: A Personal Impression." In English and Stubbs, *Mackenzie King*, 15–29.

– *Seeing Canada Whole: A Memoir*. Toronto: Fitzhenry and Whiteside, 1994.

Power, Charles Gavan. *A Party Politician: The Memoirs of Chubby Power*. Edited by Norman Ward. Toronto: Macmillan of Canada, 1966.

Prang, Margaret. *N.W. Rowell: Ontario Nationalist*. Toronto: University of Toronto Press, 1975.

Price, John. "'Orienting' the Empire: Mackenzie King and the Aftermath of the 1907 Race Riot." *BC Studies* no. 156/57 (winter/spring 2007/08): 53–81.

Quinlan, Kevin. *The Secret War between the Wars: MI5 in the 1920s and 1930s*. London: Boydell Press, 2014.

RCMP Security Bulletins, The Depression Years, Part V 1938–1939. Edited by G. Kealey and R. Whitaker. St. John's: Canadian Committee on Labour History, 1997

Reardon, Terry. *Winston Churchill and Mackenzie King: So Similar and So Different*. Toronto: Dundurn, 2014.

Reid, Escott. "Mr. Mackenzie King's Foreign Policy." *Canadian Journal of Economic and Political Science* 3, no. 1 (February 1937): 86–97.

Remack, J., ed. *The Nazi Years: A Documentary History*. Prospect Heights, IL: Waveland, 1990.

Reynolds, David. *In Command of History: Churchill Fighting and Writing the Second World War*. London: Penguin, 2004.

Reynolds, P.A. *British Foreign Policy in the Interwar Years: Europe and Africa, 1932–36*. London: Longmans, 1954.

Rhodes, Anthony. *The Vatican in the Age of the Dictators*. London: Hodder and Stoughton, 1973.

Ribbentrop, Joachim. *The Ribbentrop Memoirs*. London: Weidenfeld and Nicolson, 1954.

Riddell, Walter. *The Riddell Diaries, 1908–1923*. Edited by J.M. McEwan. London: Athlone Press, 1986.

– *World Security by Conference*. Toronto: Ryerson, 1947.

– ed. *Documents on Canadian Foreign Policy, 1917–1939*. Toronto: Oxford University Press, 1962.

Ritchie, Charles. *The Siren Years: A Canadian Diplomat Aboard, 1937–1945*. Toronto: Macmillan, 1974.

Roberts, Andrew. *Churchill: Walking with Destiny*. London: Allen Lane, 2018.

– *"The Holy Fox": The Life of Lord Halifax*. London: Weidenfeld and Nicolson, 1991.

Robertson, Esmonde. *Mussolini as Empire Builder: Europe and Africa, 1932–1936*. London: Macmillan, 1937.

Rock, W.R. *British Appeasement in the 1930s*. New York: Norton, 1977.

Ronaldshay, Earl of. *The Life of Lord Curzon*, vol. 3. London: Benn, 1928.

Rose, Norman. *Vansittart: Study of a Diplomat*. London: Heinemann, 1978.

Rowell, Newton. *The British Empire and World Peace*. Toronto: Oxford University Press, 1922.

Rowse, A.L. *All Souls and Appeasement: A Contribution to Contemporary History*. London: Macmillan, 1961.

Sanger, Clyde. *Malcolm MacDonald: Bringing an End to Empire*. Montreal & Kingston: McGill-Queen's University Press, 1995.

Schmidt, Paul. *Hitler's Interpreter*. London: Heinemann, 1951.

Segere, Claudio. *Italo Balbo: A Fascist Life*. Berkeley: University of California Press, 1987.

Shakespeare, Nicholas. *Six Minutes in May: How Churchill Unexpectedly Became Prime Minister*. London: Harvill Secker, 2017.

Shirer, William. *Berlin Diary: The Journal of a Foreign Correspondent 1934–1941*. New York: Bonanza, 1984.

Silverman, Hugh. "Newton Wesley Rowell, Lawyer, Politician, Judge." *Canadian Bar Journal*, October 1966.

Skelton, O.D., "The Imperial Conference of 1923." *Journal of the Canadian Bankers' Association* 31, no. 2 (January 1924): 153–62.

– *Our Generation: Its Gains and Losses*. Chicago: University of Chicago Press, 1938.

Sloane, Neville. "Chamberlain, Appeasement, and the Role of the British Dominions." *London, Journal of Canadian Studies* 23 (2007–2008): 67–80.

Smith, Gene. *The Dark Summer: An Intimate History of the Events That Led to World War Two*. London: Collier Macmillan, 1987.

Smith, Janet Adam. *John Buchan*. London: Hart Davis, 1965.

Soucy, Robert. *French Fascism: The Second Wave*. New Haven: Yale University Press, 1995.

Soward, F.H. *Canada in World Affairs: The Pre-War Years*. Toronto: Oxford University Press, 1941.

Speer, Albert. *Inside the Third Reich*. Translated by R. and C. Wilson. New York: Macmillan, 1970.

Stacey, C.P. *Arms, Men and Governments: The War Politics of Canada 1939–1945*. Ottawa: Queen's Printer, 1970.

– *Canada and the Age of Conflict*, vol. 2, *1921–1948: The Mackenzie King Era*. Toronto: University of Toronto Press, 1981.

– "The Divine Mission: Mackenzie King and Hitler." *Canadian Historical Review* 61, no. 4 (1980): 502–12.

– "Laurier, King, and External Affairs." In John Moir, ed., *Character and Circumstance: Essays in Honour of Donald Grant Creighton*, 85–98. Toronto: Macmillan, 1970.

– *Mackenzie King and the Atlantic Triangle*. Toronto: Macmillan, 1976.

– *A Very Double Life: The Private World of Mackenzie King*. Toronto: Macmillan, 1976.

– ed. *Historical Documents of Canada*, vol. 5, *The Arts of War and Peace 1914–1945*. Toronto: Macmillan, 1972.

Steiner, Zara. *The Triumph of the Dark: European International History, 1933–38*. Oxford: Oxford University Press, 2011.

Strang, Lord. *Home and Abroad*. London: Faber and Faber, 1957.

Strawson, John. *Churchill and Hitler: In Victory and Defeat*. London: Constable, 1997.

Swinton, Earl of, and James D. Margach. *Sixty Years of Power: Some Memories of the Men Who Wielded It*. London: James H. Heinemann, 1966.

Sylvester, A.J. *Life with Lloyd George*. London: Macmillan, 1975.

Tamchina, Rainer. "In Search of Common Causes: The Imperial Conference of 1937." *Journal of Imperial and Commonwealth History* 1, no. 1 (1972): 79–105.

Taylor, A.J.P. *English History, 1914–1945*. Oxford: Oxford University Press, 1965.

– *Englishmen and Others*. London: Hamish Hamilton, 1956.

– *The Origins of the Second World War*. London: Hamish Hamilton, 1961.

Templewood, Samuel John Gurney Hoare. *Nine Troubled Years*. London: Collins, 1954.

Thompson, John Herd, and Allan Seager. *Canada 1922–1939: Decades of Discord*. Toronto: McLelland and Stewart, 1985.

Thompson, Neville. *The Anti-Appeasers: Conservative Opposition to Appeasement in the 1930s*. Oxford: Clarendon, 1971.

– *Canada and the End of the Imperial Dream: Beverley Baxter's Reports from London, 1936–1960*. Toronto: Oxford University Press, 2013.

Thurlow, Richard. *Fascism in Britain: A History, 1918–1985*. Oxford: Blackwell, 1987.

Tolppanen, Bradley J. *Churchill in North America, 1929: A Three Month Tour of Canada and the United States*. Jefferson, ND: McFarland, 2014.

Tree, Ronald. *When the Moon Was High: Memoirs of Peace and War, 1897–1942*. London: Macmillan, 1975.

Ullrich, Volker. *Hitler*, vol.1, *Ascent, 1889–1939*. London: Bodley Head, 2016.

Underhill, Frank. "Mr. King's Foreign Policy." *Canadian Forum*, July 1938.

Vance, Jonathan. *Maple Leaf Empire: Canada and Britain and Two World Wars*. Toronto: Oxford University Press, 2012.

Veatch, Richard. *Canada and the League of Nations*. Toronto: University of Toronto Press, 1975.

Veith, June. "Joseph Kennedy and British Appeasement: The Diplomacy of a Boston Irishman." In Kenneth Paul Jones, ed., *U.S. Diplomats in Europe*. Santa Barbara: ABC-Clio, 1981.

Wagner, Jonathan. "The Deutscher Bund Canada, 1934–9." *Canadian Historical Review* 58, no. 2 (1977): 176–200.

Waite, P.B. "French Canadian Isolationism and English Canada: An Elliptical Foreign Policy, 1935–1939." *Journal of Canadian Studies* 18, no. 2 (summer 1983): 132–48.

– "Mackenzie King and the Italian Lady." *The Beaver* 75, no. 6 (December 1995).

– *In Search of R.B. Bennett*. Montreal & Kingston: McGill-Queen's University Press, 2012.

Walder, David. *The Chanak Affair*. London: Hutchinson, 1969.

Wallace, Max. *The American Axis: Henry Ford, Charles Lindbergh and the Rise of the Third Reich*. New York: St Martin's Press, 2003.

Walters, F.P. *The History of the League of Nations*. Oxford: Oxford University Press, 1952.

Wapshott, Nicholas. *The Sphinx: Franklin Roosevelt, the Isolationists, and the Road to World War II*. New York: Norton, 2015.

Ward, W.P. *White Canada Forever: Popular Attitudes and Public Policy toward Orientals in British Columbia*. Montreal & Kingston: McGill-Queen's University Press, 1978.

Watt, D.C. "Appeasement: The Rise of a Revisionist School?" *Political Quarterly* 36, no. 2 (April 1965): 191–213.

Wegenast, Franklin Wellington. *Liberty Is Dead: A Canadian in Germany, 1938*. Edited by Margaret Derry. Waterloo: Wilfrid Laurier University Press, 2012.

Wegenast, Ulrich. "Germany in Nazi Times." In Bendazzi, *Animation*, 148–50.

Whitaker, R. "Mackenzie King and the Dominion of the Dead." *Canadian Forum* 11 (February 1976).

– "Political Thought and Political Action in Mackenzie King." *Journal of Canadian Studies* 13, no. 4 (winter 1978–79): 40–60.

Whitaker, R., Gregory S. Kealey, and Andrew Parnaby. *Secret Service: Political Policing in Canada from the Fenians to Fortress America*. Toronto: University of Toronto Press, 2012.

Wigley, Philip. *Canada and the Transition to Commonwealth: British-Canadian Relations 1917–1926*. Cambridge: Cambridge University Press, 1977.

Wilgress, Dana. *Dana Wilgress Memoirs*. Toronto: The Ryerson Press, 1975.

Zeigler, Philip. *King Edward VIII: The Official Biography*. London: Collins, 1990.

Zucchi, John. "The Emergence of Fascism among Italian Immigrants." *Papers of the Canadian Historical Association*, 1984.

Index

Aberhart, William, 186

Abyssinia (Ethiopian Empire): guerilla resistance against Italian forces, 152; and Hoare-Laval Pact, 120–2, 125–6, 160–1, 196; Italian king as emperor of, 152, 153; Mussolini's invasion of, 83, 88–99, 125, 132; racist views toward, 86, 112–13; as a "sphere of influence," 87

Action canadienne française, 195

Action française, 74

Albania, 228, 229, 231, 237

Allward, Walter, 137

America First movement, 233

Amery, Leopold: on Austrian *Anschluss*, 198; on Hitler, 92; and King, 10, 23, 51, 53, 92; on League sanctions, 97, 98; on Munich agreement, 220

Anglo-German Fellowship, 143, 171

Anglo-Japanese alliance, 13, 18, 21

Annan, Noel, 162, 192

Anticosti Island, 186–7

anti-Semitism. *See under* Jews

appeasement: abandonment of, 228–9, 255; backed by rearmament, 148, 155, 201, 203, 209–10; Chamberlain's belief in, 200–1; Chamberlain's meetings with Hitler, 210–29, 231, 237; differing views on, 225–6; dominion attitudes to, 223; economic appeasement, 164–5; of Italy over Abyssinia, 120–2; King's adoption of, 7, 161–2, 206–7, 228–30, 254–5; Munich Agreement, 217–27, 228–9, 231, 237; Taylor's analysis of, 217. *See also* Czechoslovakia

Arcand, Adrien, 78–80, 112–13, 145–7, 231–2

armament. *See* rearmament and defence

Ashley, William Alfred, 1st Baron Mount Temple, 143, 171

Asiatic Exclusion League (California), 16

Asquith, H.H.: on imperial foreign policy, 34, 36, 222; reassurances to King from Beyond, 86, 99, 251

Astor, Nancy, 192

Athol, Duchess of (Katharine Stewart-Murray), 168

Attlee, Clement, 220

Australia: at 1923 imperial conference, 51; and Chanak incident, 43, 46; communications with Foreign Office, 49; and dominion autonomy, 53; at Evian Conference, 193; immigration policies, 12, 15, 20, 196; on imperial foreign policy, 36, 156, 223; and Japan, 13; Menzies's visit to Berlin, 209; and Royal Navy, 29

Austria: *Anschluss*, 92, 181, 197–200, 228, 260; and Italy, 62–3, 197; Jewish refugees from, 194

Avenol, Joseph, 117

Badoglio, Pietro, 125

Balbo, Italo, 67

Baldwin, Stanley: on appeasement, 122; Bickersteth's memorandum for, 139; on Chamberlain, 188; on Chanak incident, 45; and Hoare-Laval pact, 87, 96, 104; at 1923 imperial conference, 45, 49, 144; on joint flying training, 145; and Jones, 234; and King, 127, 144, 145; and Lloyd George, 138; on oil sanctions, 88; and Public Order Act, 92; and Ribbentrop, 164; visits to Canada, 59, 241

308   Index

Balfour, Arthur, 23, 34, 53–4
Balfour Declaration, 229
Barnes, A.J.L., 42
Beament, Henry, 146
Beaudry, Laurent, 108–9, 111, 112, 131
Beaverbrook, 1st Earl of (Max Aitken), 44–5, 72, 102, 203
Belgium, 7, 183
Bell, Leslie, 79
Beneš, Edvard, 137, 208
Bennett, R.B.: on Anticosti Island, 187; and Arcand, 145; on Asian immigration, 15; on British Commonwealth, 134; and Churchill, 73; and economic depression, 85, 102, 129, 186; foreign affairs portfolio, 3, 70; on Japanese aggression, 59–60; on King's foreign policy, 221; on League of Nations, 59–60, 73, 74, 226; on League sanctions, 89–91, 93–7, 100, 107–8, 130, 133, 253; and Ligue d'action nationale, 195; as prime minister, 68, 82; on rearmament, 203; and Riddell, 60–1, 89–90, 95, 97, 130–1; and Rowell, 74; and Skelton, 59, 91, 95, 108, 133; and Statute of Westminster, 54; trade negotiations with US, 26, 102–3; visit to London, 73
Berlin (Ontario), 9, 75, 164
Berlin Olympics, 135–6
Berton, Pierre, 136
Bethune, Norman, 190
Bickersteth, Burgon, 139, 223
Birkenhead, 1st Earl of (F.E. Smith), 42, 43, 45–6, 48–9, 94
Blair, Frederick, 194–5
Blondin, Pierre-Édouard, 79, 145
Blum, Leon, 142, 204
Bohemia, 181, 237
Bonar Law, Andrew, 44, 48, 49
Borden, Frederick William, 33
Borden, Robert: on Asian immigration, 15, 24–5; and Churchill, 47, 68; foreign affairs portfolio, 3; on imperial foreign policy, 35, 51, 53; King's offer of services to, 33, 253; on League of Nations, 56, 57, 58, 132; and Military Service Act, 37; and naval bill, 37; and Rowell, 40, 73–4; wartime government, 31–5
Bott, Bernard, 77

Bouchard, Télesphore-Damien, 147
Brazil, 133
Britain: alliance negotiations with USSR, 238–9, 248–9; Chamberlain's appeasement meetings (*see under* appeasement); conscription legislation, 229; fascist/Nazi supporters in, 73, 74–5, 92, 143, 145–6; Government Code and Cypher School, 190; guarantee to Poland, 237–9; and Hoare-Laval Pact, 120–2, 125–6, 160–1, 196; imperial centralist politics in, 34–5; Jewish refugees in, 196; MI5 and MI6, 70, 80, 123, 128, 166, 173, 251; "Peace Ballot" (1935 election), 84, 92, 121–2, 144; rearmament and defence, 144–5, 205, 220, 229; and Rhineland reoccupation, 123; Royal Air Force (RAF), 96, 145, 202, 240; Royal Navy, 14, 29, 61, 253, 259; and Spanish Civil War, 189, 190; and Sudetenland crisis, 200, 209; wartime coalition government, 41–2
– Dominions Office: information and briefings from, 6, 125, 153, 222; Massey's contacts with, 125, 134, 154–5
– Foreign Office: Bennett's attitude to, 70; information and briefings from, 70, 125, 222; and Japanese invasion of China, 126; King's attitude to, 49, 70, 73, 153–4; Massey's contacts with, 125, 154–5
– treaties and agreements: Alaska boundary settlement, 19; Anglo-German naval agreement, 91–2; Anglo-Japanese alliance, 13, 18, 21; London Treaty, 82–3; Treaty of Commerce and Navigation, 13, 15, 24
British Columbia: Asian immigrants in, 12–13, 15, 24–5, 28, 53; Social Credit government, 186; US designs on, 20, 21, 22, 24
British Commonwealth Air Training Plan, 48, 145, 202, 241, 259
British Somaliland, 153
British Union of Fascists, 80, 92, 146
Bryce, James, 1st Viscount Bryce, 24
Buchan, John. *See* Tweedsmuir, 1st Baron of
Bulgaria, 69
Bund Canada. *See* Deutscher Bund Canada
Bunyan, John, 193

Cadogan, Alexander, 126, 172
Cahan, Charles, 59–60, 88, 130

Index   309

Campbell, John, 45

Campbell-Bannerman, Henry, 85

Canada: Defence Purchasing Board, 241; fascist/Nazi groups in, 75–7, 145–7, 231–2, 239, 249, 250–1; Monroe Doctrine extended to, 205, 254; naval controversy, 29, 37, 235; neutrality for, 148–50, 152; rearmament and defence spending, 129–30, 148–51, 159–60, 235, 240–1, 259; refugee policies, 194–6, 227–8

– Department of External Affairs: creation of, 11, 229; intelligence and briefings for, 6, 124–5, 139–40, 153–4, 221–2; King's self-appointed role in, 3–4, 229–30, 246; Pearson's description of, 6, 140, 230, 235, 255–6, 259; Skelton's administration of, 6, 229–30; staff and foreign service for, 5–6, 124, 229–30; Wrong's criticism of, 6, 125, 229–30

– federal elections: in 1911 ("reciprocity"), 10, 25, 29; in 1917 ("khaki"), 32; in 1921, 37, 39; in 1925, 37; in 1930, 37, 59, 68, 79; in 1935, 37, 84–5, 93, 100–1, 102; in 1939 (1940), 186, 255

– legislation: Customs Act, 189; Foreign Enlistment Act, 189; Military Service Act, 33, 37, 74

– parliament: debates on foreign policy, 3–4, 124–5, 128–9, 131–2, 156, 190–1, 245–6, 254–5, 257; King's attitude to, 257; "Parliament will decide," 3, 9, 40, 94, 215–16, 221, 257

Canadian Broadcasting Corporation (CBC), 6, 183–4

Canadian High Commission in London (Canada House): air raid shelters for, 242; King's attitude to, 154; secretaries at (*see* Massey, Vincent; Pearson, Lester; Ritchie, Charles)

Canadian Institute for International Affairs, 66

Canadian Nationalist Party, 80, 232

Canadian Union of Fascists, 232

Cardin, Pierre Joseph Arthur, 105, 215, 228, 250

Carnarvon, 4th Earl of (Henry Herbert), 34

Casa d'Italia (Montreal), 67

Cassel, Ernest, 171

Catholic Church. *See* Roman Catholic Church

CCF (Cooperative Commonwealth Federa-

tion): in debate on Anticosti Island, 187; on defence spending, 148, 149–50, 199, 240; on neutrality, 149; pacifism, 130, 134, 150; on sanctions, 60, 130, 197

Cecil, Lord Robert. *See* Gascoyne-Cecil, Robert

Céline (Louis-Ferdinand des Touches), 146

Chamberlain, Austen, 41, 65, 191

Chamberlain, Joseph, 10, 34, 162

Chamberlain, Neville: on alliance with USSR, 248–9; appeasement and Munich agreement, 210–29, 231, 237, 245; on appeasement with diplomacy, 161–2, 200–1; on appeasement with rearmament, 148, 205; on approaching war, 188; on Bennett, 102; on Canada's support, 203; and Churchill, 192, 223, 224, 246; on Czechoslovakia, 193, 205; on dominions' foreign policy, 155; Eden's disagreement with, 191–2; and Edward VIII, 128; on French commitment to sanctions, 98, 104, 110; on Goebbels, 143; guarantee to Poland, 237–8, 247; and Halifax, 192; hatred and horror of war, 7, 201; and Henderson, 171–2, 174; on Hitler, 143, 207, 212, 218; on Hoare-Laval pact, 122, 126; and King's confidential memorandum on Hitler, 177–9, 182–3, 261; King's praise for, 162–4, 219–21; and King's visit to Berlin, 165–8; on League reorganization, 159; on League sanctions, 97, 98, 107; on League's failure, 197; and Lothian, 143; meeting with Mussolini, 231; and MI6 reports on Germany, 221–2; on Nazi persecution of Jews, 227; as a politician, 226; on rearmament and defence, 144–5; on Rhineland reoccupation, 124; on Ribbentrop, 163; and Roosevelt's peace initiative, 151, 187–8, 191; and royal tour of Canada, 166; on Spanish Civil War, 188, 189; on Statute of Westminster, 145

Chanak incident, 43–51, 65, 171, 246, 253

Chile, 117, 120, 121, 122

China: immigrants from, 14, 16, 28, 53; Japanese invasions of, 59–61, 62, 88, 126

Christie, Group Captain M.G., 180–1

Churchill, Clementine, 50

Churchill, Winston: on Abyssinia, 87; on alliance with USSR, 208, 238; and

Chamberlain, 192, 223, 224, 246; and Chanak incident, 42–51, 253; on Czechoslovakia, 213; on empire free trade, 68; on failure of appeasement, 220; on failure of sanctions, 126; on German munitions, 219; and Greenwood, 14; on guarantee to Poland, 238; and Halifax, 192; on Hitler and Nazi regime, 70, 73, 138; King's meetings with, 10, 23, 50–1, 196; King's views on, 23, 36, 162, 246; on Lloyd George, 138; on Munich agreement, 224; on Mussolini, 65–6, 126; on rearmament and appeasement, 201; on rearmament and sanctions, 96, 99; on rearmament delays, 144; and Ribbentrop, 164, 165; on Roosevelt's peace initiative, 151, 188; and Russian Civil War, 47; on "the moment with all odds against you," 234, 238; and Tree, 229

Cliveden set, 143, 192

Coldwell, Major James William (M.J.), 150, 197

common imperial foreign policy. *See under* foreign policy

communism: in Canada, 67, 80; fascism as a force against, 62, 65, 67, 71, 161; Hitler's violence against, 70; Jewish refugees linked with, 195; Skelton suspected of, 225

concentration camps, 70, 114, 228

Connaught, Duke of (Prince Arthur), 164

conscription: in Britain, 229; crisis over (1917), 32–3, 37, 40, 74, 162, 253; King's pledge on, 236, 239–40, 255

Conservative Party (Canada): on Abyssinia, 253; on conscription, 37, 240, 255; on defence spending, 149, 150; and fascist/Nazi supporters, 79, 146; and imperialism, 252–3; on League of Nations, 133; and royal tour, 243. *See also* Bennett, R.B.; Manion, Robert; Meighen, Arthur

Cooper, Diana, 113, 218

Cooper, Duff: on Chamberlain, 218; on Halifax, 192; on Henderson, 209; resignation, 224; on Sudetenland crisis, 209, 210, 212

Coughlin, Father Charles, 234

Cousandier, Giorgia Borra de, 83–4, 114–15, 129, 141

Crerar, H.D.G., 169

Crerar, Thomas C., 40, 74, 228

Croix de feu, 74

Curzon, Lord: on Chanak incident, 44, 46–7, 49, 52, 65; on imperial foreign policy, 36, 222

Czechoslovakia: Beneš as president of, 137, 208; Bren gun design, 202; creation of, 69, 219; crisis over, 200–29, 237–9; dominions' attitudes to, 155, 205, 223; French alliance with, 183, 193, 200, 209, 211–12, 214; German partition and occupation of, 213, 217–19, 237–9, 255; guarantee for, 193; King's cabinet discussions on, 205, 206, 215–16; King's views, statements, and cabinet discussions, 7, 197, 200, 207–9; M16 intelligence and warnings about, 221–2; Sudetenland and Munich agreement, 7, 174, 184, 197, 200–26. *See also* appeasement

Dafoe, J.W.: on League of Nations, 73, 134, 160; on Munich agreement, 220–1; on royal tour, 242–3

Daladier, Édouard, 212, 217, 218

Dandurand, Raoul, 58–9, 112

Dawson, Geoffrey, 127, 192, 222, 242

Dawson, MacGregor, 19

defence spending. *See* rearmament and defence

depression (Great Depression, 1930s): Bennett government during, 85, 102, 129, 186; defence budgets during, 150; dictatorships during, 69–70; New Deal legislation, 69, 103

Derby, 17th Earl of (Edward George Villiers Stanley), 164

Deutscher Bund Canada, 75–7, 80, 136, 180, 231, 232

Dexter, Grant, 142

Diefenbaker, John, 142–3

Dodd, William, 103, 232–3

Dominican Republic, 196

Douglas, Tommy, 130

Drew, George, 129, 202

Drummond, Eric, 82, 116, 117

dual foreign policy: King's basis for, 5–7, 33–4, 101, 252–3, 260; legacy of, 260–1; with "Riddell incident," 118–19; shift to single policy, 228–9, 261; with Spanish Civil War, 189. *See also* foreign policy

Dunning, Charles, 165, 208

Duplessis, Maurice, 146, 186, 187, 195

Eayrs, James, 156, 240

Eden, Anthony: at 1937 imperial conference, 157–8, 165, 167; on Abyssinia and League sanctions, 88, 106, 116–17, 118, 157–8; as foreign secretary, 122; and Henderson, 173, 175; and King's confidential memorandum on Hitler, 177–9, 182–3, 261; King's contacts with, 118, 139, 141, 165; and Laval, 96, 120–1; on rearmament, 160; resignation, 191–2, 196; on Roosevelt's peace initiative, 187, 191; and Tree, 229

Edward VIII, king (later Duke of Windsor): abdication, 144, 166; ascent to throne, 126–7, 137; King's meeting with, 143–4; pro-Nazi views, 75, 123, 127–8, 143–4, 165; visit to Germany, 185

Einstein, Albert, 194

Eisenhower, Dwight, 67

Elgin, Lord, 10, 23

Elizabeth, princess (later Elizabeth II), 128, 168, 224

Elizabeth, queen consort (later Queen Mother), 128, 224, 241, 244

Eritrea, 83, 88

Ethiopia. *See* Abyssinia

Euler, William, 136–7, 176, 215, 240, 249

Evans, Richard, 63

Evian conference, 193–6

Falconer, Robert, 7

Farr, Joseph, 80, 145, 231

Federal Bureau of Investigation (FBI), 128, 251

Ferguson, Howard: and Dafoe, 242; as high commissioner in London, 100, 119, 154; King's criticism of, 118, 158; and sanctions policy, 90, 95, 98

Fielding, William S., 35, 74

Finland, 238

First World War: Anglo-Japanese alliance, 25; Borden government, 31–5; Britain's coalition government, 41–2; conscription crisis, 32–3, 37, 40, 74, 162, 253; King's in US during, 31–3, 40, 181, 258; London Treaty, 82–3; Paris Peace Conference, 31, 35, 62, 83; Vimy Ridge memorial, 40, 137

Fiume, 65

Ford, Henry, 103, 233, 234

foreign policy: avoidance of decisions, 255;

commitment to Britain, 236, 254–5; common imperial policies, 4–5, 35–6, 141, 155–6, 168, 222–3; imperial centralist politics, 34–7; isolationist views, 51–2; King's control of, 3–4; King's goals with, 128–30, 147–8, 252–3; Pearson's criticism of, 6, 140, 230, 235, 255–6, 259; summary of, 252–62; Woodsworth's criticism of, 132, 134; Wrong's criticism of, 6, 125, 229–30. *See also specific issues*

Foster, George, 58

France: alliance negotiations with USSR, 238; alliance with Czechoslovakia, 193, 200, 209, 211–12, 214; fascist/Nazi groups in, 74; Hoare-Laval Pact, 120–2, 125–6, 160–1, 196; and Italian invasion of Abyssinia, 98, 104–5, 107, 110, 152; "little entente," 238; London Treaty, 82–3; and Rhineland reoccupation, 123; and Spanish Civil War, 189, 190

Franco, Francisco, 106, 189

Friends of the New Germany, 76

Gandhi, Mahatma, 65

Gardiner, James, 104, 228

Gascoyne-Cecil, Robert, 1st Viscount Cecil of Chelwood, 57

George V, king: death and funeral, 126–7; on horror of war, 97; and Mosley, 75; on Mussolini, 72; radio broadcasts, 183; reassurances to King from Beyond, 242; silver jubilee, 89

George VI, king: royal tour of Canada, 166, 224, 236, 241; succession to throne, 144, 151; views on Nazi Germany, 128

Gerhard, Karl, 77

Germany: Anglo-German naval agreement, 91–2; German immigrants in Canada, 75; King's visit to Berlin, 171–85; and League of Nations, 69, 133; Lindbergh's misinformation about, 233–4; Luftwaffe, 144, 202, 233–4; MI6 warnings about, 221–2; Nazi-Soviet non-aggression pact, 248–9; "Night of Long Knives," 71–2; Nuremburg rallies, 73, 92; Pact of Steel, 237, 243; persecution of Jews, 93, 193–4, 196, 228, 236, 237; plans for Anticosti Island, 186–7; prewar colonies, 184; rearmament and conscription, 89, 144, 169, 219; Reichstag fire, 70, 71, 72; Rhineland reoccupation, 123–4, 125, 139,

142, 144, 157; rise of Hitler and Nazism, 68–73; Rome–Berlin Axis, 144, 197; and Spanish Civil War, 189; Wehrmacht, 72, 238, 251; Weimar Republic, 69. *See also* Hitler, Adolf; Nazism
Gilbert, Felix, 171
Gladstone, William, 34, 85
Glazebrook, George, 38
Gobeil, Samuel, 79
Goebbels, Joseph: Chamberlain on, 143; and Hitler, 247; at Nuremburg rallies, 92; Phipps on, 172; as propaganda minister, 75, 135; and Shaw, 179
Göring, Hermann: on Czechoslovakia, 218; King's meetings and contacts with, 168, 175–6, 179–80, 184, 213; and Lindbergh, 234; and "Night of Long Knives," 71; Phipps on, 172; plans for Anticosti Island, 187
Grant, Julia, 103, 141
Grant, Ulysses S., 103
Gray, Charlotte, 8, 84
Greece, 43, 237, 239
Greenwood, Hamar, 1st Viscount Greenwood: anti-Nazi views, 171; career in Britain, 14, 23, 33; on Chanak incident, 46; on Japanese immigration, 10, 14–15, 16; and King's messages to Chamberlain, 182, 207
Greville, Mrs Ronnie (Margaret), 73
Grey, Albert, 4th Earl Grey (governor general), 21, 23, 29, 164
Grey, Edward, 1st Viscount Grey of Fallodon (foreign secretary), 19, 22, 23, 27, 85, 99
Groulx, Abbé, 195
Guastalla, Giuseppe, 83

Halifax, 1st Earl of (Edward Wood): and Dawson, 127; as foreign secretary, 191–2; and Henderson, 175, 237; on Munich agreement, 210, 224; and Ribbentrop, 165; and royal tour of Canada, 166
Halton, Matthew, 70–1, 74, 135–6
Hankey, Maurice, 165
Harington, Charles, 46, 47, 51
Harper, Bert, 31
Henderson, Nevile: as Britain's ambassador to Berlin, 171–2, 178, 190, 209; and Chanak incident, 46; and Halifax, 237; and King's message to Hitler, 211; and King's visit to

Berlin, 166, 171, 173, 174–5, 182; and Sudetenland crisis, 183, 190, 200, 209
Hepburn, Mitchell, 186
Herridge, William Duncan, 91, 94
Hess, Rudolph, 75, 76, 168, 179–80, 184
Himmler, Heinrich, 71, 72
Hindenburg, Paul von, 72
Hitler, Adolf: and Euler, 136–7; and Hollywood films, 247; King's confidential memorandum on, 177–9, 182–3, 261; King's correspondence with, 219, 236–7, 247–8, 249; King's meeting with, 176–9; King's mystic portrayals of, 178–9, 197, 199, 250, 256; Kirkpatrick's description of, 213–14; and Lloyd George, 137–8, 143, 165, 185; *Mein Kampf*, 69, 103, 161, 171, 198; Mussolini as model for, 63, 65; popular support for, 92–3; rise to power, 68–73; at Vimy memorial, 137; and Wagner, 246–7, 251. *See also* Germany; Nazism
Hoare, Samuel: and Ferguson, 90; and Laval, 96–8, 104, 110; resignation, 119; on Sudetenland crisis, 205; talks with Hitler, 89
Hoare-Laval Pact, 120–2, 125–6, 160–1, 196
Houde, Camillien, 112, 146
Hull, Cordell, 106–7, 151, 194, 227
Hungary, 214, 217, 237
Hutchinson, Bruce, 184

Ilsley, James Lorimer, 105, 215
immigration: Asian immigration controversies, 12–25, 53; German immigrants in Canada, 75; Italian immigrants in Canada, 64, 66–7, 108; Jewish refugees from Europe, 194–6, 227–8, 244, 250; Vancouver anti-immigration riot, 16–17, 18, 27
imperial centralist politics, 34–7
imperial conferences: in 1902, 29; in 1911, 34; in 1923, 34, 38, 44, 45, 48–51, 144, 226, 261; in 1926, 52–4, 226, 261; in 1933, 73; in 1936, 145, 261; in 1937, 151, 155–68, 242; King's attitude to, 155–7
Imperial Economic Conference (Ottawa, 1932), 102, 145
Imperial War Cabinet, 35
Imperial War Conference of Dominions and India, 35
India: immigrants from, 12, 13–14, 23, 28

Inskip, Thomas, 164
intelligence: from FBI, 128, 251; from MI5 and MI6, 70, 80, 123, 128, 166, 173, 251
International Labour Organization (ILO), 31, 56, 60; Chile conference, 116, 122
International Olympic Committee, 135
International Opium Commission, 27–8
Ireland and Irish Free State, 41–2, 53, 141, 176
Italian-Ethiopian Treaty, 83
Italian Somaliland, 83, 88, 153
Italy: fascism and rise of Mussolini, 62–7; and Hoare-Laval Pact, 120–2, 125–6, 160–1, 196; invasion of Abyssinia, 83, 88–9, 125, 132; invasion of Albania, 228, 229, 231, 237; Italian immigrants in Canada, 64, 66–7, 108; King's visits to, 62, 82, 83–4; London Treaty, 82–3; naval forces in Mediterranean, 231; Pact of Steel, 237, 243; Paris Peace Conference, 62; Rome–Berlin Axis, 144, 197; and Spanish Civil War, 189, 190. *See also* Mussolini, Benito

Jaffray, Robert, 16
Jamaica, 225, 226
Japan: Anglo-Japanese alliance, 13, 18, 21; bombing of Hiroshima and Nagasaki, 29; immigrants from, 12, 14, 15, 16–18, 28, 53; invasion of China, 126; invasion of Manchuria, 22, 59–61, 62, 95; King's visits to, 5, 29; and League of Nations, 69, 133; military dictatorship, 59–60; peace mission to, 29; Russo-Japanese War, 13, 16, 21, 23; Treaty of Commerce and Navigation, 13, 15, 24; and trilateral discussions on Asian immigration, 12, 19–20
Jebb, Gladwyn, 221
Jeune Canada, 79
Jewish Congress of Canada, 193
Jews: anti-Semitism in Canada, 66, 77–8, 79, 80; and Evian Conference, 193–6; Nazi persecution of, 93, 193–4, 196, 228, 236, 237; proposed homeland for, 196; refugees from Europe, 194–6, 227–8, 244, 250
Joan of Arc, Saint, 179, 199
joint flight training project. *See* British Commonwealth Air Training Plan
Jones, Roderick, 163
Jones, Tom, 234

Kellogg-Briand Peace Pact, 62
Kemal, Mustafa, 43, 46
Kennedy, Joseph, 103, 234, 243
Kent, Duke of (Prince George), 127, 128
Kerr, Philip. *See* Lothian, Lord
Kershaw, Ian, 221
Keyes, Roger, 1st Baron Keyes, 50
Keynes, Maynard, 41, 42
King, Isabel Mackenzie (mother), 8–9, 83, 99, 246
King, John (father), 10, 83
King, Max (brother), 31
King, William Lyon Mackenzie
– personal life: childhood, family, and education, 7–9; complex character and private life, 7–9, 87, 256–7; diaries, 3, 7, 256–7; finances, 33; friends, 31; international travel, 5–6; later holidays: (in Europe), 83–4; (in Caribbean), 224–5; (in US), 108–9, 151; as a royalist, 242–4, 250
– early career: editor of *Labour Gazette* (1900), 10, 62; deputy minister of labour (1900–08), 5, 10–11, 16, 29; trilateral talks on immigration (1907), 12, 19–20; minister of labour (1909–11), 5, 10–11, 27, 29–30; at Rockefeller Foundation (1914–18), 31; defeat in 1917 election, 32, 33; *Industry and Humanity* (1918), 33, 57, 140, 208, 261; election as Liberal leader (1919), 4, 5, 32–3, 37, 73–4; leader of opposition (1930–35), 68, 70, 73, 82, 86–7, 93, 96, 99–100
– spiritualism: divinely ordained role, 129, 141, 143–4, 173, 186, 190–1, 241; mystic portrayals of Hitler, 178–9, 199, 215, 250, 256; reassurances from Beyond, 8, 103, 137, 245, 246–7; from Asquith, 86, 99, 251; from Laurier, 85, 86, 100, 227
Kirkpatrick, Ivone, 213
Kristallnacht, 196, 228, 236, 237

Labour Gazette, 10, 62
Lansbury, George, 121
Lapointe, Ernest: on Canada's League membership, 56, 58, 196; on Chanak incident, 47, 48, 253; on conscription, 37, 236, 239–40; control of Quebec caucus, 37, 150; and Dandurand, 58–9, 112; on defence and Canadian participation in war, 148–9, 150,

215–16, 226, 229, 235–6, 249; on fascist/Nazi groups in Canada, 77, 79, 81, 231–2, 251; and foreign affairs portfolio, 101, 246; on imperial centralism, 36–7; at imperial conferences: (1926), 52; (1937), 165, 169; on Jewish refugees, 195, 228; King influenced by, 3, 36–7, 139, 153, 253–4; King's reliance on, 37, 55, 253; and Larkin, 49; at League of Nations, 44, 47; on League sanctions, 91, 93, 101, 104–5, 130, 153, 196, 253–4; and Petrucci, 108; and "Riddell incident," 111–13, 116, 117–18, 119, 121, 122, 131, 182; and Skelton, 39, 54, 235–6; at Vimy memorial, 137

Larkin, Peter, 33, 49, 85, 154, 245
Lateran Accords, 62, 66, 67, 113
Latin America, 5, 146, 193, 206
Laurendeau, André, 80
Laurier, Wilfrid: and Asian immigration controversy, 14–17, 19–25, 27; and Fielding, 35; foreign affairs portfolio, 3, 11, 52; and King's labour portfolio, 27; and Larkin, 49; and naval controversy, 29, 235; opposition to conscription, 32, 33, 74; reassurances to King from Beyond, 85, 86, 100, 227; resignation and death, 4, 32, 73; secret of Canadian unity, 48; support for Britain ("if England is at war …"), 235, 239; trade negotiations with US, 29–30. See also Liberal Party (Canada)
Laval, Pierre: and Hoare-Laval pact, 104, 107, 110, 120, 157; on Italy and League sanctions, 83, 96, 97–8
Law, Bonar, 44, 47, 48, 79
League for Peace and Democracy, 232–3
League of Nations: 1936 Assembly, 129, 132–3, 138–9; Canada's membership in, 4, 32, 56–61; Covenant of, 56–7, 58, 97, 139; ended with Hoare-Laval Pact, 126, 160, 161, 196; founding of, 56; and Japanese invasion of Manchuria, 59–61, 88; King's abandonment of, 115–16, 151, 253; King's criticisms of, 196–7, 198–9, 202–3, 207–8, 215; King's speech to, 129, 140–1; King's views and statements on, 4–5, 56, 57–8, 73, 158–9, 196–7; non-member countries, 57, 69, 133; and rearmament policies, 99, 160; sanctions committee, 89–90, 100–1, 104, 106, 109, 117, 119; secretary-general, 82, 117; weakness

and failure of, 69, 123, 132, 138–9, 255
– sanctions against Italy: Canadian termination of, 134–5, 150–1; King's statement on (Oct. 1935), 105–6, 109–11, 116, 118, 133; Mussolini's fear of, 106–8; US policy on, 107
League of Nations Society, 56, 58
Lemieux, Rodolphe, 17, 18–19, 24, 28, 40
Lenin, Vladimir, 225
Le Pan, Douglas, 262
Lewis, John, 32
Liberal Party (Canada): and King's foreign policy, 5, 142–3, 253–5; King's leadership of, 4, 5, 32–3, 37, 73–4; Quebec support for, 37, 68, 99, 253–4; and royal tour, 241–2, 243. See also Laurier, Wilfrid
Libya, 88
Ligue d'action nationale, 195
Ligue des jeunesses patriotes, 74
Lindberg, Charles, 68, 69, 103, 233–4
Lithuania, 231
Lloyd George, David: and Baldwin, 138; coalition government, 41–8, 51, 94; and Hitler, 137–8, 143, 165, 185; and Lindbergh, 234; and Ribbentrop, 165; on Sudetenland crisis, 205
Lloyd George, Megan, 138
Lockhart, Robert Bruce, 75
Londonderry, Lord (Charles Vane-Tempest-Stewart), 73, 143
London Treaty, 82
Lothian, Lord (Philip Kerr), 143, 165, 192
Low, David, 163
Ludecke, Karl, 78, 145, 179
Ludwig, Emil, 141

McBride, Richard, 15
MacDonald, John A., 47
MacDonald, Malcolm: on dominions' foreign policies, 155, 222; on King's mistrust of high commissioners' meetings, 154–5; King's statements to, 139, 162, 168, 181–2, 199–200, 246; and King's visit to Berlin, 168, 170
MacDonald, Ramsay, 54, 87, 95, 154
Macdonald, Scott, 90
Mackenzie, Alexander, 99
Mackenzie, Ian, 148–9, 160, 206, 215, 241
Mackenzie, William Lyon, 8–9, 242, 252
Mackenzie-Papineau brigade, 190, 236

Maclean, J.B., 129–30
McNaught, Kenneth, 257
McNaughton, Andrew, 153
Macphail, Agnes, 150–1
Macpherson, Robert, 14
Manchuria, 22, 59
Manion, Robert, 228, 240, 255
Mann, Thomas, 194
Margaret, princess, 128, 168, 224
Markham, Violet: friendship with King, 23, 33, 227; on Hitler, 168; on King's belief about Hitler and Mussolini, 257; and Tweedsmuir, 244, 257
Martin, Paul, 142
Massey, Alice, 162
Massey, Vincent: at 1926 imperial conference, 53; and Bickersteth, 139; and British Commonwealth Air Training Plan, 241; and Canada's sanctions policy, 119–20, 122, 134–5; on Chamberlain and appeasement, 216, 228, 238; as high commissioner in London, 119, 125, 154–5, 242; on Hitler, 208; King's relationship with, 139, 142, 144, 154–5, 170; on Mackenzie-Papineau brigade, 236; on Mussolini, 65; and National Liberal Federation, 84; on Skelton, 38
Medici, Lorenzo de, 86, 99
Meighen, Arthur: and Chanak incident, 47, 253; on King, 33, 34; King compared to, 3, 32, 51, 203; and League of Nations, 56, 89–90, 133
Menzies, Robert, 209
Middlemas, Keith, 42, 155
Milner, Alfred, 34
Mitford, Diana, 75
Moravia, 181, 237
Morley, John, 22
Mosley, Oswald, 74–5, 92, 145, 146, 179
Mount Temple, Lord (William Alfred Ashley), 143, 171
Mulock, William, 9–10, 17, 62
Munich agreement. *See under* Czechoslovakia
Munro, John, 258, 259
Mussolini, Benito: on Austria, 197; Chamberlain's meeting with, 231; fear of oil sanctions, 106–8; international views on, 62–5, 74–5; invasion of Abyssinia, 88–99, 106–20; invasion of Albania, 228–9, 231,

237; Italian immigrants support for, 64; King's meeting with, 64; and Laval, 104, 107; March on Rome, 62, 65, 67; occupation of Fiume, 65; portrayed in King's diaries, 256; Quebec views on, 66, 108, 112–13, 253; rise to power, 62–7; and Rome-Berlin axis, 197; Schmidt's description of, 106, 120. *See also* Italy

National Progressive Party. *See* Progressive Party
National Socialist Christian Party of Canada (later National Social Christian Party), 78, 80, 146
National Unity Party, 232, 239
Nazism: compared to fascism, 63; *Lebensraum* concept, 144, 161; spread of, 74–81; supporters in Britain, 73, 74–5, 92, 143, 145–6; supporters in Canada, 67, 75–7, 80, 145–7; supporters in US, 75–6, 103, 145–6, 233–4. *See also* Germany; Hitler, Adolf
Neatby, Blair, 176, 235
Neurath, Konstantin von, 164, 168, 179, 180, 184
neutrality, 148–50, 152
New Deal, 69, 85, 103
Newfoundland, Dominion of, 44, 169
New Zealand: and Chanak incident, 43, 44, 46; on common imperial foreign policy, 34, 53, 156, 168, 223–4; at Evian Conference, 193; immigration policy, 12, 15; Riddell in, 182; and Royal Navy, 29
Nicolson, Harold, 122, 123, 213

Offer, Avner, 12
O'Leary, Grattan, 33
Olympic Games in Berlin, 135–6
Owens, Jesse, 135

Pact of Steel, 237, 243
Pan American Union, 5
Paris Peace Conference, 31, 35, 62, 83
Patteson, Joan: on Eden's resignation, 191; King's friendship with, 31, 86, 99, 204, 248, 251
Pattullo, Duff, 186
Peace Pledge Union, 121
Pearson, Lester: on Austrian *Anschluss*, 198; and Ferguson, 91, 100; on foreign affairs

under King, 6, 140, 230, 235, 255–6, 259; at Geneva disarmament conference, 169; at League of Nations, 74, 88, 90, 95; on royal tour, 243; on Skelton, 6, 91, 224
personal diplomacy, 144, 187, 200, 210, 219, 233
Petrucci, Luigi, 107–8
Phipps, Eric: as Britain's ambassador in Berlin, 171, 172–3; on Hitler and Nazi Germany, 72–3, 123, 143, 172–3; on Ribbentrop, 163
Pickersgill, Jack, 39, 201–2, 245, 255
Poland: Anglo-French guarantee for, 192, 223, 237, 238–9, 247, 249–50, 251; and Czechoslovakia, 200, 214, 217, 237; as a dictatorship, 69; German invasion of, 222, 251
Portugal, 69
Pound, Ezra, 65, 114
Pourtales, Guy de, 246
Power, Charles ("Chubby"): isolationist views, 112; on League sanctions, 105; on rearmament and war, 148, 206, 215, 235, 250
Preston, W.T.R, 28
Progressive Party (Canada), 39–40, 41, 44, 47–8, 53, 86

Quebec: anti-Semitism in, 66, 195; and conscription crisis, 32–3, 37, 40, 74, 162, 253; under Duplessis and Union Nationale, 186, 187, 195, 228; fascist/Nazi groups in, 78–80, 146–7; King's knowledge of, 39, 54–5, 253; Liberal support in, 37, 68, 99, 253–4; Roman Catholic Church in, 113–14, 117; views on defence spending, 130, 148–51, 226, 235–6; views on League of Nations, 57, 117–18, 253–4; views on Mussolini and Italian fascism, 66–7, 108, 112–13, 253; views on Spanish Civil War, 189

Raymond, Maxime, 187, 189
RCMP. See Royal Canadian Mounted Police
rearmament and defence: appeasement backed with, 148, 155, 201, 203, 209–10; Bren gun manufacture, 202; cabinet discussions on, 148–51, 205, 235–6; in Canada, 129–30, 159–60, 240–1, 259; in Germany, 144, 169, 219; joint flight training project, 145; and League of Nations, 160; munitions production, 202, 241

Reid, Escott, 66
Ribbentrop, Joachim: Chamberlain on, 163; and Czechoslovakia invasion, 218; death, 164; and Duke of Windsor, 185; King's correspondence with, 182, 184, 190–1, 193, 204, 211, 213; King's meeting with, 164–5, 279n36; and King's meeting with Hitler, 163–8; and Lloyd George, 137; Low's cartoons of, 163; and Nazi-Soviet non-aggression pact, 248; and Shaw, 179; and Wallis Simpson, 128; years in Canada, 164, 277n36
Riddell, Walter: and Bennett, 60–1, 89–90, 95, 97, 130–1; and Cahan, 60–1; as Canadian advisor at League of Nations, 88–90, 95, 97–8, 104; and changes with King's administration, 106–12; on failure of sanctions, 126; at ILO conference, 117, 120–2; initiative based on King's sanctions statement ("Riddell incident"), 106, 109–12, 115–18, 125, 130–3, 158, 191; King's later dialogue with, 158, 182; and Simon, 87, 179; and Skelton, 100–1, 108–10, 118
Rilke, Rainer Maria, 65
Rinfret, Fernand, 228, 250
Ritchie, Charles, 154, 238, 247
Robertson, Norman, 38, 60, 169, 261–2
Rockefeller Foundation, 31, 277n36
Rogers, Norman, 105, 208–9, 228
Röhm, Ernst, 71–2
Roman Catholic Church: and fascism, 66–7, 113–14, 233; in Quebec, 113–14, 117; and Spanish Civil War, 189; Vatican and Lateran Accords, 63, 66, 113–14, 253
Romania, 69, 200, 237, 238, 239
Rome-Berlin axis, 144, 197
Roosevelt, Eleanor, 234
Roosevelt, Franklin: concern for Jewish refugees, 227–8, 244; Evian Conference, 193–6; "fireside chat" broadcasts, 183; and Kennedy, 234, 243; King's contacts with, 103, 135, 151, 205–6, 221; and Nazi supporters, 76; New Deal legislation, 69, 85, 103; peace initiative (proposed conference), 151, 187–8, 191; pledge of protection for Canada, 205, 254; and royal visit, 224, 243
Roosevelt, Theodore: King's interactions with, 24, 25–6, 28–9, 102, 103; role in Asian immigration controversies, 15, 17–22; and Russo-Japanese treaty, 21

Root, Elihu, 15–16, 19, 20
Rothermere, 1st Viscount, Harold
  Harmsworth, 75
Rowell, Newton: career, 73–4; and Crerar,
  40; on League of Nations, 57, 88, 134; on
  League sanctions, 88–9, 104, 138–9; and
  Riddell, 118
Roy, Philippe, 208
Royal Air Force (RAF), 96, 145, 202, 240
Royal Canadian Air Force (RCAF), 148, 240
Royal Canadian Mounted Police (RCMP):
  and German plans for Anticosti Island,
  187; and Italian consulates, 67; monitoring
  of fascist, Nazi, and leftwing groups, 67, 77,
  79, 80–1, 180, 232, 239, 250–1
Royal Canadian Navy, 240
Royal Navy, 14, 29, 61, 253, 259
royal tour of Canada: King's pride in, 248,
  250, 252; planning for, 166; political aspects
  of, 236, 241–2, 243; US included in, 166,
  224, 243–4
Rumbold, Horace, 45–7, 51, 172, 173
Russia: war with Japan, 13, 16, 21, 23. See
  also USSR

Sachsen-Coburg und Gotha, Duke of
  (Charles Edward), 127
Savage, Lyon, 168, 223
Schleicher, Kurt von, 72
Schmidt, Paul, 106, 138, 176
Scott, Frank, 146
Second World War: British Commonwealth
  Air Training Plan, 48, 145, 202, 241, 259;
  declaration and outbreak, 3, 168, 242, 249–
  50, 251, 255–60; Holocaust, 114; King on
  causes or reasons for, 7, 32, 202; and Nazi-
  Soviet non-aggression pact, 248–9; slaugh-
  ter of zoo animals, 175; use of atomic
  bomb, 29
Self, Robert, 222–3
Shaw, George Bernard, 65, 179
Sheppard, Dick, 121
Shirer, William, 247
Simon, John, 87, 179
Simpson, Wallis, 127, 128
Skelton, O.D.: at 1923 imperial conference,
  50–1, 54; administrative weaknesses, 6,
  229–30; attempts to "stiffen" King, 37–8, 54,
  201; and Bennett, 59, 91, 95, 108, 133; on

Chanak incident, 48–9; on defence spending, 149, 160; doctoral thesis, 225; on Evian
  conference, 195; isolationist views, 37–9, 54,
  139, 254; on King's administration, 52; and
  King's imperialism, 203, 208–9, 215; King's
  sidelining of, 217, 224–5, 244–5; and La-
  pointe, 39, 235–6; on League of Nations,
  158; on Quebec, 39, 54–5; on Rhineland
  occupation, 124; and Riddell, 100–1, 108–
  10, 118; suspicions about briefings and
  intelligence, 169, 222, 242; and US trade
  negotiations, 102, 103
Slovakia, 237
Snowden, Philip, 1st Viscount Snowden, 143
Social Credit Party, 186
Somaliland, 88, 153
South Africa. See Union of South Africa
Southern Rhodesia (now Zimbabwe), 145
Soviet Union. See USSR
Spain, 69, 145
Spanish American War, 13, 17, 18
Spanish Civil War: Canadian volunteers
  (Mackenzie-Papineau brigade), 79, 190,
  236; international responses to, 144, 188–
  90, 234; King's silence on, 193, 198; US oil
  exports for, 106
Speer, Albert, 123
spiritualism. See under King, William Lyon
  Mackenzie
Stacey, C.P., 51, 241
Stalin, Joseph, 187, 197, 208, 248–9
Stamp, Josiah, 1st Baron Stamp, 184
Statute of Westminster, 53–4, 126, 145
Stevens, H.H., 24
Stevenson, Frances, 43
Stevenson, John, 242
Strathcona and Mount Royal, 1st Baron of
  (Donald Alexander Smith), 23, 24
Streicher, Julius, 77, 92
Sudetenland crisis. See under Czechoslo-
  vakia
Sullivan, John, 79
Swastika Association of Canada, 80
Swinton, 1st Earl of (Philip Cunliffe-Lister),
  162
Switzerland, 136, 194

Taft, William Howard, 18
Taylor, A.J.P., 63, 191, 217, 248

318　Index

Touches, Louis-Ferdinand des (Céline), 146
trade negotiations and agreements, 29–30,
　102–3, 108, 159, 226–7
Treaty of Commerce and Navigation, 13, 15,
　24
Treaty of Locarno, 123, 142
Treaty of Sèvres, 42–3, 49
Treaty of Versailles: Canadian ratification of,
　35; contention about, 41; Hitler's repudia-
　tion of, 69, 142, 144; principle of self-
　determination, 205; states created by, 69,
　219; terms for Germany, 89, 136, 161, 178,
　225, 238; terms for Turkey, 43; terms on
　Rhineland, 123–4; Tweedsmuir on, 199;
　Woodsworth on, 132
Tree, Ronald, 229
Turkey, 41, 42–7, 49, 171, 237
Tweedsmuir, 1st Baron of (John Buchan):
　and Chamberlain, 163, 203; King's corre-
　spondence with, 203, 204, 213, 227; on
　King's foreign policy, 199; and Markham,
　244, 257; and royal tour, 166, 242, 243,
　244, 250

Union Nationale (Quebec), 195, 228
Union of South Africa, 5, 34, 53, 145
United Farmers Party, 39–40
United Kingdom Fascist Party, 75
United States of America: absence from
　League of Nations, 57, 69, 106–7, 133;
　Alaska boundary settlement, 19; and Asian
　immigration, 13, 16, 17–18, 20; fascist/Nazi
　sympathizers in, 75–6, 103, 145–6, 233–4;
　Federal Bureau of Investigation (FBI), 128,
　251; German immigrants in, 75; Great
　White Fleet, 20; isolationist foreign policy,
　205–6; Kellogg-Briand Peace Pact, 62;
　King's employment in, 31, 33; King's skepti-
　cism about, 22, 24, 26–7, 102; Monroe doc-
　trine, 205, 254; New Deal legislation, 69, 85,
　103; protection for Canada, 156, 205–6, 208,

224, 254; royal visit to, 166, 224, 243; terri-
　torial expansion, 12–13; trade negotiations,
　29–30, 102–3, 108, 159, 226–7
USSR (Union of Soviet Socialist Republics):
　alliance negotiations with, 120–1, 200, 203,
　208, 223, 238; as a dictatorship, 69; and
　League of Nations, 133; Nazi Germany
　as bulwark against, 71; Nazi-Soviet non-
　aggression pact, 248–9; and Spanish Civil
　War, 189–90. See also Russia; Stalin, Joseph

Vanier, George and Pauline, 170
Vansittart, Robert, 70, 143, 173
Vatican. See under Roman Catholic Church
Veatch, Richard, 257
Victor Emmanuel III, king of Italy, 64, 125,
　152
Vien, Thomas, 125
Villeneuve, Jean-Marie-Rodrigue, Cardinal
　of Quebec, 189
Vimy Ridge memorial, 40, 137

Wagner, Richard, 193, 246–7, 251
Waite, Peter, 66
Waugh, Evelyn, 113
Webb, Beatrice, 179
Weber, Anton, 174
Wegenast, Franklin, 249
Whittaker, William, 80, 145, 231
Wilgress, Dana, 137
Wilson, Horace, 172
Wilson, Woodrow, 57
Windsor, Duke of. See Edward VIII, king
Woodsworth, J.S.: on Edward VIII, 127;
　integrity and intelligence, 132; on King's
　foreign policy, 134, 246, 254; on League
　of Nations, 132; pacifist convictions, 132;
　and Riddell, 60
Wrong, Hume, 6, 125, 194, 229

Yugoslavia, 231